AN INTRODUCTION TO LAW AND SOCIAL THEORY

An Introduction to Law and Social Theory

Edited by

REZA BANAKAR

and

MAX TRAVERS

·HART·
PUBLISHING

OXFORD – PORTLAND OREGON
2002

Hart Publishing
Oxford and Portland, Oregon

Published in North America (US and Canada) by
Hart Publishing c/o
International Specialized Book Services
5804 NE Hassalo Street
Portland, Oregon
97213-3644
USA

Distributed in the Netherlands, Belgium and Luxembourg by
Intersentia, Churchillaan 108
B2900 Schoten
Antwerpen
Belgium

Hart Publishing is a specialist legal publisher based in Oxford, England.
To order further copies of this book or to request a list of other
publications please write to:

Hart Publishing, Salter's Boatyard, Folly Bridge,
Abingdon Road, Oxford OX1 4LB
Telephone: +44 (0)1865 245533 or Fax: +44 (0)1865 794882
e-mail: mail@hartpub.co.uk
WEBSITE: http//www.hartpub.co.uk

British Library Cataloguing in Publication Data
Data Available
ISBN 1–84113–208–X (cloth)
ISBN 1–84113–209–8 (paper)

Typeset by Hope Services (Abingdon) Ltd.
Printed and bound in Great Britain on acid-free paper by
Biddles Ltd, www.biddles.co.uk

Acknowledgements

We are grateful to the Oxford Centre for Socio-Legal Studies and Buckinghamshire Chilterns University College for funding the workshops we held at Wolfson College, Oxford in December 1999 and December 2000. We would also like to thank the contributors who devoted their time and creativity to making this volume possible. Finally, we wish to thank Richard Hart for his advice and encouragement.

We acknowledge permission from *Law and Social Inquiry: Journal of the American Bar Foundation* to publish material from Volume 25 (2000), which was originally published as 'Language, Law and Power', in chapter twelve.

Contents

Contributors

Reza Banakar, Paul Dodyk Research Fellow, Centre for Socio-Legal Studies, Wolfson College, University of Oxford, UK.

Nico J. Beger, Research Fellow, Amsterdam School of Cultural Analysis, Universiteit van Amsterdam, Netherlands.

Bo Carlsson, Associate Professor in Sociology of Law, the Department of Sociology, Lund University, Sweden.

Yves Dezalay, Directeur de Recherche, C.N.R.S and Maison des Sciences de l'Homme, Paris, France.

Robert Dingwall, Professor of Sociology, Director of the Institute for the Study of Genetics Biorisks and Society, University of Nottingham, UK.

Robert Fine, Professor of Sociology, Department of Sociology, University of Warwick, UK.

Ruth Fletcher, Lecturer in Law, Department of Law, Keele University, UK.

John Flood, Professor of Law, Westminster University, London, UK.

Anne Griffiths, Reader in Law, School of Law, Edinburgh University, Scotland, UK.

Alan Hunt, Professor, Departments of Law and Sociology/Anthropology, Carleton University, Ottawa, Canada.

Mikael Rask Madsen, Ph.D. Student, École des Hautes Études en Sciences Sociales, Centre de la Sociologie Européenne, Paris, France.

David Nelken, Distinguished Professor of Sociology at the University of Macerata, Italy and Distinguished Research Professor of Law at the University of Wales at Cardiff, Wales.

Jennifer L. Pierce, Associate Professor, Department of American Studies, University of Minnesota, USA.

Jiří Přibáň, Associate Professor of Legal Sociology and Philosophy, the Charles University, Prague, The Czech Republic, and Lecturer in Law at the Cardiff Law School, University of Wales, United Kingdom.

Shaun McVeigh, Senior Lecturer in Law, School of Law, Griffith University, Queensland, Australia.

Max Travers, Reader in Sociology, Buckinghamshire Chilterns University College, UK.

Gary Wickham, Associate Professor of Sociology, Murdoch University, Perth, Western Australia.

Klaus A. Ziegert, Professor of Jurisprudence at the Faculty of Law and Director of the Centre for Asian & Pacific Law at the University of Sydney (CAPLUS), Australia.

Introduction

REZA BANAKAR and MAX TRAVERS

LAW AND SOCIOLOGY have always had a close, if troubled, relationship as academic disciplines. They share common origins in the eighteenth century, as attempts to understand and regulate the social world according to rational principles. Each has recently weathered a sustained challenge, from poststructuralist philosophers and political critics seeking to undermine their foundations in Enlightenment thought. The founders of sociology all recognised the centrality of law for the modern world (and Max Weber was as much a jurist as a sociologist), and sociologists now study law from a range of theoretical perspectives. Jurists (the term we will be using for academic lawyers) have always been interested in the relationship between law and the rest of society. This interest is amply demonstrated in the sociological jurisprudence of Ehrlich, Pound and Aubert, in traditions of research such as the Law and Society movement which advocates inter-disciplinary research on law and legal institutions, and in the small but growing number of texts which introduce law to students contextually, rather than as a set of self-contained rules.

Nevertheless, despite some attempts to bring the two disciplines closer together, they remain frustratingly apart. Jurists complain that sociologists do not understand or respect the content of law, or seek to undermine law as a profession. Sociologists complain that 'law in context' courses, and the research pursued by the Law and Society movement, are not sufficiently sociological. Law is not always addressed as a topic on sociology degrees, or only as part of courses on criminology or deviance. Sociology (at least as a sociologist would understand it) is not taught in law schools, even though sociologists are employed in large numbers in departments of medicine, nursing, journalism, social work and education. There are only a handful of inter-disciplinary programmes in law and society in the world, and even here postgraduate students are not given the methodological training they would receive as undergraduates in a sociology department.

The case for a contextual law degree—which would mean compulsory courses in sociology, research methods and social policy in each year of the degree —was first made in the 1960s, but remains just as relevant today. We feel as powerless as other critics to change the nature of legal education, since a majority of academic lawyers, supported by a profession which is anxious to maintain its status in the face of competition from accountants and other professional groups, is still committed to a traditional 'black-letter' degree. By editing an up-to-date collection about the relationship between law and social theory, we would, nonetheless, hope to raise the issue for a new generation of law students and teachers.

In British higher education outside the law school, sociology (a scientific discipline concerned with studying society), and social policy (a discipline concerned with policy debates about public sector institutions and services) are viewed as separate disciplines. Within law schools, the two subjects are often confused, or presented together under the umbrella term 'socio-legal studies'. The same blurring between sociological and policy-oriented work (along with other disciplines) has occurred in the inter-disciplinary Law and Society movement in America. A further source of confusion is that critical legal studies, which is taught in some law schools, usually contains some sociology, although this is not taught in relation to empirical research and with a focus on methodological issues.

The main point we wish to make in this volume is that sociology needs to be taken seriously as a discipline in its own right, and this means paying attention to a whole range of traditions in the discipline, and how they can be used to study law. This is not to deny the need for policy-oriented studies, or to dispute the usefulness of critical theory for the examination of legal texts, but to demonstrate that there is a good deal more to sociology of law than the theoretical approaches and methodological techniques usually taught in courses on 'law in context', 'socio-legal research' or 'critical legal studies'. Although there are a growing number of law schools where these subjects form part of the curriculum, students are usually only taught a narrow range of sociological theories and perspectives, and never develop an appreciation of the relationship between theories, or the debates between them.[1]

Everyone would agree that law students benefit from viewing law in a wider social context. We would argue that the only way to do this properly is for law schools to adopt a deliberate policy of offering some kind of introduction to sociology of law, linked to optional courses on policy research, research methods, and critical legal studies, taught in a systematic way through the law degree. An introductory sociology of law course would not talk about 'context' in a general way, but introduce students to the different ways in which sociologists understand context (represented in the different sections of this book). This, we believe, would be interesting for students, and would also be good preparation for professional practice in a rapidly changing world.

1. THE DIVERSE CHARACTER OF SOCIOLOGY OF LAW

The sociology of law, both as an academic discipline and a field of research, embraces a host of disparate and seemingly irreconcilable perspectives and

---

[1] This is reflected in introductory texts on sociology of law, which usually cover a limited range of theories and approaches, whatever their other merits. See, for example, R. Cotterrell, *The Sociology of Law* (London Butterworths 1992), S. R. Anleu *Law and Social Change* (London Sage Publications 2000) and J. R. Sutton, *Law/Society* (California Sage Publications 2001), which focus mainly on structural traditions and how these can be used in studying law.

approaches to the study of law and society. This diverse character of the sociology of law is celebrated by some scholars who regard it as a source of theoretical pluralism, and criticised by others for causing the theoretical fragmentation of the socio-legal field. Whether we approve or disapprove of the theoretical state of the field, the fact remains that its diverse make-up poses difficulties of a special kind to students of the subject, many of whom do indeed perceive it as 'an incoherent or inconclusive jumble of case studies'.[2]

The starting point for sociology as a scientific discipline is the recognition that human beings are affected and shaped by, and yet at the same time influence, other people. Society exists before we are born, and will be there after we die: it was only natural for Durkheim to conceive it as having an independent existence, like the physical world, that could be studied using scientific methods. Moreover, the same can be said of the various organised and institutional groups that constitute organised social life. The legal system is, for example, a set of institutions concerned with making and interpreting legal rules. Sociologists are interested in the various groups working in legal institutions (lawyers, judges, police officers and so on), and in how laws are made through the legislative process. One encounters legal institutions and rules at various points in everyday life, from calling the police to getting divorced, setting up a company, or buying a house, and will come into contact with the technical specialists who know the law, and decide disputes. A sociological approach to law is concerned with how this institution works and the relationship between law and other areas of social life.

Unfortunately, once one begins to think about law in this way, matters quickly become more complicated. If you read any sociology textbook, it will be apparent that there are numerous ways of understanding the social world. There are all kinds of divisions, and sub-divisions, within particular traditions. There are also three general debates that cut across the whole subject. These are the 'consensus'-'conflict' and 'action'-'structure' debate, and the challenge to sociology from poststructuralism.

The consensus-conflict debate

Sociologists differ considerably in their political views, and this influences how they understand society. One influential body of social thought has argued that this must ultimately depend on maintaining a shared set of values. Law can be viewed, along with education, as the cement holding society together. If you take this view, then lawyers are not simply another occupational group: they are custodians of a cultural tradition that we largely take for granted. This balances rights and obligations, protects us from crime and makes possible the exchange

---

[2] L. M. Friedman, 'The Law and Society Movement,' (1986) 38 *Stanford Law Review* at 779.

of goods and services in a capitalist economy. Law also evolves over time in response to new social and economic circumstances.[3]

The most popular social theories today take issue with this view: they see society as based not on shared values, but on those of a culturally or economically dominant group which are imposed on subordinate groups and legitimate its own power. From this perspective, the law has an ideological character. The Marxist tradition saw the rule of law as a fraud imposed by force on the working class. One can, however, use similar arguments in relation to any subordinate group, such as women, homosexuals or ethnic minorities. The underlying assumption is that these conflicts cannot be resolved without a major shift of economic and political power. In other words, the solution to these problems lies outside the law.

Although one might assume that 'consensus' and 'conflict' theorists are forever talking past each other, or engaged in bitter political argument, in fact, the main trend in social theory in the last forty years has been towards a compromise or synthesis between the two traditions. Here one might note that in the 1960s and 1970s there seemed more chance of transforming society through youthful protest or industrial militancy, and the Soviet Union was still a superpower committed to supporting socialist revolution across the world. Today, on the other hand, neither anti-capitalist protestors nor Islamic 'fundamentalist' terrorists pose much of a threat to liberal American capitalism. Clearly, this does not mean we are at the 'end of history', since one can still organise politically around all kinds of issues. However, it does mean that most contemporary theorists accept the values of liberal capitalism, whereas they were more critical towards established institutions, including the legal system, during the 1960s.

The action-structure debate

Another reason why 'consensus' and 'conflict' traditions have tended to converge is because, despite their political differences, they adopt much the same approach in thinking about the social world. The key concept one finds in liberal thinkers like Parsons and Luhmann, left-leaning liberals like Giddens, Bourdieu and Habermas, but also in hard-line Marxists like Althusser, is that society can be understood as a system in which different elements can be related together. The terminology differs, so in Parsons one finds 'systems', whereas in Bourdieu one has 'fields', and in Althusser 'practices'. The common objective, however, is to produce a grand, synoptic model of society, that explains how different institutions fit together, and how the whole changes over time.

The most systematic theories also address the relationship between the individual and society. Parsons offers the fullest and most explicit discussion, arguing

---

[3] See T. Parsons, 'A Sociologist Looks at the Legal Profession' in *Talcott Parsons: Essays in Sociological Theory* (Collier-Macmillan Toronto 1964) at 370–85.

that human beings acquire goals and values (for example, a respect for the law) in the course of socialisation. The problem here is how to account or allow for 'free will', while at the same time retaining the notion of a social system. Anthony Giddens is the latest theorist who has attempted to incorporate 'action' and 'structure' in the same theory, through his concept of the 'duality of structure'. The basic idea is that structures, such as institutions, are produced by people through their actions, but that actions are constrained by the structural resources available to the actor (which can include cultural or material resources).

There are, however, difficult issues that are not fully resolved by attempts to solve the action-structure problem. Twentieth century critics like the ethnomethodologist Harold Garfinkel have argued that systems theory seems to require human beings who are 'cultural dopes'. Aside from the question of free will, this kind of theorising also offers an impoverished view of human action. It cannot address, for example, how people account for their actions by giving reasons or excuses, or how they make judgements about other people. From this perspective, the initial focus on structure prevents the theorist from seeing what lawyers, judges or police officers are doing in their day-to-day activities.

There is also a deeper issue here, which goes back to nineteenth century debates about the nature of sociology. Admirers of natural science like Emile Durkheim argued that sociology should produce causal laws through observing patterned human conduct: there was no reason to investigate how people understood their own actions. By contrast, the hermeneutic tradition in Germany argued that this was an inappropriate way of studying human beings. Unlike the objects studied by natural scientists, human beings can think, experience emotions and have free will. For this reason, sociology has to be concerned with interpretation and meaning.

This nineteenth century debate has never been resolved, despite attempts by theorists like Giddens and Habermas to combine or reconcile the two traditions. One can see that any systems theory must ultimately be based on a Durkheimian conception of sociology as a science, since it looks at human beings from the outside. This can be contrasted with interpretive sociologies, such as symbolic interactionism and ethnomethodology, which address how people understand their own actions. There is no need in these traditions to make an ironic contrast between our superior knowledge, and the limited or imperfect understanding of the people we study as sociologists. Instead, the objective is to explicate and describe common-sense knowledge.

The poststructuralist challenge

Although it may in retrospect turn out to have been only a short-lived, *fin de siecle* movement, one that can perhaps best be explained as the response of utopian left-wing intellectuals to the fall of communism, it is important to recognise the immense difficulties that poststructuralism has created for sociology.

Just as systems theorists felt they had made some progress in producing a model of society that combined insights and ideas from the old consensus and conflict traditions, and which solved the action-structure problem, the discipline came under attack from a different direction. A group of mainly French philosophers set out to trash the Enlightenment assumptions underpinning sociological enquiry: including the idea that the application of reason and science can produce truth and progress (an idea which is widely shared in many academic disciplines), and that it is possible to produce objective or unproblematic descriptions through using social scientific methods.[4]

Although poststructuralism does have implications for conducting empirical research,[5] it is best understood as a philosophical critique, that makes us question the authority and coherence of classic texts. Like other radical movements in the discipline, it has largely been absorbed and tamed by mainstream theorists, and subversive thinkers like Foucault are most usually understood in law and society circles as saying something similar to Marx.

2. THE STRUCTURE OF THE BOOK

Given the diversity of social theory, it is impossible to cover every tradition in a single volume, and the reader will notice some obvious omissions. There is, for example, no chapter in this volume about the work of Donald Black, the influential American theorist who has followed Durkheim in adopting a scientific approach to law. There is also no chapter on Parsons and structural-functionalism, not because we dislike this approach, but because it proved difficult finding someone who had the time and expertise to write a review.

The text is organised in six sections on 1) classical sociology of law, 2) systems theory, 3) critical approaches, 4) interpretive approaches 5) postmodernism and 6) pluralism and globalisation; and there is also a conclusion in which we discuss the relationship between law and sociology, and the prospects for sociology of law. We realise that this way of classifying particular chapters is inevitably artificial. Alan Hunt's chapter on 'the problematization of law in classical social theory' in section 1 could equally well belong to section 4 since he employs a Foucauldian approach in analysing the writings of Marx, Durkheim and Weber. We have also put Habermas in the section on 'systems theory' (as a theorist who has engaged critically with Parsons), whereas he could also have been classified as a critical theorist.

---

[4] Poststructuralism should be distinguished from postmodernism, which is the belief that human history entered a new epoch in the late twentieth century (and which is also likely to be viewed as a short-lived intellectual movement). Many commentators use poststructuralism as an umbrella term for both these intellectual movements. See for example S. Best and D. Kellner, *Postmodern Theory: Critical Investigations* (London Macmillan 1991). We explain our understanding of the distinction in section 5.

[5] See chapter eight in M. Travers, *Qualitative Research Through Case Studies* (London Sage 2000).

All the sections contain chapters in which specialists review theoretical traditions, with the exception of one chapter in section 3, which is a study of race and
gender in the organisation of law firms, and one chapter in section 5 on globalisation. These chapters illustrate how a particular theoretical perspective can be
used in studying a substantive topic. At the start of each section, we have
included an introduction, which explains the background to these theorists in
simple terms, and relates them to wider debates that are not always addressed
by the contributors.

When we commissioned these pieces, we asked contributors to write in a way
that would be accessible to the general reader, did not assume too much knowledge, and which used concrete examples to illustrate how the approach could
be used in studying law. Despite this request, many of the chapters demand a
great deal from the reader, and several authors have chosen to supply an original, and sometimes contentious, interpretation of a body of theory, rather than
a simple textbook introduction. This was, perhaps, inevitable in a text about
social theory, which is invariably written in a difficult and demanding language,
and requires us to think critically about our deepest assumptions. Whatever you
think of particular contributions, we hope that it will encourage you to read
more about different traditions, and how they can be used in studying law.

Section 1

Classical Sociology and Law

REZA BANAKAR and MAX TRAVERS

M OST UNDERGRADUATE COURSES on sociology of law begin with the three nineteenth century 'founding fathers' of sociology: Marx, Durkheim and Weber. The two sides in the consensus-conflict debate we referred to in the general introduction take their lead from these theorists, who were writing about the massive social and economic changes that took place in nineteenth century Europe that we now describe as the emergence of capitalism or modernity. Marx believed that the central dynamic of this new world would be a growing polarisation between rich and poor, that would eventually result in revolution. Weber offers a less deterministic view of human history, but one that places equal emphasis on the competition between different groups for wealth, power and status. Durkheim, on the other hand, believed that industrial unrest was simply a temporary symptom of adjustment; and that political elites could re-establish a sense of order and well-being through fostering shared values.[1]

All three theorists were interested in law and legal institutions, although only as one element in society as a whole, alongside the economy, political system, and cultural institutions. For Marx, the idea of 'the rule of law', celebrated by British jurists, was a means of promoting the ideological idea that law benefits everyone, whereas, in fact, it only benefits the ruling class.[2] Durkheim took the opposing view that law embodies shared values, and advanced his famous theory, expressed as a scientific law, of how laws change over time as society becomes more complex. Weber, on the other hand, was most interested in the development of law codes, as one example of a growing rationalisation of social life; and, in contrast to both Marx and Durkheim, offered a pessimistic vision of modernity as a soulless 'iron cage' with no prospect of liberation through reason or science (since they were themselves partly responsible).

The first contribution to this collection by Alan Hunt contains a summary of Marx, Durkheim and Weber's ideas on law, but it does rather more than this, and is best read as a wide-ranging and provocative statement about the field of sociology of law as a whole. Hunt is being provocative since he argues that the classical theorists have more in common than is generally realised: they each

---

[1] For some useful introductions, see J. Hughes, et. al., *Understanding Classical Sociology* (London Sage 1995) and. I. Craib, *Classical Social Theory* (Oxford Oxford University Press 1997).

[2] This over-simplifies matters, since the few references to law in Marx can be interpreted in different ways. See H. Collins, *Marxism and Law* (Oxford Oxford University Press 1982).

view law in a 'constuctivist' way as a tool that can (and should) be used by the state in regulating human affairs.

To give some more detail about the argument, Hunt is suggesting that there was a shift in the way intellectuals conceptualised law in the nineteenth century. Whereas in pre-modern times, law was either viewed as a 'natural' pheno-menon, deriving from tradition or ecclesiastical authority, or as representing the 'will of the sovereign', the new capitalist industrial economy required a differ-ent understanding of law. Hunt argues that what has become dominant is 'legal constructivism' (which he contrasts to the idea of naturalism): the 'intentional deployment' of law 'to promote, secure or defend specific social interests'.

At the risk of over-simplifying a complex argument, Hunt suggests that a common concern of these theorists (and also of the legal thinker Henry Maine) was the relationship between law and the state. Marx believed that law would eventually 'wither away' after a socialist revolution; but he recognised its importance for nineteenth century governments as a means of controlling popu-lations, and securing the conditions for capitalist economic relationships. Similarly, a major theme in Weber's writings was the growth of 'professionali-sation and bureaucratisation', which sustained 'the stability and security of the new capitalist order'. According to Hunt, Durkheim also saw 'modern law' and 'political democracy' as the only means of maintaining social solidarity in a complex, industrial society.

Hunt's chapter ends with some general reflections about law in the modern world, and about sociology of law itself, which he argues still sees law 'as a man-ifestation of state sovereignty'. He argues that the relentless juridification that has occurred during the twentieth century (essentially the growth of the state) has solved many problems, but creates a reaction against the grip of law. However, initiatives intended to escape bureaucracy and law, such as the alter-native dispute resolution movement or the rise of 'self-governance', end up pro-moting further juridification. Modern sociology of law should 'move beyond the state', and study 'new popular forms of engagement that reach out beyond . . . the classical period of state, law and sovereignty'.

Those familiar with Hunt's recent work will know that this is very much a neo-Foucauldian argument, and he also draws on Habermas's ideas about the colonisation of the life-world.[3] It is worth adding, however, that each of these theorists can be understood as developing and elaborating a theme that was already present in the writings of Max Weber. Juridification is, after all, one part of what Weber viewed as a process of rationalisation through human history. There is arguably a moral ambiguity in all these writers towards the state. They could imagine no alternative to liberal democracy; but were aware that excessive regulation reduced human creativity and freedom.

---

[3] See A. Hunt and G. Wickham, *Foucault and Law: Towards a Sociology of Governance* (London Pluto 1994) and Wickham's chapter in section 5. Also, see Bo Carlsson's chapter on Habermas in section 2.

One thing that will be apparent from the preceding discussion is that the classical sociologists were all concerned with the relationship between law and society, as part of a response to the emergence of a new industrial capitalist society, and the development of the modern state. In our second chapter, Reza Banakar offers a different perspective on this issue by reviewing the ideas of a group of legal thinkers, including Leon Petrazycki and Eugen Ehrlich, who were impressed by the limited impact of state law on social relationships in their own countries.

Whatever their personal response to the emergence of capitalism, the classical sociologists were impressed by the power of the modern state, and its capacity to sweep aside outdated customs and institutions. It is, therefore, interesting to read a legal thinker like Ehrlich, who was not only aware that state law had only a limited impact in his own country, but also argues that it should recognise the existence of an alternative 'living law'.

One can argue here that Ehrlich has a significantly different emphasis to Hunt in describing areas of society outside the rule of law. Hunt portrays law as extending its grip, as new institutions are created, backed by the state, concerned with 'self-governance'. Ehrlich, on the other hand, draws attention to how social life is already ordered before the development of state law; and how institutions like the family and the economy are produced and maintained by local practices that have never been codified into legal statutes.

The extent to which these models of law and society are compatible would be an interesting issue to consider on a law and society course (which would require some consideration of empirical examples). There have, of course, been many anthropological studies about customary law, and how this relates to state institutions, that support Erhlich's argument. The most interesting studies, like the Swedish examples Banakar considers in his chapter, also demonstrate that state law may only have a limited relevance to how people in developed, industrial societies conduct many aspects of their everyday lives. One might argue that the legal pluralism paradigm is potentially a means of under-cutting and re-conceptualising the whole classical sociological literature on law, although there is plenty of room for debate.[4]

---

[4] See Anne Griffiths' chapter in section 6.

1

The Problematisation of Law in Classical Social Theory

ALAN HUNT

THIS CHAPTER EXPLORES the relationship between what will be termed the 'classical tradition' of social and legal theories of the nineteenth and early-twentieth centuries and contemporary trends in theoretically oriented studies in the fields of 'law and society' and 'sociology of law'.[1] A feature which the sociology of law shares with other sub-disciplinary fields is an almost reverential acknowledgement of the 'founding fathers', in particular the familiar trinity of Marx, Durkheim and Weber. This chapter will focus on the trinity with some brief comments on Sir Henry Maine.

This undertaking will be approached by exploring the forms in which classical theory problematised law. For this purpose, I shall draw upon Foucault's reflections on problematisation as opening up a new and fruitful avenue for the historical study of the human sciences. While the key figures had very different intellectual and political agendas, it will be argued that there was an underlying shared problematisation about the configuration of economic, political and legal relations that was taking shape during the course of the nineteenth century. While the problematic of Weber and Durkheim was conceived within the perspective of liberal capitalist rule, Marx exemplified a break with the problems posed by this tradition. In that tradition the problematisation of law was preoccupied by the question of how to facilitate the possibility of an extension of the capacity of political institutions to govern the economic and social conditions of a nation and its population. The liberal tradition was concerned that the capacity to rule should be exercised without transgressing proper limits that preserved the expanded economic and political rights won in the transition from monarchical to parliamentary sovereignty.

The classical sociological interrogation of the legal field demarcates the period in which 'the social' had come to the fore as the central target for the governance of the population.[2] Marx had signalled, but did not complete, the separation of

---

[1] For present purposes nothing hangs on the differences between these fields of inquiry.

[2] 'The social' came into being in the nineteenth century; it designated 'a certain region of society, a space between the economy and the state. It was an arena of collective needs, grievances and disruptions that were related to the transformations in the economic realm'; G. Steinmetz, *Regulating the Social: The Welfare State and Local Politics in Imperial Germany* (Princeton Princeton University Press 1993) at 2.

the fields of the economic, the political and the social. This separation and the emergence of the discipline which problematized 'the social' was furthered by Weber, but he was still concerned with the political problematic of liberalism, not posed in terms of the 'limits' of law, but rather in terms of the sphere of rational bureaucracy, the vehicle through which the state regulated the social. The separation and reification of the social, dissociated from the economic, was articulated in its most complete form by Durkheim for whom law was a major agent of 'moral governance' of the social totality. It is important to recognise that sociological reflection on law still remained heavily influenced by the political problematic of 'ruling too much' and the limits of legal infringement of personal autonomy. The emergent discipline of sociology was much less preoccupied with this question.

The influence of the way in which law was problematised that paralleled the emergent preoccupation with the 'social' is exemplified with 'social law', and the link between the welfarist regulation of the population as a whole was exemplified in the concern to grasp the connection between collectivist conceptions of welfare and social rights. This set of issues dominated sociologically inspired thought about law, more especially in Britain than in the United States up until the emergence of 'law and society studies' in the 1960s.[3] This movement, without at first clearly defining its own problematic, was concerned with the limits of welfare and bureaucratic legal regulation.[4] With the eruption of the crisis of the welfare state in the late 1970s, the law and society movement, while still influential, has come under mounting criticism from both the Right, who have reinvigorated a concern with law as the guardian of individual liberty, and from the unstable radicalism of critical and postmodernist currents that have lost faith in the rational and bureaucratic potential of law.

The method to be pursued will seek to identify the problematisation of law present in theorisations of law. Problematisation serves to initiate a line of inquiry by drawing attention to the rudimentary organisation of phenomena which yields problems for investigation. I draw upon Foucault's reflections on problematisation but it should be stressed that Foucault's concept was far from completely developed. His historical method of study is a history of problematizations, that is, 'the history of the way in which things become a problem'.[5] The trajectory of his own major works can be posed as the disarmingly simply questions: How did madness, health, and sexuality come to be confronted as problems requiring intellectual work and political interventions? The present inquiry asks: How has law been problematised? Problematisation as a method-

---

[3] See also W. Novak, *The People's Welfare: Law and Regulation in Nineteenth Century America* (Chapel Hill University of North Carolina Press 1996) and J. Handler, *Law and the Search for Community* (Philadelphia University of Pennsylvania Press 1990).

[4] Its most immediate concerns were the effectiveness of law as a means of securing social rights and welfare, policing discretion, and generally utilising law as an agent to promote social change.

[5] M. Foucault, 'What Our Present Is' [1988] in S. Lotringer and L. Hohroth (eds) *The Politics of Truth* (New York Semiotext(e) 1997) at 164.

ological strategy involves a commitment to challenging the 'taken-for-granted' nature of the 'problem' of law in different historical periods. One important implication of this approach is that it intentionally avoids any attempt to produce a chronological 'history' of the treatment of law in the social sciences.[6]

1. THE CLASSICAL PROBLEMATISATION OF LAW

How did classical social theory constitute law in relation to its object of inquiry? This question must be approached in a way that does not involve the implication that law necessarily formed a primary or even explicit focus of attention for the individual theorists. This is essential because, while Weber did devote self-consciously focused attention to law with the 'sociology of law' forming an important component of his monumental *Wirtschaft und Gesellschaft*;[7] and though a similar sustained attention to the evolution of law was pursued by Sir Henry Maine (1861–1905), others did not accord law this centrality. In contrast, Durkheim devoted substantive attention to law primarily in the course of a study centred upon the transformation of the division of labour of which law served to provide convenient and accessible empirical evidence.[8] Nor did Marx ever take law as his immediate object of inquiry, although he and Engels had a great deal to say about law.

The impetus that makes human thought shift has long been (but not always) a looming sense that something about life is new and different, and that things cannot or should not be discussed in the currently conventional terms. The prescient thinkers have been those able to encapsulate these shifts in ways that put together a narrative that makes sense of an array of symptoms and binds them together into a coherent account. The most popular narrative of our age has been that of 'modernity'; a fact that is sustained, not controverted, by the recent extension of that storyline by the addendum effected by 'postmodernity'. I do not want to argue that the tropes of 'modern' and 'modernity' are wrong, but rather that they are dangerous. They are dangerous because a purely chronological label, one that distinguishes the past from the present, the traditional from the modern, is made the bearer of a whole complex of substantive dichotomous characterisations (agricultural-industrial, rural-urban, Gemeinschaft-Gesellschaft and the like) that have been the focus of early twentieth century social thought.

The concept of modernity is especially precarious when applied to the phenomenon of law. Modernist theory conceives law as one of the important stars

---

[6] This approach, which I now reject, informed my earlier discussion of the 'sociological movement in law' in A. Hunt, *The Sociological Movement in Law* (London Macmillan 1978).

[7] M. Weber, *Economy and Society: An Outline of Interpretive Sociology* (ed. G. Roth and C. Wittich) (2 vols.) (Berkeley University of California Press 1978).

[8] E. Durkheim, *The Division of Labour in Society* [1893] (trans. W. D. Hall) (London Macmillan 1984).

in the constellation of the modern. Yet it is usually remembered that law pre-
dates modernity so the treatment of law becomes tarnished with an unexamined
presentism in which the past of law is viewed as a long march towards modern
rational law; the old pre-modern (irrational) elements are gradually sloughed
off to reveal law in its glorious rational form. The great bulk of the writings on
legal history, from Maine to the present, has been marked by the seductions of
this presentism.

The issue of law comes to figure in the problematisation engaged with by classic social theory in so far as it becomes less and less feasible to treat law as a 'natural' phenomenon. The most obvious form of law as a natural phenomenon is
that captured in both substance and in name by natural law theory. It was
grounded on the presumption of a social order based on a taken-for-granted set
of institutions and values constitutive of the social order. It makes little or no
difference if these were articulated in theological form with a set of primary values stipulated in some principal religious text, or if theology was partially secu-
larized through a process of reflection upon the human condition. Typically
such reflections were expressed in terms of a generalised problem of social
order; a set of questions most powerfully articulated by Thomas Hobbes in
terms of a problem of order that could only be addressed through obedience to
a vision of a political order grounded in a unitary conception of sovereign
power.

This vision came increasingly into conflict with the challenges posed by the
emergence of a capitalist economic order. Capitalism as used here involves the
coexistence of the production of commodities, industrial forms of production
and the mobilisation of mass wage-earning labour, with these elements being
coordinated through markets. The most profound impact of these developments, even outstripping the social dislocations they caused, was the primacy of
economic markets that required nothing less than the radical separation of an
economic from a political sphere. But the self-regulating market could never
achieve full self-regulation, and continued to require inputs from the political
system to sustain and protect the market order. Law was the primary mechanism
for this linkage of the economic and political orders. The crucial fact is that lais-
sez faire itself was enforced by the state and at the same time there was a major
expansion of the state; the free market was sustained by an enormous increase in
continuous, centrally organised and controlled interventionism.

The emergence of law as an object of sociological investigation rests on the
implicit view that legal systems are essentially constructed, social creations (not
natural orders) and thus presuppose an instrumental conception of law. In line
with the Enlightenment vision of 'progress' understood as a project that gives
effect to an ever expanding realm of the human capacity to control its conditions
of existence, law comes increasingly to be perceived as a primary steering mechanism for societies marked by complex interdependence, a task that can no
longer be fulfilled by more traditional 'direct rule' through the political system.
A persistent line of thought within legal theory has counterposed a divide

between law as autonomous and law as dependent on society; this has in many accounts been presented as the core distinction between the internal perspective of legal positivism and the external perspective of the socially informed approach to law. While this distinction should not be ignored, it is important to recognise that these views of law are not antithetical; the rise of law as autonomous system increasingly separated from the political sphere is consistent with a view of law as dependent on society, in the sense of being an historical achievement, one that has wider ramifications embodied in the strange co-existent reality and mythology of the idea of the separation of powers and the rule of law.

The next step in my argument is decisive. It involves a profound reversal of F. A. Hayek's rejection of the dominant 'constructivist' vision of the dynamic of the intervention of the political order in the economic order or self-regulating market. But before attending to the reversal some attention to Hayek's theses is necessary.[9] Hayek has long been a controversial figure; despite the favour he has found by providing the theoretical grounding of modern neo-liberal politics, he was one of the most important thinkers of the twentieth century.

Hayek set out to challenge what he viewed as the ruling myth of the twentieth century, shared by both welfare liberalism and social democracy, which he designated as 'constructivism'.[10] The 'constructivist fallacy' views social institutions as potentially amenable to intentional creation, reform and intervention by means of legislation and interventionist economic strategy. His objection is based on the contention that social planning is impossible; it is impossible because it is never feasible to accumulate systematic knowledge of the actions of individuals in pursuit of their interests exemplified in the uncountable markets transactions. Only the impersonal mechanism of 'the market' is capable of aggregating these actions to produce outcomes that are not reducible to the intentions of economic actors. To intervene in ways that impact on the market with imperfect knowledge can only result in the disruption and distortion of the market in ways that, far from rendering markets calculable and controllable, result in unintended consequences.

In other words, faced with the most profound implications of the commoditisation of labour and its products that constitutes capitalism, namely, the radical disjunction of the economic and political realm, Hayek endorses the necessity of that separation and the corollary that the political realm must abstain from intervention in the functioning of the self-regulating market. Thus, it follows that for Hayek the ruling vision of modern law, particularly in the increasingly dominant form of statutory legislation as a mechanism of deliberative intervention, is fatally flawed. Law can and should do no more than give

---

[9] F. Hayek's ideas were developed through a mass of published work; they are accessible in their most concentrated form in his three volume, *Law, Legislation and Liberty* (London Routledge & Kegan Paul 1973–1979).

[10] F. Hayek, *Law, Legislation and Liberty: Vol.1 Rules and Order* (London Routledge & Kegan Paul 1973).

authoritative endorsement to the necessary conditions for the functioning of the self-regulating market such as the protection of the rights of property, free labour and capital.

This is not the occasion to engage in a critique of Hayek, but two important lines of inquiry can be indicated. While he is logically correct in claiming that full knowledge is unattainable, it is disputable whether it follows that such complete knowledge is a necessary precondition for purposive intervention; what forms and degree of knowledge are sufficient grounds for purposive intervention remain a matter of investigation. The second question is, given Hayek's radical separation between the economic and political realm, where does the concept 'society' fit into his schema; is it the mere aggregation of economics and politics or is it a field not reducible to the other constituents? What is at stake here is whether society is the passive reflex of economics and politics on everyday life, or an active arena in which through cooperation and conflict people 'construct' forms of life through which they seek to take control of their existences.[11]

The radical reversal of Hayek which I propose is that, whether we approve of its consequences, the constructivism of law, that is its intentional deployment to promote, secure or defend specific social interests is precisely what was 'new' about the legal orders that emerged in the late eighteenth century. Legal constructivism has continued to advance over the next two centuries; this fact is most simply attested to by rapid extension of constructivism into the international arena with the growth of international criminal law and human rights law. Constructivism is no aberration or accident; it is, quite simply, a social fact that law is one of the primary techniques of governance. It has displaced the two previous visions of law as either the expression of a natural social order or as the expression of the will of the sovereign. This has been a displacement, but not a disappearance. The quest for a general normative order still infuses our ongoing concerns with justice and human rights. And Foucault is right in noting that we still have not 'cut off the King's head',[12] that is law remains heavily imbricated with state sovereignty. My contention is that the problematisation of law in classic social theory was grounded in the challenges posed by the constructivist reality of law.

---

[11] Hayek's position on the question of 'society' is complex. He views the evolutionary formation of human instincts as being formed when hominids lived in small cooperative bands that survived through solidarity. He rejects Hobbes' primitive individualism as a myth. 'The savage is not solitary, and his instinct is collectivist. There was never a "war of all against all" ', F. Hayek, *The Fatal Conceit: The Errors of Socialism Vol.1 The Collected Works of F.A. Hayek* (ed. W. W. Bartley) (London, Routledge, 1988) at 12. What is significant about this argument is that it explicitly contends that social evolution runs counter to the 'instincts' formed through evolutionary processes; learned rules that promote the individualism of market relations have to overcome primitive collectivism.

[12] M. Foucault, *Power/Knowledge: Selected Interviews and Other Writings, 1972–1977* (New York Pantheon 1980) at 121.

2. LEGAL CONSTRUCTIVISM IN CLASSICAL SOCIAL THEORY

While the substantive analyses, theoretical apparatuses and political commitments of Maine, Marx, Durkheim and Weber are radically different, nevertheless they can be understood as addressing questions that are posed by the rise of constructivist law. The issues they engage with are ones in which law is no longer the expression of the will of political authority (typical of monarchist or absolutist regimes) or a concretisation of shared religious-moral values.

Maine

Maine has not acquired the same status as the other theorists under consideration. His canvas, though broad, was not as expansive as the others and his preoccupation with legal history has largely confined his reputation to this field. This fate is compounded by the fact that Maine's intellectual universe was, like so many others at the time, framed by one of the many variants of social Darwinism. For this reason I will have less to say about him than the other figures; but this does not detract from his significance. His best remembered thesis is that the history of legal evolution can best be grasped as a transition from status to contract.[13] The ascribed status attached to individuals in pre-modern societies determined the law to which they were subject. Despite recognising the huge productivity of legislation, Maine insisted that it was the emergence of the consensual contract, by means of which individuals made their own law, that is the decisive, albeit prolonged and complex, line of development that endows the law of 'progressive societies' with the innovative capacity that allows law to keep pace with the increasing rapidity of social change.

What is significant for present purposes is the implication that individual contractual activity effects a decisive shift in the location of law within social life. It marks a radical break with the identification of law with sovereignty; and this is evident in Maine's sharp and telling criticism of the 'imperative theory of law', associated with Jeremy Bentham and John Austin, who reduced all law to commands of the sovereign. What Maine advances in contrast is a model in which law is attributed a distinctively liberal role as an autonomous entity that serves, as it were, the role of neutral umpire that determines the boundaries of the relations between contracting individuals. However, Maine never took the decisive step that could complete the liberal model which would have posited a separation between law and state such that courts could mediate the relations between individuals and the state.

---

[13] H. Maine, *Ancient Law: Its Connection with the Early History of Society and its Relation to Modern Ideas* (London John Murray 1861).

Marx

Marx's relationship to the emerging liberal model of law was far more complex. Most obvious is the fact that law never presented itself as his primary object of inquiry.[14] Marx's primary concern was with the 'critique' of capitalist society. This critique involved the analysis of the mechanisms through which capitalism reproduced itself and in so doing revolutionised all social relations. It also concerned the political question of how the gross inequalities instituted through the very freedoms which capitalism promoted in overcoming pre-capitalist forms of social organization could be superseded by the revolutionary transformation of society. His primary answer is well known; it is that one of the most important creations of capitalism, the conversion of the great majority of the population into wage-labourers, the proletariat, was the only force whose potential revolutionary action could conquer capitalism and institute a realm of equality based on the collective ownership of society's productive capacity.

Marx's treatment of law exhibits two very different emphases. While he viewed capitalism as a self-reproducing economic system, he also emphasised that capitalist economic relations secure dominance over all other major fields of social and political life. In particular, he emphasised the intimate connection between law and the state. Law in this manifestation is first and foremost a mechanism of state power giving effect to the state's monopoly of the legitimate means of violence and its capacity to use legally sanctioned coercion to advance and protect the interests of capital. Indeed, he argued that 'the bloody expropriation of the peasantry' effected by laws of enclosure and vagrancy law was a primary mechanism by which the rural population was driven to accept the necessity of submitting themselves to work in the mines and factories. Marx stressed the repressive character of law in order to redress the blindness of most liberal thought which played down the role of legal repression. But in reacting against the omissions of liberal theory Marx came perilously close to simply reversing liberalism's error by equating law with repression.

Marx's account of law exhibits a second line of analysis. Capitalist relations exhibit a powerful self-reproducing tendency, one that effects the general subsumption of wider social and economic relations under the logic of commodity relations; consumption, leisure and family relations all succumb to a greater extent to the logic of the market. But Marx stressed the instability of capitalist societies, their tendency to crisis. It is in this context that he drew attention to the significant degree of law's autonomy and separation from the state. Most importantly law provides and guarantees a regime of property and of contractual exchange. The

---

[14] Because of the scattered character of Marx's engagement with law individual texts will not be cited. For general compilations and discussions of Marx's treatment of law see: M. Cain and A. Hunt, *Marx and Engels on Law* (London Academic Press 1979); H. Collins, *Marxism and Law* (Oxford Oxford University Press 1982); P. Hirst, *On Law and Ideology* (London Macmillan 1979) and R. Phillips, *Marx and Engels on Law and Laws* (Oxford Martin Robertson 1980).

expansion of the forms of capital and their circulation require a regime that protects the multiple forms in which capital circulates as legal interests. Legal relations have distinctive effects. The most important of these is the extent to which legal relations actually constitute economic relations, as witnessed in the formation of corporations with limited liability; these are legal creations in that it is the ability to confer a legal status which determines the liability of participants and thus makes the corporation a viable vehicle for the cooperation of diverse capitals.

Just as important was that legal rules and procedures make provision for regulating the inter-relations of capital, through commercial law, insurance, banking and other financial services. For Marx, these mechanisms function as background conditions which constitute the framework within which economic relations are conducted. Law also provides the central conceptual apparatus of property rights, contract and other legal relations that play the double role of both constituting a coherent framework for economic activity and providing important components of the ideological conceptions of rights, duties, and responsibilities. Legal relations share important features of capitalist economic relations in that they abstract from real life relations, and in so doing, they fetishise relations viewing them as having an existence, such as ownership or liability, disconnected from their concrete conditions. It is in this respect that Marx's critique is at its most acute. The primary way in which law participates in securing the conditions of existence for capitalist social relations takes the form of endowing legal subjects with actionable rights. Marx scathingly denounced 'the so-called rights of man' and 'the rights of egoistic man'; and called talk of equal rights, 'obsolete verbal rubbish'.[15]

Marx's problematisation of law shares with Weber, in particular, the pervasive concern with law as a mechanism of rule at a distance, as if the rules were abstracted from specific economic or political interests. He gives this problematization his own distinctive inflection by focusing on the implications of this new proximity of law and capitalist economic relations by considering its implications for the forms of rule to be envisaged in a future communist society. Marx was adamant in his refusal to speculate on utopian models of future society. But it is clear that his critique of rights is not only a criticism of the fetishism of legal rules, but is asserting the proposition that since industrial capitalism operates increasingly through the medium of law such a mechanism can play no significant role in the construction of egalitarian relations. This line of thought was taken to its logical derivation by the early Soviet legal theorist Evgeny Pashukanis who extrapolated from Marx to arrive at the conclusion that, under socialism, law would necessarily wither away.[16]

---

[15] K. Marx, 'On the Jewish Question' [1843] in *Karl Marx Frederick Engels Collected Works Vol. III* (London Lawrence & Wishart 1975) at 150 and 165, and K. Marx, 'Critique of the Gotha Programme' [1875] in D. McLellan (ed.) *Karl Marx: Selected Writings* (Oxford Oxford University Press 1977) at 565.

[16] E. Pashukanis, *Pashukanis: Selected Writings on Marxism and Law* (eds. P. Beirne and R. Sharlet) (London Academic Press 1980).

Weber

There are strong lines of filiation between Weber's treatment of law and that embedded in Marx's writings. This connection is certainly not an identity, not least because Weber was always conscious, however much common ground he might cover, of a concern to distinguish his position from Marx's in what has come to be referred to as 'the debate with the ghost of Marx'. Another crucial difference is that Weber's treatment of law is far more systematic. With Marx, we have pithy pronouncements that are left hanging, tantalising suggestions that remained undeveloped. Weber meets just about all the hallmarks of a rigorous general theory of law. Thus in drawing attention to continuities between Weber and Marx, I will attend to the differences by pointing to the way in which a problematisation of law which exhibits continuity is inflected in different directions with respect to his substantive lines of inquiry.

Weber's problematisation of law derives from his central concern to understand 'the uniqueness of the West'; how it was that in Western Europe the extraordinary economic transformation of capitalism took place. It was this question that led him into his extensive explorations of the world's great civilisations. Underlying this concern was an anxiety about the long-term viability of industrial capitalism whose continued economic advance seemed to depend on an increasingly militant and organised working class. Weber did not share the almost religious faith in the evolutionary guarantee of progress which was still such a powerful influence into the opening years of the twentieth century. Nor did he have any great enthusiasm about the advance of mass political democracy for this was endangered, particularly in the German context, by the advance of socialist parties.

Thus, the core problematic of Weber's social and political theory addressed the question of how the stability and security of the capitalist order could be sustained. The substance of this problem is readily apparent from a consideration of his tripartite model of the forms of authority.[17] Traditional authority was readily understandable; it was the force of habit, rationalised as tradition and surrounded by religious and other legitimations, that secured its authority; but an authority that was always vulnerable to conditions that could more or less rapidly undermine its legitimacy as was the fate of most of the ancien regimes of Europe and beyond. Nor could such a system take full advantage of the economic potential of nascent capitalism. Similarly, the legitimacy of the intermediate or transitional form of political authority that he termed charismatic was readily understandable. It was the response to the attributes of the charismatic leader that endowed the leader with legitimate authority; the personal

---

[17] Weber's writings on law from various sections of *Wirtschaft und Gesellschaft* are collected in an English translation in M. Rheinstein, (ed.) *Max Weber on Law in Economy and Society* (Cambridge Mass. Harvard University Press 1954).

nature of such authority is attested to by the primary difficulty encountered by charismatic regimes, namely, that of securing succession or, as Weber called it, the routinisation of charisma.

In important respects the rational or rational-legal authority that Weber identified as the key characteristic of modern forms of political authority has none of the advantages of the other forms in that it lacks a readily available symbolic figurehead; rather it was, by its very nature, a faceless impersonal order. From the Enlightenment onwards political authority systematically shifted its claims to legitimacy from tradition, emotion and religion to rational, bureaucratic and professional sources.

Rational authority had to supply its own legitimacy by making a merit out of professionalisation and bureaucratisation; by no means an easy task. Such a legitimation might prove acceptable on pragmatic grounds such as its fairness or impartiality, but it starts out as a 'weak' legitimation unlikely to command strong allegiance until such ideals as the separation of powers and due process of law can be articulated as strong constitutional doctrines. Significantly, Weber himself barely made appeal to such ideals. Rational authority as he conceived it relied largely on the capacity of rational law to generate its own legitimation, requiring obedience to law in and of itself to provide the grounds for citizen compliance. The major functional attribute which Weber saw as inhering in rational law was that it facilitated predictability. While undoubtedly significant in the self-interested calculus of the market, predictability is unlikely to provide anything more than a weak legitimation. The three substantive features of rational law that he identified were a professional judiciary (always likely to be distant from popular sentiment), a bureaucratic public service following 'the rules laid down' (also distant and impersonal) and the codification of rules (only compelling when associated with democratic legitimation).

One important feature of Weber's version of rational authority is frequently overlooked, namely, that he makes only minimal appeal to democratic legitimation. The significant strength of appeal to democracy is that it has the capacity to go a long way to bind citizens of a democratic regime by invoking the collective responsibility of the citizenry. In its simplest form, democratic legitimation derives from the assertion that one's fellow citizens have chosen a system of rule or a law to be implemented, and such a decision is binding on all by virtue of their shared status as citizens.

Weber's vision of modernity draws attention to a tension between individual autonomy and formal legal rationality. He saw the consequence of the rise of legal rationality as manifesting itself in what Habermas was later to term 'juridification processes' through which not only expanding realms of social relations become subject to legal regulation, but in a wider sense law-like processes, rules and procedures are adopted in many fields of social life. Weber saw the peculiarity of the West as centred in its legalistic rationality in which rational self-control and rational economic calculation form a unity. Rationality exhibits two dimensions, one impersonal and connected to control and mastery, and the other normative linked to choice and freedom. Legal rationality contributes to 'freedom' via purposeful self-regarding conduct. This is the root of the tension that Weber perceived between rationalisation and disenchantment.

Weber's project of solving the problem of articulating a political order for modern capitalist society capable of sustaining legitimacy is rendered more difficult by the tension which he recognised as built into the form of justice generated by rational law. There is an inescapable friction between formal and substantive justice. Formal justice generates its claim to realise justice from the impersonality of its decisions that arises solely from being the result of following the rules laid down such that any similar case would be decided in the same way. On the other hand, the claim of substantive justice requires not merely that the rules are followed, but that the results can be morally just by reference to some criteria external to the rules. Formal justice may fail to realise substantive justice, just as securing substantive justice may require the breach of the requirements of formal justice. Thus Weber tends to conflate 'law' with 'legality' and identifies 'law as order' with 'law as justice'. The 'paradox' at the heart of Weber's position is that the institutionalisation of Western rationalism raises the very possibility of its extinction in the form of a domination of means over ends that characterises the pursuit of capitalist interests.

Weber was aware of these and related problems. Its most distinctive manifestation is in his much discussed remarks about the 'iron cage' in his conclusion to *The Protestant Ethic*:

> [T]he pursuit of wealth, stripped of its religious and ethical meaning, tends to become associated with purely mundane passions, which often actually give it the character of sport. No one knows who will live in this cage in the future.[18]

It is undoubtedly true that Weber exhibited a certain pessimism or lack of hope about the long term viability of the framework of rational law and bureaucratic organisation as a stable and sustainable set of supports for rationality and capitalism. It is also evident that Weber, perhaps more than other social theorists, articulated a constructivist view of law as a conscious and intentional means of governing complex social and economic relations. And the constructivist task is firmly located in the hands of the state. Here, as will be seen, there is an important link with Durkheim, for both identified the basis of social cohesion in modernity in the primacy of the imagined community of the nation-state; it is this which goes a long way towards explaining Weber's unproblematic nationalist politics.

---

[18] M. Weber, *The Protestant Ethic and the Spirit of Capitalism* (trans. T. Parsons) (London George Allen & Unwin 1930) at 181–82.

Durkheim

While Marx and Weber directly confronted the problem of the legitimacy of capitalist social relations (Marx) and capitalist political order (Weber), Durkheim rarely used the term capitalism. Yet his problematic was in one important respect similar to those of Marx and Weber. Durkheim's abiding question was: How is it possible that modern society, lacking a cohesive religion or spontaneous morality, can sustain social bonds sufficient to offset the fragmenting tendencies associated with industrial societies? He sought to establish that the complexity of industrial society and the individualism that it fosters does not have to lead to fragmentation and class conflict. In modern society, individuals whilst becoming more autonomous, also become increasingly interdependent and, here is his crucial step, interdependence between individuals results in their depending more closely on society. One element of this rejection of Marx was the insistence that there could be no turning back from individualism which 'is henceforth the only system of beliefs which can ensure the moral unity of the country'.[19] Durkheim's problematic asked how could social cohesion be rendered compatible with advancing individualism.[20]

For Durkheim the task confronting sociology is to:

> discover those moral forces that men, down to the present time, have conceived of only under the form of religious allegories. We must disengage them from their symbols, present them in their rational nakedness, so to speak, and find a way to make the child feel their reality without recourse to any mythological intermediary.[21]

As Durkheim expressed it in one of his best-known formulations: 'The old gods are growing older or already dead, and others are not yet born'.[22] The task is to elaborate a secular morality as the source of social cohesion, and in this task law plays a significant role.

Durkheim had an ambivalent attitude towards industrialism and capitalism. He rejected Marx's strategy for the revolutionary overthrow of capitalism; but,

---

[19] E. Durkheim, 'Individualism and the Intellectuals' [1898] in W. S. F. Pickering (ed.) *Durkheim on Religion: A Selection of Readings with Bibliographies* (trans. J. Redding and W. S. F. Pickering) (London Routledge & Kegan Paul 1975) at 66.

[20] An illustration of this line of inquiry is found in Durkheim's account of the changing forms of punishment. With advancing individualism the deprivation of liberty alone becomes the normal means of social control. He identifies an historical shift from 'religious criminality' (crimes directed at 'collective things') to 'human criminality' (crimes which injure only individuals, such as homicide and theft); E. Durkheim, 'Two Laws of Penal Evolution' [1900] (1973) 2 *Economy and Society* at 285–308.

[21] E. Durkheim, *Moral Education: A Study in the Theory and Application of the Sociology of Education* (trans. E. K. Wilson and H. Schnurer) (New York Free Press 1961) at 11.

[22] E. Durkheim, *The Elementary Forms of Religious Life* [1912] (New York Collier Books 1961) at 427. There is a significant parallel between Durkheim's formulation and Gramsci's thesis that the crisis of capitalism 'consists precisely in the fact the old is dying and the new cannot be born; in this interregnum a great variety of morbid symptoms appear'. A. Gramsci, *Selection from the Prison Notebooks of Antonio Gramsci* (London Lawrence & Wishart 1971) at 276.

he recognised that the pursuit of self-interest produced adverse effects and generated conflict.

> Man's passions are stayed only by a moral presence they respect. If all authority of this kind is lacking, it is the law of the strongest that rules, and a state of warfare, either latent or acute, is necessarily endemic.[23]

This led him to argue that economic life must be regulated in order to 'have its morals raised, so that the conflicts that disturb it may have an end'.[24]

In his early work, *The Division of Labour*, Durkheim's interest in law was peripheral; the tabulation of different types of laws provided a useful measure of the prevalence of two primary forms of social solidarity, the mechanical solidarity of simple societies and the organic solidarity of complex societies. When he ceased to make use of the mechanical-organic distinction, what emerged was a more sophisticated view of the intertwining of law, morals and politics.[25] His problem was to discover a secular morality to serve as a substitute for religion; hence his interest to understand law as a moral phenomenon. His primary claim was that law expresses what is fundamental in any society's morality; thus to understand law sociologically it is necessary to explore how law articulates the basic characteristics of the society. He makes the fundamental claim that human desires must be constrained and channelled through internalised self-discipline. Law is the most visible, formalised element in processes of social regulation. Most significantly, law gives authoritative voice to morality conceived as a system of rules and sanctions that stipulate how people should act, and to behave properly they must obey conscientiously. While he recognised that law may be insensitive and oppressive, Durkheim perceived in the essential nature of law the roots of social cohesion, the ties that bind the individual to the group and its collective aspirations.

This vision of the law as the embodiment of commitment to society is somewhat naive, for it grants no effectivity to the play of power, politics or even the autonomy of the formation of the substantive content of law. I suggest that the root deficiency is that, without stating the thesis explicitly, he views law as the modern substitute for religion which is the concentrated expression of the whole collective life, since in worshipping the divine, society unwittingly worships and celebrates itself. Law is the vehicle through which modern society worships itself. Durkheim, however, emphasised the necessity of incorporating individualism as the moral basis for modern law. Individualism is not necessarily egoism (that is a distorted form, manifesting itself in anomie and other negative manifestations), but rather individualism expresses sympathy for fellow humans by demanding respect for the liberty of each. Here, more clearly than

---

[23] Durkheim, *ibid.*, at xxxiii.
[24] E. Durkheim, *Professional Ethics and Civic Morals* (trans. C. Brookfield) (London Routledge & Kegan Paul 1957) at 12.
[25] For a detailed examination of the relationship between law and morality see R. Cotterrell, *Emile Durkheim: Law in a Moral Domain* (Edinburgh Edinburgh University Press 1999).

elsewhere, Durkheim is closest to liberalism. The 'cult of the individual' provided modern law with its moral basis, but this humanist vision depends on the dubious assumption that social divisions are non-antagonistic.

It is in this context that Durkheim's views on law come into contact with his account of the state and democracy. His conception of the modern state exhibits compatibility with Weber's rational bureaucracy, but as a paternalistic organisation of disinterested specialists supervising the 'cult of individualism'. Moral leadership, governmental skill and diligent administration are needed to translate the morality of complex societies into law. He had no perception of the state as a site of conflict; politicians and experts are treated as benign agents trying to decide what is best for society.

Durkheim proposed that sectional interests and immediate forms of participation be provided through expanding the role of intermediate occupational bodies (such as guilds and trade associations, but not trade unions) as a moral force capable of curbing individual egoism by invigorating feeling of common solidarity. His key idea was that only occupational groups, guilds or corporations could carry out this function because they included all who worked in the same economic field.

His question is, can a governmental morality express the conditions of solidarity in complex societies? How does it maintain authority when collective beliefs no longer unify society? Durkheim's theory of democracy sought to provide an answer to these questions. Under representative democracy, the authority of the state not only depends upon, but encourages the attachment of citizens to society. Thus political democracy is a necessary basis for government in modern individualist societies. Modern law is the form in which the results of these communicative processes are expressed in impersonal rules in a form capable of uniting the citizens. The element which has a largely unspoken but decisive place in the solution that Durkheim proposes to the general problematisation, which holds his inquiries together, is that the nation-state and the concomitant nationalism which it stimulates function as the glue that binds the imagined community of republican France into a governable entity.[26]

3. CONCLUSION

Despite the manifest differences between their projects, their conceptual apparatus and their political agendas, there is a common core to the problematisations that underlie the work of Maine, Marx, Weber and Durkheim. There is a certain linear advance in a recognition and commitment to a constructivist vision of law and one of the primary strategies and techniques of law; Marx

[26] Much of Durkheim's work is concerned with the role of education as the governmental training of citizens into a civilized nationalism; E. Durkheim, *Education and Sociology* [1925] (New York Free Press 1956) and Durkheim, *supra* n. 24.

opposed this line of development, but Weber and Durkheim were deeply committed to this strategic vision.

I conclude with a few brief conjectures on the extent to which the problematization of law has changed over the last century. During this period there has been an academic institutionalisation of inquiries that take law as their immediate object of inquiry. There has been a demarcation into a set of overlapping sub-disciplinary fields each with their own institutional apparatuses of departments, research institutes, conferences and journals. Jurisprudence, sociology of law and socio-legal studies each have their own distinguishing marks. For present purposes I ignore these, but a fuller treatment would need to take account of the differing lines of development of these disciplinary specialisms.

The primary trajectory of social studies of law has been to carry forward a variety of versions of the constructivist project in such a way as to resonate with the dominant politics of the twentieth century, namely, the social democratic or liberal welfarist model. But over time there has been an increasing realisation of the contradictory nature of the unintended consequences of the juridification tendencies inherent in deployment of law as a mechanism of conscious social change. My suggestion is that the history of the post-classical sociology of law and socio-legal studies can be understood as a range of responses to the crisis of juridification.

The theme of a crisis of juridification has been expressed in its most developed theoretical form by Habermas.[27] The most important phase of juridification manifests an inescapable side effect of the welfare state project. The web of welfare norms were intended to cushion the effects of capitalist relations (social insurance, etc.) but, in so doing, these measures, designed as means of guaranteeing freedom, operate in such as way as to endanger the freedom of the recipients of benefits. The price paid has been a bureaucratisation that undermines the independence and self-image of welfare recipients. Thus, 'while the welfare state guarantees are intended to serve the goal of social integration, they nevertheless promote the disintegration of life relations'.[28]

Within the predominantly empiricist and policy-oriented field of socio-legal studies there is little explicit consciousness of the crisis of juridification; but its presence is evident in the continuation of the long-standing realist preoccupation with the effectiveness of law which embodies the implicit project of making legal interventions more effective to reduce popular dissatisfaction with the legal enterprise. There is also evident a newer concern which I designate as a preoccupation with legal citizenship whose self-awareness is generally articulated as a concern with 'participation' or 'inclusion/exclusion'. In its most straightforward form the concern is to make law accessible to previously excluded, disadvantaged or marginalised groups. One of the more active trends has been the alternative dispute resolution movement; which in promoting its

---

[27] J. Habermas, 'Law as Medium and Law and Institution' in G. Teubner (ed.) *Dilemmas of Law in the Welfare State* (Berlin de Gruyter 1986) and 'Tendencies Toward Juridification' in *The Theory of Communicative Action: Vol.II Lifeworld and System* (Boston Beacon Press 1987).

[28] Habermas (1986) *ibid*, at 364.

vision of 'user-friendly' alternatives to litigation has been largely unaware that rather than promoting an escape from juridification, it is an active agent of juridification promulgating law-like interventions in ever wider social fields. So whether the specific topic is legal aid and resources for the poor or with advancing gay-lesbian rights, the feature that unites these projects is a vision of law as a strategy for an inclusive citizenship through legal rights and their delivery.

There is a deep tension at the root of this style of work. On the one hand, it grapples with many important dimensions of the reformist project of legal constructivism, that is the use of law as a means of directed social change. Yet its strategy is unambiguously one of juridification. While it resists hierarchical and bureaucratic forms of juridification, it furthers an increasing legalisation of expanded fields of social life. In this respect, it exemplifies the problem which Habermas' discussion of juridification tendencies has highlighted. The problem in its simplest form is that law is both part of the problem and part of the solution. Welfarist interventions participate in the 'colonization of the lifeworld' but the expansion and deepening of legal rights consolidates advances in the promotion of normative values arrived at through democratic political dialogue. In some of his earlier formulations Habermas seemed to suggest a tension, even an opposition between the positivity of law and its promotion of values. In subsequent moves away from this suggestion he advances the view that law 'functions as a hinge between system and lifeworld'.[29] While this aspiration is attractive it seems to ignore the likelihood that in each specific context legal intervention may be skewed in one direction or the other.

There has been a marked tendency for the gap between sociology of law and socio-legal studies to widen and for there to be more open hostility or, perhaps worse, a tendency to ignore developments on the other side of the intellectual fence. This gulf may, however, be more a matter of style than of substance; the language of meta-theory has become more arcane such that the texts of postmodernism verge on the incomprehensible for all but those that have pored over the privileged texts; while empirical studies become more mundane as they rework ever smaller questions about the functioning of legal institutions and processes. It does not follow that the substantive topics addressed have necessarily diverged: certain currents pursued by theoretically informed sociology of law manifest some degree of continuity with the general trajectory of socio-legal studies as described above.

Sociology of law, like so many other areas of the humanities and social sciences, has undergone a decisive 'cultural turn'.[30] This major current has

---

[29] J. Habermas, *Between Facts and Norms: Contributions to a Discourse Theory of Law and Democracy* (trans. W. Rehg) (Cambridge Mass. MIT Press 1996) at 56.

[30] D. Chaney, *The Cultural Turn: Scene-Setting Essays on Contemporary Cultural History* (London Routledge 1994); V. Bonnell and L. Hunt, (eds.) *Beyond the Cultural Turn: New Directions in the Study of Society and Culture* (Berkeley University of California Press 1999) and F. Jameson, *The Cultural Turn: Selected Writings on the Postmodern, 1983–1998* (London Verso 1998).

promoted concern with sets of issues variously termed informalism, legal pluralism, law in everyday life, and community law. It is important to recognize that such interests are by no means 'new'. As discussed above, Maine's meta-history of law gives prominent place to deep-seated shifts in the ordering of social relations that only subsequently leave their mark on state law. Eugen Ehrlich could well have been singled out for recognition as a classical founder of law and society studies;[31] he perhaps more than anyone else pressed the claim for the cultural roots of legal ordering. Thus, it might be more accurate to speak of a 'cultural return'.

My concern is not to engage in an extended discussion of contemporary scholarship, but rather to situate it. Foucault perceptively grasped that current discussion of law still starts out from a deeply ingrained assumption that law is located as a manifestation of state sovereignty. He challenges us by chiding us about our failure 'to cut off the King's head'. Nevertheless, the sociology of law has tended to focus on the modernisation of state law as a major 'steering mechanism'. The alternative proposed by the cultural turn is that a sociology of law that has freed itself from a preoccupation with state-law can discover and elaborate 'alternative legalities' and provide a source of resistance to hegemonic state projects.[32]

The shift of attention towards an informalism and community ordering that is either beyond state legality or, more cautiously, a parallel mechanism of social ordering interest, has been the dominant focus of the sociology of law for more than a decade.[33] It is part of a much wider concern with the transformation of modern liberalism into a form conventionally styled 'neo-liberalism'. This concept has the merit of avoiding the debate which has become somewhat sterile as to whether our present is still modern or is now postmodern, or that we may indeed 'have never been modern'.[34]

Neo-liberal forms of social ordering are characterised by a complex and shifting deployment of forms of state-law regulation which seek to stimulate the self-governing capacity of increasingly individualised citizens.[35] This account of neo-liberal forms of governance has been most fully developed by the Foucauldian

---

[31] Indeed Ehrlich was only omitted on the grounds that to have included substantive discussion would have opened up the field to other claimants and resulted in transforming this essay into an encyclopaedia entry.

[32] S. Silbey and A. Sarat, 'Reconstituting the Sociology of Law: Beyond Science and the State' in D. Silverman and J. Gubrium (eds.) *The Politics of Field Research: Beyond Enlightenment* (Beverly Hills Sage 1989), at 162; see also B. Santos, *Toward a New Common Sense: Law, Science and Politics in the Paradigmatic Transition* (New York Routledge, 1995).

[33] The concept 'social ordering' is employed to contrast with 'social order'. Social ordering is a process of attempts that are never complete, that frequently fail or produce unintended consequences. Its incompleteness and failures only prompt renewed attempts at ordering.

[34] B. Latour, *We Have Never Been Modern* (Hemel Hempstead Harvester-Wheatsheaf 1993).

[35] Those people who are unwilling, unable or lack the resources and capacities to engage in self-governing are either excluded and left to eke out a liminal existence or encounter elevated levels of disciplinary control.

governmentality tradition.[36] This rigorous interrogation of the changing forms of liberal rule has yet to have realised its potential in work specifically focused on the changing forms of legal ordering. However, a particularly promising avenue is suggested by O'Malley's identification of the rise of a new 'prudentialism'.[37]

In welcoming the cultural turn in the sociology of law, I end with a cautionary observation. The rise of self-governance and enterprising individualism, does not herald either the death of the state or of 'the social'. We have not been witnessing the demise of the state or of state-law, but its transformation into new configurations with other modes of ordering. The task, having celebrated the cultural turn is, therefore, to 'bring the state back in'. The task is to grapple with the changing forms in which state law is imbricated with other forms of legal ordering. This provides a problematisation which is no longer, as in the classical tradition, essentially confined to the relationship between state sovereignty and the law, but now reaches out to new connections between forms of ordering. These new prospects are at one and the same time dangerous and exciting. They are dangerous because they herald a globalisation of power without responsibility and accountability whose primary agents are giant corporations and unelected international institution; yet they also create the possibility of envisaging new popular forms of engagement that reach out beyond the classical electoral forms of politics of the classical period of state, law and sovereignty. Marx, Weber and Durkheim, despite the obvious differences between them, all problematised law with respect to sovereignty. Modern sociology of law can and should stimulate the problematisation of law in its relation to democracy.

---

[36] N. Rose, 'The Death of the Social? Re-figuring the Territory of Government' (1996) 25 *Economy and Society* 327–56 and M. Dean, *Governmentality: Power and Rule in Modern Society* (London Sage 1999).

[37] P. O'Malley, 'Risk, Power and Crime Prevention' (1992) 21:3 *Economy and Society* 252–75.

2

Sociological Jurisprudence

REZA BANAKAR

AT THE SAME time as Marx, Weber and Durkheim were theorising about law the Polish-Russian jurist Leon Petrazycki (1867–1931) and the Austrian jurist Eugen Ehrlich (1862–1922) also began to explore the relationship between law and society using broadly conceived sociological perspectives. Petrazycki and Ehrlich worked independently of one another and yet their theories came to correspond with each other in at least one respect. Taking issue with the jurisprudence of their time they refuted natural law theories and contested the claims of legal positivism that a norm became a legal rule only if it was posited by the state. This could not be the primary source of law for the simple reason that its existence presupposed and was conditioned by the law. Instead, each in his own way argued for an empirically based concept of law, which was broader than the state law and existed independently of any outside authority. Unlike Durkheim or Weber, Petrazycki and Ehrlich did not strive to grasp the problems of modernity, but employed social sciences in order to improve the science of law. I have, therefore, chosen to introduce their works under the rubric of 'sociological jurisprudence' to distinguish their contributions from the analyses of the law which emerged out of the sociological inquiry into the nature of modernity.

The following starts by briefly describing the context in which the sociological approaches of Leon Petrazycki and Eugen Ehrlich to law were born. It then goes on to present some general features of the socio-legal theories of Petrazycki and Ehrlich. The final part provides empirical examples of the applicability and relevance of these theoretical approaches to the study of socio-legal issues.

1. THE SEEDS OF THE HOSTILITY

The idea that law and other societal forces are interconnected is hardly new and has always been an important part of any systematic reflection on the nature of the law. Having said that, it is difficult to ignore the total lack of understanding—what has at times amounted to outright hostility—which has tainted the relationship between legal scholars and the sociologists of law. For example, when in his *Fundamental Principles of the Sociology of Law* Eugen Ehrlich presented a concept of law based on the distinction between judicial decisions and statutory enactments, on the one hand, and 'living law' defined as 'the law that dominates life itself, even though it has not been printed in legal propositions',[1] on the other, he was immediately attacked by Hans Kelsen who claimed that Ehrlich had simply confused normative and descriptive analysis and his notion of law was misconceived.[2]

Kelsen's antagonism to and rejection of Ehrlich's theory of living law should be placed in the context of the relationship between law and social sciences at the end of the 19th century. As sociological theory was being developed at the turn of the previous century, and emphases were being placed on *scientific* analysis in all walks of life, a new protest movement began to take shape against the prevailing dogmatic concept of law and the ideology of legal positivism.[3] In continental Europe, feelings of 'uneasiness about the scientific state of jurisprudence' were expressed and voices were raised 'against the self-sufficient activities of legal science and the poor academic standard of jurisprudence'.[4] Critically minded scholars began to question the assumed logical unity of the law and the empirical plausibility of constructing a legal system in logical terms alone. Through the works of scholars such as William Graham Sumner, Leon Petrazycki, Eugen Ehrlich, Emile Durkheim and Max Weber, sociologically orientated studies of law were for the first time introduced and the sociology of law as an academic subject began to take form. These scholars tried to reveal the intrinsic interconnectedness of law and other societal forces, but also to illustrate the primacy of the social in relation to the legal. Their works were distinguished from similar attempts made previously by, for example Montesquieu, Savigny or Maine to study law in its social context, by the application of what can be broadly termed social scientific methods.[5]

It would be misleading to present the friction between traditional legal scholars and sociologists of law as a one-sided affair caused by lawyers' lack of appreciation of sociological insights. Timasheff, for example, argues that '[s]ociology was born in a state of hostility to law', a problem which he then attributes to Auguste Comte's belief—a belief that in turn rested upon Saint-Simon's lack of basic understanding of the law—that 'law was an emanation of the metaphysical spirit and would disappear when the positive stage of development would be reached'.[6] It is, however, a mistake to reduce Comte's attitude in this respect

---

[1] E. Ehrlich, *Fundamental Principles of the Sociology of Law* (Cambridge Mass. Harvard University Press 1936 orig. publ. 1913) at 493.

[2] D. Nelken, 'Law in Action or Living Law? Back to the Beginning in Sociology of Law' (1984) 4 *Legal Studies* 157–82, at 161.

[3] K. A. Ziegert, 'The Sociology behind Eugen Ehrlich's Sociology of Law' in (1979) 7 *International Journal of Sociology of Law* 225–273. According to Ziegert (*ibid.*, at 226) Ihering in Germany, Geny in France, Lundstedt in Sweden, Petrazycki in Russia, and Ehrlich in Austria were among those who raised their voices in protest against the prevailing state of affairs within legal science.

[4] Ziegert, *ibid.*, at 226.

[5] See A. Hunt, *The Sociological Movement in Law* (London Macmillan Press 1987). Also see *infra* n. 7.

[6] N. S. Timasheff, *An Introduction to the Sociology of Law* (Westport Greenwood Press 1974), at 45.

to his (or for that matter to Saint-Simon's) lack of understanding of law only. During this period there was a general mistrust of law and legislation, a fact captured by the critical views of the Historical School,[7] and Karl Marx's conceptualisation of the law as a part of the 'superstructure' of the society reflecting the interest of the bourgeoisie. Marx too was of the opinion that law was a transitory phenomenon, which was 'to "wither away" together with the State, after the establishment of classless society'.[8]

The seeds of this antagonism were *consciously* disseminated through the writings of at least two of the founders of the sociology of law, Petrazycki and Ehrlich, provoking hostile reactions among more traditional legal scholars.[9] To make matters worse, this new social scientific perspective on law was not always presented in the most effective way to those interested in legal theory. As Timasheff explains, Petrazycki wasted little time on academic subtlety when debating legal theory and bluntly told his students and colleagues that 'all the existing theories on the nature of the properties of law were essentially wrong because they ignored the nature of its reality' and what they considered to be the reality of the law was simply a figment of their imagination.[10]

It is interesting to note that the writings of Durkheim and Weber were not, to the same extent, perceived as a challenge to the prevailing legal thought, as those of Petrazycki's and Ehrlich's. Durkheim and Weber's discussions on law were developed as a part of their labours to resolve problems arising out of their studies of modernity. Their studies were not limited to the examination of the effects of law on social forces, but also explored legal reasoning, legal ideas and legal doctrine. Durkheim clearly believed that 'the enterprise of understanding

[7] The Historical School emerged almost at the same time as analytical positivism as a reaction to natural law theories at the beginning of nineteenth century. Two names often associated with this school are the Prussian jurist and statesman Friedrich Carl von Savigny (1779–1861) who belonged to the German 'romantic' tradition and Sir Henry Maine (1822–1888). Savigny and Maine had little in common beside their belief that one could not understand the law without grasping its historical development. The central idea of the German romantic school was that law was the manifestation of the spirit or 'the common consciousness of the people' (the *volksgeist*). Cf. F. C. von Savigny, *Of the Vocation of Our Age for Legislation and Jurisprudence* (New York Arno Press edn. 1975 orig. publ. 1831) at 28. This also implied that the legislator did not stand above the community to impose his will on them, but was part of the people and as such gave effect to their intuitions and needs. That was, incidentally, why Savigny opposed the codification of the law of the German state. Furthermore, the romantics argued that not only law did, but it also 'should vary from one country to another, since different peoples had different spirits' [J. W. Harris, *Legal Philosophies* 2nd ed. (London Butterworths 1997), at 235–36]. Expressed in sociological terms, for Savigny, custom was the universal source of law, a view that seems to be in line with the theory of 'living law' developed later by Eugen Ehrlich.

[8] Timasheff, *supra* n. 6, at 46.

[9] Georges Gurvitch (1896–1965) should also be mentioned here, because he too developed his theory of 'social law' in opposition to legal positivism. Gurvitch belongs to the generation proceeding Petrazycki and Ehrlich and I shall, therefore, not include him in the discussion here. For an introduction to Gurvitch, see R. Banakar, 'Integrating Reciprocal Perspectives: On Georges Gurvitch's Theory of Immediate Jural Experience' in (2001) 16 *Canadian Journal of Law and Society* 67–92.

[10] N. Timasheff, 'Introduction' in L. Petrazycki *Law and Morality* (Harvard University Press 1955) at xvii.

of law as a doctrine should itself become a field of sociology'.[11] Nonetheless, they did not set out to design an alternative concept of law to revolutionise jurisprudence. Instead, they described and explained the phenomenon of law within what was essentially a sociological project. Expressed in an oversimplified form, Weber focused on social action and by exploring the role of rationality in modern society, contributed to the sociological understanding of forms of action, domination and the problem of legitimacy. Weber's explorations into law, legality, legitimacy, legal training, legal profession, bureaucracy, his typology of legal reasoning, as well as his discourse on the relationship between law and economy, must be placed within the broader context of his sociological project to understand the impact of the increased rationalisation of social life. More importantly, in his attempts to unravel the anatomy of legal domination, Weber took the state law as his point of reference. Far from advancing an alternative to legal positivism, Weber affirmed its underlying assumptions by defining law in terms of state coercion exercised by a staff of people who were specialised in law work. Durkheim's theoretical preoccupations might have been formulated differently from those of Weber, but he too was in pursuit of sociological, rather than legal, knowledge. Durkheim was mainly interested in investigating the evolution of society through differentiation of labour and it was against this evolutionary backdrop that he viewed and explored the law as an 'external' index symbolising the nature of social solidarity.[12] Petrazycki and Ehrlich were, in contrast to Durkheim and Weber, specifically interested in employing social scientific methods to *develop* and *improve* the science of law. This ambition was clearly pronounced in Ehrlich's attempts to use historical analysis and empirical observations to re-evaluate legal theory in order to construct a non-doctrinal scientific approach which could inform both legal practice and education.

As pointed out before, it is a mistake to assume that jurisprudence has been hostile to the understanding of the relationship between law and society or has denied the interconnectedness of social and legal factors. For example, constitutional law has never been strictly separated from political science and has, in fact, demonstrated as much interest in the 'letter of the constitution as its practical application, and in addition to this, the nature of the body to which it was applied' i.e. the state.[13] Yet, it is important to recognise that the interest of jurisprudence in society and social facts is very much a function of its own juristic categories. It is one thing to *recognise* that social forces have an impact on law and legal behaviour, as jurisprudence does, but it is another thing completely to apply sociology as a tool to develop a new concept of law aimed to *improve* legal thinking and practice as Petrazycki and Ehrlich attempted to do. They introduced a new concept of law specifically designed to challenge the

[11] R. Cotterrell, 'Why Must Legal Ideas Be Interpreted Sociologically' in (1998) 25 *Journal of Law and Society* 171–92, at 172.

[12] E. Durkheim, *The Division of Labor in Society* (New York Free Press 1933 orig. pub. 1893).

[13] Timasheff, *supra* n. 6, at 50.

dominant understanding of the law in the West. Let us now take a closer look at the works of these two scholars before examining how their theories influenced and guided empirical research on law.

2. PETRAZYCKI'S INTUITIVE LAW

Despite the fact that Petrazycki was an influential legal theorist and social scientist of his time with original ideas concerning the study of law, his sociology of law still remains largely unknown and unrecognised.[14] In the heyday of legal positivism, he rejected both legal positivist definitions and natural law theories and joined the first handful of legal scholars attempting to develop a specific social scientific method for the study of law.[15] This led him to develop a concept of law based on the distinction between official and unofficial forms of law and legal behaviour, a contribution which to date also remains unrecognised by many proponents of legal pluralism. The legal scholars of the turn of the 19th and early twentieth century (*not* unlike many legal scholars and sociologists of today) defined law in terms of the coercion of the state, or a command backed by force. They perceived law and its societal effects in terms of the operations of the formal judicial agencies and institutions such as the courts. These decisions were, however, of secondary importance to Petrazycki who was at pains to explain that the actual foundations of legal order lay not in positive law, but in intuitive law, ie in 'those legal experiences which contain no references to outside authorities'.[16] The functions and operations of the formal agencies and institutions of the law represented by the actions of courts, juries, judges, lawyers and so on, captured only violations of the law, reflecting pathological instances of conflicts and legal transgressions. For Petrazycki, to confuse the pathology of the law with the law proper amounted to ignoring the full potential of the law.[17] By broadening the traditional concept of law, he expressed his disenchantment with the legal theory of the time and, at the same time, addressed the political need for regulation arising out of the conditions dictated by industrialisation to guide the development of society by planned policy

---

[14] Cf. J. Gorecki, *Sociology and Jurisprudence of Leon Petrazycki* (Urbana University of Illinois Press 1975) and A. Podgórecki, 'Unrecognized Father of Sociology of Law: Leon Petrazycki' in (1980) 15 *Law and Society Review* 183–202.

[15] Russian legal theorists such as N. Korkunoff (1833–1902) and V. I. Sergueyevich (1841–1910) had prior, to Petrazycki, made attempts to apply a social scientific approach to the study of law. According to Timasheff, Petrazycki was in particular influenced by Korkunoff who 'combined the sociological heritage of Comte and Spencer with the teaching of R. Ihering'. Cf. Timasheff, *supra* n. 10.

[16] Petrazycki, *supra* n. 10, at 6.

[17] Half a century later, H. L. A. Hart arrived at a rather similar conclusion. He wrote: 'The principal function of the law as a means of social control is not to be seen in private litigation or prosecution, which represents vital but still ancillary provisions for the failures of the system. It is to be seen in the diverse ways in which the law is used to control, to guide, and to plan life out of court'. See H. L. A. Hart, (reprint) *The Concept of Law* (Oxford Oxford University Press 1988) at 39.

measures. The discrepancies existing inevitably between intuitive and official law are a potential source of conflict, but also of social change.

Distinguishing Law from Morality

Petrazycki's theory of law is part of a larger theoretical construct, specifically designed for social action and includes not only a general methodology, but also elements of psychological, sociological, legal and moral theory. Yet, despite his inter-disciplinary engagement, and the fact that in much of his work he was ultimately concerned with sociological issues, there is little doubt as to the profound influence of psychology on his thought. For him law, but also morality, was to be found within ourselves and not as an independent phenomenon out there; law was a psychic phenomenon or a specific form of ethical *experience*, created partly by the state and partly by various groups and individuals. To explore this experience, Petrazycki turned to the psychology of his day and developed the notion of 'impulsion', indicating a category of psychic stimuli, which unlike emotions and sensory perceptions, both of which constituted passive experiences (and, thus, were 'unilateral' psychic stimuli), demanded both a passive and active experience. Hence, the notion of impulsion, which is incidentally Petrazycki's contribution to the psychology of his day, had a 'bilateral' or relational constitution. A person exposed to an impulsion experiences a stimulus (which causes a passive but at the same time a bilateral experience) upon which he/she is urged to respond (to act). The sense of duty, for example, constitutes such an impulsion; it consists of the awareness of a specific state (the feeling of being under obligation or somehow accountable) and an urge to do something about it. The impulsion of duty belongs, according to Petrazycki, to the broader category of *ethical impulsions*, which in turn consist of two sub-categories: those which are experienced as duties linked to another person's corresponding rights, which he calls law, and those without such a link, which he calls morality. This distinction enabled Petrazycki to separate law from morality (which otherwise belong to the same psychological category of ethical impulsions) without making any universal claims as regards the substance of such norms. The distinction is, however, contextual and essentially sociological, reflecting the existing relations at any intersection of time and place. As Gorecki explains:

> The thus identified legal and moral impulsions are among the main stimuli of the social actions of men. The moral ones are somewhat of a luxury: they stimulate exceptional rather than broadly expected behaviour. (However, in the course of social development many of them become legal: what had been perceived as a gracious obligation by the few noble-minded becomes a widespread experience encompassing rightful claims on the part of the beneficiaries; for example, the duty of equal treatment of minorities in many nations). Consequently their social role is narrower than that of the legal impulsions. Moreover, the legal impulsions are stronger: containing

not only the feeling of duty, but also of right, they tend to bring about a greater pressure on those legally bound, and stimulate those who experience their own rights—a stimulation indispensable to the creation of free citizens and to the developments of various kinds of social activities, in particular the economic.[18]

The contextual character of the distinction between law and morality, that the distinction is not carved in stone and is continuously revised and recreated in response to new social needs, turns Petrazycki's understanding of law into a dynamic theory and reveals how different his approach to law and morality was from that of the scholars of his time.

To sum up, according to Petrazycki, law and morality belonged to the same class of ethics consisting of bilateral psychological experiences. Morality was distinguishable from law because it was based on purely imperative impulsions, creating duties only. Law, on the other hand, always consisted of imperative/attributive emotions, creating mutually correlated rights and duties. A person's perception of her *rights* is a state of mind ultimately produced by law—it is a legal experience irrespective of whether or not it is upheld by the state norms—while behaviour motivated by duties alone is a function of morality. This distinction is, in fact, a sociologically useful one and was employed by Petrazycki to conduct a comparative examination of moral and legal phenomena. It was also used later as the basis of Gurvitch's sociological theory of law. More recently, it has formed an important part of the theoretical approach informing nationwide inquiries into the legal attitudes of the Polish people.[19]

The Relationship of Official and Intuitive Law

In *Law and Morality*, which consists of Petrazycki's selected writings translated into English, he argues that law includes not only much of that which lies 'outside the cognisance of the state and does not enjoy positive official recognition and protection, but also much that encounters an attitude of outright hostility on the part of the state and is to be hunted out and eradicated as contrary and antagonistic to the law officially recognized by the state'.[20] An extreme example of such a system of law, which is not recognised by the state, is that of 'the law of criminal organizations', which according to Petrazycki, consists of more or less sophisticated systems of imperative attributive norms aimed at distributing obligations among, designating functions to and bestowing rights on its members. The other example of this type of unofficial law is found among certain classes of society or religious or tribal groups which are otherwise constitutive of the state.

---

[18] Gorecki, *supra* n. 14 at 6–7.
[19] For examples see A. Podgórecki, *A Sociological Theory of Law* (Milano Dott. A. Giuffre Editore 1991).
[20] Petrazycki, *supra* n. 10.

The tribal mind holds tenaciously to certain elements of ancient law, so that—for centuries sometimes—a dual system of law continues to exist, with resulting conflicts and occasional tragedies and the imposition of more or less cruel punishments (from organs of official power which follow the official law and consider it alone "law") upon persons acting in accordance with the directions of their legal conscience in effectuating rights sacred in their opinion or in fulfilling the sacred legal duty.[21]

It is, however important to note that there is no absolute polarisation between intuitive and official law. The same discrepancies which cause conflicts between the two types of laws also create a *mutual* relationship between them through which they influence each other, thus making social engineering possible. Intuitive legal experiences can challenge official law forcing the legislature to revise its rules of application. At the same time, the official law can create the basis for intuitive legal experiences or as Gorecki explains:

> Obligations and rights, originally perceived as an outcome of the legal codes become experienced as binding and just in themselves. Thus lawmakers can purposefully shape the (positive and intuitive) legal mind of man, influence the ethos of the social group, and consequently smooth and speed up the otherwise unconsciously emerging ethical progress. This is exactly the role of social engineering through law as understood and recommended by Petrazycki . . .[22]

The recognition that there is a mutual relationship between intuitive and official law allows Petrazycki to develop a legal typology capturing the observable combinations of these two types of laws. As summarised by Podgorecki, he distinguished between:

1. *Positive official law* (law used by the courts and upheld by the state);
2. *Positive unofficial law* (e.g. a mediator or unofficial agency resolving a conflict with reference to positive law or normative facts);
3. *Intuitive official law* (e.g. a decision by English courts on the basis of equity); and
4. *Intuitive unofficial law* (people's spontaneous behaviour guided by their legal intuitions rather than by statutes or other normative facts).[23]

The distinctions made here are, as I hope to demonstrate, empirically relevant and represent an insight which is absent in other theories, such as Ehrlich's theory of living law.

Legal Experience and Legal Norm

Petrazycki's general approach is broadly speaking empirical and as such falls comfortably within the boundaries of recent socio-legal research. Yet, one aspect of his approach to law according to which legality is defined as a subject-

---

[21] Petrazycki, *supra* n. 10, at 7.
[22] Gorecki, *supra* n. 14, at 11
[23] Podgorecki, *supra* n. 14, at 191–192.

ive experience could find itself easily at odds with current socio-legal research. He argues that law can be studied as 'a real phenomenon' only in the mind of the person who *experiences* a legal judgement. He writes:

> Observation is the fundamental method of studying phenomena—whether of the physical world or of the spiritual world . . . The legal phenomena occur—and can be found for the purpose of observation—not where optical illusions lead us to suppose they are but much nearer: here within us; in our consciousness of him who is experiencing rights and duties at that given second . . .[24]
>
> The introspective method—simple and experimental 'self knowledge'—is the sole means of observation, *and of the immediate and reliable* cognition and study, of legal and moral phenomenon.[25]

Petrazycki means that only categories of such psychic phenomena which we have already experienced are accessible to our cognition. He is, of course, not interested in ideas as such, but the experience of them by the individual. Although he was acquainted with the works of the sociologists of his time, and also never denied the fact that the experience of ideas could be shared by other individuals (turning into a collective experience) he nonetheless retained his emphasis on the individual and consciously avoided developing a legal theory of collective consciousness. Subsequently, his individualistic approach would restrict us, firstly, to the subjective domain of social life and of studying attitudes to law at the expense of neglecting the structural relations which reproduce legal patterns of behaviour both at the level of the individual (agency) and institution (structure). Secondly, it might mislead us to equate opinion/attitude with action/behaviour. It is now a social psychological commonplace that there can exist a discrepancy between attitudes and behaviour. The fact that a person expresses a belief does not necessarily mean that that person will act in accordance with that belief, which is why it is often said that many people 'do not have the courage of their own convictions'. Having said that, there is undoubtedly a *link* between perception (attitude, opinions, beliefs) and action (behaviour and conduct). The Polish scholars, Adam Podgórecki and Jacek Kurczewski discuss this link in the course of their empirical research.[26] Podgórecki, for example, conducted a study in 1964 to investigate the legal perceptions of the Polish population in general and the population's attitude towards legal sanctions and the general functions of the legal system in particular. Podgórecki admitted readily that there were methodological problems pertaining to the study of the causal relationship between attitude and action and wrote that it was impossible to test how far the views held by a person were consistent with his or her actions. Nevertheless, the data that he collected showed that opinions and attitudes to law were largely determined by psychological factors.[27]

[24] Petrazycki, *supra* n. 10, at 12.

[25] Petrazycki, *supra* n. 10, at 14.

[26] Cf. A. Podgórecki, 'The Prestige of Law' in Britt-Mari Persson Blegvad (ed.) *Contributions to the Sociology of Law* (Copenhagen Munksgaard 1966) and J. Kurczewski, 'The Penal Attitude and Behaviour of Professional Judges' in (1971) 1 *The Polish Sociological Bulletin*, at 127.

[27] Podgórecki, *ibid.*

Jan Gorecki, another Polish scholar, offers an interpretation of Petrazycki's theory that is more susceptible to mainstream sociological analysis. According to Gorecki, Petrazycki did not completely reject the concept of *norm* from the language of his system and, in particular 'when speaking about law as a tool for engineering, he clearly had norms in mind, not experience'.[28] Subsequently, Gorecki suggests that, within the framework of Petrazycki's theory, both norms and experience may be considered as the legitimate subject of socio-legal inquiry, which is more in line with the way it was employed in empirical research later.[29] This interpretation links the concerns of Petrazycki with those of Ehrlich, who made the study of norms the cornerstone of his sociology of law.

In retrospect, Petrazycki's explorations into the issues of law and morality could also be regarded as an early contribution to the sociology of organisations, for by broadening the notion of law in this way he equated the organisational norms of social associations with the law proper. To put it differently, by implication he highlighted the fact that formal legal norms (or positive law in general) were simply a small and specialised part of a much more fundamental societal process of organising social life through rules and norms. In an ideological sense, he 'elevated' these organisational norms to the level of positive law, a tendency which is more pronounced in the works of Eugen Ehrlich and Georges Gurvitch in particular, but more importantly he demonstrated that for positive law to become an effective social tool it had to be understood as an integral part of the larger mechanisms of social organisation, upon which it is dependent for its existence. The validity of positive law is always a function of previous legal decisions or legislation, which in turn presuppose social organisation of some kind, while intuitive law is binding by itself, for it is an intrinsic feature of social organisation. The strength of official positive law lies in the fact that it can be exercised uniformly and its weakness is to be found in the fact that it is by definition 'lagging behind' intuitive law, i.e. there is a gap between widely experienced legal conscience and the legal norms in force.[30]

3. EHRLICH'S LIVING LAW

To what extent the Austrian jurist Eugen Ehrlich was acquainted with and influenced by Petrazycki's social scientifically oriented theory of law, which was published in German before Ehrlich's main work, is a matter of speculation.[31]

---

[28] Gorecki, *supra* n. 34, at 13.

[29] Petrazycki's ideas have been in fact used to conduct fruitful empirical research by the Polish scholar Adam Podgórecki in a nationwide study of the legal and moral attitudes of the Polish population (see Podgórecki, *supra*. n. 26).

[30] Gorecki, *supra* n. 14, at 8.

[31] The first volume of Petrazycki's introduction to legal policy (*Die Lehre vom Einkommen*) was published in Berlin in 1893 and his theory of law and state was published in *Über die Motive des Handelns und über das Moral und des Rechts* also in Berlin in 1907. Ehrlich's *Grundlegung der Soziologi des Rechts* appeared in print first 6 years later in 1913.

However, the fact remains that Ehrlich went about constructing his theory of law by distinguishing between positive and living law in a fashion that bears some general resemblance to Petrazycki's basic understanding of the law in terms of official and intuitive legal experiences.[32] Having said that, it should be mentioned that there are important epistemological differences between Ehrlich and Petrazycki's approaches to obtaining legal knowledge as a result of which Ehrlich's scholarship can in no sense be regarded as an imitation or reconstruction of Petrazycki's ideas. Whilst Petrazycki focused on the individual's experience of legal phenomenon to obtain knowledge of law, Ehrlich concentrated on social and legal norms to carry out his socio-legal analysis. In contrast to Petrazycki, who for methodological reasons and theoretical preferences, shied away from the notion of collective legal consciousness or experience and used psychological categories to devise and develop his approach, Ehrlich felt comfortable exploring the legal features of groups and associations by employing, broadly speaking, a sociological methodology.

The Inner Ordering of Associations

According to Ehrlich no amount of legislation, official enforcement and coercion could by itself transform a rule into 'law' understood in the social sense of the word.[33] For Ehrlich, who formulated his views with the help of observation and through his empirical study of the habits and customs of numerous ethno-cultural groups constituting the Austro-Hungarian Empire of his day, the state was not the source of (legal) order in human society, because order could not be established through coercion alone and the thought of compulsion by the courts did not enter the minds of ordinary men when conducting their everyday business. The order of law was, therefore, not to be found in the law books, but in how social life was *de facto* organised by social networks and groups.

Ehrlich focused on the rules of conduct that people in actual fact obeyed and, thus, in effect governed social behaviour and brought order to social life. He argued that the efficacy, legitimacy and validity of these rules were functions of their acceptance rather than coercion. Ehrlich named these rules, which were based on social behaviour rather than the compulsive norm of the state, 'living law', and argued that they were generated as part of the inner orderings of 'associations' or formal and informal social groupings of various kinds. These associations, which were created through the attempts of people to cooperate and could vary in size and function from business communities to families, constituted for Ehrlich the essence of social organisation of society. In short, according to Ehrlich, society consisted of many associations—some were official and

---

[32] *Fundamental Principles of the Sociology of Law*, which is Ehrlich's major work (*supra* n. 1), was first translated and published in English in 1936.

[33] Ehrlich, *supra* n. 1, at 21.

formal, many were informal. Positive law represented only the law of one of these associations in society, i.e. the law of the state. Furthermore, the state was not *necessarily* superior to other associations as a source of norms, and positive law could be effective only if it was in line with the inner order of associations it was to regulate.

The modern practical jurist's understanding of the word 'law' is primarily in terms of legal rules or provisions, which according to Ehrlich are norms addressed to courts to guide their decision making (*Entscheidungsnorm*) or are instructions addressed to administrative officials as guidelines to process cases (*Verwaltungsnorm*). Thus, for the lawyer's everyday practical objectives, the law is limited to formal rules for making decisions, to 'the norms for decision'. For Ehrlich, on the other hand, the domain of law is much broader than 'Legal Provisions'. Ehrlich can indeed, imagine a legal system consisting of nothing but social order, 'if only for the reason that society is older than Legal Provisions and must have had some kind of ordering before Legal Provisions came into existence'.[34]

Ehrlich is then not only shifting 'the centre of gravity of legal development' away from the state, legislation, legal science and judiciary to the society itself, but also introducing a sociologically informed concept of law which is much broader than legal science can ever permit.[35] He writes:

> The modern science of society, sociology, looks upon law as a function of society. It cannot limit itself to the legal provision as such. It must consider the whole of law in its social relations and must also fit the legal provision into this social setting. For this purpose obviously the greatest possible knowledge of the whole structure of society, of all its institutions, and not only those regulated by statutes, is prerequisite.[36]

The forces governing legal behaviour are, thus, not to be found in legal documents, doctrines, the decisions of courts or the actions of legal functionaries, but in the larger social world. Ehrlich developed in effect a theory of 'societal law in the form of organizational norms', which contrary to the state law evades conflicts and demonstrates its full social potential when it is 'pitted against a superimposed (state) law'.[37]

An Error or a Paradox?

Ehrlich's 'living law' has been often criticised for its unrestricted scope, which tends towards absurdity by including all rules of conduct as law. This tendency lies at the heart of most theories which subscribe to legal pluralism and has been interpreted as an analytical error underlying the sociological concept of law

---

[34] E. Ehrlich, 'The Sociology of Law' (1922) 2 *Harvard Law Review* 130–45, at 132.
[35] Ehrlich, *supra* n. 1, at xiv.
[36] Ehrlich, *supra* n. 34, at 144.
[37] Ziegert, *supra* n. 3, at 242.

based on the assumption that legal phenomena include also the non-legal phenomena. To express this error in a more pointed fashion, the living law seems
to claim that law is even that which is not law. Putting aside the polemical intentions inherent in such a statement, the contradiction is not entirely caused by
sociological theorising, and is indeed to be observed in the operations of the formal law, which, to give an example, under certain conditions recognises the customs and practices of certain groups as valid law. This does not, of course, mean
that all norms of organisation are then to be automatically viewed as law
proper. Yet it shows that the contradictory element in the sociological concept
of law of Ehrlich, and many proponents of legal pluralism, does not necessarily
have to be an analytical error and can, indeed, be an empirically observable
paradox. Notwithstanding such criticisms, Ehrlich's general approach, which is
based on questioning the basic ideological premises of jurisprudence and legal
practice, is still celebrated by many scholars as *the* approach to the study of law
in its social context. And needless to say, the notion of 'living law', which is not
the lawyer's formal tool in adversarial battles but the mode of social organisation *par excellence*, poses even today serious challenges to the lawyer's understanding of the law. As Alex Ziegert points out, Ehrlich's discovery of the
'organisational norms', 'idealised as it might be, has a special analytical power
and naturally runs counter to any experience of a lawyer. This is the effect
Ehrlich wanted to achieve'.[38]

Now looking back at Ehrlich's writings with the intention of placing them
in the context of his biography, we can say that it is highly probable that
the notion of 'living law' was a product of the ethnic and cultural diversity of
Czernowitz in the Bukowina, where Ehrlich worked. There, Ehrlich could
observe 'nine tribes: Armenians, Germans, Jews, Rumanians, Russians
(Lipowanians), Ruthenians, Slovaks (often taken for Poles), Hungarians,
Gypsies' living side by side.[39] He also regarded the attempts of the politicians in
Vienna to enforce their laws on the functioning normative order of this culturally diverse, yet harmonious, social group as socially detrimental. Also, being a
Roman Catholic of Jewish descent with an interest in the Jewish question in
Eastern central Europe, Ehrlich had probably experienced the tensions entailed
in living on the point of intersection of cultures, worldviews and ethnic identities. Such experiences convinced him that formal traditional law was not the
best instrument for coping with such diversity and directed him along a path
which soon took him beyond the pluralistic concerns of Bukowina. According
to Ziegert, this path set Ehrlich off on a jurisprudential quest of 'solutions to the
burning methodological questions *inside* jurisprudence'.[40] According to Nelken,
it led him to reveal the *normative* pluralism inherent in different working normative orders:

[38] *Ibid.*, op. cit.
[39] Quoted by Ziegert (*supra* n. 3, at 229) from E. Ehrlich, 'Das lebende Recht der Völker in der
Bukowina' in (1912) 1 *Recht und Wirtschaft*.
[40] Ziegert, *supra* n. 3, at 227.

The general point that emerged from his consideration of Bukowina was the claim that *lawmakers never confront a normative vacuum*. This claim remains valid today in other social circumstances than those of Ehrlich, even if his more particular views about the limited scope for the state activity now seem outdated.[41]

To assess the true impact of Ehrlich's theory of 'living law' on the formation and development of the sociology of law is difficult and cannot be stated with any historical accuracy. However, it is beyond doubt that other sociologists of law have developed ideas very similar to Ehrlich's. 'Social law', legal pluralism and its offshoot 'legal polycentricity', not to mention Roscoe Pound's call for the study of the 'law in action' are only a few examples of theories, which run parallel with and more or less simulate Ehrlich's insight into law and organisational norms, and also in the same manner question the lawyer's understanding of law and legal practice. The two examples that follow illustrate how ideas similar to those of Ehrlich have stimulated empirical research and further theorising. These examples, which are chosen from the works of the Swedish scholar Per Stjernquist, were influenced by Ehrlich's notion of law and organisational norms, yet they take us beyond identifying the discrepancies between formal and informal law.

4. BEYOND THE GAP BETWEEN FORMAL AND INFORMAL LAW

The first example is based on a historical inquiry into the Swedish legislation on sale and draws on a study which Per Stjernquist conducted during the 1930s.[42] Stjernquist interviewed elderly smallholders in the woodlands of southern Sweden to study their understanding of legal issues at the turn of the century. According to his initial findings the national law diverged a great deal from local practices on sale. In a way similar to Ehrlich, Stjernquist demonstrated that social norms existed prior to the legal norms. Yet, unlike Ehrlich, he observed that despite the fact that the formal laws diverged from the living law, the relationship between the customs and practices of the local people, on the one hand, and the laws of the state, on the other, were not defined in terms of conflict and confrontation. In fact, the legal norms were adjusted to, rather than being superimposed upon, their corresponding social norms (incidentally, this observation is in tune with Petrazycki's recognition of the possibility of a fruitful mutual relationship between formal and intuitive law). The Swedish 1905 Sales Act, which emphasised the legal primacy of the formal agreement between contracting parties, at the same time, recognised that, where no formal agreement existed, current commercial customs had the force of valid law. This illustrated,

---

[41] Nelken, *supra* n. 2, at 164.
[42] All references to Stjernquist's works are based on P. Stjernquist, *Organised Cooperation Facing Law: An Anthropological Study* (Stockholm Almqvist & Wiksell International 2000).

according to Stjernquist, that social and legal norms could form two coherent and independent systems of rules existing side by side for centuries.

This point was further illuminated in another empirical study by Stjernquist that focused on how the formal and informal rules governing corporations were developed in Sweden. Stjernquist argued that it is necessary to adopt a 'social form', such as informal company or cooperative—i.e. an association of two or more people brought together for the purpose of setting up a business endeavour—to stabilise cooperative activity. It also meant that partnership constituted a social form dependent on mutual trust and personal relations among a number of people with a common objective. That is why it does not have a legal personality of its own and partners can be held liable for the obligations and debts of the firm. In addition to this social form, a cooperative venture might also need to adopt a 'formal form' to regulate the future activities, transactions, and financial relations of the participants in the corporation. The need to balance the social form with a formal form arises when the venture expands and the number of participants increases, thus diminishing the role of trust and personal relations as the basis for conducting business. In order to guarantee a degree of stability and continuity in cooperative undertakings, the partnership can reinvent itself by adopting the formal structure of an incorporated company, which has a legal personality distinct from its members and conducts its business in the name of the company. By legally registering what was originally a partnership—ie a 'social form'—as a company, a formal form is employed to underpin the venture and enhance its long-term co-operative stability. Formal documents defining the objectives of the cooperation, the distribution of responsibilities, obligations, and the structure of relationships, are then drawn up and signed by the participants.

Through references to cases and rulings of the Swedish Supreme Court, Stjernquist demonstrated that the social and legal forms of cooperation had a *symbiotic* relationship supplementing each other in the ongoing process of stabilising societal cooperation. The expansion of partnerships (where members are liable for breaches of obligations and duties arising in the course of their mutual business transactions and dealings) necessitated the development of incorporations (where members can no longer be held responsible for business liability). This development soon led to 'innovative' practices motivated by the prevailing socio-economic conditions in society. Some businesses started to separate their activities into various branches, which were then registered under different incorporated company names led by 'dummy members' lacking any interest in the business, in order to reduce their business liability while avoiding risks. The courts initially were not inclined to recognise such constructions as bona fide incorporations. Legislators, however, were eventually resigned to the idea and accepted a limited notion of one-man companies, in the belief that a need for it existed in business. This amounts to the application of the 'formal form' of cooperation to *ad hoc* constructions, but it also demonstrates how the prevailing conditions in society, the norms and values that are generated and reproduced by these conditions, and actions that are promoted on the basis of these norms and values, can interact with the law and the legal system.

In these studies, Stjernquist was concerned with locating the place of law in the everyday life of ordinary people. Therefore, he devoted much of his attention to investigating the manner in which law may be utilised to facilitate, or alternatively impede, the cooperative efforts of ordinary people to organise their everyday life. The questions he posed and the answers he offered successfully utilised and developed not only insights intrinsic to Ehrlich's living law, but also Malinowski's understanding of social order—which as mentioned above was most probably influenced by Petrazycki—and Nonet and Selznick's concept of 'responsive law'. By taking us through modern Sweden's experience of legal regulation, Stjernquist demonstrated vividly that the activities, goals, and aspirations of ordinary men and women, social groups, communities, associations, and enterprises played a decisive role in how the law is formed, transformed, produced, and reproduced over time. Expressed in terms reminiscent of Ehrlich, official legal rules are only a part of what people take into consideration when planning their everyday cooperations, transactions, and interactions. Social or customary norms ('living law' if you will) growing informally out of the activities of communities and associations of people are also taken into account. These customary norms define patterns of behaviour and set the bases for future interactions and organised activities of individuals and groups. The legal rules are frequently developed or brought about intentionally to protect and assist these patterns of action, which emanate from the informal and often spontaneous attempts to organise social life.

These two studies throw new light on Ehrlich's theoretical insights (which had been also emphasised by Petrazycki) by, firstly, clarifying that although living law and formal law may diverge from each other, they may still exist side by side as two separate entities, without necessarily being drawn into a state of conflict. Secondly, by showing that, under politically democratic and economically stable conditions similar to those which prevailed in Sweden, and where the law and its functionaries are accepted as legitimate agents by the general public, living law and official rules of the state may be brought into interplay, creating a formal/informal symbiosis. This idea of symbiosis takes us beyond the notion of state rules as *merely* superimposed forms of legal norms and shows that studies of the living law should also investigate the interplay between formal and informal rules. The fact that living law comes into existence prior to formal law does not necessarily imply that it develops, or *should* develop, in isolation from the formal law. Neither does it mean that the formal law *should* necessarily be a mirror of the living law to become effective. The data on which Ehrlich based his studies belonged to an environment where the relationship between the official laws and informal rules of social organisation was, by definition, confrontational.

This can easily lead to an interpretation of Ehrlich's living law which emphasises the discrepancies rather than the interaction between the formal and informal rules. Stjernquist's studies were conducted under politically stable conditions, which enabled him to reveal that the formal and informal rules of organisation may enter into a symbiotic relationship generating formal rules of law which are neither the will of the Sovereign imposed from above, nor a simple articulation of the norms of conduct, generated from below. This type of law production was hardly alien to Petrazycki, who did not sharply distinguish between formal and informal law (as Ehrlich did) and developed his theory of legal policy by recognising the mutual relationship between what he called intuitive law and official law of the state, thus distinguishing between positive official law, positive unofficial law, intuitive official law, and intuitive unofficial law.[43] In this sense Petrazycki was ahead of Ehrlich. The type of law production Stjernquist describes falls within the framework of Petrazycki's third category of intuitive official law. It also demonstrates that formal/state law and living law are not necessarily two distinctly separate forms of law and that a specific form of legal regulation can, indeed, contain elements of both formal and informal law.

[43] Podgórecki, *supra* n. 14, at 191–92 and *supra* n. 19, at 11.

Section 2

Systems Theory

REZA BANAKAR and MAX TRAVERS

Oᴜʀ ᴏʙᴊᴇᴄᴛɪᴠᴇ ɪɴ this introduction is to explain how law is understood by Niklas Luhmann and Jürgen Habermas, which will help you understand the more advanced introductions by Klaus Ziegert and Bo Carlsson in this section. Each of these European thinkers can be understood as engaging with, yet at the same time making a radical departure from the systems theory that Talcott Parsons developed at Harvard during the 1940s.

There is unfortunately no chapter on Parsons in this reader, which partly reflects the fact that very few academics explicitly draw on structural-functionalism as a research paradigm today.[1] There has, of course, been a reaction against the idea that sociology can aspire to become a science since Parsons was writing in the 1940s. The interpretivists (see section 3) have always been a minority group protesting on the sidelines, but many supporters of the Durkheimian project were taken aback by the extent to which poststructuralist ideas were taken up in the 1980s and 1990s (see section 4). A generation of radical scholars have also turned against Parsons, unhappy with his endorsement of capitalism, and inability to address social conflict. Nevertheless, if one sides with those who see sociology as a science, Parsons is the key macro theorist after Durkheim: and systems theory remains the only means of thinking deeply, and systematically, about the relationship between the individual and society, and how different institutions in society fit together.[2]

In simple terms, Parsons presents society as a smoothly-functioning system, capable of meeting the four functional needs which any society (or biological organism) has to satisfy. These needs are:

A) *adaptation* to the physical environment,
G) *goal attainment*, which means finding ways to organise the system's resources to achieve its goals and obtain gratification,
I) *integration*, which concerns how the system manages internal tensions and conflicts, and co-ordinates its different parts.

---

[1] Although see A. J. Trevino (ed.) *Talcott Parsons Today: His Theory and Legacy in Contemporary Sociology* (Lanham Rowan and Littlefield 2001).
[2] See J. Holmwood, *Founding Sociology? Talcott Parsons and the Idea of General Theory* (London Longman 1996).

L) *pattern maintenance or latency* which is how the system maintains and reproduces itself over time.

There are four sub-systems which enable a society to survive. The economy adapts the system to its environment by extracting resources from the natural world (Adaptation). The political system sets goals for the system through the legislative process (Goals). The educational system and the mass media ensures that the population is socialised into shared values, such as respect for the law, and a desire to consume economic goods (Latency). Finally, the legal system binds everything together,[3] and acts as a safety net by punishing deviants who have not been properly socialised (Integration). For this reason, Parsons was a great admirer of the legal profession, and praised lawyers for fulfilling important 'latent functions' for society such as persuading clients to settle disputes without going to court.[4]

Parsons was roundly criticised by conflict theorists for offering a conservative and uncritical view of American society in the post-war period.[5] However, it is important to recognise that the model did acknowledge the existence of tension and conflict, created by inadequate socialisation and also by poor integration between sub-systems. One theme in Parsons' writings was that the economy was evolving faster than the rest of the system. Institutions and practices lagged behind economic needs, and new laws often ran into opposition from individuals and groups socialised with traditional values. Parsons, in fact, acknowledged the existence of strains and conflicts inside each sub-system, and within individuals trying to meet conflicting role-expectations. However, unlike conflict theorists, he supported the core values of American society, and was optimistic about the prospects for securing greater equality, democracy and economic growth.[6]

The systems theorists who came after Parsons all retained the basic framework of society as an evolving social system, but with a much greater emphasis on strains and conflicts between and within sub-systems. Jeffrey Alexander's neo-functionalism is probably the closest in spirit to Parsons, in that it still regards society as something that can be steered and managed by enlightened government. Luhmann and Habermas, as European intellectuals, offer a rather

---

[3] In 'The Law and Social Control' in W. M. Evan (ed.) *The Law and Sociology* (New York Free Press 1962) 56–72, Parsons describes the legal system in highly differentiated societies as 'generalised mechanisms of social control' operating through economy, polity and pattern maintenance to integrate society.

[4] T. Parsons, 'A Sociologist Looks at the Legal Profession' in *Talcott Parsons, Essays in Sociological Theory* (New York The Free Press 1964).

[5] See, for example, C. W. Mills, *The Sociological Imagination* (Oxford Oxford University Press 1961).

[6] Researchers in this tradition have often employed quantitative methods to measure outputs and inputs between different systems, conceptualised as 'feed-back loops', an example of which can be found in W. M. Evan, *Social Structure and Law: Theoretical and Empirical Perspectives* (Newbury Park Sage 1990). It was assumed that the analyst can act like a scientist or a physician in identifying faults and correcting them.

more sober assessment, one better suited to a contemporary world where we can see no alternatives to the present system, but are increasingly aware of the massive economic inequalities, environmental problems and psychological anxieties generated by capitalism.

We are fortunate in having a contribution in this section from Klaus Ziegert who knew Luhmann personally, and is familiar with many of his books that have not so far been translated into English. Some readers may well get the disturbing sense that there is a whole theoretical apparatus here that has had very little impact on the international Law and Society movement. Our own reading of the chapter is that concepts like 'recursivity', 'operative closure', 'binary coding', 'structural coupling' and, of course, 'autopoiesis' offer a powerful tool for thinking formally about the relationship between law and society. Although Ziegert would probably disagree, there is not much in Luhmann that is not already present in Talcott Parsons's structural-functionalism (which, as we have suggested, did recognise the existence of strains and tensions between systems). On the other hand, Luhmann's understanding of the manner in which systems differentiate themselves from other systems, i.e. their 'autopoietic' property, offers a distinctive way of theorising society that is particularly useful in understanding law.

Systems theorists are often criticised for producing abstract models of society that cannot be related back to the actual activities of human beings. Although this criticism can also be made of Luhmann, one can see from Ziegert's chapter how this conceptual framework can be applied in a systematic way to law. One can see, for example, how it is quite useful for understanding the interdependence, and yet also the structural tensions between law and the state, and the internal differentiation within the legal system of different specialisms. Ziegert also offers the interesting general characterisation of the law as the 'immune system' of the social system, one that steps in when things are going wrong. This is again similar to Parsons' view of law, except that Luhmann believes that legislation cannot guarantee 'a successful management of society's future'. Here one has echoes of the Durkheimian argument that the individual in modern, highly-differentiated societies suffers from anomie, a sense that there are no longer certain or shared values.

This is also, more or less, what Jürgen Habermas concludes about society and the legal system, although this hardly does justice to the systematic way he works through different bodies of theory to produce an awesome synthesis which owes as much to Marx and Weber as to Parsons. In fact, Habermas is usually described as a critical theorist and the heir to the tradition of the Frankfurt School, the left-wing intellectual movement founded in the 1930s by Max Horkheimer, Walter Benjamin, Theodor Adorno and Herbert Marcuse. Although, none of these were systems theorists, one can see from Bo Carlsson's review why we have included Habermas in this section. He gives systems theory a critical or left-wing edge, particularly in his early work, which is absent in Parsons and Luhmann.

We have already seen how both Marx, Durkheim and Weber, the sociological jurists and the systems theorists have been interested in the relationship between the modern state and the rest of society.[7] Habermas theorises this in terms of crises caused by the 'colonisation' of 'the lifeworld' by 'the system', i.e. by the growth of the market economy and modern state. Whereas in Parsons and Luhmann, there are tensions between different parts of the social system, Habermas contrasts 'the system' and 'the lifeworld'. In his early work, he identified a 'legitimation crisis' created by the growth of the state, which cannot solve problems such as social exclusion, crime and inequality. This was a politically radical agenda since he was also arguing, along Marxist lines, that the media represented the interests of the powerful, and that the crisis could only be resolved by achieving greater democracy. However, Carlsson also notes that, in his later writings, Habermas seems to have made his peace with liberal capitalism. One finds him complimenting law, in a similar way to Parsons and Luhmann, as having the 'potential to "transmit" the "democratic impulses" of the life-world to the systematic machinery of the economic and administrative state'.[8]

---

[7] See Hunt's and Banakar's chapters in section 1.

[8] W. E. Forbath, 'Habermas's Constitution: A History, Guide and Critique' (1998) 23 *Law and Social Inquiry*, at 992.

3

The Thick Description of Law

An Introduction to Niklas Luhmann's Theory of Operatively Closed Systems

KLAUS A. ZIEGERT

THE PURPOSE OF this chapter is to give an overview of the guiding concepts and objectives of a particular methodology, namely Niklas Luhmann's theory of social systems. In order to mark its radically different approach and to set it apart from the structuralist and normative tenets of earlier systems theory and from what he called 'empirical sociology' in his numerous replies to criticisms, Luhmann called his approach functional method at first, then 'comparative method', later the theory of social systems, and finally, more accurately, the theory of operatively closed systems.[1] It is in this later stage that Luhmann's work was more widely noted and branded as 'autopoietic theory' by others.[2] However, the name for his approach did not matter much to Luhmann and he occasionally used other names in his profuse work. Luhmann's indifference as to how one should label the approach—which he places squarely and deliberately in sociology rather than in legal theory or social philosophy—makes an important point which is often overlooked when the work is bluntly categorised as a 'grand theory'. I will argue that Luhmann was not interested in theory building as such but in the enlightening potential of sociological methodology.[3]

---

[1] The 'classic' systems theory is above all associated with the name of Talcott Parsons (1902–1979) and his foundational work for modern sociological theory. For Luhmann's replies to his critics see, for instance, N. Luhmann, *Das Recht der Gesellschaft* (Society's law) (Frankfurt Suhrkamp 1993) at 18, 31, 41, 45, 46, 149. On the indebtedness of Luhmann's work to Parsons see N. Luhmann, 'Warum AGIL?' (Why AGIL?), 40–1 *Kölner Zeitschrift für Soziologie und Sozialpsychologie* 127–139. For discussions on his comparative method see, for instance, N. Luhmann, 'Funktionale Methode und Systemtheorie' (Functional method and systems theory), (1964) 15 *Soziale Welt* 1–25, quoted from reprint in N. Luhmann, *Soziologische Aufklärung* (Opladen Westdeutscher Verlag 1970, 31–53) at 46.

[2] Luhmann was mildly puzzled about the rabid attention which the single word 'autopoiesis' provoked (from Greek 'self-creation' but also implying self-reference); he pointed out that a single concept (autopoiesis) could never amount to a theory, especially not systems theory; but that required a reworking of systems theory in order to make it consistent with the assumptions implied by the concept. Cf. G. Kiss, *Grundzüge und Entwicklung der Luhmannschen Systemtheorie* (Fundamental principles and development of Luhmann's systems theory) (Stuttgart, Enke, 1990).

[3] See the collection of his pathbreaking sociological essays under the title 'sociological enlightenment' which had a momentous impact on sociology at the time of their publication starting in 1967, N. Luhmann, *Soziologische Aufklärung* (Opladen Westdeutscher Verlag 1967), until 1990, *Soziologische Aufklärung 5* (Opladen Westdeutscher Verlag 1990).

His approach, then, can be better understood as a sociological methodology for theory building.[4]

I will start this overview by setting the scene for Luhmann's approach (section 1). This will be followed by an outline of the basic theoretical concepts that are generated by this approach and lead to a conceptual map of society's law (section 2). In conclusion, the methodology of Luhmann's approach and its applicability for socio-legal research will emerge as the crucial issue in understanding the objectives of the theory of social systems (section 3).

1. THE QUEST FOR A SOCIOLOGICAL THEORY OF LAW

Niklas Luhmann is arguably the most radical, certainly the most ambitious, propagator of a scientific observation and description of law. Luhmann has explicit answers to the question as to how law can be observed and described as a phenomenon. But these answers are not simple and sociologists should not expect simple answers. Above all, these answers cannot be found in legal theory or legal doctrine, and not in sociological doctrine either. That is why Luhmann branches out to the philosophy of science and works out a unitary concept of scientific knowledge with evolution theory and the theory of distinctions as the crucial link between conventional natural science and social science approaches. Many readers, especially lawyers and sociologists of law, are challenged by this broadly based scientific approach presented with his peculiar sarcastic pitch and unique style of writing. Difficulties of understanding abound even if readers understand and can read the texts in the German original. Translations compound these difficulties.[5] Uncompromising science requires uncompromising language, and here Luhmann's fondness for the finely tuned concepts of jurisprudence comes into play. Both jurisprudence and the academic design of the German language support playing with words, modifying words and meanings, simply inventing new words, or filling old words with provocatively new meaning.[6] Obviously, all of this helps to distinguish the conceptual fit of statements. But it also asks readers to be on their guard and to think for themselves.

Luhmann offers more than just a general theory in the conventional deductionist natural science paradigm. In a very particular way he moves on to what amounts—in methodological terms—to a thick description of society, including

[4] See for a more detailed discussion of the relationship with a similar method-conscious approach (grounded theory) section 2 below.

[5] For Luhmann's own comments on the difficulties with translations of his text, see the interview with P. Guibentif in Bielefeld 1991, first published (in French) in A.-J. Arnaud & P. Guibentif (eds) *N. Luhmann, 'Observateur du droit'* (Paris Librairie générale de droit et de jurisprudence (1993) 5 *Droit et société*, pp.187–229); in the German original transcript version P. Guibentif, 'Niklas Luhmann und die Rechtssoziologie: Gespräch mit N. Luhmann, Bielefeld, 7. 1. 1991' in (2000) 21–1 *Zeitschrift f. Rechtssoziologie* 217–245 at 220.

[6] See comments on translating into English in N. Luhmann, *Social Systems* (Stanford Stanford University Press 1995) at xxxviii.

its law.[7] Such a thick description of society is complex, because society is complex and it is 'thick' because it follows up conceptually and situationally every detail that happened or happens in society as it happens. What Luhmann objected to in his criticism of empirical sociology was, in fact, only one particular branch of empirical research: quantitative variable-analysis. What he actually ventured onto unwittingly, in distancing himself from this kind of empirical research, was the other branch: the content-rich, thick description used systematically in qualitative empirical research. In Luhmann's version the conceptual groundwork is much denser and interwoven than envisaged by the pragmatist, ultimately conceptually thin version of grounded theory.[8] Over the course of its development from programmatic probing[9] to meticulous mapping[10] Luhmann may have used different names for his approach, but he plotted his methodological strategy early in his work and stuck meticulously to it.[11] This methodological strategy can be summarised as follows:

1) Things or, as Luhmann prefers to say, 'states of affairs' (*Sachverhalte*) and the 'world' at large, are there and/or happen.
2) States of affairs and the world are neither obvious nor self-explanatory.
3) They can be scientifically observed and explained, and this may result in the different points of view of different observers. But the phenomena are not 'made up' by the observers and the observers can reach an inter-subjective understanding of what things 'mean'.
4) Theory which is a-priori and predictive (prognostic) is useless (impractical) for explanation. Scientific observation and explanation have to proceed empirically and by a solid grounding of theoretical concepts on accurate observations.
5) The most solid grounding and most accurate observations are achieved by a comparative approach.

---

[7] See C. Geertz, 'Thick Description: Toward an Interpretive Theory of Culture' in C. Geertz, *The Interpretation of Culture* (New York Basic Books 1973) at 3–30. See also, surprisingly, L. Mjøset, 'Stein Rokkan's Thick Comparisons' in (2000) 43 *Acta Sociologica* 381–397.

[8] See most notably B. Glaser & A. Strauss, *The Discovery of Grounded Theory* (New York Aldine de Gruyter 1967); A. Strauss & J. Corbin, Strauss *Basics of Qualitative Research. Grounded Theory Procedures and Techniques* (Newbury Park Sage Publications 1990).

[9] See the collection of early sociological essays (1962–1968) in N. Luhmann, *Soziologische Aufklärung* (Opladen Westdeutscher Verlag 1970).

[10] See the series of books on functional systems starting with the conceptual map in N. Luhmann, *Soziale Systeme: Grundriss einer allgemeinen Theorie* (Frankfurt Suhrkamp 1984; Engl. edition: *Social Systems*, Stanford University Press Stanford 1995); *Die Wirtschaft der Gesellschaft* (Society's economy; Frankfurt Suhrkamp 1988); *Die Wissenschaft der Gesellschaft* (Society's science; Frankfurt Suhrkamp 1990); *Das Recht der Gesellschaft* (Society's law; see note 9), *ibid*. Die Kunst der Gesellschaft (Society's fine art; Frankfurt Suhrkamp 1995); *Die Religion der Gesellschaft* (posthumously Society's religion, Frankfurt, Suhrkamp, 2000); *Die Politik der Gesellschaft* (posthumously Society's politics; Frankfurt Suhrkamp 2000) and ending with the grandiose account of society in the setting of global society in *Die Gesellschaft der Gesellschaft* (Society's society; Frankfurt Suhrkamp 1997).

[11] See support for this assessment by Kiss, *supra* n. 2, at 4.

6) When compared, the most distinctive features of phenomena are their functions and not their forms.

7) The most important aspect of functions is not that they are fulfilled or the fact that they exist but that they are made possible.

8) Possibilities are contingent. If something (that exists/happens) is possible, it is also possible differently (functional equivalents). The fact alone that something happens, eg social action, does not allow any inferences as to why it happened.

9) If something is possible, its appearance can be compared in different settings.

10) The arbitrariness in choosing reference points for comparisons can be limited (observations can be 'condensed') by observing functional equivalents and how they are generated.

11) Good theory (accurate observations and content-rich, careful building of theoretical concepts) must be able to answer the question as to how something can become possible, ie good theory must be able to answer the question as to how something can create its (own) boundaries in relation to the environment.[12]

12) The observation and conceptualisation of systems and system operations is a means to build good theory, because:
   12.1) systems exist;
   12.2) systems create their (own) boundaries in relation to the environment (autopoiesis);
   12.3) systems organise, reproduce and maintain possibilities and conditions for other possibilities through their operations;
   12.4) the possibilities that are provided by systems operations are determined by their functions.

13) The theory of social systems is good science because it
   13.1) observes actual (complex) system operations;
   13.2) is limited in its arbitrary selection of reference points ('topoi') by the structures which the system operations themselves have and reproduce, and therefore exhibit;
   13.3) can locate topoi empirically by areal/situational mapping.

14) Social systems are the 'research field' or 'sites' of systems theory research.

Being aware of the methodological drive behind Luhmann's use of systems theory and the strategic choice of the concept of 'system' as the empirical key element refutes the suspicion that Luhmann's theory building is an exercise for theory building's sake.

---

[12] See Luhmann, (1993) *supra* n. 1, at 15.

2. THE THEORY OF OPERATIVELY CLOSED SYSTEMS

We can start, then, from the assumption that, just like the 'understanding' approach of Max Weber is crucially guided by the concept of 'ideal type' as a methodological key element, the concept of 'system' is the methodological key element in Luhmann's approach of the theory of operatively closed systems. In this sense, the concept of system is both a theoretical concept and a methodological stepping-stone. It follows, differently from Weber's approach and also sharply in contrast to Talcott Parsons' concept of system, that a system is not an ideal type or normative projection but a concretely existing, and in this sense real, area or site for sociological mapping. In grounding his theory on the empirical reality of systems, Luhmann laid a foundation both for the thick description of systems and for further theory building. The concept of system was fully developed and locked into place both in methodology and theory by 1984.[13]

We can assume further that, because of Luhmann's professional socialization as a lawyer, the legal system has a paradigmatic position in his work. Therefore, in mapping the legal system, we can step by step unravel the complex loops of the theory of operatively closed systems, obtain a thick description of law and come to terms with Luhmann's methodology and theory of operatively closed systems.

2.1. Mapping the Legal System

Basic Assumptions[14]

For Luhmann the question is no longer 'how is social order possible?' but 'how is it that social systems make themselves possible?' The concept of system replaces the idea of society, a useless term as far as sociological theory is concerned. Does it mean: people? nations? states? countries? In contrast to the term society, systems can be defined accurately. Their constitutive (final) elements are their operations. Systems emerge from unfocussed operations becoming focussed.

For instance, the undirected nervous muscular movements (operations of the organic system) allow a newly born baby to associate (operation of the mind or personal system) certain states of her body (getting fed, warm, dry, comfortable, etc.) with certain movements that the mother makes in playing her role as mother of a baby (operations of the social system). The unfocussed operations of association become increasingly focussed on earlier operations of the same

---

[13] The date is clearly marked by the publication of his major work *Soziale Systeme* (social systems) with the programmatic subtitle *Grundriss einer allgemeinen Theorie* (Fundamental principles of a general theory) *supra* n. 10.

[14] See for a systematic introduction to these concepts Luhmann, *ibid.*

kind: the baby begins to distinguish consciously between environment (mother, food, cold, etc.) and 'self' (what mother, food, cold etc. 'mean' to 'herself'). The baby's mind (consciousness) begins reproducing and stabilising its own operations. The result is a self-concept of the mind—self, in contrast to the environment, but put on as a mask ('persona') constructed in relation to what can be gleaned ('perceived') from how other individuals present themselves as persons. The system 'mind' emerges through the recursive operations of association, drawing a distinction between the operations themselves and what they cannot operate (environment).

In our example we have been dealing with three systems and their (own) operations. There is a) the organic system (body) of the baby, b) the emerging personal system[15] (mind) and c) the social system (meaningful communication between baby and mother). The operations of each system are determined by previous operations to which they cannot but recur. They cannot be determined by operations in the environment.[16] And each system can deal with the other systems only as their being a part of an indeterminable and 'blurred' environment.

Full self-directedness of the operations of a system is achieved when it can reproduce all its operations exclusively by its own operations (operative closure) and, therefore, can draw a clear boundary between its operations and the environment. This happens, for instance, with the body at birth when the umbilical cord is severed, with the mind when full consciousness is established (from age three to five) and with the social system when communication can be established that makes 'sense'—the 'interlacing of feelings and language'. Operative closure, then, does not mean a hermetic seclusion of the system from the environment. For instance, the human body (organic system) cannot survive under water. It requires the processing of oxygen—even if technically (social system!) we can approximate a life under water with diving apparatuses and submarines and incur the risk that they may fail. The mind (personal system) cannot and does not draw on the experiences of others, and we rely on communication (the social system) to approximate the experience of others incurring the risk that we may have missed or misunderstood essential details. And communication (the social system) cannot be extended to 'talking with' the mountains or anything else in the physical environment—even if we can talk about mountains and can approximate the conversation with them, for instance, in religions (social systems) or fairy tales with the risk of disillusionment. In all these cases everything

---

[15] Luhmann uses 'personal system' and 'psychic system' (German: *psychisches System*) interchangeably—in English probably better: psychological system—for the concept of a duality of meaning generating systems (coupled personal systems *and* social systems) rather than the, meaningless unity of an individual ('subject'). Cf. Kiss, *supra* n. 2, at 24.

[16] Systems are related to their environments exclusively by the operations of the system; see Luhmann, 1984, *supra* n. 10, at 146. This argument leads to the further argument (against Darwin) that there is no 'natural selection' as such in the process of evolution because there is no nature as such which selects but only systems (which operate selectively).

that lies beyond the boundaries drawn by the operations of the respective system, ie what can be operatively closed by the system, is 'ultra vires' for the operations of the system—or remains guesswork and conjecture which are still operations of the 'meaning generating' systems (the social system and the personal systems respectively).

We have seen that *recursivity* ensures that systems can cope selectively with situations by focusing on readily available operative sequences which the system has used earlier and over which the system has exclusive disposition. In recursively reproducing such operations the system reproduces itself or, in reproducing itself, the system is not only self-referential but also creating its elements with its own elements (*autopoiesis*). Seen in a different way, we can call this sequencing of operations *operative closure*. It means that in order to operate and keep operating, systems cannot but bring into play their own operations. Operative closure does not mean that systems operate in a vacuum, or that systems do not respond to pressures, stimuli or irritations generated in the environment, for instance by other systems, or to self-irritations generated in the system itself.

Translated into the terms of the operations of the social system (communication) *normativity* presents itself as a communicative means of operative closure. Normativity provides a drastic selection of manageable operations from many more possible ones. *Normative projections* are effective operations over time because they resist change by ignoring other possibilities (ie they are *contrafactual* because they are not designed to respond to information about 'reality'). This 'refusal to learn' is their desired 'ratchet' effect.[17] This means that normative projections, as operations of the system (communication) can be maintained no matter what actually materialises. We can identify these kinds of system operations as *normative expectations*.[18] They are operations which, on the one hand, allow further operations to become possible at all and, on the other hand, ride on the radical reduction of complexity ('the ratchet' effect). The operative device for an alternative strategy would be the communication of *cognitive expectations*, that is projections of future states that signal preparedness (openness) for adjustment ('learning') in the face of contradictions and good reasons for not holding on to these particular expectations ('trial and error'). Put simply, the alternative is between insisting on norms or learning. Both are *factual* forms of communication.[19] Furthermore, the communicative design of

[17] Obviously, the projection of an 'ideal' state of affairs is not an issue of the norm design. Or, simply put, norms want to be norms and are silent about any ideal reality.

[18] More accurately, though clumsily, described they are normative expectations of expectations (of others). This reflexive relationship reflects that they are social system operations (communication) and *not* individual (personal) expectations which may or may not endorse the expectations communicated normatively in the social system.

[19] Accordingly, the frequently alleged qualitative difference between a 'normative' sphere of 'ought' (norms) and a 'factual' sphere of 'is' (facts) has no substance in sociological observation. They are just different strategies for dealing with information in communication. Note, for example, the different treatment of 'law' (norms) and 'facts' in legal procedure.

expectations makes possible a coupling effect between the social system (communication) and personal systems (minds). Through this *structural coupling* the strictly separate (autopoietic) operations in each system can become aligned with each other and rely on each other in *a parasitic relationship* of social systems and personal systems. With structural coupling of expectations in place, each system can rely on the complexity of the other system to operate its own autopoiesis. A good example of this relationship is socialisation. Socialisation means that individuals pick up the meaning of communication in their social environment (eg family, school, profession, etc.) without surrendering their own ideas, fantasies or expectations while confirming and reproducing the communication in the social system in the socialisation process. Evidently, nothing 'flows' *between* the mind (personal system) and society (social system). The operations of each system happen or they do not happen. But when they happen they always happen only on the own terms of each system and as operations of that system.

A first conclusion is, then, that the operations of communication and their recursive reproduction of the system alone constitute the social system. Any further development, for instance in a historical or evolutionary sense, is a development *within* the social system. Put differently, in order to develop new possibilities for communication, the social system can provide an environment within the system in relation to which other social systems can be (normatively) stabilized. Sub-systems operate with the social system as their environment. Such functional sub-systems specialising in providing particular functions for society (the social system) by increasing the internal complexity of society are, for instance, the political system (organising collectively binding decision-making), the economic system (specialising in exchange relations), the family system (organising coping with everyday life on an enduring base), the science system (organising collective knowledge) and the legal system.

It follows that society's differentiation of functional (sub-) systems is achieved by *selective operations* that create and then stabilise special meaning as the focus for further (specialised) communication This can happen in three directions following the three dimensions which meaning can take:[20] a) a factual dimension of meaning (ie things and contexts in the environment); b) a time dimension of meaning (ie past, future, at a distance); and c) a social dimension of meaning (ie others and their experiences and actions). As the complexity of the social system increases, not least through the proliferation of sub-systems, the specialisation of the references to these three different dimensions of meaning becomes more accentuated by the operations of the social system in special (functionally differentiated) systems which help to increase the selectivity of communication (the social system) in the face of complexity.

For instance, specializing references to the factual dimension allows stabilising *person concepts* ie how to present oneself to others, *values,* ie points of

---

[20] See Luhmann, *supra* n. 10, at 114.

preference or priority, or *roles*, i.e. aspects of the scope of the activities of others. The communication of person concepts specialises the function of families (ie the family system) and how they operate socialisation and social control by relating conduct to meaningful person concepts (for instance, what it means to behave like a man, woman, child, hero, saint, etc.). The communication of values specialises the function of political systems, including religions in facilitating the communication of points of preference to which others commit and bind themselves collectively. The communication of role concepts specialises the proceduralisation of the organisation of work, eg in trades, professions, industries etc. and makes it possible to shift social structure from a status society (in which, above all, person concepts are communicated) to a 'class society' (in which the communication of role-concepts makes possible a dramatic increase of communication events. ie 'industrial society', 'mass society'). On the other hand, communication of references to the social dimension of meaning specialises the protection from the open complexity of social relations and the unreliability of individuals. It provides with the form of *institutions* a normatively generalised, more manageable alternative to 'real people'—for instance, the judges of a court (must) hear, within their institutional obligations, all cases all the time and (must) decide without fear or favour. Finally, communication of references to the time dimension of meaning specialises the protection from the openness of time—no one can know the future for certain. Future-resistant communication provides with the form of *norms* a generalised, more manageable alternative to the 'real future'. The ratchet effect of a norm makes it possible to subscribe to a 'guaranteed' prediction of a future outcome. For instance, a speed limit sign 'guarantees' that all drivers will respect a certain speed by guaranteeing that it cannot be wrong ('embarrassing') to drive not faster than the mandated speed, even if nobody observes the speed limit (drivers rarely drive accurately at the mandated speed). While the norm cannot guarantee that the projected outcome materialises (all drivers observe the speed limit all the time), it can justify conduct retrospectively (eg after an accident) or allow litigating (eg after a hurt or 'tort'), or simply make one feel good (eg when others are stopped by an unmarked police car).

Two observations, then, are important here: a) norms 'immunize' against the unpredictability of the future but cannot control the future, and b) the functional effect of norms is not the projection of an ideal future but the projection of a 'managed' alternative to an unpredictable future. Their binding effect is achieved in relation to time and not in relation to the social dimension (integration). Norms bind time and not people. This explains why the vast majority of norms are not, and need not be, 'enforced' and why non-compliance with norms remains largely unchallenged. As a rule, norms are maintained side by side with each other, even when they contradict each other, often with considerable social costs. The time-binding design of norms also explains why the legal system as a special (functional) communication system has the stabilisation of norms as its *only function* and why it achieves this function by the differentiation of legal decision-making and not by enforcement. The legal system is the immune system of society (a system within the social system) which protects against the unpredictability of an open future.[21]

The Legal System Step-by-Step

1. The social system (*society* or *the* social system) is the autopoietic unity of all human communication. In coping with its complex environment (everything outside communication operations), the social system selectively increases its own complexity by differentiating (specialising) communication operations which, in turn and as operatively closed systems, create their (own) environments within society.
2. Law is society's law and society has always had law. A specialised practice (communication) of legal decision-making of secondary observers of society (elders, chiefs, moots, kings, priests, administrators, judges, etc.) can always refer—normatively—to *tradition* (custom, 'our way of life') as earlier law.[22]
3. Operative closure of legal communication is achieved when the decision-makers base their decisions exclusively on law as validated by earlier decisions (legal decisions). *Positive law* is operatively closed legal communication which refers normative legal decisions exclusively to previously stated legal communication (decisions, legal documents, legal texts). Historically, this is a relatively late development and happens only under the specific historical conditions of European society.
4. The (only) function of specialised legal communication (law, the legal system) is the improvement of the selectivity of normative expectations in society in relation to the time dimension (stabilisation of normative expectation).[23] This improvement is practically achieved by using the selectivity of the legal system's own operations for the endorsement of specific norm projections which, as 'valid' law, immunise against the openness of the future.
5. Law is always created and never 'found'. The operations of legal decision-making must continuously (and consistently) reproduce the selectivity of legal communication and, therefore, add normative communication (distinctions, rules, principles, laws, statutes, and codes) in the process. These cannot be 'found' in the environment(s) of the legal system or the social system and they would not exist at all in society (the social system) without the operations of the legal system.
6. All legal communication (legal norms, legal documents, legal decision-making and their effects/impact) must be understood in the terms of this

---

[21] See Luhmann, (1993) *supra* n. 1, at 566.
[22] *Ibid.*, at 138.
[23] *Ibid.*, at 132.

self-created production of an intrinsic 'added value' (*Eigenwertproduktion*) by the operations of the legal system and only the legal system.

7. Law is a functional (sub-) system of the social system that acts as the immune system of the social system. In the case of a disturbance or deficiency of normative expectations—disappointments, blame, claims, contradictions, conflicts, impasses, accidents, in short: 'cases and controversies'—society provides a 'proxy solution' in the operations of the legal system, observing the legal system as to the consequences of the disturbance *for the legal system*. In each case the consequences are a (further) legal operation (decision, new legislation, legal change).

8. The function of an immune system (stabilisation of normative expectations) is achieved by the operatively closed *self-steering* of the legal system. All assumptions of social engineering by law or social steering by law which are widely held in the literature of sociology of law, overlook the specific differentiation of legal communication in relation to the time dimension (binding time not people) and the fact that, by design, legal operations can only 'control' legal operations but not conduct or behaviour in their environment. In this strict sense, all legal postulates of 'norm conforming' behaviour are *acratic*, ie project a performance that they cannot really control.[24] Other systems (including personal systems) can only be irritated or stimulated by the operations of the legal system but their operations remain 'ultra vires' for legal communication. The operations of other systems are exclusively controlled by those systems themselves.

9. While the unity of the legal system is constituted by an increasingly consistent and complex use of self-references, the unity of the system is a 'blind spot' within the system which can only be represented and operated by a symbol. Internally, the legal system represents its unity, ie the paradox of its self–created unity, through the symbol of 'legal validity'.

10. The autopoietic drive of legal communication is a drive to an internal differentiation of the legal system, reflected in the 'voracious appetite of lawyers for legal propositions' (Ehrlich), or simply in the proliferation of 'cases'. Also, this is an indication that legal communication is not concerned with people but with the stabilisation of normative expectations, reflected in the (self-) observation of cases (decisions) as system operations.[25] 'Equal treatment' translates for law into equal treatment of cases (not people), ie treating equal cases alike and different cases differently from each other. The (self-) observation of cases is a learning device (*cognitive opening*) for the legal system that drives its differentiation to higher levels of internal complexity (ie a better selectivity with regard to the complexity found in the environment of the legal system). Nevertheless, the references in these

---

[24] Acratic, orig. in Greek moral philosophy meaning 'lack of (self-) discipline'. See K. A. Ziegert, 'Courts and the Self-Concept of Law: The Mapping of the Environment by Courts of First Instance' in: (1992) 14 *Sydney Law Review* 196–229.

[25] See Luhmann, (1993) *supra* n. 1, at 271 and 375.

'learning' operations still lie with the (self-) reference to law and not references to the environment. The latter only provides the pressure or motivation for differentiation internalised (operated as legal references) as 'facts'.
Without doubt, however, facts are also constructions of the legal system
(legal operations) and not a materialisation of the environment in the legal
system, as any external (scientific) observation of court proceedings and
their treatment of evidence can demonstrate. Also, the observation of the
environment—the facts of the case—is an operation of the legal system in
the legal system.

11. There is an obvious correlation between the increase of the complexity of
this kind of 'lawyers' law' and the increase of complexity in the social system ('society') at large and other social systems (economy, political system,
science, etc.). This relationship can be called parasitic. The more normative
expectations are reproduced in these other systems, as a condition of their
differentiation, the more pressure is put on the legal system (ie the more
cases) to selectively make decisions which, in fact, 'change the law'. In turn,
these legal decisions motivate other social systems to realign their communication of normative expectations.

12. This duality of legal norm selection and social norm projection can be called
the double modality of law or the dual-mode performance of law.[26] The
drive of the decision-making operations reproduces a special *decision-
making system within the legal system*. It is the latter that seduces legal doctrine, legal theory and then legal education to assume that law is the
exclusive domain of lawyers and that the legal propositions and texts are
'the law'. This internal view underestimates the selective relationship of
legal decision-making with normative reflexivity in society at large, which
ground the structures of meaning in society. This sense that law makes or
not is the other mode of law to which legal decision-making responds.
Nevertheless, while the 'centre of gravity of law' may very well be found 'in
society itself'[27] (and not in legal propositions or the 'law in the books'), its
operative closure is only achieved in the decision-making system.

13. The dramatic increase of the operations of the decision-making system in
advanced legal organisations witnessed, for instance, in Roman Law and
early English common law, is reflexively tied to the 'hardening' of the
boundaries of the legal decision-making system. This means that the
increasing refinement of the distinctions used in deciding cases produces an
increasing refinement in the basic delineation of the unity of law—what is
law, what is not law (*quaestio iuris*). Such refinement leads, in the process,
to the point of a *sharp binary distinction* that allows only two values to be
used in legal communication: law and non-law. This basic distinction (*coding*) is carried concurrently in all legal operations and provides the means to

[26] See Luhmann, (1993) *supra* n. 1, at 147.
[27] This is the classical formulation of E. Ehrlich, *Fundamental Principles of the Sociology of Law*
(Cambridge Mass. Harvard University Press 1936 orig. publ. 1913). See Foreword.

identify legal operations compared with operations that are not. A strict binary code facilitates the operative closure of legal decision-making as *positive law*, for instance as case law in English common law. Legal regimes on the European continent and elsewhere have struggled for a long time and are still struggling, for instance in East-Asian countries, with the problem of third values—law, non-law and x. Historical examples for a third value are divine law, equity, nature, reason, the American Creed (the constitution), the State (or reason of state), the Communist party, and the national interest. While it may be politically expedient for the legal system to operate codes with three or more values, the selectivity of legal operations is clearly reduced and the attractiveness of legal decision-making diminished. This means, ultimately, that the stabilisation of normative expectations in society is maintained by or reverts to devices which bind people (through status, nomenklatura, 'dirty togetherness'[corruption] and so on) rather than time. Put simply it means the 'rule of men' rather than the rule of law.

14. The 'harshness' of a strictly binary coding of legal operations in order to make decisions consistent, not least with a view to future decisions, has been recognised early in the development of legal decision-making systems as 'unjust'. Accordingly, attempts have been made to 'soften' the unpalatable social consequences of legal decisions. Thus Roman law complements the ordinary legal decision-making with a highly discretionary Praetorian law which allows for a third value 'equity' to be adopted by legal operations. Similarly, English common law develops a branch of 'equity' decision-making that is, initially, not subject to the harsh binary coding of legal decision-making. However, arguably the operation of the third value 'equity' does not withstand the strong centripetal pull of the legal decision-making system over time and is reigned in as merely another, even if arcane and peculiar, form of legal decision-making in English common law. The same development can be observed in more recent attempts to 'soften' the harshness of strictly binary coded legal operations by, for instance, informal decision-making arrangements like industrial tribunals or community justice centres. Also, here procedures and decision-making become increasingly 'legalized'. This development is indicated, for instance, by an increasing use of lawyers in the decision-making processes, not least where appeals lie ultimately with the ordinary higher courts.

15. The harshness of the binary legal code may also be unacceptable in cultures where traditional and familial social control values of harmony, hierarchical subordination and acquiescence are pervasive in social system operations.[28] Thus law in Asia, ie particularly China, Korea, Japan, and Vietnam, has never become positive law, in spite of the relatively early codification of legal texts, mainly in penal codes in China and Vietnam; and attempts at modernisation of law have been made by the importation of

---

[28] See Luhmann, *supra* n. 1, at 191.

European civil and penal codes to China, Japan and Vietnam in the nineteenth and twentieth century. It must be assumed that even today the legal operations especially in China and, in a different political environment also Japan, are encoded with a third value (party political order and traditional 'informal' elite order respectively). This compounds, with a diminished attraction of legal decision-making in favour of 'informal arrangements', the lack of a fuller functional differentiation of the operations of the social system at large while, at the same time, upholding a high level of stability (unchangeability) of social structures.

16. As far as law is concerned, a more successful alternative for coping with the consequences of the rigidity of binary coding and positive law is internal differentiation of devices which 'mobilize' legal change without loss of selectivity and consistency by legal operations. Such devices are predominantly *programmes and procedures*.[29] This means that legal decision-making systems learn to distinguish between operations of coding (reproducing the unity of the legal systems, eg typically when the '*quaestio iuris*' is asked) and operations of programming which provide 'additional semantics for generating further points of view'.[30]

17. The most prominent forms for programming legal operations are legislative programmes (laws, statutes, codes) and legal procedures. Their sensitivity for the time dimension is reflected in the fact that the legal system operates exclusively conditional programmes. Conditional programmes can mobilise (proceduralise) legal operations in a typical combination of operative closure (references to the binary code) and cognitive openness (references to the associated consequence) in the form of 'if x then y, z, and å'. Seen in a temporal perspective, the conditional programme provides the certainty/consistency of legal operations by placing the condition in the present, and binding consequences to the legal operation—in a future which cannot be reliably known—to the legal operation in the present. What might be in the future is 'ultra vires' for legal operations and, therefore, outside the purview of the legal system. Therefore, goal oriented programmes—so much preferred in the political system ('policies') but also medicine ('therapy')—are useless for legal operation because their (speculative) projection of operations in the future is far too open and unacceptable as a basis for legal operations, for instance, a decision. Law does not speculate about the future, it binds time and thus the present's future. It is above all this development of the distinction between binary code and programmes and the combination of operative closure and openness for future contingencies in the form of conditional programmes, which has propelled the evolution of law to a much higher level of internal complexity. This, in turn, has significantly raised the attraction of

---

[29] See Luhmann, *supra* n. 1, at 189.
[30] *Ibid.* at 189.

legal communication for the social system and other systems (functional sub-systems but also personal systems).

18. Political systems, and above all governments, put pressure on the legal system, through their legislative programmes. These, cannot, however, control legal operations. At best, they can motivate legal operations and, at worst, irritate the legal system. The legal system is protected against such pressures and irritations by its operative design of distinguishing centre and periphery. In this design, the centripetal pull of the legal-decision making system locates the selective operations of legal decision-making (courts) in its centre and relegates legislation to the periphery of the legal system. As there is no communication *between* the political system and the legal system (but only communication *in* the respective systems), there is no relationship, and certainly not a hierarchical one, between these systems but rather a *functional* co-operation in which each system controls its own operations (see also point 26 below). For instance the 'irritating' political intentions in the legislative programmes (eg 'tougher law') are subject to filtering by legal operations in the periphery, for instance legal academic debates and doctrinal dissertations and the highly selective operations of *legal* decision-making in the centre of the legal system. In turn, the 'formalistic' or 'legalistic' application of legislative norms in the legal system and especially in the courts 'irritate' the political system and motivate changes in the legislation or even law reform, and so on.

19. The highly selective asymmetric form of the conditional programme (operative closure *and* cognitive openness) recurs in the form of *legal procedures*. Procedures are organised in the form of temporally well-defined *episodes*.[31] These episodes start with the lodging of a claim and end with a decision. Legal communication achieves operative closure by controlling the temporal aspects of the episode (start, end) and cognitive openness by allowing any matter whatsoever to be heard in court and all its aspects presented to the court, as long as the matter satisfies the criteria of a case. By organising the processing of cases in this formally controlled episodic form, legal communication is open to 'learn', ie sequester information from the redundant operations of the procedure, case by case. The tension between the operatively closed operations of the binary code (*quaestio iuris*) and the cognitive openness of the proceedings produces the episodic uncertainty of legal proceedings. Proceedings use the uncertainty as 'a medium for their own autopoiesis'.[32] The openness of proceedings invites contributions from participants and motivates participation by offering prospects of chances and opportunities, but not of results. It motivates and captures with the participation in the communication the acknowledgment of participants that they have participated. 'In the end, [participants] are prisoners of their own

---

[31] *Ibid.*, at 208.
[32] *Ibid.*, at 209.

participation in the proceedings with only few prospects left to challenge the legitimacy of the proceedings ex post-facto'.[33]

20. The observation of the structural design of legal proceedings allows seeing *juridical argumentation and legal reasoning* in a different light, namely in relation to the openness of legal proceedings in the centre of the selective operations of the legal decision-making system.[34] Juridical argumentation and legal reasoning do not follow a particular 'juridical logic' but the selective design of redundancy and variety of legal terms in, ultimately, communication in courts as the autopoiesis of the legal system. Redundancy of legal terms confirms and condenses their use in legal communication; variation (*distinction*) opens the way to new legal terms and possibly legal change under the protection of both the formal control of legal proceedings and the operative closure with references to the binary code. Juridical argumentation and legal reasoning as legal operations in this 'nested form' (operations *within* proceedings *within* the binary coded decision-making system *within* the legal system) is highly selective (*productive*) because it is operatively closed. In this sense, variation of legal terms is incremental and circumspect, building on the layered internalisation of references to the state of affairs outside the legal system. For instance, the distinction between 'formal' and 'substantive' law can be understood as a distinction between self-references of the legal communication (formal) and other-references (substantive), while remaining firmly a legal operation. Similarly the concepts of 'interests' or 'customs' are such other-references which can be easily incorporated in juridical argumentation and legal reasoning because they are operations of the legal system.

21. The legal profession and its communicative style are a crucial part of the legal operations in the centre of the decision-making system. The professional organisation of lawyers is centrally important for the functioning of the legal system. In specific historical cases, like the Roman law and English common law, the fact that lawyers were drawn from a particular status group in society (aristocracy) became the organisational launching-pad for the differentiation of an operatively closed legal communication and the development of a strictly binary code. The aristocratic status of lawyers added authority, legitimacy and validity to the developing decision-making system. Even in the modern common law regimes, the function of lawyers as facilitators of legal communication, ultimately in court proceedings, and their professional but privatised control of the legal system is still obvious. This important function of lawyering is not so clearly visible in other legal regimes where the communication between dominant legal functionaries is organised differently. For instance, the lack of political integration in medieval continental Europe led to a dominance of legal academics and

---

[33] See Luhmann, *supra* n. 1, at 209.
[34] *Ibid.*, at 338.

legal academic doctrine in continental Europe. Conversely the dominance of political integration in the Nordic European countries, but also China and Japan, led to a dominance of the role of governmental legislators and administrators (bureaucrats) and their administrative instructions in legal communication. Finally, specialised legal roles for lawyering are altogether absent in religious law regimes like Islamic law, Canon law or Hindu law.

22. The central importance of lawyering is additionally obfuscated by legal ideologies promoted by these other law functionaries. For instance the legal doctrine of the sources of law in continental European law, especially in France but also all other 'civil law' regimes, including Nordic countries, allows assumptions of 'binding' legal texts (codes, legislation) for legal decision-makers. This emphasises the (ideally 'gapless') production of legal texts, especially legal codes, and assumes a precise 'application' of these texts ('juridical-logical' deduction from norms and principles) by the decision-makers. Such an ideological overvaluation of the periphery under-estimates the important role of lawyers in the centre of the legal system. Nevertheless, also in these legal regimes, notwithstanding the higher ideo-logical status of codes and legislation (binding sources of law) applied by career judges, the autopoiesis of the legal system happens only through the selective operation of the redundancy and variety of legal terms in courts. This may become more evident in the European context with European integration and the important role of the European courts (European Court in Luxembourg, European Courts for Human Rights in Strasbourg, etc.) and in the international context with global integration and the important role of International Courts. These processes reflect on the overall process of the differentiation of global law through the decision-making in courts rather than through the (peripheral) legislative operations in nation states.

23. The observation of legal operations, including the self-observation and self-description of law in legal doctrine, legal theory, legal reasoning and juri-dical argumentation supports the finding mentioned above (point 18) that the legal system is organised in the form of centre and periphery. Seen in relation to the evolutionary dynamics of selection and variation, legal com-munication is routed through the centre in order to achieve high selectivity combined with consistency and certainty, but cognitively open through its communication in the periphery. Typical operations in the periphery are, as we have seen above, legislation, legal doctrine, legal theory (including also reflexive legal theories like critical legal studies, sociological jurisprudence, legal realism, feminist jurisprudence etc.). They also include legal opera-tions 'in the shadow of the law' like contracts, wills, mediation, arbitration, negotiation, delegated administrative decision-making and diversions of criminal justice like family-conferences and community shaming. The his-torical individuation in concentric legal decision-making systems (legal organizations, legal regimes) is the result of the differentiation of the global

legal system (*the* legal system). Global law produces in this form an environment in which the different legal regimes/organisations (French law, Japanese law, Judaic law etc) can treat each other both as separate *and* connected. Just as the unity of the social system (world society) is bounded by the world-wide communication of humans but reproduced locally, the legal system is a global communication system bounded by world-wide legal communication that is reproduced locally.

24. The evolution of law, then, is the autopoietic management of its internal complexity in progress. In this view the principle of 'justice' is just another possibility, together with the principle of legal validity, to refer to the unity of the legal system. Justice, like validity, is not a 'third value' for coding the legal operations (ie law/non-law/justice) but a *formula for the contingency of* (social) outcomes of legal operations, ie a formula for other-references (equity, interests), leaving the operative closure which is achieved by binary coding intact, and operating internal correlates of 'justice' instead ('procedural justice', certainty/ consistency of decision-making, equal treatment of cases, and so on).

25. Similarly, concerns for *social justice* are externalised where they cannot be operated as legal terms and referred to *the periphery of the legal system.* It is important to note that, while such voiced critical concerns (reflexive legal operations) at various stages and at different points of time in history attempt to distance themselves from the law *as it is perceived to operate,* they are still operations in the legal system and thus operations of the legal system. Depending on how virulent the stimulation or irritations are which the legal system inflicts here upon itself, these communications may or may not lead to higher degrees of differentiation and/or more complexity of the legal system. Most importantly, however, these critical movements also show that the legal system makes self-irritations possible in the form of the operations of the legal system and reacts to them only in the form of operations *in* the legal system.

26. The impossibility of communication *between* systems but the apparent historically varied correlations between the legal system and various other social systems require a more accurate observation as to how such relationships become possible and what form they take. The co-evolution of social systems leads in particular historical sequences in some cases to the co-operation of the legal system with other functional systems, for instance with the economic system and the political system (see above point 18). This co-operation appears to be facilitated by the mechanism of *structural coupling* mentioned above. This means, that each system adjusts its own operations in response to the performance of the other system(s). Obviously, this can only happen if the respective systems have achieved operative closure (binary code for the legal system, state for the political system, money/banks for the economic system) and a relatively high level of internal complexity. However, once social systems are sufficiently differentiated (evolved), they can enlist the complexity of

another system for the operation of their own autopoiesis and co-evolve further parasitically on each other's complexity.

27. In the development of (European) law two such parasitic relationships are particularly notable: the co-evolution of law and economy and the co-evolution of law and politics.[35]

28. The structural coupling of law and economy is evident in devices such as contract and property. Each enhances the autopoiesis of both systems. More exchanges in the economic system mean more cases in the legal system. Even though this coupling is particularly clear in the English common law, private law in all legal regimes and international law can be identified as the most dynamic performance of the legal system. It creates more self-irritations for the legal system (litigation!) than other performances (for instance, criminal law) and in contrast to irritations caused externally (for instance social welfare legislation or administrative regulations).

29. Another momentuous structural coupling is that of law and politics, particularly in the form of state and law. The coupling device here is the constitution, which has at its political side the operations of the state and on its legal side the operations of law in constitutional law. Also, here, it is notable that the parasitic alignment can only happen at an advanced stage of the differentiation of both systems. The different developmental patterns explain the comparatively much later historical occurrence of the coupling of law and state in contrast to the relatively early coupling of law and economy. Historically, the coupling of law and state, once it can happen, is conceptualized as the *rule of law* in common law and the state of law (*état de loi, Rechtsstaat*) in European continental law. Understood as coupling of law and state the concept of the rule of law has a clear functional meaning. It is not just an ideological fabrication of jurisprudence and legal theory and indicates an irreversible point in the development of the autopoiesis of both the political system and the legal system. However, seen in this functional perspective, the rule of law does not require the 'sovereignty' of states in order to be operative. 'Sovereignty' has never been an issue in the autopoiesis of the political system in contrast to the issue of how political decisions can be made collectively binding. In this view, the rule of law may have occurred when state power was historically at its peak and unchallenged by other organisations. However, it is not under threat by the increasing internationalisation of political communication (and 'loss of sovereignty' of national states) and, on the contrary, is reinforced by the increasing differentiation of international law in the (global) legal system.

30. The most important consequences of the structural coupling of law and politics (rule of law) for legal communication are increases in the internal differentiation of legal decision-making. These are *the independence of judges* (courts) and, as its flip-side, *the prohibition of the denial of justice*. With

---

[35] See Luhmann, *supra* n. 1, at 459.

guaranteed access to state power and the monopolisation of violence by state coercion, the operative closure of the legal system is expressed in the independence of judges. The price for this independence from political decision-making is the finer delineation of the speciality of legal decision-making (*principle of the prohibition of the denial of justice*—ie the right to be heard in a court). This means that legal decision-making is compulsory once proceedings have started and judges have to find a decision no matter how hard or 'impossible' the case presented to them may be.

31. The functional specialisation of the legal system as a global system of legal decision-making and communication means that law is not only unique in being communication that binds an open future but also in making it binding that a legal decision be made. There is no functional equivalent for such a high level of selectivity in establishing meaning in the social system. This explains the increasing attraction of law and legal decisions in the process of the ever-increasing, confusing complexity of the global society.

3. CONCLUSION

The reception of Luhmann's approach in socio-legal research so far has been, at best, patchy. This is not surprising, given the difficulties outlined above and in view of the fact that the theory of operatively closed systems has not yet become a widely accepted paradigm for sociological theory in mainstream sociology. Here the various denominations of social action theory, including symbolic interaction and various ethno-methodological approaches, and the nineteenth century concept of the individual human actor as 'subject' and indivisible 'atom' of a society made up by actors and social action, including communicative action, are still the dominant paradigms in spite of the apparent impasses in providing robust explanations for much more complex patterns of social relations and conditions.[36] The, by far, most successful reception of Luhmann's approach happened in legal theory and here, above all, through the work of Gunther Teubner.[37] In fact, it was Teubner's profuse work that promoted the concepts of reflexive law and autopoietic law and led legal and socio-legal scholars, especially in English speaking countries, to the concepts of the autopoiesis and operative closure of law.[38] However, it is clear from the creative use that Teubner makes of Luhmann's approach that we are dealing here with reflexive legal

---

[36] See G. Kiss, *supra* n. 2, at 3.

[37] For the reception of Luhmann's approach outside sociology, including law and legal theory see H. de Berg and J. F. K. Schmidt (eds.) *Rezeption und Reflexion:Zur Resonanz der Systemtheorie Niklas Luhmanns ausserhalb der Soziologie* (Reception and reflexion: on the resonance of NL's systems theory outside sociology, Frankfurt Suhrkamp 2000).

[38] For examples of such work published in English see G. Teubner, 'Substantive and Reflexive Elements in Modern Law' in (1983) 17-2 *Law and Society Review* 239–286; G. Teubner (ed.) *Dilemmas of Law in the Welfare State* (Berlin, de Gruyter 1986); G. Teubner (ed.) *Autopoietic Law: A New Approach to Law and Society* (Berlin de Gruyter 1988) and G. Teubner (ed.) *Global Law Without a State* (Aldershot Dartmouth Gower 1997).

theory and not socio-legal research, ie Teubner's construction of arguments is a series of legal operations. As such they are, in Luhmann's terms, a transfer of topoi and themes into the periphery of the legal system for the self-irritation of the legal system with new arguments and terms. This is a possible use of Luhmann's approach but it deliberately leaves aside, and must leave aside, the essential thrust of this approach as a scientific methodology.

If one takes this methodological aspect into account, it is evident that Luhmann offers the most powerful and systematic theory yet devised for understanding the relationship between law and society, in keeping with the latest developments of the philosophy of science, which can no longer separate phenomena in those of the world of 'nature' and those of the world of 'humanities'. The very assumption of the self-description of social systems in their operations suggests that a wealth of data can be tapped by adopting Luhmann's 'grounded theory' methodology, giving 'voice' to the deep structures of the operations of social systems. The advanced conceptualisation of those structures in Luhmann's theory design can help to circumvent the somewhat naïve assumptions of inductive research but retain the discursive 'thickness' of qualitative theory designs towards a testing, confirming and condensing of the concepts used in building sociological theory.

The 'best fit' of the approach of the theory of operatively closed systems is evident in the currently emerging global perspective on law. While it may take courage to talk of *the* (one and only) *legal system* in view of the dazzling array of legal regimes, legal organisations and legal communication worldwide, it seems to be a robust argument—which can be tested—that the latter are only the historical and local operations of a functional system which operates as widely as a global society communicates. At the same time, and notwithstanding the macro-sociological coverage, the approach makes it possible to start research from the bottom up, and to look for law in the irritations caused by it to families, business firms and political parties; or to look into the practice of lawyers' sequestering what is 'legal' and protecting the law against contamination with 'social trash'. Even finer yet, the approach makes it possible to track legal decision-making from its opening stages of legal argument to the vital '*quaestio juris*' and legal reasoning as an effort of construction and the selection of the requisite variety of legal operations. Most importantly, the approach makes it possible to trace the evolution and the globalisation of law as conditioned by and conditioning the individualisation of humans and their individual rights, and the corresponding breaking-up of accustomed and deeply entrenched social structures. In doing so, the sociological mapping of society's law picks up the theme of 'living law' again. But the outlook is no longer so optimistic. The major driving force of society's law is the fact that society cannot know its future and that legal decisions promise certainty by making society's future binding in the present. In an utterly complex society, this only means that nothing in society can happen without law and, that even with law, a successful management of society's future in the future is not guaranteed.

4

Jürgen Habermas and the Sociology of Law

BO CARLSSON

JÜRGEN HABERMAS (1929–), the most influential social theorist associated with the Frankfurt School today, has written voluminously in defence of reason. Amongst the ideas he has developed is a concept of a public sphere elaborated in terms of moral justification through communicative action, which in turn has led him to develop a theory of procedural rationality.[1] Habermas ultimately aims to diagnose the ills of the contemporary world against the backdrop of moral and rational developments of modern societies; a task which he accomplishes on a meta-theoretical level and in normative terms. Subsequently, his approach is both highly complex and normative, making his theory difficult to operationalise. This chapter takes on the challenge of bringing into empirical focus the socio-legal relevance of these meta-theoretical ideas.

Due to the complexity of Habermas's theoretical approach, any short introduction to his theory will necessarily be selective. This chapter focuses on his ideas concerning emancipation, legitimation crisis, the public sphere, and the relation of system and lifeworld, as well as on his writings on law and morality and deliberative democracy. I shall use examples from Swedish sociology of law to illustrate how his ideas can be applied in studying legal topics.

1. A BACKGROUND IN THE 'FRANKFURT SCHOOL'

Habermas's initial theoretical development can be traced back to the Frankfurt School. As a response to the Stalinist vulgarisation of Marxism, Theodore Adorno and Max Horkheimer developed a humanistic form of Marxism when

---

[1] For examples of introductions and commentary texts to Habermas's theory see: T. McCarthy, *The Critical Theory of Jürgen Habermas* (Cambridge Polity Press 1978), J. B. Thompson and D. Held (eds.) *Habermas: Critical Debates* (London Macmillan Press 1982), S. K. White, *The Recent Work Of Habermas: Reason, Justice and Modernity* (Cambridge Cambridge Univ. Press 1998), S. Benhabib and F. Dallmayr (eds.) *The Communicative Ethics Controversy* (Cambridge Mass. MIT Press 1990), A. Honneth and H. Joas (eds.) *Communicative Action* (Cambridge Polity Press 1991), C. Calhoun (ed.) *Habermas and the Public Sphere* (Cambridge Polity Press 1992), and M. Deflem (ed.) *Habermas, Modernity and Law* (London Sage Publications 1996).

they took charge of the directorship of the Max Plank Institute. They aimed to integrate the psychology of Freud and the sociology of Weber with the ideas of Marxism, in order to develop an emancipatory science or critical theory. But Hitler's Germany was not a particularly friendly environment for Adorno and Horkheimer, who also happened to be Jewish. In the United States, where they took refuge from Nazis, they continued their emancipatory project by producing *Dialectic of Enlightenment* as their diagnosis of (instrumental) reason. However, they were soon disillusioned by American culture which they described as 'the air-conditioned hell'. Their general 'rage against reason brought them to the brink of irrationalism' and drove the Frankfurt School into slumber until Habermas was appointed to Horkheimer's chair in 1965.[2]

The central theme in Habermas's studies is *emancipation*; ie the conception of free individuals in a free society. Habermas's approach is rare in the sense that not only does he regard modernity as an unfinished project, but he also insists that 'the Enlightenment got it mostly right',[3] thus, challenging those who reject the quest for emancipation.[4] Contrary to postmodern ideas, 'Habermas wants to show us how a stronger form of democracy is still a genuine and achievable goal, even in complex and pluralist societies'.[5] In that sense, 'no one living social theorist has worked harder or produced more on behalf of progress(ive) universalism and grand theory than Habermas'.[6] There is, therefore, no doubt as to Habermas's humanitarianism.[7]

Another theme in Habermas's work is the rationalisation of society. In the face of Weber's sociology and his teachers' rage against reason, Habermas claims that the rationalisation of society is a blessing of civilisations and a curse of the culture. He holds fast to the critique of instrumental reason and its social pathologies, but asks 'whether there was not something more in Enlightenment rationality than the destructive logic unveiled and indicted by his mentors'.[8] As a solution, he develops his communicative rationality as a broader and more interactive alternative concept to that of Weber's 'individualistic' conception of rationality. Habermas has tried to devise a theory based on the notion of symbolically structured lifeworld 'without relapsing into moral relativism'.[9]

---

[2] W. E. Forbath, 'Habermas's Constitution: A History, Guide and Critique' (1998) 23 *Law and Social Inquiry*, at 981.

[3] Forbath, *ibid.*, at 969.

[4] D. Abraham, 'Persistent Facts and Compelling Norms: Liberal Capitalism, Democratic Socialism, and the Law' (1994) 4 *Law & Society Review* 939–46.

[5] J. Bohman, 'Complexity, Pluralism and the Constitutional State: On Habermas's Faktizität und Geltung' (1994) 4 *Law & Society Review* 897–930.

[6] Abraham, *supra* n. 4, at 939.

[7] B. Z. Tamanaha, 'The View of Habermas from Below: Doubts About the Centrality of Law and the Legitimation Enterprise' (1999) 4 *Denver Univ. Law Review*, at 1007.

[8] Forbath, *supra* n. 2, at 981.

[9] E. J. Palti, 'Patroklos's Funeral and Habermas's Sentence' (1998) 23 *Law and Social Inquiry*, at 1018.

2. AN EMPHASIS ON EMANCIPATION AND COMMUNICATION

Mankind's historical and fundamental struggle for emancipation from structural constraints and other barriers constitutes the cornerstone of Habermas's social theory. Hence, Habermas investigates the development of knowledge in relation to human interests, human actions and their cognitive and moral competencies.[10] He discusses the empirical-analytical sciences which, he claims, originate from the aspiration for technical control resulting from the manipulation of the objective world. The hermeneutic sciences are directed towards exposing confusions in our communication, and attaining mutual understanding. But, Habermas claims that they are not sufficient for constructing a critical science capable of illuminating and exposing communicative misunderstanding and communicative obstacles between individuals, traditions or cultures. In as much as hermeneutics accepts the active individual's own definition of the meaning of his/her actions, it is not able to apprehend systematically constructed misunderstandings.[11]

A critical science must expose power and ideology. In this respect, the works of Marx and Freud can be viewed as contributions to the creation of critical and emancipatory sciences.[12] According to Habermas, the social sciences demand a depth hermeneutics, which confronts tradition and other barriers in a way which reveals the source of oppression and distorted communication. In this sense, the concept of self-reflection becomes an important element in the development of Habermas's critical theory. The strength of self-reflection is that knowledge and interests are brought together. It is through this process that reason can be perceived as governed by interests.[13]

This insight led to a fundamental analysis of the concept of action, and the difference between the process of creating and justifying action. This, in turn, resulted in the theory of communicative competence, according to which our language is dependent on and directed towards the idea of a genuine consensus, which can occur only discursively. The analysis of such a consensus involves taking into account the normative element intrinsic to the model of an 'ideal speech situation'. This normative foundation becomes the starting point for Habermas's critical theory. It is the assumption that an ideal discourse provides the prospect of a critique of ideology. The emphasis on an ideal discourse is not, Habermas declares, arbitrarily chosen, because 'our first sentence expresses unequivocally, the intention of a universal and an unconstrained consensus'.[14] Furthermore, 'if we assume that the human species maintains itself through the

---

[10] J. Habermas, *Knowledge and Human Interests* (London Heinemann 1975).

[11] J. Habermas, 'The Hermeneutics Claim to Universality' in Bleicher (ed.) *Contemporary Hermeneutics: Hermeneutics as Method* (London Routledge 1980).

[12] J. Habermas, *Theory and Practice* (London Heinemann 1974).

[13] Habermas, *supra* n. 10, at 212.

[14] Habermas, *ibid.*, at 314.

socially co-ordinated activities of its members and that this co-ordination has to be established through communication [. . .] then the reproduction of the species also required satisfying the conditions of a rationality that is inherent in communicative action'.[15]

Habermas's analysis points to the existence of four 'validity-claims' that every competent speaker must satisfy in order to engage in communicative action. Firstly, an utterance (a speech act) must be intelligible; secondly, it must be true; thirdly, it must be performed correctly; and finally, its intentions must be sincere. Each of these 'validity-claims' provide a reflexive basis for evaluating the intelligibility, truthfulness, sincerity and accuracy of actions and utterances, thus creating opportunities for detecting and rectifying mistakes and to start a learning process. However, as Habermas points out, since these claims cannot be settled trustworthily in everyday communicative action, a public forum is required to resolve disputes.

3. A FOCUS ON THE PUBLIC SPHERE

From the outset Habermas has been preoccupied with issues arising out of the structural transformation of the public sphere in the liberal state.[16] He has, in particular, tried to investigate the development and the disintegration of the public sphere.

The development of the liberal public sphere during the seventeenth and eighteenth centuries became, according to Habermas, the foundation for modern societies based on rational communication. During this time the state and society, public authorities and the private sphere, were brought together in a particular way. Habermas focuses on the positive emancipatory nature of this development, and regards the early liberal public sphere as the foundation for critical reflection; communication was transformed from parlour conversation to critical reasoning, in literary clubs, critical political journalism and coffee shops. This public discourse became the standard for the 'truth' of law, justice and legitimacy in the liberal (bourgeois) world view.

However, according to Habermas's diagnosis, the public sphere has, since the middle of the nineteenth century, lost its critical function. Instead of a consensus founded on the basis of a rational discourse, the focus has gradually shifted to reaching compromises based on the relative strengths of temporary coalitions. The pursuit of a rational life based on ethics is in retreat and is being replaced with what is politically possible. The public has been transformed from a culturally and politically argumentative force, to a consuming audience. The

---

[15] J. Habermas, *The Theory of Communicative Action, vol. I* (Cambridge Polity Press 1984), at 397.

[16] J. Habermas, *The Structural Transformation of the Public Sphere* (Cambridge Mass. MIT Press 1989).

language of commercial interests permeates the public sphere; and ideas are subjected to fashion trends.

The structural transformation of the public, social and private spheres has been accentuated by the welfare state. State intervention in the private sphere seems to dissolve the boundaries between the state and the market, the state and the community and the public and the private. In this transformation the private domain has been brought under the control of the public authorities. Habermas argues, for instance, that a number of functions are increasingly removed from the family reducing its importance from an institution responsible for upholding features of social integration to a sphere of intimate relations.

When interpersonal conflicts occur in the private realm, the search for a solution is frequently and increasingly carried out in the public sphere by professional agents and public institutions. As a result, an increasing institutionalisation and professionalisation occurs in the wake of a structural transformation of the public and private spheres.

4. LEGITIMATION CRISIS

Habermas focuses on various tendencies towards crises that arise from the operation of the economy and administration in contemporary society. Drawing on Durkheim's sociology, he distinguishes mechanisms of system integration from mechanisms of social integration and highlights the necessity of legitimation and motivation for social systems.[17] These kinds of crises occur when the organisational principle of a society does 'not permit the resolution of problems that are critical for its continued existence'.[18] Habermas points out that 'crisis occurrences owe their objectivity to the fact that they issue from unresolved steering problems'.[19]

Modern societies are no longer legitimated through traditional values such as religious beliefs. Instead, legitimation depends on public acceptance of the justice of the market (and state administration). Hence, the liberal capitalist process of production is at the same time 'a dialectic of the moral life'.[20] The liberal market system now faces a serious crisis. In order to repair functional gaps in the market economy, the state has to intervene in the process of capital accumulation. Consequently, 'the steering mechanism is no longer a self-regulating market, but a state apparatus that has taken on a market-replacing and market-complementing function'.[21] In turn, the (welfare) state also faces an economic and administrative crisis. The crisis in the public finances is the result of the increasing costs of more socialised production (eg transport, health care and social security). The need to

---

[17] J. Habermas, *Legitimation Crisis* (London Heinemann 1976).
[18] McCarthy, *supra* n. 1, at 361.
[19] Habermas, *supra* n. 17, at 4.
[20] McCarthy, *supra* n. 1, at 363.
[21] McCarthy, *ibid.*, at 365–6.

secure legitimation for governmental activity becomes crucial. This legitimation crisis is, according to Habermas, not a system crisis, rather an identity crisis; and as such, a direct threat to social integration. In order to secure a motivated population, interest in consumption is developed, and new areas of consumption are introduced. This is a dilemma, because the expanded activity of the state produces a need for justification of government intervention into new areas of life, increasing the need for legitimation.

5. SYSTEM AND LIFEWORLD

Developing the Durkheimian ideas of system integration and social integration, Habermas makes a distinction between the system and the lifeworld in *The Theory of Communicative Action* (*TCA* hereafter).[22]

The *TCA* has two themes: firstly, the gradual separation of the system from the lifeworld; and secondly, the system's colonisation of the lifeworld. The integration of the system is based on instrumental and strategic action/rationality. A system becomes 'more rational as its complexity increases, that is, as its range of adaptation to environmental changes is enhanced'.[23] In the context of systems' complexity, legal regulations—according to Habermas's distinction between 'law as a medium' and 'law as an institution'—are used as a steering medium and control.[24] The coordination of actions in this sphere of society depends on either the market or the political system, by more or less 'functional' mechanisms, which appear to work independently of the actor's knowledge of them. The social infrastructure of consumption, for instance, drives economic growth by incessantly converting luxuries and privileges into necessities.

The lifeworld, on the other hand, represents the production ground for social norms, moral values and world views. The self-productive spheres of the lifeworld consist of the areas of socialisation, social integration and cultural reproduction. The social integration of the lifeworld is based on communication and presupposes intersubjectivity and a mutual understanding among the actors. Social integration in this perspective refers to the participants' own concept of everyday life. The lifeworld works as a cultural framework, which connects individuals to society, thus mediating a common world view in which the individual as well as the collective receives an identity.

The lifeworld has a twofold meaning:

> on the one hand, the horizon-forming contexts of culture, society and personality within which communicative action takes place, and, on the other hand, the resources

---

[22] Habermas, *supra* n. 15, and J. Habermas, *The Theory of Communicative Action, vol II* (Cambridge Polity Press 1987).

[23] White, *supra* n. 1, at 104.

[24] J. Habermas, 'Law as a Medium and Law as an Institution' in G. Teubner (ed.) *Dilemmas in the Welfare State* (Berlin Walter de Gruyter 1985).

of possibilities from which participants in communicative action can transmit and renew cultural knowledge, establish solidarity and build social identity.[25]

The lifeworld is a horizon of experiences and knowledge that we implicitly have at our disposal, but will be explicitly expressed only when the situation brings unaccustomed subjects into focus. We are always situated in the context of the lifeworld, and can never decide to ignore the lifeworld.

Habermas's diagnosis of the development of modern society appears ambivalent because of his attempt to see both positive and negative developments in the lifeworld:

1. He has found an ongoing and increasing proceduralisation of law which corresponds with the communicative structures of the lifeworld. According to Habermas this is a positive trend.

2. At the same time, he has found mechanisms in the system which colonise the communicative structures of the lifeworld. This is the negative feature of Habermas's diagnosis.

Habermas's second point implies the subordination of the lifeworld to system imperatives, as a result of which an increase in bureaucratic control takes place at the expense of a decrease in freedom. This gain in control restricts the development of moral-practical values. Having said that, an understanding of 'reason as essentially instrumental and strategic is fatally one-sided',[26] even though, 'it is indeed the case that those types of rationality have achieved a certain dominance in our culture'.[27] In this respect, the subsystems in which steering is institutionalised, ie in the economy and government administration, 'have increasingly come to pervade other areas of life and make them over in their own image and likeness'.[28] This kind of monetarisation and bureaucratisation of life is what Habermas calls the colonisation of the lifeworld.

In accordance with his discourse on ethics, and his emphasis on the communicative structure of the lifeworld, Habermas makes a distinction between a 'normatively ascribed agreement' and a 'communicatively achieved understanding'.[29] To cope with the changing structures in the lifeworld and to deal with ordinary people's experience, it is sufficient, according to Habermas's communicative ethics to set up a procedure which will enhance the mutual understanding and learning process. Law should install or correct the channels of communication in a self-regulated democratic process of decision-making. On the other hand, when law is employed not as a mechanism to enhance

---

[25] M. Deflem, 'Introduction: Law in Habermas's Theory of Communicative Action' (1994) 4 *Philosophy & Social Criticism*, at 4.

[26] T. McCarthy, *Ideals and Illusions: On Reconstruction and Deconstruction in Contemporary Critical Theory* (Cambridge Mass. MIT Press 1991), at 52.

[27] McCarthy, *ibid., op. cit.*

[28] McCarthy, *ibid., op. cit.*

[29] Habermas, *supra* n. 15, at 70

mutual understanding but as an instrumental steerage, the lifeworld suffers from systematically distorted communication and becomes colonised by system.

According to Habermas, the welfare state operates insensitively and 'the legal-bureaucratic regulatory regime is too intrusive, too clumsy'.[30] The expansion of welfare services presupposed the reduction of the citizen to a consumer of expertise. This signifies that, for instance, the legal process transforms individuals into 'subordinated subjects of the proceedings rather than participants in them'.[31] This form of denial and insensitiveness is a method of creating passive individuals. It 'isolates individuals, depersonalises social relations, masks domination under the guise of efficiency, destroys interpersonal connections and intimacy, and fragments lives'.[32]

6. THE THESIS OF JURIDIFICATION

Habermas's analysis of substantial social welfare programmes has highlighted the problematic tendencies in the colonisation of the lifeworld. The welfare net, which is created by substantial social reforms, is meant to diminish the (negative) effects of the market. The more closely this net is tightened, the more ambivalent it appears. As Habermas points out it is, 'the very means of guaranteeing welfare and freedom that endangers the freedom of the beneficiaries'.[33]

By introducing the theme of juridification, Habermas directs his analysis to the 'rapid expansion of law'.[34] However, the discussion of juridification should not be understood exclusively in quantitative terms. An adequate diagnosis of the extent of juridification requires some qualitative judgement as to the effects of law. For instance, the proven psychological shortcomings of judicial decision-making practices result, Habermas writes, 'not so much from an inadequate professional training of jurists for this task, as from a juristic formalisation which requires a different type of treatment'.[35]

The concept of juridification becomes an important instrument when it is used to show the effects of the welfare state and regulatory law. The threat of juridification can be observed in the effects of the welfare state's purposive interventions in various social areas. In social security law and family law, for instance, it can be observed that juridification endangers the self-productive spheres of the lifeworld. This implies that juridification can be described as a

---

[30] J. Handler, *Law and the Search for Community* (Pennsylvania Pennsylvania Univ. Press 1990), at 48.

[31] Habermas, *supra* n. 24, at 217.

[32] Handler, *supra* n. 30, at 71.

[33] Habermas, *supra* n. 22, at 362.

[34] G. Teubner, 'Juridification: Concepts, Aspects, Limits, Solutions' in Teubner (ed.) *Juridification of the Social Sphere* (Berlin Walter de Gruyter 1987).

[35] Habermas, *supra* n. 24, at 217.

process whereby the welfare state intrudes in areas of social life in such a fashion that it restricts the autonomy of individuals and their ability to determine their own affairs.

The juridification of family life, for instance, does not mean 'the densification of an already existing network of formal regulations' but rather legally supplementing a communicative context of action 'through the superimposition of legal norms'.[36] This formalisation of relationships within the family implies an objectification of relationships, which leads the members to conflict situations where they will encounter one another as legal subjects 'in an objectivating success-oriented attitude'.[37] It also generates new disturbances:

> If the structure of juridification is dependent on administrative and juridical controls, which do not merely supplement socially integrated contexts with legal institutions but convert them to the medium of the law, then functional disturbances arise.[38]

Habermas's analysis of juridification has generally been made in critical terms. The concept puts the finger on (1) the juridical system's detachment from social life, (2) the juridical system's call for autonomy, (3) the juridical system's important influence on other systems and everyday life, and (4) the juridical system's 'passivisation' and disabling of individuals. Social concepts—such as child and parent—become redefined by the law and get a juridical content and significance. This means that the juridical system and the implementing bureaucracies must reduce reality to a set of legal categories.

> The situation to be regulated is embedded in the context of a life-history and of a concrete way of life; it has to be subjected to violent abstraction not merely because it has to be subsumed under the law but in order that it can be handled administratively. The implementing bureaucracies must proceed very selectively and *choose* those instances of social needs which, using the means of a legally-proceeding bureaucratic rule, can be brought under the legal fiction.[39]

To sum up: The process of juridification is based on instrumental and strategic rationality, which neglects 'norms and contexts of action that from functional necessity are based on communication as a coordinating mechanism'.[40] In a juridified world the rules of law are applied without paying due respect to the social context of the individuals' everyday life.

7. LAW, MORALITY AND RATIONAL DISCOURSE

Discussing law and morality, Habermas claims that Rawl's theory of justice is sociologically naive and 'shares the ambiguity with the tradition of natural

---

[36] Habermas, *ibid.*, at 216.
[37] Habermas, *ibid.*, *op. cit.*
[38] Habermas, *ibid.*, *op. cit.*
[39] Habermas, *ibid.*, at 210.
[40] Habermas, *supra* n. 15, at 369.

law'.[41] Furthermore, Luhmann's system theoretical approach 'is rejected because he eliminates the question of normativity altogether',[42] subsequently, collapsing into legal positivism, which derives 'the "validity" of law only positivistically from existing law'.[43] Habermas argues that the law must do more than reduce complexity in society; it must also support democracy. Besides, Habermas criticises all individualistic reductions of morality. He also decisively abandons the notion that morality relies upon a shared substantial consensus.

Central to Habermas's theory is his claim that law cannot be separated from morality. However, he is not an advocate of substantive morality because law 'cannot provide us with unambiguous substantive norms of justice'.[44] Instead, he talks of communicative ethics as grounds for procedural rationality. Still, Habermas defends a moralistic conception of law; ie the institutionalisation of moral argumentation as the key to procedural rationality. At the same time he disapproves of the 'overmoralisation' of regulatory law.

The discursive project can be described as minimal ethics. Habermas writes: 'What moral theory can do and should be trusted to do is to clarify the universal core of our moral intuitions, thereby refuting value scepticism. What it cannot do is to make any kind of substantive contribution'.[45] In addition, morality must emphasise the rights of the individual by postulating equal respect for the dignity of everyone. Moral principles must also protect the intersubjective relations of mutual recognition by which individuals survive as members of a community. Thus, Habermas's minimal ethics corresponds to the principle of justice and solidarity. As he explains: 'Every morality revolves around equality of respect, solidarity and the common good. Fundamental ideas like these can be reduced to the relations of symmetry and reciprocity presupposed in communicative action'.[46]

Communicative ethics is based on a principal revision of moral theory in general, that is to say, 'the shift of the frame of reference from the solitary, reflecting moral consciousness of the Kantian ethics to the community of subjects in dialogue'.[47] This means a shift, on the one hand, from predictability (formalism) to mutual understanding (communication) and, on the other hand, from instrumental rationality to communicative rationality. The goal of Habermas's ethics is, therefore, a community of subjects in dialogue. In this manner, 'Habermas replaces the social contract model with a view of the legal community constituting itself on the basis of discursively achieved agreement'.[48]

---

[41] J. Habermas, *Justification and Application* Cambridge Polity Press 1993), at 27.
[42] D. M. Rasmussen, 'How is Valid Law Possible?' (1994) 4 *Philosophy & Social Criticism*, at 27.
[43] Rasmussen, *ibid.*, *op. cit.*
[44] White, *supra* n. 1. at 73.
[45] J. Habermas, 'Morality and Ethical Life: Does Hegel's Critique of Kant Apply to Discourse Ethics' (1988) 83 *Northwestern Univ. Law Review*, at 53.
[46] Habermas, *ibid.*, at 44.
[47] McCarthy, *supra* n. 1, at 327.
[48] Forbath, *supra* n. 2, at 990.

In addition, Habermas asserts that 'participants in argumentation cannot avoid the presupposition that [. . .] the structure of their communication rules out all external or internal coercion other than the force of the argument and thereby also neutralises all motives other than that of the cooperative search for truth'.[49] This implies a stress on the principle of *universalisation*. This principle postulates that '[f]or a norm to be valid, the consequences and side-effects of its general observances for the satisfaction of each person's particular interests must be freely accepted by all'.[50] Or, 'just those action norms are valid to which all possibly affected persons could agree as participants in a rational discourse'.[51] In this way, the principle of universalisation formally governs those conditions which must be met if the claim of legitimacy is, in fact, justified.

The other principle is *intersubjectivity*, because as Habermas, points out, only an intersubjective process of understanding can generate an agreement that is reflexive; only then can all participants know that the argument has convinced all.

8. A RATIONAL DISCOURSE

Habermas speaks of the standards of a 'rational discourse' and an 'ideal speech situation' which will ensure a 'communication free from domination'. The guide for a rational discourse is 'the force of the better argument', and it means that with the exception of the mutual search for truth, all other motives will have to be abandoned. If the discourse is to be characterised as a communication free from domination, then all individuals must have a real chance of participating in the discourse. At the opposite end, a consensus marked by power and money or by delusion, illusion, stratagem and fraud is regarded as a distorted communication.

The model presents (ideal) standards that are necessary for fair and rational discourse. Consequently, the model can direct an empirical critique of different agendas (forums) of communication in everyday life. Only by a careful analysis of the prerequisites for a communication free from domination is it possible to estimate whether or not an agreement is reached by distorted communication. A rational consensus can be 'ascertained only dialogically in unrestricted and unconstrained discourse'.[52] A rational discourse model of argument is grounded on the force of the better argument. In this respect, the *rationality* of Habermas's discourse model relates to a consensus or an agreement based on the force of the better argument.

---

[49] J. Habermas, *Moral Consciousness and Communicative Action* (Cambridge Mass. MIT Press 1990) at 89.
[50] Habermas, *supra* n. 45, at 40.
[51] J. Habermas, *Between Facts and Norms* (Cambridge Polity Press 1996) at 107.
[52] McCarthy, *supra* n. 1, at 237.

In order to develop this conception of a rational discourse, Habermas has applied the theoretical insights of Mead's interactionism to the Weberian paradigm of rationality. The analytical action theory (ie the Weberian paradigm) was limited to 'the atomistic model of action by an isolated actor and does not consider the mechanisms for co-ordinating action through which interpersonal relations come about'.[53] Instead of being based on a constraining concept of instrumental and strategic rationality, similar to the Weberian paradigm, the concept of communicative rationality realises a model of discourse capable of examining validity claims of arguments concerning different domains of reality. Accordingly, rationality does not only belong to the domain of efficiency in the objective world (instrumental rationality). In communicative ethics, the question of rationality belongs to different spheres of life; that is, the truth or the efficacy of teleological action in the objective world, the rightness of norms of action in the social world, truthfulness in the subjective world, and the adequacy of standards of value in the aesthetic life.

A rational discourse model of argument is grounded on, or redeemed by, the force of the better argument. A rational consensus can be 'ascertained only dialogically in unrestricted and unconstrained discourse'.[54] Rationality in the discourse model relates to a level of consensus based on the force of the better argument.

The discourse model thus transforms what Mead viewed as individual role-taking into participation in a public sphere; 'practised intersubjectively by all involved'.[55] The normative model of an ideal speech situation of discourse requires an intersubjective recognition and 'a putting out of play of all motives except that of a willingness to come to an understanding'.[56] As a result, discourse ethics have replaced the ethics of obligation (for example, the Kantian categorical imperative), by a procedure of moral argumentation among free subjects.

Habermas has repeatedly focused on communicative action in relation to the emancipation of mankind. He presents different progressive social movements (eg peace movements, environmental protection activists and women's liberation groups) in our everyday life as social phenomena, which stand for and carry on the 'emancipating' rational discourse. The rational discourse is likewise conceived as a learning process, as the image of an open conversation; that is a conversation in which one is obliged to listen to other voices. Such conversation is 'ultimately to be seen as a continual learning process in which different experiences are shared in the process of recognising more clearly who we are and who we want to become'.[57]

---

[53] Habermas, *supra* n. 15, at 273.
[54] McCarthy, *supra* n. 1, at 327.
[55] Habermas, *supra* n. 45, at 41.
[56] T. McCarthy, 'Introduction' in Habermas, *Legitimation Crisis* (London Heinemann 1976) at 8.
[57] White, *supra* n. 1, at 82.

9. AN INSTITUTIONAL DESIGN: THE LAW AND DELIBERATIVE DEMOCRACY

In the 1960s, the target of Habermas's diagnosis of society was the transformation and the decline of the public sphere in the wake of a commercialisation of
politics and culture. Later, he attempted to rehabilitate the liberal public sphere
and its institutions, because, as Habermas presents it, it is through the public
sphere that new subjects and agendas are directed into the state administration;
ie where communicative actions are transformed into administrative power.[58]
In this project he looks at the (liberal and constitutional) law and seems to find
US legal proceduralism more acceptable than before.

Habermas has been criticised for neglecting the institutional condition of
rational discourse. In *Between Facts and Norms* he 'compensates for the practical deficits of the idealisations of his previous theory by going in the direction of
a "realistic" theory of social institutions, one which makes democracy fit the
conditions of social complexity'.[59] In this manner, Habermas takes his theoretical project from social and moral theory to the domain of law and constitutions, creating *a discourse theory of law and democracy*. What Habermas has in
mind is a form of government where the citizens govern themselves through participation in a legitimate and institutionalised process of law-making, and
where only a consensus which receives all the participants' approval in a free
discourse receives legitimation.

In Habermas's present works, the law plays a central role. He apprehends law
as a dominant social force, capable of integrating the societal community. This
means that law 'serves as the intermediary between citizens and the powerful
institutions that implement decisions in a complex world'.[60] In a modern differentiated and democratic society, face-to-face interactions must be transmitted
into interactions among anonymous strangers. Law is, according to Habermas,
the only legitimate instrument by which this may take place. However, law's
potential to consolidate actions and expectations depends on its capability to
support actions in a legitimate manner. Expressed differently, laws must pass
muster under the principle of democracy, which specifies a process of legitimate
lawmaking. This means that only those laws can claim legitimate validity which
can achieve the agreement of all citizens in a discursive process of legislation.

Moreover, Habermas argues that 'modern law is the key lynchpin that mediates the relationship between system and lifeworld'.[61] In this respect, law has a
unique position. It works as the primary source of normative integration in
modern society *as well as* a steering medium in the economy and regulatory
state. Thus, Habermas's position is that 'law has the potential to "transmit" the

---

[58] Habermas, *supra* n. 51.
[59] Bohman, *supra* n. 5, at 927.
[60] Bohman, *ibid.*, at 898.
[61] Tamanaha, *supra* n. 7, at 990.

"democratic impulses" of the lifeworld to the systematic machinery of the economic and administrative state'.[62]

In complex societies, Habermas states, unfettered communicative action cannot bear the burden of social integration. Hence, Habermas assumes that law is the only medium that can carry out integration in society and at the same time remains rooted in communicative interaction. The argument is that the 'law removes the task of social integration from the actors and, at the same time, sets the medium through which communicative action can become operative in the context of highly differentiated social environments'.[63] Consequently, law obtains a cardinal position, which Habermas describes as the *great transformer,* linking different subsystems with lifeworld and converting communicative action (ie social integration) into administrative power. Law satisfies this central function due to its double nature. It is both universal and particular and as a subsystem, 'it develops its own inner logic, but given its validity claims, it is internally linked to the lifeworld'.[64]

In addition Habermas presents the law as 'the medium for transforming communicative power into administrative power'.[65] Notwithstanding Habermas's faith in (liberal) law, the administrative system (and the law) still needs to be tied to communicative interaction. Thus, administrative power 'cannot simply reproduce itself (as systems tend to do), but [can] only be permitted to regenerate [itself] from the conversion of communicative power'.[66]

Habermas, therefore, presents a proceduralist conception of deliberative democracy. This means that Habermas in his conception of *democratic deliberation* connects 'negotiations and pragmatic deliberations together with ethical and moral discourses, under conditions that warrant a presumption that procedurally correct outcomes will be ones with which free and equal citizens could reasonably agree'.[67] For Habermas, the principles of the democratic constitutional state present the institutional conditions in which 'rational deliberation can be implemented both in official governmental arenas and in unofficial arenas of the political public sphere'.[68]

10. THE THEORY OF COMMUNICATIVE ACTION VERSUS *BETWEEN FACTS AND NORMS*

From a socio-legal point of view we can either focus on the diagnosis of law in *The Theory of Communicative Action* or on law's normative foundation in *Between Facts and Norms*. In the former work, Habermas was interested in

---

[62] Forbath, *supra* n. 2, at 992.

[63] Palti, *supra* n. 9, at 1021.

[64] Palti, *ibid., op. cit.*

[65] Habermas, *supra* n. 51, at 169.

[66] Forbath, *supra* n. 2, at 993.

[67] T. McCarthy, 'Kantian Constructivism and Reconstructivism: Rawls and Habermas in Dialogue' (1994) 105 *Ethics*, at 48–9.

[68] McCarthy, *ibid.*, at 49.

sociologists such as Mead, Durkheim, Parsons, Schutz and Weber, while in the latter work this interest has vanished and he is now concerned with the legal philosophies of Hart, Rawls and Dworkin as well as John Hart Ely's proceduralism, Frank Michelman's and Cass Sunstein's civic-republican proposals and Bruce Ackerman's thesis on law-making.[69]

For those who have regarded Habermas as an advocate of radical democracy, *Between Facts and Norms* will appear as a strikingly liberal work. His reconstruction of the constitutional state may even appear as uncritical. And his previous critical diagnosis of the colonisation of the lifeworld by markets and state bureaucracy are generally absent. From this perspective, his present position is a retreat from his original emancipatory concerns. Now the democratic process and law have replaced any conception of 'popular sovereignty moving toward a communicative ideal'.[70] At the same time he is 'less committed to a substantive democracy he championed two decades ago'.[71] In the political sphere he now chooses publicity and equality over participatory democracy, which means that his previous radical approach is replaced by an optimistic and celebratory view of law and liberal constitutionalism.

11. CRITICAL REFLECTIONS ON HABERMAS

Complex theories are attractive targets for criticism. In this respect, Habermas's theory of communicative action and universalistic ethics is no exception. He has, for instance, been warned against 'risking sophism', ie the situation in which language, instead of becoming a vehicle of emancipation, becomes an end in itself.[72] Luhmann criticises Habermas for confusing law and morality and paying too much attention to morality, while postmodernists and critical theories criticise him for ignoring the significance of power. He has also been criticised for the apparent unrealism in his rational discourse model on the basis that such a discourse can never exist in everyday social practices. This criticism is somewhat misleading because, as Bauman points out, the model 'is not a generalisation of practice, but the definition of its idealised horizon'.[73] The ideal speech situation should not be regarded as a condition which can be finally reached in human affairs, but as a dynamic and evolving condition: a matter of degree.[74]

---

[69] W. Rehg, 'Translators Introduction' in Habermas *Between Facts and Norms* (Cambridge Polity Press 1996).

[70] Abraham, *supra* n. 4, at 942.

[71] Abraham, *ibid.*, *op. cit.*

[72] R. Bubner, 'Habermas's Concept of Critical Theory' in Thompson and Held (eds.) *Habermas: Critical Debates* (London Macmillan Press 1982).

[73] Z. Bauman, *Hermeneutics and Social Sciences* (London Hutchinson 1978) at 243.

[74] Cf., D. Cornell, 'The Poststructuralist Challenge to the Ideal of Community' (1987) 8 *Cardozo Law Review*, 989–1022.

One criticism is that the model neglects local differences and local beliefs. As a matter of fact, 'the barrier of localised differences, not to mention the limits of rationality itself, are far more obstinate than Habermas seems willing to acknowledge'.[75] In other words, he fails

> to give due consideration to the particular linguistic, cultural, and cognitive competencies by which those who advocate the norms in question, and those whose actions are judged accordingly, construct their own disparate senses of self and social reality.[76]

From this perspective, 'Habermas's notion of an ideal speech condition, [. . .] fails to account for the diverse ways in which discrete cultural, cognitive, and linguistic constructs give rise to various kinds of meaning making'.[77] According to this argument, 'it simply will not do to impose abstract notions of "the right", "the just", and "the true" from the top down, [. . .], without inquiring into how those notions (and conflicting ones) are actually understood at the level of local belief, discourse, and practice'.[78]

A similar critique originates from 'the below'. The rational discourse model put excessive demands on the citizens, for instance, expecting them to eagerly participate in the struggle over public relevance and interpretations of their own needs. In this respect, the model 'asks too much, and forces a burdensome obligation upon the ordinary citizen'.[79] The model relies on a version of an elitist reason.

Habermas is said to be overly optimistic regarding the possibility of achieving consensus in respect of important norms. Hence, 'communicative ethics must be wedded to a more pragmatic temper regarding plurality and difference', and to make the model less demanding.[80] Besides, there 'is no logical way to move from a procedure to a morally correct outcome'.[81] The target of the criticism is that 'a morally worthy procedure does not [. . .] entail any guarantee of doing the right thing'.[82] Nevertheless, a morally excellent procedure is more advantageous.

The analysis of the relation between system and lifeworld has faced a similar critique. The theory has two prerequisites: the gradual separation of system from the lifeworld, and, secondly, system's colonisation of lifeworld. In this context Habermas proclaims that system integration cannot replace the social integration of lifeworld, without pathological effects. However, Habermas finds it difficult to present good reasons for why such a replacement will have pathological consequences. There is no need for a sharp line between system and lifeworld. In other words, the distinction between system and lifeworld is

---

[75] R. K. Sherwin, *When Law Goes Pop: The Vanishing Line between Law and Popular Culture* (Chicago Chicago Univ. Press 2000) at 236.
[76] Sherwin, *ibid., op. cit.*
[77] Sherwin, *ibid., op. cit.*
[78] Sherwin, *ibid., op. cit.*
[79] Tamanaha, *supra* n. 7, at 1003.
[80] Forbath, *supra* n. 2, at 1114; cf., Bohman, *supra* n. 5 and Tamanaha, *supra* n. 7.
[81] Tamanaha, *supra* n. 7, at 1002.
[82] Tamanaha, *ibid., op. cit.*

claimed to be 'empirically indiscernible'.[83] The analysis of the thesis of juridification might even move in another direction. The thesis of juridification and internal colonisation of lifeworld, then, 'seems to neglect the possibility that law as an institutional complex of the lifeworld can be restructured by systems to bring about a colonization of law, rather than that the law is itself a colonizing medium'.[84]

Habermas's focus on law as *the* integrative mechanism in modern society has been questioned. According to this criticism, Habermas neglects the force of other integrative mechanisms (eg customs, the market, spontaneous social organisation and shared language). No doubt, 'law is an attractive candidate for solving the problem of social order'.[85] This accepted truth is, however, never subjected to socio-legal analysis. It can be argued that 'society may be ordered without law (though not without rules), although law cannot exist without an already organized society'.[86] After all, 'the notion that law stabilises behavioural expectations in modern society is highly questionable'.[87] The most effective laws are those laws 'which happen to coincide with what people do anyway'.[88]

12. EMPIRICAL APPLICATION OF HABERMAS'S THEORY

As I argued before, *TCA* provides better bases for conducting empirical research than *Between Facts and Norms*, even though the later publication is more concerned with the law.

Several studies in the Swedish sociology of law have been inspired by Habermas's idea about communicative rationality and the colonisation of the lifeworld. These include a study of the regulation of the environmental protection and civil disobedience,[89] a study of distorted communication in medical malpractice cases,[90] a study of the limitations of law in eliminating ethnic discrimination,[91] and, finally, an investigation into custody disputes.[92] All of these studies

---

[83] Palti, *supra* n. 9, at 1022.

[84] Deflem, *supra* n. 25, at 11.

[85] Tamanaha, *supra* n. 7, at 993.

[86] Tamanaha, *ibid.*, at 995.

[87] Tamanaha, *ibid.*, at 997.

[88] Tamanaha, *ibid.*, *op. cit.*

[89] L. Ericsson, *Ett surt regn kommer att falla* [A Hard Rain is Going to Fall] (Lund Scandinavian Studies in Sociology of Law 1985); Lars Ericsson 'Civil ohörsamhet' [Civil Disobedience] (1989) 5 *Tidskrift för Rättssociologi*, 55–76.

[90] B. Carlsson, *Hälsa, kommunikativt handlande och konfliktlösning* [Health Communicative Action and Dispute Resolution] (Lund Scandinavian Studies in Sociology of Law 1989) and Bo Carlsson 'Communicative Rationality and Open-ended Laws in Sweden' (1995) 4 *Journal of Law and Society*, at 480.

[91] R. Banakar, *The Doorkeepers of the Law* (Aldershot Ashgate 1998).

[92] B. Carlsson and A. Rejmer, 'The Swedish Way of Dealing with Custody Disputes' in Carlsson *Social Steerage and Communicative Action* (Lund Series in Sociology of Law 1998).

deal with open-ended laws (*ramlagar*) with a procedural character and an emphasis on communication and participation. Here I focus on two of these studies.

Environmental Protection Law

The Environmental Protection Law (*Naturskyddslagen*), 1969, is an open-ended
law, which means that it does not stipulate what has to be done in detail, as a
result of which its interpretation becomes unclear. The legislature tried in 1976
to remedy this problem through the notion of participation and communication. Environmental protection groups and the general public were invited to
participate, and to put forward arguments and counter-arguments. The established interest groups did not support this idea and, in fact, did their utmost to
limit such participation.

By increasing the participation of the general public, the decision-making
process, controlled by the Swedish National Environmental Protection Board
[Koncenssionsnämnden] became, at least in theory, open to value judgements
concerning the nature and the concept of a good life. However, these arguments
were caught up in mechanisms of instrumental action and civic privatism that
were oriented to career and consumption.

This study showed that instrumental rationality dominated the decision-
making process. Both authorities and corporations were basically interested in
economic growth and promoting consumption, as a result of which interests in
conserving nature were not taken seriously, especially if the production of consumer goods and full employment were threatened. As a result the environment
and values pertaining to its protection became transformed into a cost-benefit
analysis. As a rule, local inhabitants and their environmental protection groups
played no role in the decision-making process.

Since society was not responsive to the arguments of the environmentalists,
they were left no option but to use civil disobedience. They organised street
protests and occupations which brought them into confrontation with the police.
Criminal courts which heard their cases were not interested in arguments about
the environment and evaluated their actions in isolation from the nature of their
protest. The cases were decided in special proceedings and, to the activists' great
disappointment, only four minutes were devoted to hearing each defendant. This
demonstrated that the National Environmental Protection Board was superfluous
in 1995, and participation in the legal decision-making process can have nothing
in common with what Habermas expects in the rational discourse model.

The Medical Responsibility Board

During the 1980s there was an official interest in strengthening the patients'
position in the Swedish health care system by legal means. One of the aims of

the new legislation was to stimulate the process of communication and democratisation. The keywords in the Swedish Service Act (*Hälso- och sjukvårdsla-
gen*), were integrity, vicinity, accessibility, the right to self-determination and
the right to be informed. Consequently, the quality of communication between
the patient and the system was recognised as an important factor, in everyday
care and medical treatment, as well as in communication about malpractice
claims. Despite a clear policy statement, patients have no explicit rights in the
Service Act, and, hence, are essentially allowed to participate in a malpractice
process to vindicate their rights, as formulated by the Supervision of Health
Personnel Act [*Tillsynslagen*] and processed by the Medical Responsibility
Board [*Hälso- och sjukvårdens ansvarsnämnd*]. This means that the outcome of
complaints is to some degree conditioned by the communication set in motion
by the Service Act's 'procedural rationality' and, ultimately, by how cases are
judged.

The effect of the law, however, and its capacity to facilitate a learning process
within the medical care and health system is dependent on the complainant's
will and ability to produce reasonable arguments, the quality of the medical
records, the will of the medical staff to produce valid counter-arguments and the
Board's power to investigate or to hold a specific doctor or nurse responsible.
To investigate opportunities for patients to participate in the Swedish malpractice process, you have to ask how the Medical Responsibility Board handles
complaints. Does the Board handle all the complaints equally? And, does every
complainant have the opportunity to present an argument to the board?

A study of the Board in the 1980s indicated that a large portion (25 per
cent) of complaints by patients or relatives were regarded as incomplete or
inadequate. The Board, as a matter of interest, did not examine the facts in these
complaints. This was due to the quality of the complaints, but it also depended
on the Board's formal competence. For example, a malpractice claim had to be
issued and brought to the Board's attention within two years after the reported
ill-treatment had occurred; the claim had to be related to mistakes by a distinct
individual among the medical staff; and the claim could not be regarded as
economic compensation. This 'formalism' produced an entangled decision-
making process, and in some cases blocked the Board's capacity to stimulate a
learning process.

A further difficulty arose from the tendency of the Board to 'medicalise' problems that originated with poor communication on the part of doctors. This
again obstructed patients from having a real influence on the legal process.

13. CONCLUSION

To make an empirical study possible, abstract theory must be operationalised.
The transformation of Habermas's conceptualisation of forms of rationality to
something that can be observed and analysed using social scientific methods

might, however, jeopardise analytical elements which are central to the theory's coherence and reliability. Questions also arise as to whether the result of the empirical investigation is already settled in advance. Will the theory govern both the collection and interpretation of the material? The MRB study did, however, illustrate the system's colonisation of the lifeworld and distorted communication and showed that Habermas's ideas can be employed to design methods of detecting distorted communication.

As mentioned earlier, Habermas's theory of communicative action is complicated and demanding. This introduction has necessarily neglected different constituent elements of Habermas's theory, such as his references to linguistics (universal pragmatics), symbolic interactionism and his reconstruction of historical materialism.

Notwithstanding my positive view of *The Theory of Communicative Action*, which can bring qualitatively important inspiration to empirical studies in the field of sociology of law, I still find Habermas's emphasis on communicative action and discourse ethics too abstract and demanding when it comes to designing or conducting empirical studies. His theory also falls short in addressing the individual's existential desire to become 'socially acknowledged'. Social phenomena such as altruism or egoism as well as enviousness, pride or shame, which must be understood as significant aspects of the nature of human life, are not sufficiently acknowledged in Habermas's discourse ethics. Habermas would probably argue that when one feels pride or shame, these should be regarded as forms of distorted communication. If they are, they still exist and appear to have an important integrating function in everyday life.

Section 3

Critical Approaches

REZA BANAKAR and MAX TRAVERS

THE LARGEST AND most influential tradition in law and society studies, at least in the English speaking world, is critical theory. The chapters in this section cover Marxism, feminism, critical race theory and queer theory, and it will be apparent that there are all kinds of debates taking place within these traditions. They all, however, view social life in terms of a power struggle between dominant and subordinate groups, and see law as fully implicated in economic exploitation, unfairness and injustice.

The best place to start in understanding the critical tradition is with the ideas of Karl Marx, and the first chapter in this section by Robert Fine provides a thoughtful and authoritative introduction to the views of a range of Marxist theorists on law. His central theme is the debate between those who view law as irredeemably bad—as implicated in relations of power and domination, and in the capitalist system of commodity production—and those who believe that law is necessary for a good society. Fine sides with humanistic Marxists like Lukacz and E. P. Thompson who see law as essential for the protection of individual liberties. From this perspective, the 'abstract and utopian' view that law will 'wither away' under communism 'ultimately [points] in a lawless and even totalitarian direction'. The problem with taking this view, however, is that it involves accepting, and even celebrating, liberalism; which follows once you accept that no radical transformation of society is either morally desirable or politically possible.

We particularly like this piece because it acknowledges the difficulties facing Marxism, but also makes one think about the problems facing its liberal and postmodern critics. Fine argues that those motivated by 'the rightful desire to construct a relation to law that has no kinship with totalitarianism', are usually also suspicious of '*social* theory'(his italics). The strength of Marxism is that it does address 'social questions' about the relationship between law and society. Because of this, it is more difficult to assimilate Marxism into the 'dominant positivisitic and natural law traditions in Western legal thought'; although one might also argue that when Marxists start accepting and celebrating the rule of law, they are also vulnerable to the charge of sliding into liberalism.

The Marxist insight that law reflects and maintains the position of dominant economic groups was taken up in law schools during the 1970s and 1980s by the Critical Legal Studies movement. In reviewing this area of legal scholarship,

Jiří Přibáň again focuses on the debate between 'radical' and 'moderate' critics of the rule of law. Radicals like Duncan Kennedy 'dismiss the concept of rights . . . as useless because they . . . reproduce the existing social and political inequalities and power relations'. Liberals like Roberto Unger prefer to 'critically evaluate and use the rights and rule of law doctrine for the purposes of social, political and legal transformation'.

One important development in critical scholarship over the last forty years has been the recognition that there are other social divisions unrelated to social class. The next three chapters by Fletcher, Pierce and Beger are concerned with the subordination of women, ethnic minorities and homosexuals. It would be worth starting here by reading Pierce's vivid, and morally-driven empirical study about discrimination against black people and women in American law firms. This employs a qualitative case-study approach to identify the widely-shared prejudices that frustrate equal opportunity legislation (see also Max Travers' chapter on symbolic interactionism in section 4). It is assumed that black men are not intellectually capable of working in elite law firms, and that middle-class women educated in Ivy League universities are not 'tough enough' to take the pressure.

Critical theorists who have tried to think systematically about forms of discrimination and oppression not based on social class, usually recognise a tension between 'radical' and 'reformist' approaches to law in the same way as Marxists. They are also, however, centrally concerned with the postmodern concept of difference. Fletcher shows, for example, how the feminist movement came under attack during the 1970s and 1980s from black and working class women who felt that their voices and experiences were not being represented. She is also aware of the political and epistemological problems that follow once one accepts that there are women with all kinds of identities and experiences. Once one embraces 'radical plurality', it becomes difficult forming 'some sort of unified base among feminists to ground arguments'.

Beger who is a post-structuralist (and so could as easily have been included in section 5 on Postmodernism) goes further in employing the concept of difference to challenge the liberal order. He suggests, for example, that 'concepts of queer . . . are at their best where they defy definition and where they concentrate on disruptions of the normal—the normal being male, heterosexual, white, bourgeois, but also normal business in the academy or taken-for-granted gay and lesbian identity politics'. The target here is not simply law reform that benefits homosexuals, but the subversion of conventional ideas about sexuality, what Beger calls 'the logic of a heteronormative binary gender system'.

Despite his radical-sounding post-structuralist language, Beger is saying much the same thing as reformist Marxists when they acknowledge the need to work within liberal institutions, while maintaining a critical distance from liberalism. It seems unlikely, on the face of things, that cultural activism by intellectuals will have much impact on society, without a mass political movement also developing against capitalism. There seems to be little sign of this happening at present, although it is possible that a future global economic or ecological crisis could create the conditions for this to take place.[1]

Finally, we come to the last contribution in this section, which is an introductory essay about Pierre Bourdieu's ideas on law by Mikael Madsen and Yves Dezalay. This is presented by these authors as a variety of systems theory (see section 2), which affords an overview of different elements of society and how they develop over time. However, it is important to remember that Bourdieu, like Habermas, is also a critical theorist. His ideas draw on elements from Marx, but also from Max Weber and the phenomenological tradition, so that like Habermas he has a central interest in resolving the gap between 'structure'and 'action'(or in his terminology 'objectivity'and 'subjectivity').

Madsen and Dezalay's review focuses on the role of the legal profession as an organised group that holds and exercises power, and is not simply a tool used by the state or economic elites. This view of lawyers originates with Weber's conception of society as the struggle for power, status and economic resources between a multitude of different groups (as opposed to the two blocs who are usually opposed in Marxist theory). One might add here that Weber allows one to conceptualise difference in a similar way to the post-structuralists (since he recognised multiple over-lapping identities). Weber, however, did not believe that any great economic or cultural transformation of society was likely, given the entrenched power of existing interests.

---

[1] Přibáň notes that critical scholars risk becoming a 'religious sect', when they turn their backs on law, prone to the pursuit of 'theoretical purity' and 'political correctness'. In practice, most manage to maintain a critical distance from liberalism, while still campaigning for legislation that will benefit subordinate groups.

5

Marxism and the Social Theory of Law

ROBERT FINE

MARXIST THEORY OF law remains relatively undeveloped in comparison with Marxist critiques of political economy. One reason is that Marx himself never returned to the project he set himself in his youth: to complement his critique of political economy with a critique of jurisprudence.[1] There are asides in Marx's scientific works, the *Grundrisse* and *Capital*, where he raises juridical issues of right and law and provides clues as to how the method of his critique of political economy might be transposed to the field of jurisprudence.[2] There are political texts in which Marx reveals something of his practical approach to questions of law,[3] and there are texts by Engels in which he summarises his and Marx's approaches.[4] This said, there is no possibility of discovering a *theory* of law and legal relations ready-made in Marx's works.

Learning from Marx is also made more difficult by equivocations in Marx's own analysis of law. In some texts Marx appears to offer a negative criticism of legal rights, presenting them as mere forms without substantive content, and an antinomian view of communism as a political order superseding all juridical and constitutional limits. In other passages Marx shows an appreciation of the value and durability of legal forms whose contradictions he analyses without normative preconception of what ought to replace them. In his scientific works there is no clear-cut answer to the question of what constitutes a 'positive supersession' of modern law, as opposed to its merely 'abstract negation'.[5] Even in early texts like *On the Jewish Question*, where Marx at first sight appears unequivocally critical of civil rights as icons of egoism and separation, the thrust of his

---

[1] Marx wrote: 'I shall therefore publish the critique of law, morals, politics, etc. in a series of separate independent pamphlets and finally attempt in a special work to present them once again as a connected whole, to show the relationship between the parts . . .' (preface to the 'Economic and Philosophical Manuscripts', in L. Colletti (ed.) *Karl Marx: Early Writings* (Harmondsworth Penguin 1992) at 281.

[2] See B. Fine, *Democracy and the Rule Of Law: Liberal Ideals and Marxist Critiques* (London Pluto 1995), ch. 4 'Law, state and capital'.

[3] See M. Cain and A. Hunt, *Marx and Engels on Law* (London Academic Press 1979); A. Hunt, 'Marxism, law, legal theory and jurisprudence' in P. Fitzpatrick (ed.) *Dangerous Supplements: Resistance and Renewal in Jurisprudence* (London Pluto 1991).

[4] F. Engels, *Anti-Dühring* (London Lawrence and Wishart 1943).

[5] The terms are drawn from Marx 'Economic and Philosophic Manuscripts of 1844' in R. Tucker, (ed.) *The Marx-Engels Reader* (New York Norton 1978).

work was to defend the rights of Jews against a form of radicalism which declared that Jews ought not to be granted political emancipation unless and until they abandoned their Judaism.[6] Perhaps the one thing we can say about Marx's conception of modern legality is that he never abandoned the desire to look more closely into the matter. Often critics of Marx have displayed a rather crude and stereotyped view of what Marx wrote about jurisprudence, and there is no denying that some forms of Marxism, especially those connected with the state power of Stalin and his successors, have lived up to these images. But to identify Marx as a precursor of a totalitarian destruction of law, as many critics do, would be no less of a travesty than to identify any of the other great nineteenth and early twentieth century rebels against tradition: be it Hegel or Nietzsche or even Weber.[7]

One thing which makes Marx's great works, the *Grundrisse* and *Capital*, into 'classics' is that, when we actually read them, we find original and unexpected elements that surpass all our previous conceptions of what they contained and that force us to question the images we have of them. The texts themselves never seem to exhaust what they have to say to us and the common use of terms like 'Marxist' always seems inadequate in relation to what we read. To discover what animated Marx and what makes him significant for our own times, we need to shake off what Italo Calvino has called 'the pulviscular cloud of critical discourse' which so often surrounds his works.[8] For me, the key to understanding Marx's critique of jurisprudence is to see that his task was not to posit communism as an abstract ideal built on the ruins of law, redeeming past injuries and violence through the prospect of future reconciliation, but rather to resist all forms of historicism, dispel all teleologies of progress, in short, to criticise all claims to perfect harmony which conceal real social antagonisms beneath sanctified juridical categories.

The contribution of Marxism to our understanding of law lies in its determination to uncover the social relations expressed, mediated and obscured in legal categories such as private property or state property, constitutional government or the workers' state, representative government or the general will, individual right or collective right. Here the name of Marxism indicates a commitment to a *social* theory of law: one which investigates why and with what consequence definite social relations assume determinate legal forms. Conversely, the contemporary repudiation of Marxism may signify a move away not just from socialism but from any idea of the social. In opposition to natural law theory and legal positivism, Marxism is a declaration that the idea

---

[6] In this text Marx rejected the spurious reasoning of certain young Hegelians that Jews were only concerned with the acquisition of money, lacked any wider sense of national loyalty and were therefore undeserving of political rights. His basic argument was that modern society as a whole is a money society in which self-interest usually trumps wider social concerns, so why pick on the Jews? See Marx, 'On the Jewish Question' in Colletti, *Karl Marx: Early Writings, supra* n. 1.

[7] See H. Arendt, *Between Past and Future* (Harmondsworth Penguin 1977) at 26–27.

[8] I. Calvino, *Why read the classics*, trans. Martin McLaughlin (London Jonathan Cape 1999) at 6.

of right is not a natural or rational attribute of individuals, nor is it merely a product of sovereign legislation, but a social form of the subject which emerges under given historical conditions. In this sense, Marxism does not make an 'ism' of the social in the sense that it stands for the abolition of legal forms in the name of social transparency, but rather traces the immanent development of the forms and shapes of law—from the simplest forms of abstract right to the most complex and concrete forms of state and international law—as a flexible and radically incomplete system open at every point to political action. Marxism names the perception that if there is one thing worse than the idealisation of law and its absolution from critical inquiry, it is hatred of law even when, or perhaps especially when, that hatred is expressed in the name of 'the people'.

1. MARX'S CRITIQUE OF RIGHT

Marx's most important insights into law are to be found in his marginal comments on the idea of 'right' in works focusing on the critique of economic forms.[9] In these asides Marx argued that the kind of society which gives rise to the commodity form, money relations and capital also gives rise to modern forms of right, law and state. They are two sides of the same coin. His argument may be reconstructed thus. In a society based on production by *independent* producers, whose contact with one another is mediated through the exchange of products, producers are *free* to produce what and how much they wish, *equal* in that no producer can force others to produce or expropriate their products against their will, and *self-interested* in that they are entitled to pursue their own private interests. Relations with other producers take the form of free and equal exchanges in which individuals alienate their own property in return for the property of another for the *mutual benefit* of each party. Exchange relations make no reference to the circumstances in which individuals seek to exchange nor to the characteristics of the commodities offered for exchange. They appear as self-sufficient relations, divorced from any particular mode of production and enjoyed by free and equal property owners who enter a *voluntary contract* in pursuit of their own mutual self-interests.[10] The parties to the exchange must

---

[9] See J. D. Balbus 'Commodity form and legal form' (1977) 2 *Law and Society Review* at 571–588; G. Kay and J. Mott, *Political Order and the Law of Labour* (London Macmillan 1982); D. Sayer, *The Violence of Abstraction: Analytical Foundations of Historical Materialism* (Oxford Blackwell 1987).

[10] In an exchange relation, Marx writes, 'each confronts the other as owner of the object of the other's need, this proves that each of them reaches beyond his own particular need . . . as a human being and that they relate to each other as human beings . . . there enters in addition to the quality of equality, that of freedom. Although individual A feels a need for the commodity of individual B, he does not appropriate it by force, nor vice versa, but rather they recognise one another reciprocally as proprietors, as persons whose will penetrates their commodities. Accordingly, the juridical moment of the *Person* enters here . . . all inherent contradictions of bourgeois society appear extinguished . . . and bourgeois democracy even more than the bourgeois economists takes refuge in this aspect'. Marx, *Grundrisse, supra* n. 10, (Harmondsworth Penguin 1973) at 243 and 251.

place themselves in relation to one another as *persons* whose will resides in those objects and must behave in such a way that each does not appropriate the commodity of the other and alienate his own, except through an act to which both parties consent.[11] The presupposition of exchange, however, is an organisation of production which *forces* producers to exchange their products. Their *interdependence* means that they cannot survive except by exchanging the products of their labour. Both the form of their relations, that of a contract between two private parties based on the exchange of property, and the content, the terms on which such contracts are made, are beyond the will of individuals and become a power over them. Individuals are *formally* independent but the relations they enter, far from being an abolition of relations of dependency, are rather the 'dissolution of these relations in a general form . . . *Individuals are now ruled by abstractions*, whereas earlier they depended upon one another'.[12]

The illusion of a free and equal relationship is dissolved once we explore the *content* of exchange. Where commodity production is sporadic or peripheral and exchange takes the form of an occasional barter between communities, the terms of the exchange are determined by the producers themselves and each party has a right to defend its property by force of arms. With the generalisation of commodity production, competition between producers ensures that commodities exchange at or around their values, according to the socially necessary labour time that enters their production. Since there is no guarantee that the actual labour-time taken by the producer corresponds with socially necessary labour-time for the goods in question, equal right in these circumstances entails that some producers exchange their commodities for more than their value and some for less. This leads to extremes of impoverishment and enrichment, but if one party grows impoverished and the other grows wealthier, then this is, as it were, of their own free will. Under these circumstances producers are forced to be free, that is, to observe the rules governing the exchange of commodities.

Relations between capitalists and wage-labourers continue to take the form of free and equal exchanges, but the form and content of these exchanges now change.[13] On the surface the relation between capitalist and worker remains a simple exchange, but it is distinguished by the entry into the market of a new commodity, labour-power, whose historical presupposition lies in the double

[11] Marx writes: 'The sphere of circulation of commodity exchange, within whose boundaries the sale and purchase of labour power goes on, is in fact a very Eden of the innate rights of man. It is the exclusive realm of Freedom, Equality, Property and Bentham. Freedom because both buyer and seller of a commodity, let us say labour-power, are determined only by their own free will . . . Equality because each enters into relations with the other as with a simple owner of commodities and they exchange equivalent with equivalent. Property because each disposes only what is his own. And Bentham because each looks only to his own advantage. The only force bringing them together is the selfishness, the gain and the private interest of each'. Marx, *Capital* 1, *supra* n. 11 at 280.

[12] Marx, *Grundrisse, supra* n. 10, at 164.

[13] Marx writes: 'a worker who buys a loaf of bread and a millionaire who does the same appear in this act as simple buyers . . . all other aspects are extinguished . . . the content of these purchases appears as completely irrelevant compared with the formal aspect' (Marx, *Grundrisse, supra* n. 10, at 251).

freedom of individuals—their freedom to own their own body, mind and capacity to work, and their freedom from other means of subsistence or production than their labour-power. The buyer of labour-power is no longer a simple buyer who wishes to use it as an object of personal consumption but a capitalist who uses it specifically for the production of surplus value. The secret behind the exchange between capital and labour is that workers receive in the form of wages a value equivalent to the value of their labour-power (ie the labour time socially necessary for the reproduction of the labourer) and not equivalent to the value of the products they produce on behalf of the capitalist. In this context, the unequal appropriation of unpaid surplus labour becomes the *substance* of equal right.

Turning to the reproduction of capitalist society, Marx argues that the social content of the exchange between capital and labour changes once more. Looked at individually, the exchange between capital and labour consists of the expropriation of part of the product of the workers' labour by the capitalist. The capitalist says that the capital which he exchanges with labour-power is his own property—perhaps because he worked hard for it or because it is the product of his own earlier labour. This may be true of primitive accumulation but ignores the role of violence and international pillage. In any event after several cycles of production the entire capital owned by the capitalist will consist only of capitalised surplus value, that is, of the product of the labour of workers expropriated by the capitalist and turned into capital. It is now revealed that the exchange between capital and labour is no exchange at all, since the total capital is but a transmuted form of the expropriated product of workers from a previous period. On the surface, free and equal exchange carries on as before. Beneath the surface there is the appropriation of the property of one class by another without equivalent.[14] The law which presupposes that we own the products of our labour 'turns . . . through a necessary dialectic into an absolute divorce of property and appropriation of alien labour without exchange'.[15] Marx's argument reaches its climax in the conclusion that *in this context* abstract right becomes a 'mere semblance', a 'mere form . . . alien to the content of the transaction', a 'mystification', 'only a semblance and a deceptive semblance'.[16]

Perhaps the most original proposition in this account of Marx's social theory of right is that the social relations of production which give rise to the commodity or value form of the products of human labour also give rise to the right

---

[14] Marx writes: 'Originally, the rights of property seemed to us to be grounded in man's own labour . . . Now, however, property turns out to be the right on the part of the capitalist to appropriate the unpaid labour of others or its product and the impossibility of the worker of appropriating his own product. The separation of property from labour thus becomes the necessary consequence of a law that apparently originated in their identity'. (Marx, *Capital* 1, *supra* n. 11, at 729)

[15] Marx, *Grundrisse, supra* n. 10, at 514.

[16] Marx, *Capital 1, supra* n. 11 at 729–730.

or person-form of the producers. Both economic and juridical categories, as well as the split between them, appear as the results of certain social relations of production. We might say that Marx's theory of *modernity* is a theory of the separation of subject and object, person and thing, right and value. Yet the difficulty Engels alluded to, that he and Marx 'neglected the formal side of political, juridical and other ideological notions—the way in which these notions come about—for the sake of their inner content', was not addressed.[17] For all the sophistication of the analysis, we are left with the presentation of right as a mere form, a semblance, an empty illusion, a *mirror* of economic relations. While the forms of value are understood as *real* appearances, the forms of right are caught within a *logic of illusion* from which it seems that Marx did not escape. Yet if the surface form of a thing is as real as its social content, as Marx recognised in his analysis of the value form, there is no reason to think that the appearance of a subject—as a person, a possessor of right, a human being—is not also as real as its social content.

In short, Marx left a rich but incomplete legacy of juridical criticism. The task of developing his critique of jurisprudence was left for others to fulfil. It has not proven easy.

2. SPLITS WITHIN MARXISM AND THEIR EFFECTS ON LEGAL THEORY

With the historical split of Marxism into Social Democratic and Bolshevic wings, Marxist legal theory was also torn apart. On the revolutionary side, the writings of the Soviet legal theorist, Evgeni Pashukanis, represented an important attempt in the 1920s to apply the method of Marx's critique of political economy to jurisprudence.[18] Pashukanis was one of the first to draw upon the systematic connections Marx observed between the commodity and the juridical subject, and on this basis generated a commodity form theory of law in opposition to both legal formalism, which abstracts the legal form from social relations, and to legal reductionism which ignores legal form in favour of an analysis of political interests or economic functions. Pashukanis argued that law is a determinate social form, signifying relations of mutual competition between juridical subjects who affirm their private rights against one another and are otherwise indifferent to the needs of others. He argued that law arose in the modern bourgeois era, was indelibly marked by its origins, and would wither away under socialism.

Pashukanis' commodity form theory of law represented an important step forward in recovering Marx's critique of right, but the result of his investigations

---

[17] Engels, 'Letter to Mehring', 1893, in Marx and Engels, *Letters on Capital*, trans. by E. Drummond (London New Park 1983).

[18] E. Pashukanis, *Law and Marxism* (ed. and introduction by C. Arthur) (London Pluto 1983); E. Pashukanis, *Selected Writings on Marxism and Law* (ed. and introduction by P. Beirne and R. Sharlet) (London Academic Press 1980).

was a one-sided critique of law as a power which operates on the basis of atomistic social relations between juridical subjects. His disinterest in rights and freedoms played into the hands of the evolving Stalinist regime and his thesis concerning the withering away of law under socialism served to justify the Soviet regime's disregard for legal procedure. Like many intellectuals Pashukanis was useful for a totalitarian movement in its period of ascendancy, but once the Stalinist regime sought to legitimise terror legally, as it did in the 1936 constitution, then Pashukanis and his work were soon dispatched. A productive reconstruction of Pashukanis' theory was attempted in the 1970s by New Left critics of law in an attempt to revive the revolutionary tradition of Marxist legal criticism, but the theoretical and political limitations of his work have become increasingly apparent.[19]

On the other side of the Marxist divide, Social Democratic legal theorists like Karl Renner in Austria were not interested in overcoming the legal form but in actualising it and giving it a socialist content. For Renner, legality is like a bottle in which different social contents can be poured. The stronger version of his argument is that it is *only* under socialism that the rule of law can be realised since under capitalism law is corrupted by private interests. The transition to socialism is taken to mean the extension of legal regulation into previously considered private spheres—through legislation on health and safety, minimum wages, trade union rights, unemployment benefits, the nationalisation of privately owned services, etc.—and the democratisation of legislative representation and procedure.[20] This idea of the progressive socialisation of law was buried under the weight of aggravated class conflicts and then of totalitarian forces, but perhaps its main internal weakness was a failure to recognise the justified revulsion that can arise at the gulf between legal ideals and the sea of human misery to which they fail to respond—a revulsion which totalitarian movements were quick to exploit. When Social Democracy re-surfaced after the war, its legal theory became largely independent of Marxist underpinning.

A more direct confrontation with the rise of fascism and Stalinism in the 1930s was to be found among Critical Theorists of the Frankfurt School. They sought to rehabilitate Marx's critique of law by reconsidering it in relation to the tradition of natural law and by contrasting it with the destructive hatred of law expressed in totalitarian movements and with the ideas of 'people', 'leader', 'nation', 'blood' and 'soil' found in National Socialist ideology. They argued, for example, that Hegel and Nazism were impossible bed-fellows, since the

---

[19] See, for example, C. Arthur, 'Toward a materialist theory of law' (1976–7) 7 *Critique*; P. Binns 'Law and Marxism' (1980) 10 *Capital and Class*; B. Fine, *Democracy and the Rule of Law, supra* n. 2 at 155–169; Alan Norrie 'Between structure and difference: law's relationality' in M. Archer et al. (eds) *Critical Realism: Essential Readings* (London Routledge 1998), 19XX; R. Sharlet, 'Pashukanis and the withering away of law in USSR' in S. Fitzpatrick (ed.) *Cultural Revolution in Russia 1928–31* (Indiana University Press 1974); R. Warrington, 'Pashukanis and the commodity form theory', (1981) 9 *International Journal of the Sociology of Law*.

[20] K. Renner, *The Institutions of Private Law and their Functions* (RKP 1949).

claims of a philosopher who stood for legality, individual rights and a bureaucracy based on rational and calculable norms conflicted with the ethnic claims of the Nazi movement. By contrast, they argued that Marx's critique of Hegel's *Philosophy of Right* both rejected its authoritarian tendencies and revealed that this philosophical authoritarianism mirrored the political proclivity of contemporary liberalism, faced with increasing class inequalities and conflicts, to turn the state into an independent power. According to Herbert Marcuse, Hegel had no choice but to betray his philosophy of freedom since he conceived the system of right as a closed ontological system identical with the end of history.[21] Marx by contrast moved beyond Hegel's 'abstract, logical, speculative expression of the movement of history' and rediscovered the 'possibility and truth' immanent within the modern state: that humankind can become the conscious subject of its own development. Marcuse saw Marx as developing an historical materialism which would foster new forms of individualism beyond abstract right, new forms of association beyond civil society, new forms of regulation beyond law, and new forms of self-determination beyond the state.

Franz Neumann endorsed Marx's critique of Hegel's *Philosophy of Right*, describing the latter as an 'inexcusable paean' to the Prussian state, 'the state of broken promises' and interpreted this as a defence of rational law against both revolutionism and legalism.[22] Neumann argued that Marxism can explain the decline of rational law as the result of the transition from competitive to monopoly stages of capitalism. Rational law was necessary for the predictability of market exchanges in a competitive capitalist economy but less needed by monopoly capital for which planning and control substitute for free exchange. If the major social functions of law are to secure the dominance of capital, make economic processes calculable, and guarantee the individual a minimum of freedom, the decline of the first two functions still left the third intact. While capital lost interest in maintaining rational law (fascism being one expression of this), the defence of rational law was all the more necessary for labour. Neumann sought to integrate Marx and Weber by linking Weber's opposition to the introduction

---

[21] H. Marcuse, *Reason and Revolution: Hegel and the Rise of Social Theory* (Boston Beacon Press, 1979) at 294–315. For a critical assessment of this way of reading Hegel, see R. Fine, *Political Investigations: Hegel Marx Arendt* (London Routledge 2001), ch. 1.

[22] Social Democracy's reliance on the constitution which no longer had real guarantees behind it, had the ambiguous effect of legalising class struggles and allowing a hostile judiciary to determine their outcomes. See F. Neumann, *The Democratic and Authoritarian State* (London Macmillan 1957); *The Rule of Law* (Oxford Berg 1986); *Behemoth: The Structure and Practice of National Socialism* (London Gollanz 1942). See also O. Kirchheimer, *Political Justice: The Use of Legal Procedure for Political Ends* (Princeton Princeton University Press 1961) and *Politics, Law and Social Change: Selected Essays of Otto Kirchheimer* (ed. F. Burin and K. Shell) (New York Columbia University Press 1969); W. Scheuerman (ed.) *The Rule of Law under Siege: Selected Essays of Franz L. Neumann and Otto Kirchheimer* (Berkeley University of California Press 1996); M. Salter 'The visibility of the Holocaust: Franz Neumann and the Nuremberg trials' in R. Fine and C. Turner (eds) *Social Theory after the Holocaust* (Liverpool University Press 2000); William Scheuerman *Between the Norms and the Exception: the Frankfurt School and the Rule of Law* (Cambridge Mass. MIT Press 1994).

of substantive legal principles to Marx's analysis of the changing character of capital. His conclusion was not to surrender to doctrines which divorce justice from legality, but to fuse the idea of socialism with that of rational law, while supporting the use of extra-legal methods to defend legality. Arguing that rational law by its very nature must possess certain formal qualities of generality, specificity, non-retroactivity, etc. and must contain certain substantive freedoms of speech, movement, religion and association, Neumann attacked tendencies to subordinate *ratio* to the *voluntas* of state sovereignty. While totalitarian movements turned law into a means of exercising arbitrariness and terror, Marxism could not be blind to the fact that rational law was not merely a 'lesser evil' but a genuine repository of democratic values.

3. THE POST-WAR RESURGENCE OF MARXIST CRITICISM

A resurgence of Marxist criticism of law took off in the latter half of the 1950s, gathered strength with the rise of the New Left in the 1960s and became linked to new social movements in the 1970s. This critique was diverse but it shared a more or less anti-authoritarian radicalism directed East at the party-state, West at cold war militarism and everywhere at imperial domination. It was driven by a sense of profound disillusionment at the gulf between what law ought to be and what it actually is. One expression of this feeling was to be found in the then influential works of Louis Althusser, Nicos Poulantzas and their admirers who formed the school of *structural Marxism*. They focused on the manifold functions which law plays in the reproduction of capitalist relations of production, including functions of repression and violence, the legitimation of the existing order, organisation of the dominant classes, fragmentation of the subordinate classes, de-politicisation of social movements, institutionalisation of class relations, individuation of collective struggles, etc. Marxism combined at first with sociological structural functionalism and then with the more radical post-structuralism of Michel Foucault.[23]

In *State, Socialism, Power* Poulantzas argued that in the modern political order law *appears* as a limitation on the violence of the state, but this appearance gives rise to an *illusory* opposition between law and terror—illusory because the bloodiest of empires have historically been founded on constituent

[23] In his essay 'Ideology and Ideological state apparatuses (notes toward an investigation)' Althusser located law within the repressive and ideological superstructure of the state, determined in the last instance by the economic base and functioning to secure the reproduction of capitalist relations of production [Althusser, *Lenin and Philosophy and Other Essays* (London Monthly Review Press 1971) at 134–158]. In *Fascism and Dictatorship* (London NLB 1974) N. Poulantzas modified this functionalist account of law, arguing that law perpetuates and sanctions class rule by regulating political power through a system of general, formal, abstract norms, and by imposing limits on the exercise of state power. While he denied that the fascist or totalitarian state is the antithesis of the liberal state, he also argued that in the former arbitrariness reigns and law is no longer the limit of power, at 320–322.

rules and because the alliance of law and terror furnished by Stalin's 1936 constitution was paraded as the most democratic in the world. Poulantzas opined
that 'nothing could be more mistaken than to counterpose the rule of law to
arbitrariness, abuse of power and the prince's act of will' and that such a vision
corresponded to a 'juridical-legalistic view of the state'. It was allegedly mistaken because the modern state 'holds a monopoly of violence and ultimate
terror' and law is 'an integral part of the repressive order' which 'organises the
conditions for physical repression'.[24] Poulantzas granted that direct violence is
not practised within the core capitalist societies as much as it once was and
attributed this in part to the functions law plays in constituting individuals as
juridical subjects. Since law fragments and individualises the ruled, cements the
social formation under the aegis of the rulers, and organises the apparatuses of
administrative and judicial power, the direct employment of violence is no
longer so urgently required. Poulantzas insisted, however, that the connection
between law and terror is not severed, even when law 'organises and sanctions
certain *real rights* of the dominated classes' and even when formal liberties are
secured as 'conquests of the popular masses'.[25] There was a certain equivocation in this critique of law—whether emphasis was put on the determination of
law in the last instance by economic forces or on the relative autonomy of law—
and part of its appeal was predicated on its ideological flexibility. It provided a
conceptual framework in which legal processes could be examined for their
effects on the wider social order—albeit from a top-down, functionalist standpoint.

Under the title of *state-derivation* and *capital-state* theories, some contemporary Marxists have focused on the place of law in the dynamics of capital
accumulation in a less functional mode.[26] They recognise that class relations
should be seen as relations of production in a wider sense than economic determinism allows and that capitalist relations of production necessarily present
themselves in mediated forms that are at once economic and juridical. They re-
read Marx's critique of capital not only as a theory of the exploitation of labour
by capital but as a theory of capitalist society as a whole, including the juridical
forms in which class relations between labour and capital are reproduced.[27] The

---

[24] N. Poulantzas, *State, Power, Socialism* (London Verso 1980) at 76.

[25] Poulantzas, *ibid., Socialism* at 92.

[26] See J. Holloway and S. Picciotto (eds) *State and Capital* (London Edward Arnold 1978);
W. Bonefeld 'Social constitution and the form of the capitalist state', *Open Marxism* volume 1,
W. Bonefeld, R. Gunn, K. Psychopedis (eds) (London Pluto 1992) at 93–132; R. Gunn 'Marxism and
mediation', (1987) 2 *Common Sense*; R. Gunn 'Rights' (1987) 77 *Edinburgh Review*; M. Postone
Time, Labour and Social Domination: a re-interpretation of Marx's critical theory (Cambridge CUP
1996).

[27] A flavour of the state-derivation approach may be had from Bonefeld's comments on the social
constitution of the capitalist state: 'the relation of the state to society' implies that 'private individuals exist as abstract individuals endowed with standardised rights and as such treated as abstract
citizens. This treatment complements politically the processing of class as wage labour. This re-
assertion of the right of property denies the existence of class . . . The formal safeguarding of rights
inverts into the substantive guarantee of exploitation . . . The mode of existence of the state . . . in

problem of the isolation of law from productive relations is addressed by seeing capital not merely as an economic category but as a more general principle of explanation. Their core proposition is that in a capitalist society the commodity is not only the general form of the product but the fundamental social form that structures social life as a whole—including the state, law, rights and even legal philosophy.

A perhaps more radical critique of the structuralist approach came from Marxists who focused on popular struggles from the bottom up and gave themselves the name of *Marxist humanism*. Their critique was directed at a 'Marxism' which considered human beings merely as units in a chain of determined circumstances and which denied the creative agency of human beings. It was this denial that the Marxist historian, Edward Thompson, called a 'heresy against man' and associated both with official Communism and structural Marxism. Workers are not mere 'bearers of capitalist relations of production', he wrote, and 'contrary to the view of some theoretical practitioners, no worker known to historians ever had surplus value taken out of his hide without finding some way of fighting back'.[28] Thompson's approach to law was brimming with 'bloody-minded distrust' of power and dismissive of an authoritarian legalism which equates law with the will of government. He urged Marxists to recover their moral imagination from the numbing language of party-speak which had also entered into academe. Thompson emphasised the *social* character of Marx's critique of political economy, but argued that even Marx was trapped within the circuits of capital and only partly sprung that trap in *Capital*. While Marx could not be blamed for the deformations of Marxism, Thompson acknowledged that there was no 'virgin untouchable purity of original Marxism to which Stalinism owes no kinship'.[29]

Thompson rejected a model of modern society which forcibly isolates law as part of the superstructure from the economic relations which make up the base, and the 'age-old academic procedures of isolation which are abjectly disintegrative of the enterprise of historical materialism, the understanding of the full historical process'. Referring to his own eighteenth century historical studies, he wrote:

terms of law . . . eliminat[es] social conflict in and through the instantiation of human rights, that is, law and order control . . . The legalisation . . . of social relations implies at the same time their stratification . . . which aims at the development of the social relations of production in politically supervised, legally controlled, non-conflictual forms . . . the content of which is the perpetuation of the slavery of labour . . . The attempt of the state (and capital) to harness class conflict into bourgeois forms of legality . . . implies not only the legalisation of social relations . . . it denies the existence of the working class as class . . . The historical composition of the state during fascism cannot be seen as an 'exceptional' form of state . . . Rather the coercive character of the state exists as presupposition, premise and result of the social reproduction of the class antagonism . . .' (Bonefeld, *Open Marxism, supra* n. 26 at 116–120).

[28] E. Thompson, 'Poverty of Theory' in *The Poverty of Theory and Other Essays* (London Merlin 1978) at 345.

[29] Cited in R. Fine 'The rule of law and Muggletonian Marxism: the perplexities of Edward Thompson' (1994) 21 *Journal of Law and Society* at 197.

I found that law did not keep politely to a 'level' but was at *every* bloody level; it was imbricated within the mode of production and productive relations themselves (as property rights, definitions of agrarian practice) . . . it contributed to the self-identity both of rulers and of ruled; it afforded an arena for class struggle within which alternative notions of law were fought out.[30]

Class relations are at once legal, political and cultural as well as economic, so that if the base-superstructure metaphor is to be retained at all, it should be recognised that the base is not economic but social—human relationships involuntarily entered into in productive processes. The problem with orthodox Marxism is that it inverts the spirit of Marx's critique of capitalist society: instead of confronting the inhumanity of a society which preaches economic determinism, it postulated economic determinism as its own doctrine.

Thompson's approach to law was driven by the conviction that capitalist society offers an inhuman form of political community and that this inhumanity was mirrored in existing socialist states. This conviction led him along a variety of theoretical and empirical paths at different stages of his writing. In his historical writings he sought to recapture the moral community of eighteenth century plebeian movements committed to upholding traditional use rights against modern laws of private property, seeing them as 'a last desperate effort of the people to re-impose the older moral economy as against the economy of the free market'.[31] In other writings Thompson defended the rule of law as an 'unqualified human good' and as a crucial 'inhibition on power'.[32] He thought it essential for Marxism to put its own house in order: this meant above all abandoning its dismissal of law as a mere instrument of class rule. He commented with some acerbity on how in the twentieth century even the most exalted thinker ought to be able to tell the difference between a state based on the rule of law and one based on arbitrary, extra-legal authority, and he attacked the essentialism of Marxist critiques of law which substituted a platonic notion of the true, ideal capitalist state for actual capitalist states, and turned law into no more than a confirmation of existing property relations. Law should be seen rather as a *mediation* which imposes effective inhibitions on power and defends the citizen from power's all-inclusive claims. In yet other phases of his journey Thompson looked for inspiration to the antinomian communities of love upheld by certain radical Protestant sects in opposition to the violence of law. This attitude was expressed in his Spring 1968 lecture at Columbia University when he declared himself a 'Muggletonian Marxist'. The Muggletonians were a Protestant sect which maintained that Legality or the 'Moral Law', as exemplified in the Ten Commandments, is a code of repression and that its prohibitions are not binding on Christians committed to the Gospel of Forgiveness,

---

[30]   Thompson, 'Poverty of Theory' *supra* n. 28 at 286–8.

[31]   E. P. Thompson, *The Making of the English Working Class* (Harmondsworth, Penguin 1986) at 73.

[32]   E. P. Thompson, *Whigs and Hunters* 'The rule of law' (London Penguin 1990) at 268.

Love and Mercy. Law may discover sin but it cannot remove it, for 'it changeth not the heart' and its principle is 'envy'. The Gospel of Love was to usher in the New Jerusalem after the fall of Rome. Where God lives in the heart, laws are relegated to mere ordinances. Thompson saw in this antinomian tradition a challenge to 'the authority of the ruling ideology and the cultural hegemony of Church, Schools, Law and even of "common-sense" Morality'.[33] Taken as a whole, the strength of Thompson's alliance of Marxism and humanism was to face up to the burden of history without proclaiming the innocence of Marxism, to hear the voices of the oppressed in all their inconsistency, and to address historically the equivocations of law.[34] Perhaps the main limitation of his approach is that, despite itself, it too sometimes ended up dissociating law from productive relations and treating law and economics as belonging to distinct or even opposed logics.

The dissociation of law from productive relations has been the unresolved thematic of contemporary Marxism. The central contention of Critical Theory, that the commodity form should be seen as the structuring principle of capitalist society as a whole, including its legal aspects, may be traced back to Lukács' judgement in *History and Class Consciousness* that the chapter in *Capital* dealing with the fetish character of the commodity 'contains within itself the whole of historical materialism', that at this stage in the history of humankind 'there is no problem that does not ultimately lead back to that question', that 'there is no solution that could not be found in the solution to the riddle of the commodity structure'.[35] Lukács presented the commodity as the *universal category* which determines the world in all its dimensions, and proceeded from the notion that workers can only become conscious of their actual existence in capitalist society when they become aware of themselves as commodities, not as individual bearers of rights. He treated the possession of 'right' as in essence a right over things: an expression of the instrumental domination of 'man' over 'nature'.

We might say that Marxist theory has followed the difficult path between Lukács and Thompson, that is, between the association of law with and its dissociation from commodity relations. Most Marxists tend to present their own particular resolutions as a recovery of the authentic Marx from traditional Marxism, but the important part of Marx's argument (at least after 1848) is that the modern *subject* is neither a commodity nor a human being in the abstract, but an owner of commodities, a possessor of at least his or her labour power, and in this respect a subject of right, a person, a human being in the substantial sense of the term. For Marx, this quality of personality marks the beginning of the long

---

[33] E. Thompson, *Witness against the beast: William Blake and the moral law* (Cambridge Cambridge University Press 1993) at 5, 19 and 225.

[34] I discuss empirically the equivocations of law in Bob Fine and Robert Millar (eds) *Policing the Miners' Strike* (London Lawrence and Wishart 1985); and R. Fine, Francine de Clercq and Duncan Innes 'Trade Unions and the State in South Africa' (1981) 15 *Capital and Class* at 79–114.

[35] G. Lukács, *History and Class Consciousness: Studies in Marxist Dialectics* (London Merlin 1971) at 83 and 170.

and arduous journey in the development of self-consciousness which takes producers beyond their status merely as workers to their human emancipation.

4. MARXIST LEGAL THEORY TODAY

As I write this paper in 2001, confronted with the difficult task of comprehend-
ing new forms of terror and counter-terror, there is no denying that Marxism is
a marginal force in contemporary legal criticism. I do not intend to investigate
the reasons for this decline but only to say that in its various shapes Marxism
has been a rich source of social theorising about law and that it would be pre-
mature to announce its death. Behind the will to declare it dead, we may find a
rightful desire to construct a relation to law that has no kinship with totalitarianism, but the rejection of Marxism not only mis-identifies the origins of totalitarianism, it may also express a deeper distrust of *social* theory—whether from
the standpoint of natural right or legal positivism or a continuous deconstruction that goes beyond law's social underpinnings to an elusive moment of alterity and justice.

Marxist legal theory has not resolved the difficulties it has encountered in its
efforts to understand the relations that hold between law and society. One such
difficulty has been the proclivity of Marxists to construct this or that 'ism'—be
it functionalism or instrumentalism or humanism or formalism or critical realism—as the royal road to the truth of law. There is nothing wrong in exploring,
say, the functions of law for capital accumulation, or the social interests and
backgrounds of those who enforce the law, or popular conceptions of law held
by the labouring classes, or the inhibitions on economic and political power
imposed by the law, or the connections that tie the form of law to that of the
commodity, or indeed the immaturity expressed when individuals relate to one
another exclusively on the basis of their rights. There is every reason to examine these issues and the strength of Marxism has been to take up the social questions that others have neglected. The weakness of Marxists, however, has been
to turn their particular concern into an exclusive concern and denounce the concerns of others. Perhaps it is time to abandon the 'ism' of Marxism itself, whose
unity is in any event illusory, and see Marx alongside the great nineteenth century critics of tradition as one source of critical thinking among others.

Today there is a new engagement of Marxists with legal theory. It has taken
off in numerous sites and from numerous standpoints. It has attached itself to
the struggle for a democracy in which human rights have pride of place. And
from very different standpoints it has immersed itself in reading legal texts. For
example, in *Toward a New Common Sense* Boaventura de Sousa Santos
explores the plurality of legal forms as a basis for his critique of the dominant
positivistic and natural law traditions in Western legal thought. He identifies
different forms of law relating to different structural sites—the household, the
workplace, the marketplace, the community, the citizenplace, the worldplace—

and argues that by prioritising the citizenplace over all other sites, Western legal thought loses sight of the connections which constitute the whole. Defining the citizenplace as 'the set of social relations that constitute the "public sphere", the vertical political obligation between citizens and the state', de Sousa Santos acknowledges that in the core capitalist societies it tends to be a place of formal legal freedoms and democratic procedures.[36] However, he argues that the restriction of democratic rights to this single site 'allowed for the shifting of the global emancipatory promises of modernity to the promise of state democratisation'—a far narrower ambition which left despotic forms of *social* power in other sites unhindered and obscured. According to the broader conception of social or human emancipation which de Sousa Santos identifies with Rousseau and Marx—a conception involving the affirmation of *social* equality and the delegitimation of class differences—we must raise the question of links between the functioning of law in the citizenplace and the forms of social power exercised in other sites. He speaks of *interlaw* to express a sense of the connectedness of the whole, the incompatibility of capitalism with the radical democratic claims of modernity, and an expanded, ultimately anti-capitalist conception of human rights to embrace the forgotten spheres of the social.[37]

To take another example, in *Empire* and other writings Michael Hardt and Antonio Negri argue that the social constitutions of the late modern period were founded on a recognition of labour and premised on a conflictual model of political life whose juridical expression was that of legal realism: a theory of law which holds that those who command over society secure their hegemony by means of law in such a way that the law is continually modified, open to conflict and reformed in line with changes in social life. According to Negri, the presupposition of legal realism is that law is a living part of the superstructure, but he argues that this has now imploded. The increasing integration of the economic and the legal has radically transformed this context of constitutional reference. A revolution from above has destroyed not only the pre-existing structures of social democracy but also the working class as one of the subjects of this relationship. It has resulted in what Negri calls, following Foucault, a 'biopolitical' model of disciplinary arrangements that differs from that outlined by Foucault only in that it is now marked by the 'imperial hierarchies' of a global system. For Negri the impact of this social revolution from above on legal studies is not only to render legal realism redundant, but also those open, anti-authoritarian Marxist tendencies whose beliefs in a strong reformism and in the alternative

---

[36] B. de Sousa Santos, *Towards a New Common Sense : Law, Science and Politics in the Paradigmatic Transition* (London Routledge 1995) at 421.

[37] This approach has led to the criticism from within the Marxist tradition that notwithstanding his radicalism de Sousa Santos does not penetrate the law of the citizenplace itself, nor question its positivistic self-understanding, nor acknowledge the forces of denial, suppression, conflict and confrontation which operate *within*. Alan Norrie argues that de Sousa Santos's pluralistic conception of sites of law lacks 'structural depth' and does not enable us to understand the articulation of structures which constitute these sites as a capitalist totality. See A. Norrie, 'Between structure and difference', *Critical Realism, supra* n. 19 at 729–30.

uses of law were predicated on a social and political situation which is now ended. For Negri, the postmodern claim that the dynamics of law and the dialectic of enlightenment are over, is basically correct. There is no outside—no other place from which to base the overcoming of what is now going to rack and ruin. Negri attaches Marxism to the conceptual framework of post-structuralism to argue that in contemporary capitalism law has lost whatever normative autonomy it might once have possessed. It has become identical with the regulated and disciplined sphere of the social.

In this new social situation Negri maintains that the subject of change is no longer the working class but the multiplicity of immaterial workers (defined by their plasticity), intellectuals, temporary labourers, female workers, immigrant workers, etc. He calls them a 'multiplicity' (a term drawn from Spinoza) to express the manifold desires that set them in opposition to capitalist biopower, and argues that this multiplicity no longer mediates its activity through the democratic system of political representation, a system which no longer works at any level, but through a plurality of movements and sites of struggle, against a plurality of forms of exploitation and oppression, according to a plurality of ideas of life and freedom. The challenge Negri poses to lawyers and politicians is the construction of a new 'constitution of liberty'—one which no longer starts from the enigma of political representation and no longer separates politics from the whole of social life, but recognises the right of all citizens to a social wage adequate for their reproduction, legitimates the exercise of counter-power, guarantees the right of mobility and welcomes foreigners. Marxism is linked here both to the post-structuralism of Foucault, Deleuze and Guatarri, and to a radicalised struggle for universal human rights outside the conventional system of democratic representation. Not for nothing is Negri sometimes presented as an organic intellectual of the anti-capitalist movement.[38]

These radicalised views of the struggle for human rights constitute a rich strand in contemporary Marxism. Many other critical writers have re-assessed relations between Marxism and the law. Notably, Jürgen Habermas has addressed what he sees as the intimate connections linking the legal rights championed within modern natural law and the radical democracy championed within Marxism;[39] and the rise of new forms of global justice and cosmopolitan

---

[38] This account is drawn from M. Hardt and A. Negri, *Labor of Dionysus: A Critique of the State Form* (Minneapolis University of Minnesota Press 1994) and from 'Postmodern global governance and the critical legal project' (paper presented at the Critical Legal Conference, University of Kent, September, 2001). Criticism of this paper has focused on the possible inconsistency of the denouncement of law in the first half and the re-affirmation of constitution and human rights in the second. If Franz Neumann was right in claiming that all law contains objective and subjective dimensions—those of regulation, authority and sovereignty on one side and rights, freedoms and agency on the other—Negri splits this unity in claiming that in the present law has become purely objective and that in the future it can become purely subjective.

[39] J. Habermas, *Between Facts and Norms* (Cambridge Polity 1997); J. Habermas, *The Inclusion of the Other* (Cambridge Mass. MIT Press 1997); R. Fine, 'Kant's theory of cosmopolitan right and Hegel's critique', *Philosophy and Social Criticism*, 2002, forthcoming.

right designed to arrest the new forms of terror and atrocity with which the modern world has become acquainted in the last century. Some are addressing the problematique of legal regulation of international business in a context of globalised capital accumulation.[40] Some have sought to develop the more directly social rather than political aspects of Marxist legal theory, in particular by relating it to feminist social critiques of law.[41] Some, like myself, have been re-examining the relation between Marx and the classical tradition of jurisprudence, including Hegel's undervalued critique of the forms of right in his *Philosophy of Right* and its connections with Marx's critique of the forms of value in *Capital*.[42] The legacy of Marx is alive in all these investigations, but it is increasingly difficult to demarcate the boundaries of what Marxism is and is not. In recompense, we now have a rich engagement between social theories of law and legal philosophy which promises much for the future.

---

[40] See, for example, S. Picciotto and J. McCahery (eds) *Corporate control and accountability: changing structures and dynamics* (Oxford Clarendon Press 1993).

[41] This line of inquiry was developed early on by Catharine MacKinnon in *Toward a feminist theory of the state* (Cambridge Mass. Harvard University Press 1989) and in *Feminism unmodified: discourses on life and law* (Cambridge Mass. Harvard University Press 1987).

[42] R. Fine, *Political Investigations*, *supra* n. 21; A. Wood 'Hegel and Marxism', in Frederick Beiser (ed.) *The Cambridge Companion to Hegel* (Cambridge CUP 1993); A. Warminski, 'Hegel/Marx: Consciousness and Life' in Stuart Barnett (ed.) *Hegel after Derrida* (London Routledge 1998); G. Rose, *Mourning Becomes the Law: Philosophy and Representation* (Cambridge Cambridge University Press 1996); D. MacGregor, *Hegel and Marx: after the fall of communism* (Cardiff University of Wales Press 1998); I. Fraser, 'Two of a kind: Hegel, Marx, dialectic and form', (1997) 61 *Capital and Class* at 81–106.

6

Sharing the Paradigms? Critical Legal Studies and the Sociology of Law

JIŘÍ PŘÍBÁŇ

THE CRITICAL LEGAL studies movement represents a radical critique of the rule of law and modern legal science which is theoretically, methodologically and historically often close to the sociology of law and its paradigm. During the 1970s and 1980s, critical legal studies was established as an independent paradigm of legal theory first in the United States,[1] and later in the United Kingdom and other countries. The main goal of the CLS movement has been to undermine legal formalism and elaborate an alternative methodology and concept of law. In fact, the critical legal studies movement has never been a theoretically and ideologically uniform intellectual movement. It rather represents a very rich and differentiated school of legal thought, ranging from radical post-Marxist and feminist activists to left-wing liberal, humanist legal scholars, and adherents of the postmodern turn in legal theory. This great variety of intellectual and ideological influences makes it difficult or almost impossible to establish what unites critical legal scholars in terms of legal doctrine or theory. However, the unifying element is the political dimension of the critique of legal system and doctrine which predominantly draws on the notions of radical democracy and social justice.

The critical legal method introduced by theorists such as Roberto Mangabeira Unger, Duncan Kennedy and Alan Hunt immediately reminds us of Nietzsche's concept of critical history which has the primary task to judge, condemn and overcome the past.[2] Critical legal scholars also aim to dismantle the politics of the rule of law with its liberal ideological background and propose a radical legal

---

[1] In the United States, the first annual Conference on Critical Legal Studies was held in the spring of 1977. It was established by a small group of scholars including Roberto Mangabeira Unger, Mark Tushnet, Richard Abel, David Trubek, Duncan Kennedy, Morton Horwitz and Rand Rosenblatt. Abel and Trubek were among the professors who had to leave Yale Law School in the late 60s and early 70s (the university made the rare decision of not turning their six-year appointments into tenure positions). Kennedy was Trubek's student and co-*enfant terrible* at Yale. Robert Gordon, Mark Kelman and Peter Gabel joined the group later. From the very beginning, the CLS group defined itself as an anti-establishment tradition in legal scholarship attacking the mainstream liberal legal doctrine, teaching methods, and social and political hierarchies entrenched in the existing legal system. For this genealogy, see M. Tushnet, 'Critical Legal Studies: A Political History', (1991) 100 *Yale Law Review*, at 1515–44.

[2] F. Nietzsche, *Untimely Meditations* (Cambridge Cambridge University Press 1997).

and political reform, or even revolution.[3] The primary target of the critical method is the political neutrality and objectivism of the Western liberal rule of law. This critique is accompanied by a radical critique of the legal science which supports such a value-free and neutral concept of law.

The CLS movement has established itself against the liberal doctrine of legal rights and principles in the field of public law, and against the law and economics movement in the field of private law. Law does not stand above politics and cannot be treated as a non-ideological tool for the settlement of social conflicts. The CLS position may be formulated in two simple sentences: *law (and legal science) is politics*; *law (and legal science) is ideology*. In this chapter, we will therefore focus on the historical context and theoretical and political implications of this position, and its connection with the sociology of law and socio-legal studies.

1. CRITICAL LEGAL STUDIES, LEGAL REALISM AND CRITICAL SOCIAL THEORY

Historically, the CLS movement builds on the methods and concepts introduced into legal doctrine by the school of legal realism. Legal realists such as Roscoe Pound and Karl Llewellyn in the United States or the Scandinavian legal realists in Europe are also considered the founding fathers of the sociology of law. This school originally used the philosophy of pragmatism to criticise the empty formalism of legalist thought and the absence of social and political dynamics in legalist doctrine and methodology. The 'realist critique' of legalist formalism and its inability to conceive law in its social context, political role and historical changeability was also a formative force of the sociology of law. Normative and rational closure and political autonomy of the rule of law was to be replaced by the sociological analysis of 'law in action'[4] and ideological critique of legal discourse. Legal realists, inspired by pragmatism, returned law to its social and political context and perceived it as one of many social institutions dependent on its environment, rather than a system of autonomous concepts and norms. The sociological analysis of law was thus introduced into legal science as a critique of dominant legal theory and practice.

Another inspiration, which is common both to critical legal studies and sociology of law, is the Frankfurt school of critical social theory. In the works of Franz Neumann, Max Horkheimer, Herbert Marcuse and Jürgen Habermas, social theory meets political, ideological and legal critique and knowledge is taken as politics. The post-Marxist critique of law and politics was typical mostly of the early stage of the CLS movement. Unger criticises the Marxist critical method for its holistic concept of history and calls for the intellectual

---

[3] R. M. Unger, *The Critical Legal Studies Movement* (Cambridge Mass. Harvard University Press 1983), at 116.

[4] 'Law in action' is one of the constitutive concepts of the sociology of law, the modern use of which originates in the school of legal realism.

destruction of the notion of history and society as a compulsive 'metaorder' which would condemn any act of free political will. Nevertheless, he adopts the imaginative and transformative power of Marxism and defines *the method of critical thought* as:

> [t]he method that, interpreting the formative institutional and imaginative contexts of social life as frozen politics, traces each of their elements to the particular history and measure of constraint upon transformative conflict that the element represents. This method must wage perpetual war against the tendency to take the workings of a particular social world as if they defined the limits of the real and the possible in social life.[5]

This trust in the transformative power of social and legal theory and possibility of combining the legal method with political imagination is typical of critical legal theorists and is closely linked to *the historical method* of critical writing. While criticising the concept of history as a force to which people have to adapt (the adaptationist theory, one historical school of which is also Marxism), the critical legal historical method seeks to prove that: a) legal norms can be analysed and discussed only with regard to changing social conditions and b) legal and political facts taken currently for granted have their historical dynamics, and their political and theoretical status may be questioned, shaken and changed.[6]

Critical legal historians such as Robert Gordon put law into its historical context through analysis of how specific class and social dominations became historically entrenched in law.[7] Sociological analysis is, therefore, considered a necessary supplement to historical study and helps to overcome the concept of law as an expression of one unified culture and society at a particular historical moment. Critical legal doctrine adopts the constitutive principle of the sociological theory of law, according to which adequate knowledge about the nature of law and legal doctrine is impossible without the sociological study of law.[8]

Critical legal doctrine is a normative science which contests the existing structures of law and power. It is based on the 'visionary ideal'[9] and provides a prescriptive theoretical framework for political action going beyond the limits of the liberal doctrine of legal rights and principles such as represented in the theoretical works of Ronald Dworkin. Critical legal theory seeks to reconstruct the Western model of democracy and builds on the notion of social and legal science as a *normative commitment*. It takes upon itself the difficult political task of changing the legal discourse and defining the legal context as a political context.

---

[5] R. M. Unger, *supra* n. 3, at 108.

[6] See M. Kelman, *A Guide to Critical Legal Studies* (Cambridge Mass. Harvard University Press 1987), at 213.

[7] See, for example, R. Gordon, 'Historicism in Legal Scholarship', (1981) 90 *Yale Law Journal*, at 1017–56; or R. Gordon, 'Critical Legal Histories', (1984) 36 *Stanford Law Review*, at 57.

[8] R. Cotterrell, *Law's Community: Legal Theory in Sociological Perspective* (Oxford Clarendon Press 1995), at 71.

[9] R. M. Unger, *supra* n. 3, at 56.

This commitment itself may be taken as a part of the legal realist tradition which critical legal studies shares with the 'realistic' sociology of law. Socio-legal researchers understand legalist thought and jurisprudence as a deformation of the reality of law and a source of pathological law, not real and normal law.[10] The role of the sociological interpretation of law is to disclose and demystify legal doctrine, discourse and law's understanding of itself. A number of theoretical schools within the sociology of law seek to provide a 'realistic' perspective on law and, therefore, the chance to overcome the ideological nature of legal scholarship. Similarly, like CLS scholars, some sociologists of law use words such as 'must' and 'moral vision' when defining the paradigm of their discipline. Sociology and sociological methods enjoy not only the status of a realistic science, but also of a moralist vehicle which can reveal pathological elements and thus contribute to the improvement of social and legal reality.

However, theoretical implications of the critical legal method distinguish it from mainstream 'realistic' sociology of law. The critical legal method comprises the imaginative elements and political vision of the radical transformation of the Western liberal democracies with their system of the rule of law. On the other hand, sociological theories of law usually do not give such a theoretical priority and importance to a particular political programme in spite of their own political contexts and commitments.

Critical legal doctrine advocates a more radical departure from the Western liberal democratic rule of law. In his manifesto *The Critical Legal Studies Movement*, Unger speaks about the urgent need to reconstruct institutions of market and political democracy and comes up with the concept of a permanently self-revising and revolutionising state:

> from the idea of a state not hostage to a faction, existing in a society freed from a rigid and determinate order of division and hierarchy, we might move to the conception of an institutional structure, itself self-revising, that would provide constant occasions to disrupt any fixed structure of power and coordination in social life. Any such emergent structure would be broken up before having a chance to shield itself from the risks of ordinary conflict . . . [A] successful resolution of this dilemma must provide ways to restrain the state without effectively paralyzing its transformative activities.[11]

The state and its law as social institutions must be used to accomplish complex transformation of liberal democratic societies into a new historical stage which is perceived as *alterity* to modernity and referred to as a *superliberalism* or *post-liberal society*.[12]

---

[10] J. Carbonnier, *Flexible droit. Pour une sociologie du droit sans rigueur* (Paris L.G.D.J. 1988), at 20ff. For an older view see, for example, H. Lévy-Bruhl, *Aspects sociologiques du droit* (Paris Marcel Rivière et Cie 1955).

[11] R. M. Unger, *supra* n. 3, at 30–1.

[12] For these concepts, see R. M. Unger, *supra* n. 3, at 41; R. M. Unger, *Law in Modern Society: Toward a Criticism of Social Theory* (New York Free Press 1976), at 192.

2. THE SPIRIT OF COMMUNITY AND THE CRITICAL LEGAL DOCTRINE

If law and legal doctrine are politics, they must be made part of the life of a political community. Taken from the perspective of political and social philosophy, the CLS movement represents one stream of communitarian theory which opposes liberal political theory in the field of legal science. Putting legal rights and principles into their social and communal framework is then another feature common both to the sociology of law and critical legal studies. However, while sociologists of law often look at social and communitarian aspects of law and talk about 'law's community',[13] critical legal scholars focus on the communitarian critique of the legal system, doctrine and education in liberal democratic societies.

The CLS movement is sceptical about the liberal doctrine of the rule of law and legal rights. This *rule scepticism* attacks the liberal notion of law as a mechanism for regulating public space and political power which prevents the oppression of individuals and social groups both by political institutions and other individuals or social groups. The rule scepticism of the CLS movement is inspired again by the older school of legal realists who, from a political point of view, were supporters of the New Deal social experiments and engineering attempted by the American President Franklin D. Roosevelt. The legal realists criticised the legal formalism of the judiciary which effectively paralysed the New Deal social welfare legislation in the name of universal principles and impartial legal rules, and thus overruled the political will of the democratically elected institutions. According to the 'rule skeptics' in the movement,[14] legal rules have a political meaning and law must be analysed as a political instrument.

Critical legal scholars similarly claim that the declared *principle of neutrality* of the liberal rule of law is impossible because the social institutions in liberal democratic regimes serve the economic interests of dominant social classes. In a pluralistic liberal society, it is both politically necessary and impossible to construct politically neutral institutions and normative orders. Formal legal rules are originally devoid of any social meaning and, therefore, can be filled with political content through a process of interpretation which is not neutral because it requires political authority. The rule of law turns out to be politically biased, normatively pre-determined and, therefore, violates the liberal neutrality principle in spite of the fact that it pretends to be its foundation. The 'rule of law' serves to maintain existing power relations, and the notion of government by law, not people, protects the social and political interests of the powerful.[15]

[13] R. Cotterrell, *supra* n. 8.

[14] J. Frank, *Law and the Modern Mind* (Gloucester Mass. Smith 1970). In the preface to the sixth edition of 1948, Frank refers to the legal realist movement as 'constructive skepticism' and makes a distinction between the 'rule skeptics' such as Karl Llewellyn and politically and intellectually more radical 'fact skeptics' such as Thurman Arnold.

[15] For many examples, see, for instance, D. Kairys (ed.) *The Politics of Law: a progressive critique* (New York Pantheon Books 1982).

The liberal doctrine of political rights, which draws on the principle of the politically neutral rule of law, claims to guarantee a zone of human freedom from state institutions on the basis of legally defined rights and responsibilities.[16] On the other hand, the CLS critique of the rights doctrine is established on the notion of law as a social field of permanent political struggles, contradictions, indeterminacies and confrontations. Approaches toward the doctrine of civil and human rights, however, vary a lot within the CLS movement, from attempts at reconstruction to radical and dismissive criticisms. Duncan Kennedy represents a type of critical scholar determined to 'trash' liberal legalism and revolutionise legal and political reality. He proposes to penetrate different parts of society with radical resistance politics and oppose social and political hierarchies. For Kennedy and other radical critics, the study of 'law in action' becomes not just concerned with 'politics in action', but a form of 'revolution in action' which is governed by the visionary ideal of social equality. For others, such as Peter Gabel (who opposed some of Kennedy's radical views in their famous intellectual exchange 'Roll over Beethoven' in 1984)[17] and Roberto M. Unger, the concept of liberal rights may be transformed into actual forms of a communal life. This means that political freedoms and rights are not abolished, but rather extended and made a part of a broader social environment and political *community*. Instead of denying the importance of individual and political rights, this stream of critical legal doctrine defends the standpoint that further social mechanisms and instruments must be implemented for their protection. The republican tradition of communal life goes hand in hand with the individuality of human life as represented in the liberal tradition.[18]

We might consequently distinguish two kinds of criticisms: *radical* and *moderate*.[19] The radicals build on the tradition of substantive democratic values and dismiss the concepts of rights and rule of law as useless because they do not protect individual liberty and even reproduce the existing social and political inequalities and power relations. On the other hand, the more moderate strand in the CLS movement prefers to critically evaluate and use the rights and rule of law doctrine for the purposes of social, political and legal transformation. While criticising the liberal premise of law's political neutrality, this moderate approach admits that a legal framework does constrain the state and avoids political arbitrariness. The rule of law may not be able to depoliticise conflicts, contradictions and power relations in modern societies, but it can still contribute to the democratic culture and be used for the purpose of political and social transformation.[20]

---

[16] This idea is typical not only of the legal rights theorists such as Ronald Dworkin, but also of legal positivists opposing the doctrine of human rights. See, for example, H. L. A. Hart, *The Concept of Law* (Oxford Clarendon Press 1994), at 113.

[17] P. Gabel and D. Kennedy, 'Roll over Beethoven', (1984) 36 *Stanford Law Review*, at 1.

[18] M. Tushnet, *Red, White, and Blue: A Critical Analysis of Constitutional Law* (Cambridge Mass. Harvard University Press 1988), at 23.

[19] A. Altman, *supra* n. 16, at 18–21.

[20] See J. Přibáň, 'Beyond Procedural Legitimation: Legality and Its "Infictions"', (1997) 24 *Journal of Law and Society*, at 331–349.

The main shortcoming of liberal rule of law doctrine is then seen in its inability to distinguish between formal legality and broader social values, that is, to formulate it in Kennedy's terms, between the form and substance of law, or between rules and standards.[21] Standards are substantive social and political objectives. Legal rules must conform to them. Formal legal rules fail to protect vulnerable social classes and, therefore, may become socially harmful. On the other hand, standards are tied to a substantive ethical view which may be characterised as altruism and represents communal values and moral duties to others.[22] Reconstruction of the law must be then based on respect for these communal values. Moral duties respecting the priorities of a political community must replace the individualist morality represented by the liberal doctrine of the rule of law.

The moderate critique of the liberal doctrine of legal rights and principles also comes with a demand for fundamental legal and political reconstruction. This demand is formulated for instance in Unger's 'deviationist' theory of *destabilisation rights*.[23] The doctrine of destabilisation rights wants to change the prevailing understanding of law as a system of rules ordering and protecting society against social instability. Destabilisation rights reflect the enormous social dynamic and will of contemporary democratic communities. They also promote this dynamic, enhance it and operate as a tool of political change which can effectively respond to the changing social and political needs of a democratic community. The democratic state is defined as a state permanently transforming itself. Law is consequently not a system of rules unified by fundamental principles. It rather consists both of principles and counter-principles and, therefore, must be perceived as a political battlefield in which different values, standards and principles are permanently contested and confronted.[24]

The priority of communitarian principles over the individualist liberal approach is common both to the radical and moderate critique of the liberal doctrine of the rule of law. Another common feature is the political importance of social analysis and its role in legal analysis. The CLS doctrines are mostly established on the assumption that *the social world is a social and political construction* and therefore subject to the transformative powers of human will. In other words, society is entirely a product of human will and not an expression of objective or metaphysical human nature. For the business of political transformation and reform/revolution of the rule of law typical of the CLS movement, it is therefore necessary to have knowledge about transforming political societies.

The CLS scholars take very seriously Francis Bacon's statement that 'knowledge is power' and perceive legal and political doctrine both as a source and

---

[21] D. Kennedy, 'Form and Substance in Private Law Adjudication', (1976) 89 *Harvard Law Review*, at 1712.

[22] *Ibid.*, at 1685–1778.

[23] R. M. Unger, *supra* n. 3, at 43.

[24] R. M. Unger, *supra* n. 3, at 88.

instrument of political power and change. Building on the assumption of the social world and social theory as constructs, Mark Kelman, for instance, says that:

> The Critics certainly do *not* believe that the world around us can be perceived in some untainted, unmediated, direct, and "accurate" form. All our thoughts are, and seemingly must be, language mediated, and as soon as we name, we invariably reify in the sense of ascribing identical traits to objects or situations we could otherwise imagine differentiating simply because we have given them the same name. We treat the external world as if it determines our ideas, ascribing false concreteness to the categories we have in fact invented.[25]

Refusing to accept the notions of philosophical or legal objectivism, CLS scholars deliberately get involved in this business of 'the invention of categories, doctrines and ideologies', which they use as weapons in the battlefield of the legal and political system. They view legal theory and doctrine as a strong *legitimating force* for the system of positive law. In other words, changes in legal theory must be made first in order to change both the legal system and political society. Critical legal doctrine seeks to make law and politics less authoritative and more responsive to the needs and standards of a political community. The doctrine must have both the capacity to deconstruct the existing power structures and ideologies dominating the legal system, and to reconstruct the ideals and values of radical democracy within this system.

Social theory consequently comes in as an important political tool and ideological background for this programme of political and legal transformation. Substantive social analysis must replace formalist legal analysis. Law can be made, applied and changed only on the basis of knowledge about the social and political needs and preferences of a particular political community. The old demand of legal realists to study 'law in action' instead of 'law in books' is to be once again secured by sociological and social theory methods which overcome the shortcomings and ideological implications of formal legal analysis and rule of law doctrine.

3. THE CRITIQUE OF LEGALISM AND LEGAL EDUCATION

The CLS belief that legal doctrine is political power has serious consequences for the political strategy of the whole movement. Concern about the state and development of the legal education has become a central issue for the CLS movement.

This critique of legal education and scholarship was also influenced by the older doctrine of legal realism which rejected the traditional view of law as a system of texts and instead promoted the study of law in action. Karl Llewellyn in the mid 1930s criticised the American system of legal education for being

[25] M. Kelman, *supra* n. 6, at 269–70.

empty and effectively blinding those seeking to enter the legal profession.[26] Instead of studying the legal texts and rules expressed in them, law professors and students should focus on studying the actual judicial decision-making process, behaviour and social and political motives behind judicial reasoning. According to the legal realists, legal education should abandon its political function consisting in the justification of existing laws.

Critical legal theory also objects to the orthodoxy of legal scholarship and education. They are seen as merely justifying existing legal rules and legitimating the liberal democratic legal and political system.[27] According to Alan Thomson,

> [C]ritical education, like all critical activity, initially establishes itself through negative critique. So in order to reveal a countervision of critical legal education one must begin with a critique of the dominant models of education currently operating in legal education.[28]

The principles of neutrality and determinacy of liberal law taught at the universities are discarded as methods that only reproduce the political power and influence of the legal professions. Legal education and law schools are criticised for the reproduction of 'false consciousness' of the legal profession, academics and, generally speaking, citizens living in the Western liberal democratic bourgeois societies who accept and believe in the 'rule of law'.

Critical legal scholars often retreat to religious metaphors when they talk about the 'faith' and 'priesthood' of their colleagues teaching law at universities and the 'prophecies' made by the system of legal education. Their attack on legal education and doctrine is political because law schools are described as institutions producing ideas and beliefs that support the legal and political establishment and hierarchies.[29] By changing legal education, critical legal scholars seek to change law's reality. A transformation in teaching law and legal practice is supposed to promote the idea of democratic government, political emancipation of the disadvantaged and discriminated classes, minorities and the self-realisation of individuals and different communities. As Duncan Kennedy proposes:

> There should be a substantial representation of all numerically significant minority communities on American law faculties. The analogy is to the right to vote, which we refuse to distribute on the basis of merit, and to the right of free speech, which we refuse to limit to those who deserve to speak or whose speech has merit. The value at stake is community rather than individual improvement.[30]

---

[26] K. Llewellyn, 'On What is Wrong with so-called Legal Education', (1935) 35 *Columbia Law Review*, at 651.

[27] M. Tushnet, 'Post-Realist Legal Scholarship', (1980) *Wisconsin Law Review*, at 1389.

[28] A. Thomson, 'Critical Legal Studies in Britain', in P. Fitzpatrick and A. Hunt (eds) *Critical Legal Studies* (Oxford Blackwell 1987), at 192.

[29] D. Kennedy, 'Legal Education as Training for Hierarchy', in David Kairys (ed.) *The Politics of Law: a progressive critique* (New York Pantheon Books 1982), at 40.

[30] D. Kennedy, *Sexy Dressing etc.: Essays on the Power and Politics of Cultural Identity* (Cambridge Mass. Harvard University Press 1993), at 41.

The critical analysis of this false legal consciousness and disclosure of legal doctrine and education as political ideology is intended to reveal political discrimination which is concealed by the structures of a legal system. Unfortunately, the second step, namely from critical analysis to synthesis of a different way of educating lawyers, turns out to be more difficult. The much criticised liberal doctrine of the rule of law is highly resistant to the critical legal scholars' 'trashing business'. Radical political critique of the rule of law and liberal legalism may work at the level of the analysis and critique of ideology, yet it seems hard to transform it into a legal doctrine and education which could replace the existing legal academy and legal practice and overcome 'false consciousness' of the legal professions.

Critical analysis of the social role and ideological content of law is difficult, if not impossible, to translate into an alternative legal education. The radical language and colloquial expressions, such as 'fucking oppression' and 'bullshit', which were used for the critique and 'trashing' of law, certainly fulfilled their purpose to outrage mainstream legal scholars.[31] However, this language was not sufficient for the creation of a new legal doctrine. The ambitious outline of a 'countervision' of critical legal education, when confronted with mundane legal and political reality, only turns legal analysis into a political agenda. For example, after a complex critique of the dominant models of legal education, Thomson suggests that:

> Perhaps one of the most useful general approaches in creating a critical legal education is the historical understanding not of the past but of the present . . . In grasping the hidden history of the present appearances, one has a powerful tool to reveal how things could be otherwise and thus to overcome powerlessness.[32]

Instead of a counter-visionary education model, what is usually proposed is that conventional legal education should be supplemented with historical and social scientific methods in order to prepare students for the power struggle going on inside the legal system and academia. Sociological methodology and theory are to be employed in understanding law as a social construction which itself constructs specific forms of social organisation, conflicts and divisions.[33]

The bombastic and sometimes shocking rhetoric used by radicals provoked a reaction by moderates in the CLS movement, who wanted to achieve change by

---

[31] For examples of this radical language see, for instance, M. Kelman, 'Trashing' (1984) 36 *Stanford Law Review*; P. Gabel, 'Reification in Legal Reasoning', in J. Boyle (ed) *International Library of Essays in Law and Legal Theory (Schools 4) Critical Legal Studies* (Aldershot Dartmouth 1992); or P. Gabel and D. Kennedy, 'Roll over Beethoven' (1984) 36 *Stanford Law Review*, at 1.

[32] A. Thomson, *supra* n. 29, at 195.

[33] This critique of the rule of law in *A Critical Introduction to Law* by Mansell, Meteyard and Thomson and intended as a textbook for critical legal courses, is heavily influenced by sociological interpretations of social and political order as worked out by Peter Berger and Thomas Luckmann. See W. Mansell, B. Meteyard and A. Thomson, *A Critical Introduction to Law* (2nd edn) (London Cavendish Publishing 1999), at 19–27; see also P. Berger and T. Luckmann, *The Social Construction of Reality* (Harmondsworth Penguin 1967).

reforming the existing legal system.[34] While the radicals enthusiastically went about trashing law, the moderates eventually come to the conclusion that, as formulated by Gabel in his 'Roll over Beethoven' exchange with Kennedy, it might be better to use rights doctrine and rhetoric for the critical political goals of radical democracy. The original attempt of critical legal scholarship was to

> light the world views encoded in modern legal consciousness and expose that which is false. When this is done, the blinkers will fall from our eyes, and we will be free to create new systems of meaning and thus new relationships.[35]

According to the moderates, this attempt cannot be achieved and must be replaced by the different tactic of taking small pragmatic steps and making specific changes to the system drawing on its own rhetoric, concepts and structures of education.

Although critical legal scholars often describe legal academics as priests with a false faith, liberals argue that CLS itself represents a religious sect that wants to change the existing law without touching it. Certainly, the theoretical dogma associated with critical legal studies has driven even some critically minded academics away from the movement.[36]

4. THE POSTMODERN TURN WITHIN CRITICAL LEGAL STUDIES

The statement that law is politics and ideology also involves a number of political difficulties for the paradigm of critical legal studies. Liberal legal theory, such as presented in Kelsen's pure theory of law, the analytical legalism of H. L. A. Hart and many other streams of legal positivism, contrasts law and politics because it intends to separate the liberal and democratic political order from autocracy and tyranny. Laying down legal rules for people and political authority means that law constrains political power. The legal positivist search for a pure legal theory and the integrity of legal science stands in direct opposition to twentieth century totalitarian ideologies claiming the law to be merely a political instrument used by the working class or a master-race in order to achieve their goals.[37] Even though they separate laws and morals, theories of liberal legal positivism contrast the rule of law to the rule of arbitrary terror and inhuman political violence.

The CLS attack on liberal legal doctrine launched under the slogan 'law is politics', therefore, raises questions about the ideological and political status of critical legal theory. Moreover, the status of theoretical knowledge itself has

---

[34] M. Tushnet, *supra* n. 1, at 1515–44.

[35] D. M. Trubek, '"Where the Action Is" Critical Legal Studies and Empiricism', (1984) 36 *Stanford Law Review*, at 593.

[36] See, for instance, M. Tushnet, *supra* n. 1, at 1530.

[37] R. Cotterrell, *The Politics of Jurisprudence: A Critical Introduction to Legal Philosophy* (London Butterworths 1989), at 116.

been questioned within the CLS movement and the role of theory as a basis of critical activity has diminished. Instead, politically radical pragmatic actions have been favoured which can succeed in everyday political struggles, competition and co-operation. The critical ethos keeps challenging the establishment, institutional framework and liberal 'color-blind meritocratic fundamentalism',[38] but it does so without any utopian and theoretically formulated alternative. Action seems to take precedence over knowledge. This attitude and enjoyment of Nietzscheian 'philosophising with a hammer' was always latent, for instance, in Kennedy's work and it is not, therefore, surprising that, in the first half of 1990s, he specifies the need for political action in the following terms:

> The workplaces of the intelligentsia are authoritarian, hierarchical, and repressive when judged by the standards that psychological humanism sets for group life . . .
> . . . The next step is the formation of left minorities and the exercise of some real power in office politics, as opposed to the current situation of radical grumbling at the fringe.[39]

Theory without political action is just grumbling. Legal and academic institutions should be directly used to advance the particular political agenda of critical legal scholarship. One might be talking from the position of 'a straight white male middle-class radical',[40] but it does not matter so far as the primary target remains the false neutrality of liberal politics and the rule of law, and the primary goal is affirmative political action favouring different communities and minorities. Politics is not neutral and all individuals are rooted in their cultures, communities and minority identities. Instead of the neutrality principle, law must reflect and respect the multi-cultural character of political societies and enhance the access of different minorities to the instruments and institutions of political power. Legal normativity is important only to the extent it responds to the different normativities and cultural plurality of our society.

Kennedy's later work inspired by the ideas of Michel Foucault, and Alan Hutchinson's writings inspired by the postmodern version of pragmatism of Richard Rorty are typical of the CLS movement in the late 1980s and 1990s. The re-conceptualisation of critical legal studies, drawing on postmodern theory, has radicalised the critical project developed by the CLS, and extended it to become a critique of legal theory itself. The postmodern turn is, therefore, the second stage of critical legal studies in that researchers move now to criticise their own theoretical foundations. Postmodern critical legal studies accepts the notion of law's indeterminacy and its contradictory character as worked out by critical legal science in the late 1970s, yet the postmodern project rejects the formerly popular concept of 'false consciousness' which may be analysed by

---

[38] D. Kennedy, *supra* n. 31, at 34.
[39] *Ibid.*, at 30.
[40] This is Kennedy's popular statement when he wants to emphasise his social and cultural background in respect to other communities and minorities. See, D. Kennedy, *ibid.*, at 126.

theory and substituted by a 'true' legal and political consciousness. The concepts of truth and theory have lost their persuasive and argumentative power for critical legal scholars.

Discussions about the status of theory within CLS have consequently moved into a polemical debate between the adherents of a 'soft' postmodern legal theory and their opponents who advocate a 'hard', 'anti-theoretical' position and refuse to attribute any practical meaning to legal theory. One finds a scepticism towards theory in the later work of Duncan Kennedy and the radical pragmatism of Alan Hutchinson[41] inspired by the anti-theoretical pragmatic jurisprudence of Stanley Fish.[42] It is marked by the belief that theory has no special social and intellectual status. It is merely an outcome of the practices of different communities.

However, this radical departure from critical theory represents only one of many current streams of critical legal scholarship. Different forms of postmodern theorising about law and postmodern jurisprudence continue to flourish. The postmodern turn was accepted as a mode of departure especially by the British critical legal studies movement which was formed in the second half of 1980s and represented by scholars such as Costas Douzinas and Ronnie Warrington, Peter Fitzpatrick, Peter Goodrich and others. These postmodern critical legal scholars accept the commonly shared critical legal argument that the general language of law, its formal structures and impersonality, in fact obscure social and political inequalities and injustices. The liberal concept of formal justice as equality of all before the law produces new injustices. It is just a mask of specific strategies of social control and discipline.[43] In fact, legality has never been a unified discourse and always contained a heterogeneity of vocabularies.[44] Non-legal elements such as the theological, moral, aesthetic or historical discourses are embedded in the legal system. Law is not a distinct and closed discourse of 'pure' legal arguments. It must be treated as an 'intertext' in which different discourses overlap.[45] The political function of the liberal rule of law is only to disguise the existing plurality and *contingency* of the political world by the seemingly neutral and normative language of legality.

The task of a postmodern critical legal science is to reveal the instability, contingency and heterogeneity of the legal and political order. This 'disclosure' job is what unifies postmodern critical jurisprudence with the critical legal tradition. However, the postmodern epistemological position is different because it seeks to change legal doctrine and professional legal practices from the position

---

[41] See A. Hutchinson, *It's All In the Game: a nonfoundationalist account of law and adjudication* (Durham N.C. Duke University Press 2000).

[42] See S. Fish, *Doing What Comes Naturally* (Durham Duke University Press 1989); *There's no such thing as free speech . . . and it's good thing too* (Oxford Oxford University Press 1994).

[43] See especially P. Fitzpatrick, *The Mythology of Modern Law* (London Routledge 1992).

[44] P. Goodrich, *Languages of Law: from logics of memory to nomadic masks* (London Weidenfeld & Nicolson 1990).

[45] C. Douzinas and R. Warrington with S. McVeigh, *Postmodern Jurisprudence* (London Routledge 1991), at 143.

of *the other* within law and society. According to this position, critical legal science must think 'the difference of law'.[46] The emphasis is on the plurality of differences which makes it impossible to work out a grand alternative to mainstream legal theory.

There is, however, a communitarian ethos and emphasis in postmodern 'anti-theoretical' critical legal studies on the multiplicity of different radical political practices.[47] The role of theory, however, remains one of 'demystifying' the world of legality. The richness of law's images and differences may be revealed if the grammar of modern legality is deconstructed. In contrast to Jacques Derrida's original radical conception of deconstruction as a tool for challenging theory, postmodern critical jurisprudence suggests that deconstruction is a theory which may be used to establish counter-ideologies which have the power to change the dominating paradigms of legal theory.[48] Some postmodern critical legal scholars also reject the intellectual cynicism attributed to some streams of the project of law's deconstruction. They take deconstruction as coeval with 'constructionist claims'[49] and alternative politics of law which are typical of older schools of critical legal studies or socio-legal studies.

5. A POST-SCRIPTURAL SUMMARY OF THE CRITICAL LEGAL STUDIES MOVEMENT

Critical legal theory, its postmodern version and anti-theoretical critical legal scholarship all have in common their struggle against existing law, legal doctrine and ideology. The postmodern turn in critical legal studies brought a much greater emphasis and respect for the contingency and heterogeneity of our current social and political condition. This respect usually has a political form of communitarian or anarchist ideologies, but it is also possible to detect the postmodern liberal ideology within the critical legal studies movement.

Deconstructing legality and disclosing the law's otherness may, therefore, reveal the falsity and ideological function of the concept of human rights and the rule of law. Nevertheless, it also deconstructs the possibility of achieving a true

---

[46] P. Goodrich, *Oedipus Lex: psychoanalysis, history, law* (Berkeley University of California Press 1995), at 13.

[47] For the communitarian interpretation of the postmodern fragmented social reality see, for instance, N. Lacey, 'Closure and Critique in Feminist Jurisprudence: Transcending the Dichotomy or a Foot in Both Camps?' in A. Norrie (ed) *Closure or Critique: New Directions in Legal Theory* (Edinburgh Edinburgh University Press 1993), at 208. For the critical legal elaboration of the paradoxical concept of 'liberal communitarianism' and its use in current radical politics, see R. M. Unger, *What Should Legal Analysis Become?* (London Verso 1996), at 153.

[48] C. Douzinas and R. Warrington with S. McVeigh, *Postmodern Jurisprudence* (London Routledge 1991), at 146

[49] See, for instance, P. Fitzpatrick, 'Distant Relations: The New Constructionism in Critical and Socio-Legal Studies', in P. Thomas (ed) *Socio-Legal Studies* (Aldershot Dartmouth 1997), at 147. Fitzpatrick, himself a postmodern critical legal scholar, argues that constructionism is coeval with deconstruction and therefore detectable even in the postmodern turn within critical legal and socio-legal studies.

and politically correct reading of law and politics. Belief in theory and its power to produce a better world has disappeared in the same way as the belief lawyers and social scientists once had in the extraordinary political role of modern law. The claim that law is politics has been extended so that everything has become politics. However, if law is consequently everything, it also means that its social and political importance has disappeared. If it is everything and nothing at the same time, why do we still bother?

This question is the *realist* question which inspired and initiated the whole movement of critical legal studies in the mid 1970s. The legal realists and, later, critical legal scholars refused to accept dominating images of law, legal doctrine and scholarship. Instead, they suggested an alternative approach which involved the political analysis and ideological critique of law and legal concepts as a force securing economically and politically dominant groups in society. Sociological perspectives and their realism were intended to establish a politically and morally better, and socially more reflexive, law. Critical legal science accommodated the original job of the sociological analysis of law which contrasted common sense and expert legal knowledge and wanted to control the latter by the social, moral and political virtues of the former. It extended the argument of this hierarchical model of different knowledge and wanted to subject law to politics and its rules. The postmodern turn makes this critique of law more problematic, since instead of being challenged and confronted by an omnipotent Law, according to some critical legal scholars, we cannot detect law in contemporary societies at all. This looks like an unsatisfying conclusion to the original propositions of the critical legal studies project since, according to critics of the postmodern turn, the same theoretical problems and political inequalities that inspired the original movement still exist. On the other hand, the postmodern critical legal project dialectically works as a force reviving and transforming the original powerful critique of liberal democratic legality, its doctrine of human rights and the rule of law, and therefore constitutes an inseparable part of the critical legal tradition.

7

Feminist Legal Theory

RUTH FLETCHER

FEMINIST ENGAGEMENT WITH law has taken a variety of forms over the years. Through litigation, campaigns for legal reform and legal education, feminists have engaged explicitly with law and the legal profession. In taking on the provision of specialist advice services, women's groups have played a role in making law more accessible to those in need. By subjecting legal concepts and methods to critical analysis, feminists have questioned the terms of legal debate.

A commitment to challenging gender disadvantage unites the individuals and organisations who engage in some or all of these activities. But feminists do not necessarily agree on the explanations for gender disadvantage or on the priorities for countering it. As a result feminism is a very diverse body of thought and action. Some of these differences are theoretical; others are strategic. But they all point to the futility of treating feminism as if it had one main objective. Therefore, the aim of this chapter is to clarify some of the key ideas which have arisen from feminism's encounter with law.

1. LAW, LEGAL METHOD AND LEGAL STUDIES

The diversity of perspectives on feminist objectives is matched by a diversity of approaches to law. Law became a site for feminist engagement initially because legal rules presented obvious barriers to women's free and equal participation in society. Rules such as those which required married women to give up their jobs were patent examples of discrimination against women as women. As the effort to reform sexist laws became a campaign to prevent their adoption in the first place, feminists turned their attention to the membership of legal institutions. They argued that the dearth of women in legislative and judicial positions contributed to the formation of male biased laws. If legal rules were to become more woman-friendly then the places of their formation would have to become more woman-friendly first. Feminist campaigns to encourage women to take up prominent positions as lawyers, judges and politicians were not only about increasing women's public profile, they were also about increasing women's influence on policy-making.

In struggling to seek accommodation of women's experiences in law and policy, feminists came up against three main obstacles. In the first place legal method did not always lend itself well to feminist argumentation.[1] The legal system justifies its capacity to oblige individuals to act in a certain way, eg pay a fine, by claiming objectivity and neutrality in its application of rules to people. Judges are expected to be impartial in their determination of cases, and law itself is expected to rise above subjective personal interests. Law is said to lose its legitimacy if it is shown to favour one person's wishes over another. In the abstract, such adherence to objectivity and neutrality seems fair and proper. Why would individuals trust the legal system to settle disputes if they did not have faith in its impartiality? How would the legal system avoid caving in to powerful people if it did not have an obligation to be neutral in its dispensation of justice?

But feminists among others have argued that the legal ideals of objectivity and neutrality are in fact a major problem for those seeking to represent groups which have been discriminated against historically. Some feminists think objectivity is a problem because it is actually a mask for masculine interests.[2] On this view when law claims to be objective it is actually reproducing bias in favour of men. Others argue that objectivity itself is an impossible ideal. Anything which claims to be objective will always obscure in some way the diversity of desires and needs in society.[3] Much feminist work has focused on demonstrating ways in which law has actually perpetuated bias against women through its claim to objectivity, neutrality and impartiality.[4]

Secondly [T]he need for feminist legal engagement to address problems with law's conceptual apparatus also became obvious through the process of challenging legal content and legal method. In order to advocate reform of legal rules and legal practices feminists understandably appealed to values underpinning law, most notably those of equality, justice and freedom. They argued that equality was not achieved by privileging masculine attributes over feminine ones,[5] that justice was not served by gender discrimination,[6] that freedom was not endorsed by idealizing heterosexual motherhood.[7] But some of the

---

[1] See M. J. Mossman, 'Feminism and Legal Method' (1986) 3 *Australian Journal of Law and Society* at 30–52, reprinted in M. Albertson Fineman and N. Sweet Thomadsen (eds) *At the Boundaries of Law: Feminist and Legal Theory* (New York Routledge 1991).

[2] C. MacKinnon, 'Toward Feminist Jurisprudence' in D. Kelly Weisberg (ed) *Feminist Legal Theory: Foundations* (Philadelphia Temple University Press 1993) 427–436, at 432. See also C. MacKinnon, 'Feminism, Marxism, Method and the State: Toward Feminist Jurisprudence' (1983) 8(2) *Signs* 635–658. Carol Smart identifies this as the 'law as male' school of feminist thought, C. Smart, 'The Woman of Legal Discourse' in her *Law, Crime and Sexuality* (London Sage 1995) 186–202.

[3] See further N. Lacey, 'Feminist Legal Theory Beyond Neutrality' (1995) 48(2) *Current Legal Problems* 1–38.

[4] The adoption of gender neutral rules in family law is one particular example. See M. Albertson Fineman, *The Neutered Mother, the Sexual Family and other Twentieth Century Tragedies* (New York Routledge 1995).

[5] See further K. O'Donovan, *Sexual Divisions in Law* (London Weidenfeld and Nicolson 1985).

[6] See further S. Moller Okin, *Justice, Gender, and the Family* (New York Basic Books 1989).

[7] See further C. Pateman, *The Sexual Contract* (Stanford Stanford University Press 1988) and C. Smart, *The Ties that Bind: Law, Marriage and the Reproduction of Patriarchal Relations* (London Routledge & Kegan Paul 1984).

responses that they met demonstrated that values themselves had a history; that they had been defined in ways which excluded women's experiences. I will deal with this issue in more depth in the section on equality and difference where I will discuss the various ways in which feminists have engaged with equality debates. For now, suffice it to say that feminist work has emphasised the need to question the norms and values of law.

Thirdly [E]ntering debates over the meaning of values such as equality, justice and freedom required a substantive engagement with other disciplines such as those of politics, sociology and philosophy. Efforts to develop gender sensitive models of freedom, for example, could not stop at the disciplinary boundaries of law.[8] Questions related to the appropriate level of governmental regulation, the influence of social networks and the balance between freedom and responsibility all become relevant to the legal task of defining a conception of freedom that respects intimacy without condoning harm. This was one of the ways in which feminist legal theory became conscious of the need for inter-disciplinary scholarship.

The importance of extra-legal discourses also became obvious as reform strategies which prioritised legal intervention failed to achieve all that was hoped for them. The legal changes which permitted women access to abortion, for example, did not remove the barriers imposed by the attitudes of the medical profession.[9] The tools of media and education were easily as important as those of law in bringing about an understanding of women's needs. At the same time as feminists themselves engaged in public relations exercises on television and radio and in educational programmes with citizens and professionals alike, a critical awareness of popular culture, media technology and their influence on law grew.[10] The practice of engaging in many interlinking kinds of strategies was reflected in a growing theoretical interest in the relationship between law and culture.[11]

As feminist thought helped to make law's location within the humanities and social sciences more explicit, the parameters of legal research broadened. The study of legal rules was augmented by a particular concern for their context. Although the term 'socio-legal' is problematically broad, its use does signify an acknowledgment that law is a social phenomenon which cannot be understood by attention to internal technical detail alone. The hope was that more complex questions would produce more complete knowledge. The main disadvantage of these changes was the prospect of the field becoming so broad that a certain depth of analysis would be sacrificed. However, particular conceptual paradigms developed which helped to organise feminist inquiry. I am going to

---

[8] See further W. Brown, *States of Injury: Power and Freedom in Later Modernity* (Princeton Princeton University Press 1995) and C. Vance, *Pleasure and Danger: Exploring Female Sexuality* (London Pandora 1992).

[9] S. Sheldon, *Beyond Control: Medical Power and Abortion Law* (London Pluto 1997).

[10] M. Macdonald, *Representing Women: Myths of Femininity in the Popular Media* (London Edward Arnold 1995).

[11] S. Sage Heinzelman, and Z. Batshaw Wiseman (eds.,) *Representing Women: Law, Literature, and Feminism* (Durham Duke University Press 1994).

focus on three examples of such paradigms, the sex/gender distinction,[12] the public/private distinction[13] and the equality/difference distinction.[14]

2. SEX/GENDER

Women as the object of feminist analysis

At an intuitive level, most people associate feminism with struggles by and on behalf of women. In general terms, feminism has become associated with campaigns for women's rights and women's liberation. In particular, feminism has become known for taking a stand for reproductive control, sexual freedom, and equal pay, and against sexual violence and the feminisation of domestic labour. Through the formulation of demands on behalf of women, feminism has assumed the right to speak for women. The practice of representing women's needs was initially reactive, however. Speaking for women only became necessary because women were being ignored, taken for granted or represented in ways which harmed them. Thus, for example, feminist groups such as Women's Aid came into being as an organisation which sought to provide and speak for the needs of abused women.[15] Over the years, feminism's demand that women be heard and accommodated has become proactive as well as reactive.

However, feminism only became able to represent women's needs because women had come together to share their experiences. Through various informal networks, women sought to tackle a sense of isolation and individual responsibility for the circumstances in which they found themselves. As women organised over such issues as sharing childcare, or accessing financial resources, they lived out the idea that they had something in common as women. One of the tenets of feminism thus became the notion that women shared experiences as women,[16] and one of the means of becoming aware of those shared experiences was 'consciousness-raising'.[17]

---

[12] For an overview see M. Gatens, 'A Critique of the Sex/Gender Distinction' in J. Allen and P. Patton (eds.) *Beyond Marxism? Interventions after Marx* (Sydney Intervention Publications 1983), reprinted in S. Gunew (ed.) *A Reader in Feminist Knowledge* (London Routledge 1991) 139–157.

[13] M. Thornton (ed.) *Public and Private: Feminist Legal Debates* (Melbourne Oxford University Press 1995), N. Rose, 'Beyond the Public/Private Division: Law, Power and the Family' (1987) 14 (1) *Journal of Law and Society* 61–75.

[14] G. Bock and S. James (eds.) *Beyond Equality and Difference: Citizenship, Feminist Politics, and Female Subjectivity* (London Routledge 1992).

[15] E. Pizzey, *Scream Quietly or the Neighbours will Hear* (Harmondsworth Penguin 1979).

[16] See further J. Wallach Scott, 'Experience' in J. Butler and J. Wallach Scott (eds.) *Feminists Theorize the Political* (New York Routledge 1992) 22–40.

[17] C. MacKinnon, 'Consciousness Raising' in her *Toward a Feminist Theory of the State* (Cambridge Mass. Harvard University Press 1989) 83–105.

Another way in which feminism has acted out its connection to women as a group, has been through studying women; their history,[18] their cultural activities,[19] their social roles.[20] As well as producing knowledge about women for its own sake, such research sometimes also plays the strategic role of providing evidence of women's agency, and therefore the possibility of alternatives.[21]

All of these feminist activities—lobbying for women, creating spaces for women to share their experiences, researching women—have contributed to a situation in which feminism is assumed to be about representing women's interests as a group. This assumption has come under different levels of attack over the last thirty years or so. At one level (as I discuss in the section on difference below), many women began to question feminism's authority to speak on their behalf. For example, sex workers and domestic workers were groups of women who had worked 'outside the home' for generations.[22] Each began to argue in their own way that the women's issues with which feminism seemed preoccupied were not their issues. Sex workers have argued against a dominant strain of feminism which regards prostitution as inherently exploitative, and instead demanded its decriminalisation and protection of their occupational health and safety.[23] And domestic workers have argued that the commodification of household chores does not necessarily liberate women. Other people's homes have been the site of their labour, and the means of their low wages.[24] Some feminists also argued that the experiences which women were assumed to share, such as a lack of fertility control, did not play out in the same way in all contexts. While the campaign for abortion rights became a central part of the feminist agenda in much of Western Europe and North America for example, women in India argued that access to abortion was less a problem for them than the promotion of abortion and sterilisation.[25]

---

[18] M. Lyndon Shanley, *Feminism, Marriage, and the Law in Victorian England 1850–1895* (London Tauris 1989), J. Wallach Scott, *Feminism and History* (Oxford Oxford University Press 1996) and D. Riley, *'Am I that Name?': Feminism and the Category of Women in History* (London Macmillan 1988).

[19] E. Showalter, *The Female Malady: Women, Madness and English Culture 1830–1980* (London Virago 1987), R. Sunder Rajan, *Real and Imagined Women: Gender, Culture and Postcolonialism* (London Routledge 1993) and T. Davis, *Actresses as Working Women* (London Routledge 1991).

[20] M. Z. Rosaldo and L Lamphere, (eds.) *Women, Culture, and Society* (Stanford Stanford University Press 1974), L. Dube, E. Leacock and S. Ardener (eds.) *Visibility and Power: Essays on Women in Society and Development* (Delhi Oxford University Press 1986) and Cambridge Women's Studies Group, *Women in Society: Interdisciplinary Essays* (London Virago 1981).

[21] S. Rowbotham, *Hidden from History: 300 years of Women's Oppression and the Fight against it* (London Pluto 1973).

[22] J. Walkowitz, *Prostitution and Victorian Society: Women, Class and the State* (Cambridge Cambridge University Press 1980).

[23] See further E. McLeod, *Women Working: Prostitution Now* (London Croom Helm 1982).

[24] M. Silvera, *Silenced: Talks with Working Class Caribbean Women about their Lives and Struggles as Domestic Workers in Canada* (Toronto Sister Vision Press 1989) and T. Schecter, *Race, Class, Women and the State: The Case of Domestic Labour in Canada* (Montreal Black Rose Books 1998).

[25] R. P. Petchesky and K. Judd (eds.) *Negotiating Reproductive Rights: Women's Perspectives across Countries and Cultures* (London Zed Books 1998).

Gender as the category of feminist analysis

Such critiques have had the benefit of making certain feminist assumptions explicit and of generating a more reflexive feminist practice. They have also contributed to shifting feminism's analytical focus from women to gender.[26] Rather than speaking about women per se, feminist enquiry now tends to ask how womanhood is defined in a particular context. This form of enquiry responds to the need to understand how assumptions about appropriate behaviours for men and women were formulated and sustained. As part of the intellectual task of making such practices transparent so that they could be challenged, feminists began to adopt the sex/gender distinction as an analytical tool.[27] Sex was understood to refer to the biological status of men and women. The two sexes were differentiated from each other primarily by reference to sexual and reproductive organs. The presence of a penis and testes sexed a person as male, while the presence of a vagina, ovaries and womb sexed a person as female. Gender on the other hand was understood to refer to the social status of men and women. The genders were differentiated by reference to the social roles of masculinity and femininity. Whether one was gendered masculine or feminine depended on the practices one adopted in playing out one's social role. A person in late twentieth century Western society was gendered feminine through the adoption of caring practices, for example, while a person was gendered masculine through behaving as a breadwinner.

The usefulness of this distinction was that it provided a means of interrogating the ideological assumption that treating men and women differently was justified because they were sexually different in the biological sense. For example, it allowed feminists to argue that just because a woman was biologically capable of conceiving and giving birth, did not necessarily mean that the birth mother should have the primary social responsibility for rearing children. Sexual difference did not cause gender difference. Sex did not make men incapable of changing nappies and women incapable of flying aeroplanes. Rather gender had a certain autonomy in its prescription of the social roles deemed appropriate for men and women.

The development of the sex/gender distinction was a major advance in feminist studies because it provided a means of questioning the supposed naturalness of women's responsibility for domestic tasks and men's responsibility for public tasks. Using gender analysis, feminists argued against the 'essentialism' of

---

[26] For a review of the emergence of gender as a category of analysis see: J. Wallach Scott, 'Gender: A Useful Category of Historical Analysis', (1986) 91 *American Historical Review* 1053–1075. For a review of the various ways in which gender analysis has been implemented in feminist legal studies see: C. Smart, *supra* n. 2.

[27] A. Oakley, *Sex, Gender and Society* (London Gower 1972), P. Caplan, *The Cultural Construction of Sexuality* (London Routledge 1987).

conservative, and some feminist, views about women.[28] Against conservatives, they argued that women's potential was not limited by so-called biological destiny. The only barrier to women actually taking on roles that had formerly been denied them was the institutionalised expectation that they were not up to the task. If society changed its understanding of gender, then gender in turn would change its organisation of masculine and feminine roles. And against those feminists who argued that women needed to be liberated from their biology,[29] they argued that women's reproductive and sexual lives needed better social accommodation.

On the whole, women were disadvantaged and men were advantaged by a social system which valorised and rewarded masculine attributes and practices at the expense of feminine ones. The remedy lay not in changing women per se, but in changing the means by which women were disadvantaged. Thus gender analysis switched the focus from women to the institutions, ideologies and discourses which limited women's potential. Challenging gendered practices in this way also had the consequence of explicitly recognising men as gendered beings.[30] Gender did not act on women alone, it also acted on and through men. Rather than identify men as *the* cause of women's oppression, gender analysis asked men to take responsibility for the advantages that accrued to them through the valorisation of masculinity. If women were to take on roles which had been gendered masculine, then men would also have to take on roles which had been gendered feminine. Gender analysis also recognised that the practice of denying men certain experiences, such as intimate relationships with their children, represented a loss for many men.[31] In these ways, the sex/gender distinction provided a framework for tracing the different ways in which social practices became attached to biological sex, and thus for explaining how gender privilege had come into being. The sex/gender distinction also provided a touchstone for imagining alternative social expressions of one's status as a sexed person, and for constructing a society in which happiness and equality were open to all, irrespective of gender.

As academics and activists argued for the need to distinguish sex from gender, biology from culture, nature from nurture, gendered assumptions about sexual desire also came to the fore.[32] The idea that women naturally desire sexual relationships with men was just as vulnerable to critique as the idea that women

---

[28] E. Spelman, *Inessential Woman* (London Women's Press 1990) and D. Fuss, *Essentially Speaking* (London Routledge 1989).

[29] S. Firestone, *The Dialectic of Sex: The Case for Feminist Revolution* (London Paladin 1972).

[30] L. Segal, *Slow Motion: Changing Masculinities, Changing Men* (London Virago 1990), P. Nardi (ed.) *Gay Masculinities* (London Sage 2000), R. Collier, *Masculinity, Law and the Family* (London Routledge 1995) and R. Collier, *Masculinities, Crime and Criminology: Men, Heterosexuality and the Criminal(ised) Other* (London Sage 1998).

[31] See further B. Hobson (ed.) *Making Men into Fathers: Men, Masculinities and the Social Politics of Fatherhood* (Cambridge Cambridge University Press 2002).

[32] C. R. Stimpson and E. Spector Person (eds.) *Women, Sex and Sexuality* (Chicago University of Chicago Press 1980).

naturally clean and cook.[33] The struggle against heterosexism found an ally in feminism for two main reasons. On the one hand lesbianism was positively represented as a political alternative to oppressive relationships with men. And on the other hand, recognising same sex desire was part of celebrating sexual freedom and challenging the perception that sexual practice should always have reproduction in mind. Erotic love between men and between women began to claim public visibility and to resist the practices by which it had been repressed, marginalised and stigmatised by gendered societies.

Although this understanding of sex/gender as a distinction between biology and culture, essentialism and constructivism, was very important in the development of feminist critique and is still significant as an analytical framework, it has not gone without criticism.[34] On the one hand, some feminists have argued that the dominant conception of gender is too limited: gender is still employed as if it had only two primary expressions: masculine and feminine. But if there is nothing essential about gender, why have feminists not traced more plural forms of gender articulation?[35] The concept and practice of gendering itself had assumed a binary opposition so that gender analysts tended to see things primarily in terms of masculinity and femininity.

A second major critique of gender as a category of analysis was that it presumed that sex was primary in the sex/gender relationship. By revealing the various ways in which sex was constructed through gender, gender analysis assumed that sex pre-existed gender. In so doing gender analysis could not fully account for the ways in which gender itself predetermined sex. If language and discourse were necessary for the comprehension of sex, and if language and discourse were gendered as social constructs, then how could sex avoid having to pass through gender in order to be comprehensible? One concrete example of this was the practice of operating on children who were born with both female and male genitalia in order to make them 'more female' or 'more male'. Doctors literally altered the physical sexual characteristics of some young children because of the social pressure to conform to gender.[36]

This example also illustrates the limits of thinking of biological sex as if it only had a binary form.[37] As people with both (or parts of both) kinds of genitalia, intersexuals began to campaign for their distinct sexual autonomy and

[33] A. Rich, *Compulsory Heterosexuality and Lesbian Existence* (London Onlywomen Press 1981) and E. Blackwood and S. E. Wieringa (eds.) *Female Desires: Same-sex Relations and Transgender Practices across Cultures* (New York Columbia University Press 1999).

[34] In particular see J. Butler, *Gender Trouble* (New York Routledge 1990).

[35] G. Herdt (ed.) *Third Sex, Third Gender: Beyond Sexual Dimorphism in Culture and History* (New York Zone Books 1994) and K. Bornstein, *Gender Outlaw: On Men, Women and the Rest of Us* (New York Routledge 1994).

[36] A. Domurat Dreger, *Hermaphrodites and the Medical Invention of Sex* (Cambridge Harvard University Press 1998) and S. Creighton and C. Minto, 'Managing Intersex' (2001) 323 *British Medical Journal* 1264–5.

[37] M. Hird, 'Gender's Nature: Intersexuality, Transsexualism and the Sex/Gender Binary' (2000) 1(3) *Feminist Theory* 347–364.

against the medical practices which sought to 'clarify' their sex. Transsexuals also challenged the idea that sex was binary and fixed.[38] As individuals living in bodies sexed masculine or feminine while identifying as feminine or masculine respectively, transsexuals began to demand that biology adapt to gender identity, rather than the other way around. In this way it became clear that social gender was not as easy to change as all that,[39] and that biological sex itself was not simply reducible to the categories of men or women.

One response to these critiques of the sex/gender distinction has taken the form of an argument for a more radical approach to sex and gender, which broadly speaking takes the form of transgender critiques.[40] Radical transgender approaches advocate the celebration and acceptance of any and all consensual sex/gender identities. Neither sex nor gender is limited or limiting. Sex is something which is changeable and complex, as is gender. Such transgender approaches contest the idea that there is such a thing as a lesbian or gay or straight or feminine or masculine identity. By holding out the possibility that one can pick and choose sex/gender, transgender critique seeks to liberate people from the constraints imposed on them by social expectations to sexually conform. As such, it is liberatory and imaginative. However, the radical diversity of this approach risks negating the extent to which sex/gender identity may operate as a protection against stigmatisation. While society continues to marginalize certain sexual identities in particular, people will find it necessary to organize around those sexual identities for solidarity and to resist that marginalisation. Others have responded less radically to the critique of the sex/gender distinction by issuing a gentle reminder that sex/gender is a relationship.[41] On this view the sex/gender distinction only becomes problematic if gender analysis is applied in such a way as to forget its constant relationship with sex. Gender analysis can maintain a radical potential if it is not divorced from the actual historical context in which gender and sex act on each other.

3. PUBLIC/PRIVATE

One of the primary mechanisms through which the relationship between sex/gender and law has been mediated is the public/private distinction. Although this distinction has been a central focus of feminist critique over the years, it has not always been used consistently. This is in part because the phrase

[38] I am using transsexual in its narrow sense, to refer to those individuals who desire an operation in order to change his/her physical sex and align it with his/her psychic sex. I use the term transgender in a broader sense to refer to those who want to queer sexual and gender identities to the extent that they become plural and diverse, and something which can be adopted and adapted.

[39] S. Whittle, *The Transgender Debate: The Crisis Surrounding Gender Identity* (London Garnet 2000).

[40] A. Sharpe, *Transgender Jurisprudence: Dysphoric Bodies of Law* (London Cavendish 2002).

[41] An example of work which I think implicitly takes this approach is R. Hennessy, *Profit and Pleasure: Sexual Identities in Late Capitalism* (New York Routledge 2000).

public/private divide is deceptively simple. The term itself assumes that there are recognisable entities called the 'public' and the 'private', and that they are separate from each other. However, there is substantial disagreement on the nature of the public and of the private, and on how they relate to each other.[42]

Therefore, part of the reason why researchers may mean slightly different things when they refer to the public/private divide is theoretical: the definition of 'public/private' depends on the explanatory framework within which the author is working. For feminists, the 'private' generally refers to the domestic, familial realm, but liberals generally use it to refer to the market. Another part of the reason for the confusion is historical. Relations between public and private have changed over the years and between societies, and continue to change. Conceptions of the private from nineteenth century Britain are unlikely to accurately describe private relations as they existed in twentieth century Southern Africa. Therefore, I shall clarify some of the main different ways in which the public/private divide has been considered in feminist thought, and to specify how the relations between these different aspects may be changing.

Public/Private spheres

One of the simplest and most consistent ways in which the public/private divide has been used in the feminist literature is to distinguish between those affairs into which the state is permitted to intrude ie the public sphere, and those into which it is not ie the private sphere.[43] Feminists have criticised this public/private divide for its justification of non-intervention into the domestic realm of interpersonal relationships. Under the rule of law, people are generally permitted to search out their own version of the good life except where that would harm others. This idea that people are entitled to make their own personal choices without legal interference has contributed to the characterisation of personal relations as a site of legal non-intervention. The feminist slogan 'the personal is political' was meant to call attention to the 'personal' as a site of oppression, which warranted a political response. If problems such as violence against women were to be tackled seriously, they would require legal intervention into the private realm since women's interpersonal relationships were a site of such violence.

One particular example of a law which provided evidence for this argument was the common law immunity against marital rape. Until 1991 the law in England and Wales held that a married woman could not be raped by her husband. This general principle was first documented by Hale and was clarified by

---

[42] Thornton *supra* n. 13.
[43] N. Lacey, 'Theory into Practice? Pornography and the Public/Private Dichotomy' in A. Bottomley and J. Conaghan (eds.) *Feminist Theory and Legal Strategy* (Oxford Blackwell 1993) 93–113, at 94.

Geoffrey Lane LCJ in *R v Steele* (1976) 65 Cr App Rep 22. Unless there was evidence of separation by mutual agreement or court order, the law would not consider the possibility of marital rape. The rationale behind this immunity was that a woman gave her general consent to sexual intercourse with her husband when she married. A wife's particular refusal to engage in sexual intercourse at a certain time and place could not invalidate this general consent. This legal rule was clearly informed by a view of marriage which did not regard husband and wife as equals. Rather, as far as the law was concerned, a wife gave herself to her husband on marriage. She had a duty to accommodate his sexual desires even where they conflicted with her own.

As feminist critics argued for the abolition of this immunity, one of the obstacles they came up against was a reticence on the part of legal reformers to intervene in the marital relationship. For example, the Criminal Law Revision Committee argued in 1984:

> Moreover, a prosecution for rape might necessitate a complicated and unedifying investigation of the marital history . . . Some of us consider that the criminal law should keep out of marital relationships between cohabiting partners—especially the marriage bed—except where injury arises, when there are other offences which can be charged.[44]

This disinclination to interfere in the marital relationship, in the private sphere, made it more difficult for feminists to challenge legal definitions of marriage and of rape. In order to argue that marital rape ought to be regarded as a type of injury in itself, one had to call for legal intervention into the private sphere. Finally, the House of Lords responded to such arguments by holding in *R v R* [1991] 4 All ER 481 that legal immunity from marital rape was an anachronistic common law fiction which was unacceptable in its depiction of marital relations.[45]

However, the idea that the public/private divide maps onto a sphere of regulation and a sphere of non-regulation also has several problems as a feminist analytic distinction. First, as Fineman has argued, a decision to refrain from intervening in some aspect of familial life is still a form of intervention.[46] It is a conscious response which has effects on the object to which it is directed. Allowing the status quo to persist is a regulatory decision. Second, this characterisation is more of an ideological proposition than an accurate value-free description. The claim that the family is uniformly the object of non-regulation justifies a minimal regulatory position at the same time as it obscures certain kinds of intervention into familial relations. The property rights of middle class families, for example, have been the object of state regulation for a long time.

---

[44] Criminal Law Revision Committee, 15th Report, Sexual Offences (Cmnd 9213, HMSO 1984) para 2.69; as cited in N. Lacey and C. Wells, *Reconstructing the Criminal Law: Text and Materials* (London Butterworths 1998) at 382.

[45] See also *S v HM Advocate* [1989] SLT 469, where the High Court of Justiciary in Scotland held that the marital immunity from rape was no longer a tenable legal position.

[46] Albertson Fineman *supra* n. 4.

Thirdly, one of the consequences of the separate sphere conception is a lack of clarity about the family's relationship to other social, economic and political institutions. As Fraser comments, when the expression 'public sphere' is used by feminists to 'refer to everything that is outside the domestic or familial sphere . . . [It] conflates at least three analytically distinct things, the state, the official-economy of paid employment, and arenas of public discourse'.[47] Further evidence of confusion is evident in those versions of separate sphere critique which make the market analogous to the family, as both are perceived as sites of non-intervention.[48] Yet on other occasions, separate sphere critique assumes that the market is part of the public sphere, because market participants have independent access to financial resources.[49]

One way for feminism to reformulate the conception of public/private as separate spheres so as to address some of these concerns would be to be more emphatic in identifying 'sphere' as a metaphor. If the term 'separate spheres' lost its literal interpretation and instead was used as a device to illustrate a particular kind of difference, then it would be more useful as an analytical tool. As metaphor, separate spheres do not have the same content all the time. Rather they provide a means of showing us how private relations are defined in a particular context by distinguishing themselves from public relations, and vice versa.

Public/Private norms

A second kind of feminist critique of the public/private divide differs from the above in arguing that the issue is *how* the family is regulated, not the question of *whether* it is regulated or not.[50] Rather than identify public and private in an almost physical sense as separate spheres, this critique emphasises the difference between public norms and private norms. On this understanding the problem is less that the private is not subjected to public regulation, and more that public and private are subjected to different norms of regulation.

Certain norms, such as those of financial independence, emotional self-sufficiency, physical distance, cultural formality and sexual restraint have come to be dominantly associated with the 'public', while norms of dependence, care, closeness, informality and indulgence have become emblematic of the 'private'. By identifying public and private in terms of the normative expectations they

---

[47] N. Fraser, *Justice Interruptus* (New York Routledge 1997) at 70.

[48] Lacey *supra* n. 43.

[49] F. Olsen, 'The Family and the Market: A Study of Ideology and Legal Reform' (1983) 96 (7) *Harvard Law Review* 1497–1578.

[50] See N. Lacey's discussion of public and private values in the article cited *supra* at n. 43; see further D. Cooper, 'And You Can't Find Me Nowhere: Relocating Identity and Structure within Equality Jurisprudence' (2000) 27(2) *Journal of Law and Society* 249–272 and T. Murphy, 'Feminism, Family and Constitutionalism in Transition' Paper presented at Modern Law Review Seminar on Constitutionalism, 5 July 2001, University of Leeds.

impose, feminist critique can develop a more complex account of the relationship between public and private.

Legal rules such as the marital exemption from rape could be re-characterised as reflecting certain private norms, rather than as depicting a philosophy of non-intervention. One such private norm is the idea that the home is a sanctuary in which only good happens. Another is that domestic authority resides in the father figure. The marital immunity from rape adopts the norm that a home ought to be a happy haven in such a way as to refuse the possibility that women may be mistreated there. Thus the problem with such rules from a feminist perspective is the effects of the norms which underpin them. In order to get law and public policy to respond appropriately to domestic violence, feminism had to challenge the normative expectations that familial relations were always pleasant and that fathers were always right. Once law and public policy did begin to make this shift, such norms lost their hegemonic status, although they did not disappear. Therefore, an advantage of conceptualising the relationship between public and private in terms of norms is that it permits feminists to trace complexity and change in the regulation of 'private' affairs.

Another advantage of analysing in terms of norms is that it allows feminists to make the argument that while the cult of domesticity may well have been oppressive for many women it is neither always nor exclusively so. Black feminists in particular have criticised mainstream feminism for assuming that the familial home is a negative space for women.[51] They have argued that the home has provided an important refuge for black women against racism in the public arena. In other words, public racism made the norm of domestic happiness important and relevant for them. Home did operate as a site of sanctuary from and resistance to systemic discrimination. Categorising public and private in terms of norms provides feminism with a better framework for addressing this critique because it does not have to assume that certain norms are necessarily associated with the public or the private.

Thinking in terms of public and private norms also provides a means to show how social groups are stigmatised for their perceived breach of the norms of public or private conduct. As Cooper has argued, on the one hand public norms count gay men out by not accommodating fully their citizenship rights.[52] On the other hand gay men are criticised for living out so-called private norms in public. A disadvantage of this conception however, is that it does not account for the ways in which norms become institutionalised, or for the forces that make some norms more important than others, or more likely to be associated with the public or private.

---

[51] H. V. Carby, 'White Women Listen! Black Feminism and the Boundaries of Sisterhood' in Centre for Contemporary Cultural Studies, *The Empire Strikes Back: Race and Racism in 70s Britain* (London, Hutchinson, 1982). See further A. Davis, *Women, Race and Class* (New York Random 1982) and M. Kline, 'Race, Racism, and Feminist Legal Theory' (1989) 12 *Harvard Women's Law Journal* 115.

[52] D. Cooper, *supra* n. 50.

Public/Private relations

A third kind of feminist critique of the public/private divide is similar to the latter in that it also envisages a plurality of publics and privates. But it differs from the emphasis on norms in that it is still concerned with the institutional codification of public and private. In that sense it has something to share with the separate spheres version of the public/private critique. As Boyd has argued the public/private divide may be constituted through relations between state and family, market and family, state and market, state and community,[53] and, one might add, between market and community. Especially given women's increased presence in public domains, market regulation is as capable as familial regulation of impacting on so-called 'domestic' activities. The 'relations' version of the public/private critique, therefore, is concerned with analysing how changing norms of gender appropriate behaviour are brought about through the interaction of state, family, market and community.

This form of critique provides a framework which can accommodate such changes to the relationship between public and private as are posed by certain moves towards integrating same sex relationships into marriage. Through their campaigns for legal rights and against discrimination on the basis of sexual orientation, gay men and lesbians have been demanding access to and inclusion within the public realm.[54] One of these campaigns has taken the form of a demand that spouse be redefined so as to permit same sex couples to marry.[55] Through marriage same sex couples could gain access to many of the benefits (pensions, insurance) which they are presently denied. These campaigns have met with limited success. But they have also generated substantive resistance since they pose a fundamental challenge to the idea of the marital family as necessarily a site of reproductive sex. In other words, the idea of same sex marriage demands the reconceptualisation of the private.[56]

The struggle to expand the definition of marriage has by no means met with universal approval among feminists and gay and lesbian thinkers and activists, however. One critique has been that this development simply assimilates gays into heterosexual marriage and fails to problematise marriage as a social institution. Another critique which is particularly important for thinking about

---

[53] S. Boyd (ed.) *Challenging the Public/Private Divide: Feminism, Law and Public Policy* (Toronto University of Toronto Press 1997).

[54] D. Herman, *Rights of Passage: Struggles for Gay and Lesbian Legal Equality* (Toronto University of Toronto Press 1994), D. Cooper, *Sexing the City: Lesbian and Gay Politics within the Activist State* (London Rivers Oram Press 1994) and C. Stychin, *Law's Desire: Sexuality and the Limits of Justice* (London Routledge 1995).

[55] R. Wintemute and M. Andenaes (eds.) *Legal Recognition of Same-sex Partnerships: A Study of National, European and International Law* (Oxford Hart 2001)

[56] See further J. Weeks, B. Heaphy, and C. Donovan, *Same Sex Intimacies, Families of Choice and Other Life Experiments* (London Routledge 2001).

public/private relations is that the expansion of the concept of spouse is problematic because it represents a privatisation of social reproduction. As Boyd has argued, the fact that some states are making moves to allow gay couples to claim benefits from each other is not necessarily a result of progressive pro-gay attitudes.[57] Rather gay marriage would expand the category of people who can be held privately responsible for care of each other within the domestic arena, thus relieving the state of responsibility for providing for that care. In other words, moves towards same sex marriage represent a shift in the relations between state, family and society, and are redrawing the boundary between public and private.

4. EQUALITY/DIFFERENCE

The value of equality has operated as the principal rationale behind much feminist critique. Policies and practices which discriminate against women have been criticised on the basis that they deny women equal citizenship and the means to achieve it. Arguments to the effect that human beings are of equal moral worth and should be treated as such, are appealing to many. The difficulty in making equality a lived reality for women (and indeed other disadvantaged groups), however, is twofold. First, how do you achieve equality when women have diverse needs and desires? Secondly, how do you bring about equality in the here-and-now when in order to do so we need to tackle inequalities, which have built up over a long period of time.

In thinking its way through such problems feminism has developed certain critiques of anti-discrimination policies and of the concept of equality which informs them. The first critique asks that equality not be reduced to sameness. This in turn has two aspects, that sameness should be neither the means nor the end of equality. In other words, many feminists have argued that neither 'same treatment' as a means, nor 'same individuality' as an end, represents a feminist conception of equality. Treating women the same as men will not bring about equality because it would, among other things, simply perpetuate already existing inequalities. The goal of equality should not be the production of 'sameness' in individual people either. As Smart has commented, it is by no means clear that androgyny is a feminist goal.[58]

These developments in feminist thinking about the concept of equality have in turn produced questions about how we should understand 'difference'. The main concern has been how to accommodate and indeed celebrate difference without allowing it to be used derogatively against people. This feminist concern

---

[57] S. Boyd, 'Family, Law, and Sexuality: Feminist Engagements' (1999) 8(3) *Social and Legal Studies* 369–390, see also S. Gavigan, 'Legal Forms, Family Forms, Gendered Norms: What is a Spouse?' (1999) 14(1) *Canadian Journal of Law and Society* 127.

[58] Smart *supra* n. 2.

with difference has responded to two main pressures. On the one hand, the voices who became dominant within the women's movement tended to be white, straight and middle class. They represented, albeit unconsciously, the problems of the dependant middle class housewife as *the* issue for feminism. In due course, Black women, ethnic minority women, lesbians and working class women, criticized middle class women for assuming that their experiences were representative of women in general.[59] As different groups of women articulated the needs and desires which they wanted feminism to reflect, it became clear that if it was to be sustainable feminism would have to be diverse and to value diversity among women.[60]

The other main impetus for feminist thinking about difference was the problem identified with using men as the constant comparator for feminist goals.[61] Women started to argue that they did not want to become psuedo-men in order to achieve their goals. They wanted to be accepted on their own terms. If feminists were to challenge the ways in which masculine practices had been institutionalized in workplaces and in social spaces, they would have to demand a positive accommodation of femininity in all its diversity. For some feminists sexual difference, and women's sexual and reproductive powers in particular, was not something to be negated. Rather sexual difference was positive and irreducible.

Two main trends have developed in the literature in response to these debates about difference. One trend argues that it is not difference per se that is the problem when it comes to women's oppression, but the fact that difference has been systematically constructed as disadvantage. Another trend regards difference as a positive, and regards women's bodies as a source for rewriting patriarchy.

Equality as Sameness

The formal ideal of equality prescribes that likes should be treated alike and non-likes should be treated differently. While in principle this ideal sounds fair and just, problems arise when trying to determine what are 'likes'. Historically, women were excluded from the category of human 'likes' on the grounds of their difference from men and their perceived closeness to nature. When differ-

---

[59] B. hooks, *Ain't I a Woman? Black Women and Feminism* (Boston, South End, 1981), D. Cheney, 'Valued Judgments?: A Reading of Immigration Cases' in A. Bottomley, and J. Conaghan (eds.) *Feminist Theory and Legal Strategy* (Oxford Blackwell 1993) 23–38, D. Allison, *Skin: Talking about sex, class and literature* (London Pandora 1995) and G. C. Spivak, 'Can the Subaltern Speak?' in P Williams and L. Chrisman (eds.) *Colonial Discourse and Post Colonial Theory* (New York Harvester Wheatsheaf 1994).

[60] B. hooks, 'Sisterhood: Political Solidarity Between Women' in S. Gunew (ed.) *A Reader in Feminist Knowledge* (London Routledge 1991).

[61] W. Williams, 'Equality's Riddle: Pregnancy and the Equal Treatment/Special Treatment Debate' in D. Kelly Weisberg (ed.) *Feminist Legal Theory: Foundations* (Philadelphia Temple University Press 1993) 128–155.

ence from men was the excuse used to deny women rights, it was almost inevitable that women would argue that they were like men in order to access those rights. The idea that women are the same as men in the sense that they share membership of the human species was, and still is, a powerful tool in the face of dehumanising tactics.

One key problem with the equality as sameness approach is its inability to accommodate actual differences between men and women, such as women's reproductive capacity. When women are constantly being compared to men in order to assess whether they have been treated equally or not, the fact of pregnancy can operate as a reason for difference and unequal treatment. Or it can serve as a basis to pathologise women through comparisons between pregnant women and sick men.[62] The debate over accommodating pregnancy and maternity in the workplace has driven home the inadequacy of a formal conception of equality. The use of the male as comparator normalises his experiences and means that women's experiences will also have to measure up to male standards. On the other hand, a request for the special treatment of pregnant women risks reproducing gendered stereotypes by characterising women as needing protection.[63]

Another problem with liberal anti-discrimination polices has been their narrow understanding of 'sex' discrimination. Both the European Court of Justice and the Court of Appeal have ruled that 'sex' means 'gender' and not 'sexual orientation'.[64] In so ruling the courts denied gays and lesbians the ability to use sex discrimination policies against harassment and in order to claim spousal benefits. In different factual scenarios each court determined that because a lesbian would have been treated in the same way as a gay man, there was no discrimination on the basis of sex. As well as problematically conflating sex and gender, such rulings demonstrate the limits of a narrow focus on particular axes of discrimination.

In a comparative context, Black feminists in the US have criticised antidiscrimination policy for its inability to deal holistically with discrimination against African American women.[65] Faced with legislation against racial and sexual discrimination, courts have felt the need to slot the deed in question under one or other head of discrimination, thus either degendering it or deracialising it. In response to such legal inadequacies, feminists such as Kimberle Crenshaw have argued for the need for feminists to adopt an 'intersectional'

---

[62] See further C. McGlynn, 'Ideologies of Motherhood in European Community Sex Equality Law' (2000) 6(1) *European Law Journal* 29–44.

[63] L. Findley, 'Transcending Equality Theory: A Way out of the Maternity and Workplace Debate' (1986) 86 *Columbia Law Review* 1118.

[64] Case C-249/96 *Grant v South West Trains* [1998] ICR 449, for an analysis of the Grant case see C. Stychin, 'Granting Rights: The Politics of Rights, Sexuality and European Union' (2000) 51(2) *Northern Ireland Legal Quarterly* 281–302, and *Pearce v Governing Body of Mayfield Secondary School* [2001] EWCA Civ 1347.

[65] A. Harris, 'Race and Essentialism in Feminist Legal Theory' (1990) 42 *Stanford Law Review* 581.

approach, that is to acknowledge the way in which race, class, gender and other systemic oppressions work through rather than alongside each other.[66] Some feminists, such as Drucilla Cornell,[67] have even been prompted into advocating the abandonment of gender altogether as a particular head of discrimination. Cornell thinks that gender as a legal and analytical tool is ultimately counter-productive because it ends up asking women to strip their experience of its so-called non-gender elements.

Therefore, while the equality as sameness approach had something to recommend it when women were denied rights on account of their "nature", it did not prove sufficient to the task of achieving substantive equality for women. Equality must value and accommodate difference if it is to be meaningful.

The Question of Difference

One important strategy which feminists developed in confronting gender discrimination was to argue that difference should not of itself imply hierarchy. The fact of sexual difference did not have to have the normative implications that one sex was better or worse than the other. The problem was that sexual difference had become construed in hierarchical terms so that femininity was materially and symbolically denigrated while masculinity was materially and symbolically privileged.

MacKinnon in particular has argued that difference is disadvantage as far as women are concerned.[68] She has famously described women as the objects of sex while men are the subjects. Men fuck while women get fucked. While it is clear that MacKinnon believes that men's dominance has turned sexual difference into a disadvantage for women, it is less clear whether she thinks that difference could ever become either neutral or advantageous for women. MacKinnon's particular concern with sexual violence, whether as rape or pornography, has meant that she thinks of sexuality as a site of danger and exploitation for women.

While one of feminism's main sites of activity has been activism against and analysis of sexual violence, two particular concerns with a MacKinnon-like approach have been identified. The conceptualisation of heterosex as *necessarily* a relationship of domination in which women get fucked, squeezes out the possibility of women's agency and of women's pleasure in such a context. In order to work against the objectification of women through sexual practice we

---

[66] K. Crenshaw, 'Demarginalising the Intersection of Race and Sex: A Black Feminist Critique of Antidiscrimination Doctrine, Feminist Theory and Antiracist Politics' [1989] *University of Chicago Legal Forum* 139.

[67] D. Cornell, *The Imaginary Domain* (New York Routledge 1995).

[68] C. MacKinnon, 'Difference and Dominance' in her *Feminism Unmodified* (Cambridge Mass. Harvard University Press, 1987) 32–45, reprinted in D. Kelly Weisberg (ed.) *Feminist Legal Theory: Foundations* (Philadelphia Temple University Press 1993) 276–287.

must be able to at least imagine the possibility of women's sexual subjectivity, even in relationships with men. Characterising heterosex as domination and sexual difference as disadvantage also alienates those straight women who do identify themselves as agents of their own sexual desire.

Another strand of feminism has focused on sexual difference in a very 'different' way to those who have characterised it as disadvantage. Rather than identify difference as a negative, post-structuralist feminists tend to regard difference as a positive. Helene Cixous, for example, believes that feminine writing is a type of writing which works on difference, and in so doing seeks to displace patriarchal binary thought.[69] On the surface at minimum, this approach rejects the idea that femininity is fundamentally related to sexual difference: feminine writing is not writing by women. The feminine/masculine binary is part of the patriarchal and phallogocentric system of meaning in which one side of the binary must negate the other in order to express itself. Therefore a new system of meaning cannot be feminine in the sense of not masculine. However, when Cixous tries to articulate what such an alternative system of meaning would be like, she draws on female body-centred imagery.

Thus there is a fundamental tension in this sort of feminist theory between the rejection of femininity on the one hand, and the celebration of femininity as the source of an alternative form of language on the other. Some feminists have aligned such post-structuralist feminist thought with those forms of difference feminism—Black feminism, post-colonial feminism—which reject the need for a universal notion of womanhood.[70] In their celebration of difference these sorts of combinations represent the most positive aspects of this feminism which seeks to imagine alternatives for womanhood by playing on and with meaning. Yet, the problems with such approaches return us to some of the central questions which face contemporary feminism. How can feminism avoid the accusation of biological essentialism if it theorises from the body?[71] How is it possible to formulate arguments in the name of feminism if the task is to embrace difference and to play on meaning?

5. CONCLUSION

The various threads of feminist legal thought which have been outlined in this chapter take diverse stands on a subject of shared interest: the effect of sex/gender on the legal regulation of human activity. In thinking through the ways in which this effect is mediated by public and private, equality and difference, feminist engagement with law has tried to imagine the possibility of gender justice

---

[69] H. Cixous, 'The Laugh of the Medusa' in E. Marks and I. de Courtivron (eds.) *New French Feminisms* (New York Schocken 1981) 245–264.

[70] R. Kapur, 'Imperial Parody' (2001) 2(1) *Feminist Theory* 79–88.

[71] T. Moi, *Sexual/Textual Politics* (London Routledge 1985).

while challenging the reality of gender injustice. The struggle to move beyond the constraints of the present without minimising the actual effects of such constraints has meant that feminism has had to constantly reassess its commitments. This self-reflexive practice is one of the strengths of feminism and allows it to be reinvented in order to better accommodate the particular needs and interests of specific groups in specific locations at specific times. This practice also provides a means for feminism to overcome one of its most significant challenges.

A new generation of men and women will not experience gender constraint in the same way. Just as feminism has had to learn to accommodate cultural differences, so it has to accommodate age differences. Reinvention in the light of new membership, however, is not the same as starting over. If and when young women and men need to challenge the way in which their lives are constrained by gendered ideas and practices, they will have a rich history of feminist struggle on which to draw. The diversity of feminist approaches to law reflects both a complexity in feminist thought and the multidimensionality of its engagement with law. As feminist critique has evolved and matured, so has its appreciation for the particular obstacles which law poses. The challenge which remains is the struggle to make law, legal method, and legal studies more gender sensitive without becoming complacent in assuming what that might entail. Unless law becomes better able to respond to systemic disadvantage and to accommodate gender diversity, its role in facilitating human equality and human happiness will be limited.

8

'Not Qualified?' or 'Not Committed?' A Raced and Gendered Organisational Logic in Law Firms

JENNIFER L. PIERCE

D ESPITE CLAIMS THAT affirmative action programmes are no longer neces-sary, white women and people of colour continue to be under-represented in the professions and to face discriminatory treatment in promotion and hiring and in pay differentials in the United States.[1] For example, an examination of EEOC complaints from 1967 to 1994 reveals that white women were more likely to file complaints about discrimination in promotion to higher level positions, whereas Blacks were more likely to complain about discrimination in hiring.[2] And, another study relying on data from the General Social Survey and the National Organizational Study of the University of Illinois shows that once hired, Blacks encounter far more obstacles to promotion than white employees do.[3] These large scale studies suggest not only that white women and people of color continue to face considerable obstacles to professional success, but that there may be different mechanisms at work that affect white women and Black men in distinctive ways.

To consider these implications, this chapter focuses on the experiences of white women and Black men who work in corporate law firms as trial lawyers or litigators. Both white women and African American men are numerical minori-ties or tokens within this work context and face many of the problems that soci-ologist Rosabeth Moss Kanter has associated with 'tokenism'.[4] Specifically, Kanter argued that because tokens are different from the dominant group, they often attract more attention, are evaluated more severely, receive less support and are more likely to be viewed as a disruptive force in the workplace. Although Kanter applied her explanation to white women in a large corporation,

---

[1] D. Tomascovic-Devey, *Race and Gender at Work* (Ithaca Cornell University Press 1993); B. Reskin and I. Padavic, *Women and Men at Work* (Thousand Oaks Pine Forge Press 1994).

[2] S. Bartlett, 'Trends in Equal Employment Opportunity Complaints: 1967–1994' (Department of Sociology, University of Minnesota, unpublished paper, 1998).

[3] S. Baldi and D. McBrier, 'Do Determinants of Promotion Differ for Blacks and Whites?' (1997) 24, 4 *Work and Occupations* at 478–97.

[4] R. Kanter, *Men and Women of the Corporation* (New York Basic Books 1977).

her theory of numerical proportions has also been applied to racial-ethnic minorities, and has been confirmed in studies of African American professionals as well as in studies of white women.[5]

Contrary to Kanter's assumption that the experiences of tokens are similar, this chapter demonstrates that there are also significant differences in the experiences of white women and Black men that have to do with the ways race and gender shape the meaning of what they do at work and the assumptions employers and co-workers make about their commitment and expertise. Based on in-depth interviews conducted with northern California litigators in 1988 and 1989 and thirty-three from the original group of forty-three, ten years later in 1999, my study highlights the mechanism or organisational logic that reproduces racialised and gendered patterns of inequality at the micro-level of face to face interactions. Further, it demonstrates not only the ways in which race and gender interact and intersect within this professional context to produce different life chances and opportunities for white women and African American men, but emphasises the cultural meanings that race and gender bear in this particular historical time and place. Drawing upon the extended case method,[6] my objective is to extend and reconstruct existing theory, rather than make general claims about the experiences of Black men and white women in litigation.

The first section of the chapter focuses on the stratification of the legal profession and of corporate law firms by gender and by race in the United States. It briefly highlights some key findings about the experiences of white women and Black men in corporate law firms to provide a context for this study. The next section discusses the background of the study and the methods employed. The final sections look at how a racially formed and gendered organisational logic plays out in the work lives of two different trial lawyers: Randall Kingsley, an African American man and Susan Nelson, a white woman. As a woman and a professional, Susan struggles with being seen as 'not committed' by her colleagues, while Randall, as a Black man, struggles with being regarded as 'not qualified'. As I will argue, these phrases—'not committed' and 'not qualified'— become shorthand expressions for a gendered and racialised logic about the presumed relationship between women, work, and family on the one hand, and Black men and work, on the other.

---

[5] S. Collins, *Black Corporate Executives: The Making and Breaking of the Black Middle Class* (Philadelphia Temple University Press 1997); D. Izraeli, 'Sex Effects or Structural Effects: An Empirical Test of Kanter's Theory of Proportions', (1983) 62 *Social Forces* at 153–65; S. M. Nkomo and T. Cox, 'Factors Affecting the Upward Mobility of Black Managers in Private Sector Organizations', (1990) 19 *Review of Black Political Economy* at 39–57; G. Segal, *Blacks and the Law: Philadelphia and the Nation* (Philadelphia University of Pennsylvania Press 1985).

[6] M. Burawoy et al., *Ethnography Unbound* (Berkeley University of California Press 1991).

1. GENDER AND RACIAL STRATIFICATION IN THE LEGAL PROFESSION

In the United States, the legal profession, like other occupations and professions, is stratified by gender and by race.[7] 28 per cent of all lawyers are women, while only 4 per cent are African American.[8] Furthermore, European American men predominate in the private sector where the highest paying corporate jobs are, whereas white women and women and men of colour are more likely to be employed in the public sector in jobs such as the public defender or district attorney's office which are among the lowest paid legal positions in the United States.[9] Not only are white men concentrated in the highest paying sector of the legal profession, but they also hold positions of greatest influence. In 1999, 85 per cent of the partners in the nation's 247 largest law firms were men.[10] The numbers of white women in these positions are much smaller—15 per cent; and minuscule for African Americans—3 per cent.[11]

The corporate law firms examined in my study, for example, are in the private sector which has long been dominated by white men in the United States, whereas the non-attorney stratum of such organisational hierarchies which includes paralegals, legal secretaries, receptionists, duplicating operators, and janitors is more likely to be occupied by white women and people of colour.[12] In the two San Francisco Bay Area law firms I studied in the late 1980s, more than 95 per cent of lawyers were white and 88 per cent were male. Among the most elite members of this group, senior partners, 98 per cent were white and male. On the other hand, 93 per cent of secretaries were female and more than 99 per cent were white. Among paralegals, 85 per cent were women and 95 per cent were white and the vast majority of workers on night time clean-up crews were women of colour or recent immigrants to the United States.[13]

Not only do white men predominate in numbers and in positions of power, but private elite law firms represented, in sociologist Cynthia Fuchs Epstein's words, 'the quintessential upper-class', and I would add *white*, 'male culture'. 'Nowhere is the "old boy" network so characteristic of the formal and informal structure of an occupation as in the "establishment bar"'.[14] Articles in the legal trade press such as the *National Law Journal* and *American Bar Association*

---

[7] B. Reskin and I. Padavic, *Women and Men at Work* (Thousand Oaks Pine Forge Press 1994).

[8] Statistical Abstracts of the United States. Occupational and Industry Employment, No. 675 (Washington D.C. 1999).

[9] E. Higginbotham, 'Employment for Black Professionals in the Twentieth Century' in C. Bose and G. Spitze (eds.) *Ingredients for Women's Employment Policy* (Albany State University of New York Press 1987); G. Segal, *Blacks and the Law* (Philadelphia University of Pennsylvania Press 1985); J. Heinz and E. Laumann, *Chicago Lawyers* (New York Russell Sage Foundation 1982).

[10] 'The Talk of the Profession', (January 10, 2000) *National Law Journal* at A6.

[11] *Ibid.*; A. Davis, 'S.F. Bar Frets Over Race Stats; Minority Attrition Rate', (10 June 1996) *National Law Journal* at A4.

[12] J. Auerbach, *Unequal Justice* (New York Oxford University Press 1976); Pierce, *infra* n. 13.

[13] J. Pierce, *Gender Trials* (Berkele, University of California Press 1995) at 30–31

[14] C. F. Epstein, *Women in Law* (Urbana University of Illinois Press 1993) at 178.

Journal suggest that little has changed since Epstein conducted her first study in the late seventies.[15] In a California study conducted by the State Bar Women in Law Committee, 88 per cent of the women surveyed believed there is a 'subtle pervasive gender bias' in the legal profession and two-thirds of the respondents said that women are not accepted by their male peers.[16] Hearings conducted by the American Bar Association Commission of Women in the Profession in the late 1980s as well as more recent findings reported in the *National Law Journal* drew similar conclusions.[17]

Studies show that white women and racial-ethnic minorities still have a hard time gaining admission to these professional networks. White women, for example, face serious obstacles in dealing with their predominantly male clients in the corporate world. A trade press article titled 'New Trouble for Women Lawyers', found that women have more difficulty than men bringing clients into the firm because clients are still more likely to turn to a man. As one woman lawyer said, 'It wouldn't occur to them to call up a woman. They'll call up a law school buddy'.[18] Another female attorney recalled chatting with a prospective male client at a business dinner about her work, her husband and her children. She felt confident that she was on the way to making a good business contact until the client tried to kiss her good bye. And a partner from a prominent San Francisco firm recalled meeting with a client who refused to make eye contact with her, even when she asked him direct questions. Rather than responding to her, the client turned to the junior associate, a man, who had been sitting silently next to her.[19]

Women I interviewed at corporate firms in the late 1980s, encountered similar problems in recruiting new clients. Men of colour and white men from working-class backgrounds did not find it easy to bring in business, but for different reasons than women did. Men from upper class backgrounds with family money, connections and 'cultural capital' found it easy to establish pre-existing family business connections and to make new ones. Their broad cultural knowledge and familiarity with upper-middle class social etiquette made socialising with elite CEO's and company presidents easy for them. The few men from lower middle-class and working-class backgrounds simply did not feel at ease in these situations. Men of colour also expressed discomfort in these situations. As one Black lawyer said:

---

[15] G. Hazard, 'Male Culture Still Dominates the Profession', (19 December 1988) *National Law Journal* p. 13 at 24; M. Goldhaber, 'Macho Territory', (February 2000) *National Law Journal* at A1.
[16] M. Bay, 'Poll: Sex Bias Pervades the State's Legal Profession' (13 September 1989) *The Recorder* at 1.
[17] L. Salaman, 'Progress for Women? Yes, But . . .' (April 1, 1988) 18 *American Bar Association Journal*; L. Johnson, 'Corporate Counsel—Catalyst for Progress, Responding to the Diversity Challenge' (January 2000) *The Metropolitan Corporate Counsel* 334; M. Goldhaber, (7 February, 2000) 'Macho Territory' *National Law Journal* at A1.
[18] H. Chiang, 'More Trouble for Women Lawyers' (April 9, 1990) *San Francisco Chronicle* at 1.
[19] *Ibid.*

They have an affirmative action program here . . . So, there are more Blacks, and women too. But look at who makes senior counsel. I have been here six years and I see the writing on the wall. I don't socialize with CEO's. They probably wouldn't want to socialize with me. I've never even met one of them. I'm just not a company man. The only Black man who made senior counsel did so after eight years of service with the threat of a discrimination suit.[20]

The comments made by these women and men suggest that wooing clients requires a degree of acceptance on the part of the client and an ease in sociability on the part of the lawyer. White women as well as lawyers from minority or working-class backgrounds often do not feel completely at ease socialising with corporate executives. As one women said, 'These people belong to the Bohemian Club.[21] How is that supposed to make me feel?' On the other hand, clients who work in homogeneous corporate environments are unused to working with people of colour and white women as equals. The fact that the corporate world is still unable to accept women and men who do not fit into this white, upper-middle-class male culture has serious negative repercussions for lawyers whose intra-firm mobility is based on recruiting new clients.

Not only is the culture of law firms strongly male, but the model of the professional career itself is distinctly male. In her classic article, 'Inside the Clockwork of Male Careers', sociologist Arlie Hochschild argues that academic institutions support careers which are implicitly based on the male life cycle. If the male professor has a family, the underlying assumption is that his wife will devote her time and energy to managing the potential disruption this could create in his career. Hochschild writes: 'Other things being equal, the university rewards the married, family-free man'.[22] Law professor Geoffrey Hazard makes a similar argument about the legal profession.

> This model of a professional career is distinctly male, and does not work for most women. Apart from everything else in life, a woman's biological clock has a different setting. Most women who become lawyers follow the same pathway as men until they complete college at about age 21 . . . Only a few women these days are firmly committed to having no children . . . a decision male lawyers need not impose on themselves. If women wish to keep open the option of having children, they face strategic choices in relating professional career to personal life.[23]

In sum, these studies suggest that white women and men of color, who work in these predominantly white and male organisations, face many obstacles that white, middle-class men do not.

[20] Pierce, *supra* n. 13, at 111.

[21] The Bohemian Grove is an exclusive upper class, all-male retreat in the San Francisco Bay Area. For a discussion of the cohesiveness of upper-class retreats such as the Bohemian Grove, see W. Domhoff, *The Bohemian Grove and Other Retreats: A Study in Ruling Class Cohesiveness* (New York Harper and Row 1974).

[22] A. Hochschild, 'Inside the Clockwork of Male Careers' in F. Howe (ed.) *Women and the Power to Change* (New York McGraw Hill 1975) at 67.

[23] G. Hazard, 'Male Culture Still Dominates the Profession' (December 1988) *National Law Journal* at 24.

2. METHOD

Data were collected over a two-year period from 1988–1989 and again over a one year period in 1999 in a large in-house legal department with more than 150 lawyers within a large company in the San Francisco Bay Area that I call Bonhomie Corporation. Over the past 30 years, this company has been one of the largest and most successful businesses in the Bay Area. Positions within its corporate hierarchy range from entry level factory, sales, and clerical work to jobs at higher levels requiring college and professional degrees such as an MBA or a law degree. Compared to other large companies with an in-house counsel, what makes this one unique is its federally mandated affirmative action program which was created in the early 1970s when a federal court had ordered the corporation to implement an affirmative action programme in response to a lawsuit filed against it for race and sex discrimination.

The first phase of my study was an ethnographic investigation focusing on the gendering of occupations and legal workers. Data were collected through three means: nine months of fieldwork as a participant observer in the legal department; informal interviews and formal in-depth interviews with lawyers; and an analysis of company documents, such as records about the affirmative action program, and lawyers' resumes.[24] From my initial fieldwork in the late 1980s, it was clear that there was an organisational climate of hostility directed against affirmative action, white women, and racial ethnic minorities. My field notes record page after page of negative comments about the alleged effects of the program. In the legal department, some of the white lawyers complained about 'those unqualified clerks in the file room' who, as they observed, 'just happened to be Black or Latino [and female]'. In fact, the adjective 'unqualified' popped up time and time again in public conversations as a code word for racial or ethnic minority employees. Job candidates with unremarkable previous job histories were 'unqualified' when they were African American, but could use a 'boost up' when they were white men. Bad jokes about affirmative action abounded: 'It's our quota system for lazy people'. For the most part, these jokes were told by white employees to other white co-workers in less public settings, like someone's office.

Historically, it is important to note that in 1989 when I began my fieldwork, a backlash against affirmative action was already well under way across the United States. At this time, the media focused its attention on the culture wars on college campuses, the attack on multi-cultural education, and so-called 'reverse discrimination' and the 'plight of the white male victim'. At the same time, there was a resurgence of a conservative agenda with Reagan and Bush in

---

[24] For the initial study, I studied two law firms and interviewed not only lawyers, but paralegals and secretaries as well. For a complete discussion of methods and data collection, see Pierce, *supra* n. 13.

the 1980s which led the assault against the welfare state, welfare recipients, and affirmative action.[25] In addition, the small gains African Americans made in the corporate world through affirmative action of the 1960s and 1970s were being eroded by the decisions of a more conservative Supreme Court during the Reagan and Bush years.[26] In the 1980s and 1990s, the numbers of African Americans in corporate managerial positions in the United States declined sharply. Then in the fall of 1996, the majority of California voters endorsed the so-called California Civil Rights Initiative (or Proposition 209) which was designed to end racial and gender-based preferences in employment and education in the state. California was followed by other states, such as Texas, that began to consider initiatives to repeal affirmative action programs and considerations. In this light, a California corporation provides an intriguing and timely window into raced and gendered workplace dynamics in the post civil rights era.

By 1989, Bonhomie Corporation had improved the representation of racial and ethnic minorities as well as white women in the lower echelons of the corporate hierarchy in sales and in factory work. However, the corporation had been less successful in meeting goals and timetables for managerial positions at higher levels. In the litigation department where I conducted my fieldwork, three attorneys were African American and forty were of white or European American ancestry. Nine attorneys were women: eight white and one African American.

In 1999, the second phase of the study involved contacting the 43 lawyers who had worked at Bonhomie Corporation in 1989 when I first met them and re-interviewing them. The turnover rates for both African Americans and white women were higher compared to those of white men: 100 per cent, 75 per cent, and 60 per cent respectively. Of the three African American lawyers who had worked there in 1989, all three had left the firm. I eventually located these three individuals and interviewed them (see Table 1.) Of the eight white women who had been there, six had left. I interviewed the two who remained at Bonhomie Corporation as well as five of the six who had resigned. Of the thirty-two white men, thirteen were still employed at Bonhomie Corporation. Nine of the thirteen agreed to be interviewed, and I located and interviewed fourteen of those of the nineteen who had departed for other positions. Overall, thirty-three of the original 43 individuals who had been in the litigation department in 1989 were interviewed. Among the ten people I was unable to interview, one had retired and moved away from the Bay Area, several others claimed to be too busy, another cancelled interview after interview, and finally, there were six individuals who had moved onto other jobs whom I was unable to locate.

[25] L. Chavez, *The Color Bind* (Berkeley University of California Press 1998).
[26] S. Collins, *Black Corporate Executives* (Philadelphia Temple University Press 1997).

TABLE 1
Interviews with Lawyers Who Stayed or Left (N = 43)

	White women	White men	Black women	Black men
Original number	8	32	1	2
Stayed	2	13	0	0
Left	6	19	1	2
Interviewed	7	23	1	2
Unable to interview	1	9	0	0

Interviews began as job histories and often lasted from one to two hours. Some of the questions included: What has your professional trajectory been since I last interviewed you in 1989? How would you characterise your current practice? Why did they stay (or leave) Bonhomie Corporation? How would you characterise Bonhomie Corporation's policies for women and minorities? Names of individuals and organisations were changed at their request to protect confidentiality.

My analysis highlights the experiences of white women and African American men who *left* the litigation department after I first interviewed them in 1989. The personal narratives presented in the next two sections were chosen because each one best represents the experiences of the white women and African men who chose to leave.

3. 'NOT QUALIFIED?'

One of the lawyers who left the litigation department was Randall Kingsley, an African American lawyer and Hastings law school graduate who describes himself as 'a sort of jack of all trades'. He has a modest two person law office in downtown Oakland, California and most of his cases are employment disputes, but he also does the occasional personal injury case, a simple will for a friend, or provides advice about getting a divorce. Though he enjoys his independence as a solo practitioner and finds his work interesting, he complains that 'it's often difficult to make ends meet'. His annual salary in 1998 was $47,000. Ten years earlier, in 1989, when I first interviewed Randall at Bonhomie Corporation, he was making $45,000.

Randall's work history narrative, like those of many other Black professionals, began with the opportunities opened up by affirmative action programmes and policies in the late 1960s and early 1970s.[27] In 1985, after he finished law school, he applied for jobs in several big firms in employment law,

---

[27] S. Collins, *Black Corporate Executives* (Philadelphia Temple University Press 1997); K. Scott, *The Habit of Survival: Black Women's Strategies for Life* (New Brunswick Rutgers University Press 1991).

and he ended up getting offered one position in the District Attorney's office in Oakland and another in the litigation division within the Legal Department at Bonhomie Corporation. Both places had good reputations for diversity in hiring practices and successful affirmative action programmes. He decided to take the position at Bonhomie Corporation because 'the salary was better and the opportunities seemed greater'. Four years later, when he left Bonhomie Corporation, his initial move was not up, but rather a lateral one to a legal department in another large corporation in the South Bay. His salary was commensurate to what he had been making at Bonhomie Corporation. 'It had a good reputation as a kind of progressive place, but it turned out to be pretty conservative'. In 1993, he decided that he 'had it' with the corporate environment and opened his own practice with an old friend from law school who is also African American. Randall's reasons for leaving Bonhomie Corporation are, in his words, 'a long story'.

> Part of it has to do with how they hype their affirmative action program there. [He adopts a booming announcer voice] We have the best affirmative action program and we are all one happy family. Diversity is excellence. Rah, rah, rah . . . [He returns to regular voice] But, they don't really believe that. It's just assumed that if you are Black then you can't possibly be qualified for the job.

> *So, did you feel like affirmative action was a kind of stigma there?*
> Yeah. In their heads, it went something like: minority equals affirmative action hire equals unqualified. I don't mean everyone thought this way, but enough people did to make it matter . . . So, yeah, it was disappointing. I mean part of the reason I went there was because they have a reputation for having a good [affirmative action] program. You know, it's like they made mistakes in the past, but they did something about it . . . And, uh, to be completely fair, they did improve a lot some areas like clerical, sales, and craft [factory]. But there still aren't a lot of women and minorities in management level positions. In litigation, I was one of three African Americans in the entire department . . .

> *So, why did you leave?*
> It started with a lot of small stuff, and the small stuff just added up. . . .

The small stuff began when Sam, the head of the litigation section, whom Randall described sardonically as 'pretty liberal for a white guy', gave him his first assignment, legal research in an area that lay outside Randall's area of expertise. Randall expressed some concern, but Sam told Randall not to worry about his inexperience in this area. 'There's a whole department here of folks to help you out'. 'So, I decided against my better judgement to take it on and get some help from some of the other litigators in the department. . . .'. When Randall first approached Bill, he was cool and brusque, and told him that he was 'too busy'. Randall who says he felt he was 'being brushed off' by Bill, decides to approach other senior lawyers in the department for help.

These men react indifferently or negatively to him and began to make a few jokes among themselves about Randall's style and manner. Randall experiences this undercurrent of resistance in different ways. One attorney lost a key memo Randall had spent days researching, another made jokes whenever Randall came into his office, still another ignored his remarks in meetings and another 'forgot' a lunch date he made with him. He began to see these multiple interactions as many small acts of discrimination and harassment. Moreover, it was clear to him that the new junior associate who is European American was not treated in the same way. He began to feel alienated from his colleagues, isolated, and angry. His story of leave-taking continues:

> So, I finally decided to call them on it. First, I went back to Sam and asked him why he had given me this assignment at the beginning. I wanted to know why my first project was outside my area. I mean I had been hired to do labor law and they had me working on a patent case? He got really defensive and he had all these excuses. Then I said that I felt like no one was really mentoring me, you know that they weren't helping me. And, I knew that Todd [a young white male attorney] was getting all kinds of help. He made more excuses. I said that I wanted to know what was going on. You know, because this was an incident of differential treatment. I used those words, 'differential treatment', very carefully. Oh, he got so mad. He started yelling, 'Are you calling me a racist?' And then [later] he tells everyone else in litigation that I said he was a racist and they all start acting weird—really nice, but really defensive . . . Suddenly, Bill who is like, you know, a cold fish, is like, saying hello all the time and telling me how he was really busy when I stopped by asking for advice. And, how he was really sorry if there was any misunderstanding. And by the way, did I know that he belongs to the ACLU? . . . And Ralph, kept saying over and over that he really forgot that lunch date with me, 'it doesn't have anything to do with [pause], you know . . .'

> *It doesn't have to do with the fact that you are African American?*
> Yeah, that's what he meant, but he wouldn't say it. So after that they all started doing it . . . And things just got weird. It seemed like either I did the wrong thing or people just reacted weirdly to me . . . And, so I decided to move on.

The stories the European American attorneys tell about Randall's career trajectory since he left the company as well as their professional interactions with him are quite different from his own. For example, Bill Fisher, a European American lawyer, said that Randall had 'cashed in on all the opportunities available for minorities' and had landed a much higher paying job at another firm. He also confided to me in his interview that he found Randall 'demanding' and 'abrasive' and doubted Randall's 'qualifications from the beginning', but hastened to add that 'this assessment has nothing to do with the fact that Randall is African American'. Other lawyers told me that Randall had taken a much better job somewhere else, though they could not tell me the name of the firm. One remarked that he knew Randall must be doing well because 'he's driving one of those BMW convertibles now' (Randall actually owned a Japanese economy car). Although they all agreed that Randall was a 'go getter', they joked among themselves about the way he dressed—'he's too flashy'—and complained about his requests for help—'he's too demanding'. For these white men each of whom has had two, maybe three interactions with Randall, the issue is one of style and personality and Randall just doesn't 'fit in'. He wears the wrong clothes, he says the wrong things, and he's much too obvious as a 'go getter'. For them, each individual meeting with Randall is an isolated incident.

Looking at the problem from the standpoint of the two groups—the perspective of the white male attorneys and Randall's perspective as one of the three African Americans—demonstrates that what looks 'individual' to members of a dominant group is often 'experienced as systematic bias by non-dominant group members'.[28] This helps to explain, in part, why many of the white men I interviewed claimed to be innocent of racism. They are 'innocent' in the sense that they are oblivious to the consequences of their actions. As individual white men, they simply do not experience the sum total of their actions toward Randall or their statements about him. Because they treat each meeting as an isolated incident, it is difficult for them to see how behavior such as making jokes or comments about Randall's style of dress can be construed as racist. They simply act out of a sense of their right to act. As a consequence, they fail to see how they participate collectively in constructing a hostile work environment.

Their explanation for Randall's experiences fits neatly within the framework of individualist thinking. The lawyers look at everything Randall does as an individual action, a product of 'free' choices, individual will, and hard work. Randall does not succeed, because he chose not to 'fit in', or as Bill contends because Randall lacks the qualifications to begin with. On the other hand, as a Black man in a predominantly white environment, Randall has a different understanding of the quotidian. He recognises *patterns* of behavior, rather than *individual* actions, and he sees how these patterned and systematic forms of exclusion create a hostile working environment for him as a token African American man. In this way, we can see how race shapes Randall's experiences of exclusion and marginalisation as a token Black man among his predominantly white and male co-workers.

4. 'NOT COMMITTED?'

Before the *Family and Medical Leave Act* became federal law in the United States in 1993, maternity leaves or, the more gender neutral term, parental leaves were not an option in most American workplaces.[29] With the advent of the *FMLA*, workplaces are now required to provide women and men six weeks of *unpaid* family leave from work for the birth of a new baby or a serious illness in the family. Furthermore, the Act guarantees that their job will be there when employees return from their leave. By contrast, European countries have had parental leaves for quite some time. In 1974, Sweden was the first to pass such

---

[28] L. Calvert and V. Simmons, 'Speaking as Female and White: A Non-dominant/Dominant group Standpoint' (1996) 3, 4 *Organization* at 470.
[29] M. Fried, *Taking Time: The Parental Leave Policy and Corporate Culture* (Philadelphia Temple University Press 1998).

legislation followed by other European countries in the mid-1980s and unlike
the United States, sixteen European nations and Canada provide an average of
thirty-three weeks of *paid* parental leave for women and men with new
infants.[30]

Of the two law firms in the San Francisco Bay Area that I studied in the late
1980s, one had a maternity leave policy, while the other did not. Even in the firm
where they had a formal policy, many women lawyers complained that while
men were able to obtain part-time work assignments for 'health reasons', they
were unable to work part-time *after* having their first baby. Sandi Brown, a
white woman lawyer and a single mother, confronted the managing partner
with this double-standard. He told her that 'the men had families to support'.
The other firm had no official maternity leave policy. 'They do it on a case by
case basis', explained Susan, a 31-year-old white women in her sixth month of
pregnancy. She added, 'I have no idea what's going to happen after I have the
baby. The management committee hasn't decided my case yet. I am facing this
big transition in my life, and I don't even know if I will have a job after I have
the baby'.[31]

Susan eventually left the firm after having her baby and when re-interviewed
in 1999, almost ten years later, she was working, like many other women
lawyers, as an attorney in the public sector. She describes her reasons for leaving her high-paid corporate position in litigation:

> I moved because the hours were just insane. There was incredible pressure to put in
> those hours, like you know, 60 hours a week. I was never home. I was always work-
> ing. I mean what kind of life is that? And, so few women made partner then. There
> were only two women partners in the entire department. What did that mean for me?
> Then, when I got pregnant, I started to seriously reevaluate my life. What's really
> important, you know? My career, my family, my friends? And, I could see how hard
> it would be to work full time after my daughter was born because, you know, the firm
> didn't have much of a maternity leave policy . . .
>
> And, anyway, I realized that I wasn't happy. I wanted to work and I wanted a fam-
> ily, but that just wasn't doable there . . . So, I came here. The work isn't all that inter-
> esting and I still work a lot. Sometimes, I work weekends, but I don't work sixty hour
> weeks anymore. The most is 50, and really that's pretty unusual. It's probably more
> like forty or forty-five. It's just a more humane kind of work schedule. So, I have time
> to spend with my daughter and with my husband. I have a more balanced life.

What is your salary like? Lawyers are usually paid less in the public sector.
Oh, yeah, it is a lot less money, but I also have more time.

---

[30] Commission of the European Communities, Childcare in European Communities, 1985–1990
(London, Commission of the European Communities, 1990); International Labor Office and
Women's Legal Defense Fund, Women at Work (Washington, D.C., 1988); P. Moss, *Childcare and
Equality of Opportunity, Consolidated Report of the European Childcare Network, EEC* (Brussels
European Commission 1988); K. Wever, 'The Family and Medical Leave Act: Assessing Temporary
Wage Replacement for Family and Medical Leave' (Cambridge Radcliffe Public Policy Institute
1996).
[31] Pierce, *supra* n. 13, at 112.

How would you characterize the policies for women and minorities in your work-place?
Well, I work for a federal agency, so affirmative action is the policy here for recruitment, hiring, and promotion. And, there's just a lot more women and minorities here [than in the private firm]. In fact, my former boss [in this department] whom I really liked was a woman. And that really makes a difference for things like mentoring . . . I mean it's not perfect. I still feel sometimes like there's pressure not to talk too much about my family at the office. Like if I need to leave early to take my daughter to the doctor or something like that, I usually say *I* have an appointment because there's still this idea that women put family before career, you know, women aren't *committed* to their jobs. So, yeah, I still worry about things like that. But, really that's more from the old guard, you know these older guys with the wives at home, they just don't get it (Author's italics).

In Susan's case, the long hours and the limited prospects for women in partnership were eventually what drove her to seek employment elsewhere. In the public sector, she found work, by her own admission much less well paid work, but she felt she was better able to balance her career with her family life though her worries about appearing to be committed to her job continued. In her earlier 1989 interview, she talked about how putting in long hours at the office was a way to demonstrate commitment.

It's really a macho thing, you know, all the guys sit around and brag about how many hours they put in, about their late nights and weekends in the office, pulling all nighters, and how many billable hours they have on their monthly time sheets, who had the most billable hours last month. So, there's like a culture of lots and lots of billable hours—long hours in the office . . . It's like there is always this suspicion that you aren't working hard enough, that you aren't really committed. And, I think that's especially something that women have to face because I mean, here I am six months pregnant and I know if I talk about taking maternity leave or getting part time work schedule or anything like that, the first thing the managing partner will say to me is 'Susan, are you committed to this job, because you know what we value is commitment'. I mean what am I supposed to do, file a brief while I deliver my baby?

Susan had more to say about the meaning of commitment at work in her most recent interview:

We were interviewing several people for the job and one of them was a woman. They [the hiring committee] kept asking about her over and over, 'But do you think she's really committed?' I finally said 'What about these guys [who were being interviewed], what about them, do you think they're really committed?' Everyone got real quiet. And, I think they got my point, that you know, that they were assuming that women are less committed than men. So, yeah, it's still there. It's still there all the time.

In her study of a large corporation with family friendly policies in Boston, sociologist Mindy Fried describes what she calls an 'overtime work culture'.[32]

---

[32] M. Fried, *Taking Time: The Parental Leave Policy and Corporate Culture* (Philadelphia Temple University Press 1998) at 1.

Employees were expected to put in long hours at the office and those who did not adhere to this norm were viewed as less committed to their jobs. Despite the fact that policies were specifically designed to be flexible to the needs of families, most women and men in upper management did not take advantage of flexible hours, part-time work options, or family leaves because they knew they would appear to be less committed which in turn might jeopardise salary increases, promotions, and with downsizing, conceivably, their jobs. As one mother and middle manager said: 'It's always the women who take off . . . so just going out to have the baby, people think [that] takes away from your job, [and they think] the commitment you have to give to your family also takes you away from your job'.[33] Such a workplace culture and its consequences are not unique. In another study, an employee of a large corporation reports:

> The culture is that you get credit for long hours . . . There is no forty-hour week; if you are not doing at least fifty, you are not a team player. It's a sign of dedication, [and it] doesn't matter if there's work to do . . . If there are two people of equal performance the promotion will go to the one who has put in the overtime.[34]

Like Fried, this scholar also found that employees felt pressured not to work shorter hours or to take parental leaves. In her popular and influential book *Time Bind*, Arlie Hochschild discovered similar problems for employees, particularly women, who want to take time off from work in her research on a large New York-based corporation.[35] And, Cynthia Fuchs Epstein and her colleagues' recent study of women lawyers who work part-time in order to better balance family and career found that these women are taken less seriously in their professional lives because they are seen as less committed than their male counterparts.[36]

What these studies suggest is that the meanings attached to gender play a significant role in shaping how women are viewed by their employers. For many employers, women are regarded as mothers—whether they are actually mothers or not—and mothers, they assume, will put family before career. For such employers, 'not committed' becomes a shorthand expression for their gendered assumptions about the relationship between women, work, and family. It is the woman lawyer interviewed for the job whose commitment is questioned, as Susan reminds us, not the men's. Although the one man who takes advantage of family leave in Hochschild's study is regarded suspiciously by some (after all this is not the behaviour of a typical male) it is not until he takes the leave that others begin to ask questions about his commitment. In other words, he does not enter the workplace facing the same kinds of assumptions about his commitment to work that women do.

---

[33] M. Fried, *Taking Time: The Parental Leave Policy and Corporate Culture* (Philadelphia Temple University Press 1998), at. 53.

[34] L. Bailyn, *Breaking the Mold: Women, Men, and Time in the New Corporate World* (New York Free Press 1993) at 81.

[35] A. Hochschild, *The Time Bind* (New York Vintage Books 1997).

[36] C. Epstein, C. Seron, B. Oglensky, and R. Saute, *The Part Time Paradox* (New York Routledge 1999).

According to the majority of white men who remained in the legal department, Susan left for 'family reasons'. One, in particular, spoke in derogatory terms about her pregnancy: 'Here she was wondering around the office eight months pregnant, talking to clients, going to court . . . It just didn't look good. You always have to wonder what comes first for *women like that*, their career or their family' (emphasis in original). A few mentioned that she couldn't take the 'high pressure' of the big firm. As the managing partner told me, 'Susan was really a good lawyer. She went to Stanford, I think, and she wrote good briefs, but I just don't think she was tough enough to take the pressure'.

Interestingly, though these men doubted Susan's commitment to the job—the very criticism she herself feared—they did not call her qualifications into question. In fact, most of the lawyers I interviewed told me that Susan was a good lawyer. If anything, she was regarded by many in her office as highly qualified because she received her law degree from Stanford, an elite private university, whereas most of the lawyers in her office got their degrees from less prestigious, local night schools. Like Randall, she had to contend with being the member of a numerical minority in her first job in the litigation department. And, like Randall, Susan recognised the difficulties of being a token achiever. However, the meanings attributed to Susan and Randall's work are quite different. Whereas Susan struggles with the challenge of being seen as 'not committed' and 'not tough enough', Randall is considered 'unqualified', 'too flashy', and 'overly aggressive'. What this suggests is that even though Black men and white women may both be tokens numerically in their respective jobs, they will be evaluated differently because 'Blackness' and 'femininity' mean different things in American culture. As Randall himself observes, 'minority equals affirmative action hire equals unqualified', a recognition that the term 'unqualified' has become a racialised, derogatory shorthand expression for the relationship between Black men and work, just as 'not committed' expresses a gendered cultural understanding of the relationship between women, work, and family. Given this cultural logic, it is not surprising that no one doubts Randall's commitment. He is, after all, a man. Conversely, no one doubts Susan's qualifications because Susan is white and whiteness is associated with a multitude of personal and social privileges, including entitlement to respectful treatment in social interactions, a good education, a good standard of living, and property in the United States.[37]

5. CONCLUSION

These personal narratives demonstrate how race and gender as systems of stratification intersect in ways that present different life opportunities for each

---

[37] G. Lipsitz, *The Possessive Investment in Whiteness* (Philadelphia Temple University Press 1998); C. Harris, 'Whiteness as Property', (1993) 106, 8 *Harvard Law Review* at 1709–91; D. Roediger, *The Wages of Whiteness* (New York Verso 1991).

individual. Racial status as white and occupational status as a lawyer grant Susan numerous advantages in her life, though her gender disadvantages her in some ways professionally. As a lawyer and as a man Randall enjoys modest financial success, but as an African American he faces discrimination. In addition, these case studies show that race and gender are not only systems of stratification, but categories animated by a cultural logic that provides particular meanings in the lives of each of these people. In other words, the intersection of race, class and gender do not merely represent fixed positions within a 'matrix of domination'[38] determining life chances, but these categories also bear cultural meanings in a particular historical time and place for a particular individual. If we lived in a culture where Blacks were not assumed to be poor workers and women were not assumed to put family before career, no one would question Randall's qualifications or Susan's commitment to her work.

Significantly, the language of choice, commitment and qualifications that I have described also fits neatly within Americans' larger cultural ideology of individualism.[39] The underlying assumption of individualist thinking is that we can make choices about what kind of career we want to pursue, the professional school we hope to attend, or the number of hours we dedicate to work. By utilising this language, individuals like Randall and Susan are blamed when they don't succeed, rather than the institutions and social processes which exclude their participation. Furthermore, American professional worlds are so infused with this discursive understanding, that it is difficult for individuals to find appropriate language when they have encountered discrimination. Consequently, as sociologist Susan Chase[40] found in her study of women school superintendents, though many women experienced sex or race discrimination in their professional lives, they were unable to convey what had happened to them within the cultural logic of individualist thinking—except in very halting and awkward terms. For Chase, this 'halting language' reflects a larger tension in American cultural life between individualist ideals and the reality of material inequality and discrimination.

These findings have important theoretical and practical implications. Theoretically, this study demonstrates how an intersectional approach improves upon approaches which consider either race or gender. Research that has considered how organisational logics are gendered[41] misses the subtleties and nuances that a raced and gendered approach provides. For instance, while gender appears to be most salient in Susan's experiences as a lawyer, whiteness as an invisible normative shield also provides additional privilege and status

---

[38] P. Collins, *Black Feminist Thought* (New York Routledge 1990).

[39] R. Bellah, R. Madsen, W. Sullivan, A. Swidler, and S. Tipton, *Habits of the Heart: Individualism and Commitment in American Life* (Berkeley University of California Press 1985).

[40] S. Chase, *Ambiguous Empowerment* (Amherst University of Massachusetts Press 1995).

[41] J. Acker, 'Hierarchies, Jobs, Bodies: A Theory of Gendered Organizations' (1990) 4, 2 *Gender & Society* at 139–158; D. Britton, 'Gendered Organizational Logic: Policy and Practice in Men's and Women's Prisons' (1997) 11,6 *Gender & Society* at 796–818.

that buffer her from the pejorative meanings that are attributed to Randall's qualifications. The privileges and status conferred by race in American society are what historian David Roediger has called 'the wages of whiteness'.[42] For Roediger, whiteness is not simply an identity, but an aspect of unequal structural relations in society which benefit white Americans and disadvantage people of colour. Future research needs to consider the ways whiteness interacts and intersects with masculinity and femininity to reproduce and mask gender and racial inequality in American workplaces.

Finally, this study has important policy implications. The current backlash against affirmative action and the arguments made by conservatives that race (or gender) no longer matter play a central role in current policy debates in the United States. By contrast, this research shows that race and gender *continue* to *matter* in professional contexts such as the legal profession. Moreover, it demonstrates that race and gender matter in *distinctive* ways. The fact that African American men are regarded as 'not qualified' and white women are seen as 'not committed' suggests that affirmative action policies and programs need to consider the ways these seemingly neutral terms are applied in racially and gender specific ways. In other words, policies must give more attention to the *coded ways* that racial and gender specific forms of stereotyping and discrimination persist.

---

[42] D. Roediger, *The Wages of Whiteness* (New York Verso 1991).

9

Putting Gender and Sexuality on the Agenda: Queer Theory and Legal Politics

NICO J. BEGER

IN THE LAST 30 years Europe has seen the rise of social movements fighting nationally and transnationally for participation rights in society. Minority rights and identity related rights have consequently become an important aspect of legal studies. Gay, lesbian, bisexual, and transgender rights movements are one example of these increasing legal demands. In addition—particularly in the wake of the AIDS crisis—sexuality has become central to modern politics in general. Academic theorists have increasingly paid attention to the epistemological and ontological roles gender and sexuality play in the creation and maintenance of political, social, economic, and legal domains. However, in the daily process of arguing for and about rights the centrality of those roles is mostly hidden from view in official legal discourses. In this chapter I seek to trace gender and sexuality as central markers of the juridical in European legal traditions. To assess this centrality, I analyse the connections between equality and the hegemony of the juridical. I, then, proceed to introduce queer theory as an important critique of traditional rights politics paying specific attention to 'queer law' as one of the more recent critical approaches to legal studies.

The conventions of identity-based rights politics dominate the field of minority movements and the official politics of governments in relation to issues of social justice, equality, and anti-discrimination. In the history of lesbian and gay movements, change of the status quo through reform—social and legal—has always been the most successful rallying point of mobilisation. The first phase related and relates usually to a de-criminalisation of homosexual (male) offences, age of consent, sodomy laws and other coercive state practices, such as police harassment, neglect to prosecute hate crimes, and rights of speech and assembly. The second phase was and is usually a shift from 'keeping the state off

[1] The principal contents of this chapter have been published in different chapters of Beger, 'Que(e)rying Political Practices in Europe' in *Tensions in the Struggle for Sexual Minority Rights* (Berlin CopyPrint 2001).

our backs' to a rights movement that demands partnership rights and positive re-enforcement in employment, as well as social and legal protection from all forms of discrimination. For European gay and lesbian movements today both of these phases are still current in various regions of the geographic continent of Europe. None of these demands, from simple de-criminalisation to gay and lesbian marriage or adoption has become entirely obsolete in any European country.

The achievement of reform in the social, legal, political, and economic domains is doing more than encourage gays, lesbians, bisexual and trans-gendered people to 'come out'. The struggle for these rights has promoted a feeling of pride, self-worth, public subculture, and community identity. It has also produced a politicising process that facilitates public awareness, mobilisa-tion, and the development of a specific gay, lesbian, and bisexual as well as transgender practice and theory. While this holds true, to my mind an unquali-fied praise of rights and reform is questionable without analysing the status quo of gender and sexuality as ordering principles. For lesbians and gay men, legal rights and lobby politics have, on the one hand, won rights of survival, expression and social acceptance. On the other hand it is precisely those identity-based politics which have created problems for the inclusion and accep-tance of alternative sexualities into a norm(ality) that is ultimately set up to signify and exclude difference.

In response to this insight, activists in the USA developed a form of queer pol-itics in the early nineties.[2] At the same time theorists in the field of sexuality and gender in many countries started to use post-structuralist thought to investigate the epistemological, ontological, legal, economic and social conditions of identity-based rights politics and movements. The focus shifted away from chal-lenges to political or legal rules and moved towards challenges of analytic cat-egories and explanatory systems in politics. To be precise, they moved towards the way gender and sexuality are psychologically and socially realised and main-tained in a hierarchical order in the first place. Following ideas coming from the field of literary and film studies, a substantial set of philosophical, sociological, political and legal writings has arisen, in which the connection between theory and practice—an issue at the forefront of gay, lesbian, bisexual, and transgen-der studies[3]—is questioned. What becomes clear from the literature is that let-ting go of legal rights and equality entirely will not do; but taking them for granted and as unquestionable will not do either. What concerns me here, there-fore, is promoting the ability of legal studies to deploy a queer analysis of the gendered and sexualised implications of rights, equality, and justice.

---

[2] See L. Berlant and E. Freeman, 'Queer Nationality' (1992) 2 *Boundary* at 150–180.

[3] I have explored the consequences of this connection and the debate for and against queer theory in Beger, 'Mind the Gap: Hybridity and the Antagonistic Relations of Queer Theory and Gay/Lesbian Political Practice' in Neef and Goggin (eds.) *Travelling Concepts. Text, Subjectivity, and Hybridity* (Amsterdam ASCA Press 2001) at 145–158.

1. EQUALITY AND THE HEGEMONY OF THE JURIDICAL

Social movements claim rights—positive and negative rights—by an allegation of specific, but widespread, forms of discrimination that persist throughout Europe. The European branch of the International Lesbian and Gay Association (ILGA-Europe), which enjoys consultative status with the Council of Europe and its European Court of Human Rights, once addressed the Parliamentary Assembly of the Council of Europe in 1999 with a comprehensive discrimination report. The report was introduced like this:

> On the threshold of a new millennium it is manifestly necessary that the Parliamentary Assembly again assert the right of lesbian, gay and bisexual persons to freedom from discrimination as an expression of the fundamental principle of equality and recommends actions to governments and the Council of Europe that could help finally bring to an end hundreds of years of persecution and intolerance.

This formulation is a good example of the way in which legal change—in this case anti-discrimination laws—are demanded. The formulation 'to end hundreds of years of persecution and intolerance' 'on the threshold of a new millennium' makes use of the successful shift of boundaries within legal liberal constructions of homosexuality. In Europe the gay and lesbian movement has achieved a conceptual move 'from the "deviant and dangerous offender", to the "minority" subject of human rights protection, to the "spousal" recipient of social benefits previously available only to heterosexual couples'.[4]

The wish to 'end hundreds of years of persecution and intolerance' and the address to equality as a fundamental principle of the identity of the Council of Europe, is clearly an appeal to liberal legal ideology. The discourse of liberal legal equality in European democracies inhabits an authoritative dominance within European institutions to the extent of excluding or marginalising other possible concepts of equality from debate. This liberal legal ideology of equality—strongly bound to the principle of human rights—produces a consensus within which lesbian and gay equality is defined and permitted to some extent.

The appeal to the liberal legal tradition of European institutions in political practices that utilise a language of discrimination is firmly connected to a hope of progress and future change. 'On the threshold of a new millennium' hundreds of years of discrimination can be ended through anti-discrimination legislation. This quest for anti-discrimination legislation is premised upon a particular understanding of society: namely that it contains a variety of diverse minority-like populations, each of which suffers a kind of antiquated prejudice no longer tolerable in liberal democracies. The state or the pan-European institution then acts as a neutral protector, facilitating the eradication of what is

---

[4] D. Herman, *Rights of Passage: Struggles for Lesbian and Gay Legal Equality* (Toronto University of Toronto Press 1994) at 8.

seen to be *individual* aberrations through the passage and enforcement of anti-discrimination measures. The hope of progress and change, which forms the central theme of arguments for rights legislation, is based on a set of concrete visions of change. The law and the state are, then, addressed as the most significant agents of political and social change. This address and the logic of hope affirm the political hegemony of the juridical.

When I speak of the juridical here, I mean to imply the discursive structure of social-legal regulation: everything that belongs to the discursive institutional processes of regulating and maintaining power over societies as sets of social networks. This includes concrete practices of institutions such as the law and the legal arena. The latter contains law-making bodies, courts, lawyers, and legal documents, as well as the discursive order of legality in parliamentary democracies in Europe. The juridical adds the ideological and discursive structures that assign power and truth to these institutions and maintain their rank of superior opinion. The juridical is, therefore, more than the written law and more than the practices of court rooms: it extends into the political and into the way individuals understand themselves as members of a social community, as well as into the mechanisms, the histories, the predicaments, and the workings of rights within democracies. The law itself is structured in its very existence by this ideological support from the juridical. It is the juridicial that assigns the law a certain singular power to define and speak with physical consequence.[5]

However, the rules of the juridical are a historical fact not a philosophical absolute nor a tangible entity. They are a discursive relational and contextual practice that takes shape in opposition to whatever is locally and ideologically conceived as the public and as the political. In European cultures the juridical ideologically grants liberal freedom, fitted to an economic order in which property and citizenship are not equally distributed, and this freedom is conveyed by rights against arbitrary state power, on one side, and against anarchic civil society or property theft, on the other.[6]

Through the address to the state and the law, the juridical becomes the dominant and central discursive site to effectively speak about discrimination as political capital and the site to receive alleviation. This dominance is maintained by the institutional prerogative concerning speech and silence. The law can serve to command speech and to preserve the ontological comforts of silence.[7] The power to apply both tactics, that of speech and that of silence, is a power that those who speak within the legal arena receive through the historical hegemony of the juridical in the politics of modern democracies. Both these tactics are the means to draw important distinctions between courts and publics. That

---

[5] R. Cover, 'Violence and the Word' (1986) 95 *The Yale Law Journal* at 1595, 1601–1629, 1611.
[6] W. Brown, *States of Injury. Power and Freedom in Late Modernity* (Princeton Princeton Paperbacks 1995) at 6.
[7] J. Goldberg-Hiller, 'Entitled to be Hostile: Narrating the Political Economy of Civil Rights' (1998) 7 *Social & Legal Studies* at 517–538, 521.

has significance for the question whether discrimination is acceptable, indeed whether it exists as a recognisable structure at all, and whether the dominance of the definitional power of the juridical, and thus its political hegemony, can be maintained or not.

This means that any legal interpretation is not only practical, but is a practice in itself in that the institutional context—and Foucault might add, the historical claim to ultimate truth that characterises the law—ties the language act of practical understanding to the physical acts of others in a predictable, though not logically necessary way.[8] The power and violence of the word spoken, or not spoken within law-making institutions and court rooms, is the essence of maintaining the prerogative of political definition. Any political practice that addresses the law—that speaks and claims consequential speech to be made on somebody's behalf—needs to locate itself somewhere within the juridical and its hegemonic discourses of institutional power and intelligible difference. No political practice can remain outside the hegemony of the juridical if it wants to address law.

As one significant part of the juridical, the legal arena is an obvious target of political negotiation about difference. In European cultures and modern democracies, the law functions as assurance of individual and property rights as well as ordering the duties of social belonging. For this reason 'lesbian and gay rights movements, from their inception, have engaged in legal struggle partly on the basis of what changes in legal provision *signify* more generally'.[9] Didi Herman names the defeat of bigotry and the moral majority, safety to come out, feelings of self-worth, citizenship, and community identity as themes that are seen to be influenced by legal changes. The legal arena is, thus, said to provide a space for negotiating which differences are genuine and, hence, acceptable reasons for differentiation in treatment.

The logic of hope and change is, therefore, seemingly a realistic logic in the European political climate. The hegemony of the juridical promises that equal treatment in law will reap rewards on an ideological and a material level. This promise is part of how the juridical is maintained as hegemonic. The first step the logic of hope and change takes is to assure equal treatment in law. In order to make discrimination visible and understood as such, comparisons are needed. In legal discourse, discrimination occurs where one person who does not share one particular feature is treated unfavourably, all other aspects being the same. Discrimination is most commonly written and spoken about in personal testimony and numbers, i.e. evidence of discrimination is supported as much as possible by a combination of personal witness, reviews of mainstream human rights organisations, academic assessment, existing judgements and statistical proof. Discrimination is rendered factual in that it contains a truth claim. That truth claim is maintained through a reference to the principle of equality and the

---

[8] Cover, *supra* n. 5 at 1611.
[9] Herman, *supra* n. 4 at 4.

seemingly agreed upon common sense judgement about what differentiation should be acceptable and what differentiation should not.

The definition of acceptability, however, is a central part of what counts as normal in any given legal context that assesses the social domain. Therefore, an investigation of the ways in which something is deemed normal or acceptable is strongly needed. Queer theory, in the field of gender and sexuality studies, is one important way of addressing the regime of the normal in its consequence for the legal realm.

2. QUEER THEORY

Queer is an old and also quite recent phenomenon in gay, lesbian, bisexual, and transgender (l/g/b/t) contexts. It has been a slang term for homosexuals while also being used as a form of homophobic abuse. Since about 1990 queer has become an umbrella term for all sorts of things: a substitute for gay and lesbian, a descriptive term for all unruly sexualities, the hip title, noun, verb, or adjective for everything in relation to gays, lesbians, bisexuals, and transgender people, for example, journals, parties, demonstrations, politics. It is fundamentally connected to AIDS activism and has become the infamous name of the ACT UP spin-off QUEER NATION as well.[10] While being all these things, queer has also turned into the brand name for numerous new academic theories and practices of writing.[11] The queer community is, so to speak, an oxymoronic community of difference.[12] The term carries with it an excess of meanings, which it can never fully recognise or fulfil. By the end of the decade, it seems as if the layers of complication in attempting to define queer as a political or a theoretical concept are never ending; the more the term spreads, the more it becomes *something*, the less anybody can define it. And alongside its abundance of meaning, it is also a profoundly Anglo-American term that has become common currency in many international l/g/b/t cultures without ever taking on board all its Anglo-American contents, while at the same time being enriched by new meanings in different language contexts.

However, for the sake of clarity, the usage of the term queer in an academic context should not be left unexplained. The term queer is best used in this context to demarcate a specific form of theoretical thinking that has implications for legal politics. It should not be applied to describe an identity, a subculture, or a specific form of radical activism. In fact, to my mind, queer as an identity

---

[10] ACT-UP is an activist group founded in the US, campaigning for radical AIDS politics. It has become famous for explicitly addressing sexuality and race in relation to AIDS. ACT-UP has sister groups in different European countries. Queer Nation was a splinter group that formed itself, in the US only, in response to the marginalisation of gay men in ACT-UP.

[11] M. Warner, 'From Queer to Eternity: An Army of Theorists Cannot Fail' (1992) 106 June *The Village Voice Literary Supplement* at 18–19, 18.

[12] L. Duggan, 'Making it perfectly Queer' (1992) 22 *Socialist Review* at 11–31, 19.

makes little sense whatsoever, even if queer is understood to reach far beyond gay, lesbian, bisexual, and transgender communities. In common language use throughout Europe, queer has become a substitute term for gay and lesbian, and sometimes it functions as the umbrella term for the l/g/b/t connection. While I firmly believe in the connection between gay and lesbian issues and transgender issues, I see no need to assign a new identity to that connection. A new identity suggests a form of sameness that has already been destabilised for gay men or lesbians as a group from the vantage point of gender, race, class, or culture. Experience in Europe shows that the label queer, as an identity, more often than not only functions as a substitute for gay. In that way it marginalises lesbians once again, and does not even consider bisexuals or transgendered people, nor is it capable of addressing the intersections among homosexuality, gender, race, and class that are so relevant for critical law. While I hesitantly, and with a constant sense of trouble, continue to use the terms gay men and lesbians—since they continuously carry linguistic relevancy in a legal context—I never use queer as an identification for a group of people.

Michael Warner once called queer theory 'a largely intuitive and half-articulate theory' that, for him and Lauren Berlant, barely existed in 1995.[13] Indeed, the first time it was used academically was in 1991 by Teresa de Lauretis in the infamous 1991 issue of *Differences: A Journal of Feminist Cultural Studies*. Yet, by 1995, Linda Nicholson and Steven Seidman had also already offered a tenable summary of queer theory:

> Queer theory shifts the center of analysis from viewing homosexuality as a minority identity to a cultural figure. The hetero/homo binary is imagined, parallel to the masculine/feminine trope, as a symbolic code structured into the texts of daily life, from popular culture . . . to disciplinary knowledges, law, therapeutic practices, criminal justice, and state policies. It frames the way we know and organize personal and social experience, with the effect of reproducing heteronormativity. Queer theory aims to expose the operation of the hetero/homo code in the center of society and to contribute to destabilizing its operation.[14]

Concepts of queer, thus, are at their best where they defy definition and where they concentrate on disruptions of the normal—the normal being male, heterosexual, white, bourgeois, but also normal business in the academy or taken-for-granted gay and lesbian identity politics. Queer theory has no stable referential content and pragmatic force. However, when reading legal texts through a queer-theoretical glass, I follow Seidman and Nicholson's path of assuming gender and sexuality to be a binary, hierarchised structure firmly embedded in European political orders. In fact, gender and sexuality are assumed to be a decisive frame

---

[13] Warner, *supra* n.12 at 19; L. Berlant and M. Warner 'What does Queer Theory teach us about X?' (1995) 110 *PMLA: Publications of the Modern Languages Association of America* at 343–349, 343.
[14] L. Nicholson and S. Seidman, *Social Postmodernism: Beyond Identity Politics* (Cambridge Cambridge University Press 1995) at 18.

of all political orders that influence legal procedure, be they in law-making or in court rooms. Although these assumptions have been thoroughly argued by feminist researchers over decades, they are not self-evident to the extent that they need no clarification.

Provisionally, queer theory could be characterised as framed by post-structuralism, or postmodernism. As such, it works from the vantage point of discourse as the meaning-creating system, which pre-exists and, consequently, shapes and signifies the formation of subject positions, identity, and, indeed, reality. Queer theory, thus, maps an unstable, non-essentialist, non-transparent or non-coherent, and anti-humanist understanding of sexuality and gender identity. Queer theory is fundamentally a critique of identity. Accordingly, queer as a theory emerged out of 'access to the post-structuralist theorisation of identity as provisional and contingent, coupled with a growing awareness of the limitations of identity categories in terms of political representation'.[15]

Post-structuralism itself is not a monolithic bloc or a fixed school of thought either, but a re-definable and fluid set of understandings, a practice and process of theorising.

> Rather, 'post-structuralism' indicates a field of critical practices that cannot be total-ized and that, therefore, interrogates the formative and exclusionary power of dis-course in the construction of sexual difference. This interrogation does not take for granted the meanings of any terms or analytic categories, including its own. . . . Poststructuralism is not, strictly speaking, a position, but rather a critical interroga-tion of the exclusionary operations by which 'positions' are established.[16]

Consequently, post-structuralist critiques are not new in themselves, but draw on what has been discursively produced about identities. They, thus, form an identity critique in the sense of destabilising the one most naturalised cultural category each of us inhabits: the sense of oneself as being *something*, belonging to a certain defined group, in fact, the very sense of human existence *as some-thing*. And that something is in its primary principle male or female; gender is the first category each human is assigned at birth.[17] Gender is very obviously a central mark of being human.

Queer theory emphasises that there is no such thing as a universal gender identity. According to Madan Sarup[18], every person's identity is a site of strug-gle between conflicting discourses. Sarup draws—as does queer theory in gen-eral—on a Foucaldian concept of discourse that led to the disruption of natural, universal identities. Joan Scott summarised this concept of discourse as

---

[15] A. Jagose, *Queer Theory: An Introduction* (New York London Routledge 1996) at 77.

[16] J. Butler and J. Scott, *Feminists Theorize the Political* (New York Routledge 1992) at xiii/xiv.

[17] Wherever that is not possible—such as in the case of intersexuals—clear gender assignment is forced into existence through mutilating operations and compulsory hormone treatment for infants in all European countries.

[18] M. Sarup, *Identity, Culture and the Postmodern World* (Edinburgh Edinburgh University Press 1996) at 73.

. . . any system—strictly verbal or other—through which meaning is constructed and cultural practices organized and by which accordingly, people represent and understand their world, including who they are and how they relate to others.[19]

According to Scott, the analysis of discourse then provides a starting point for conceptualising how social relations are understood, how they work, how they are institutionalised and how collective identities are established. This is an understanding of discourse as the fundamental place in which social relations are formed, defined, and contested. Individual subjectivity and identity are located and constructed in culturally, socially, and historically specific ways in discourse.

Individuals do not create or contest meaning as unified, autonomous subjects from an essential human core, but always from already being positioned in several discourses. This does not mean that discourses are constructed outside of actual relations and then placed on passive individuals. The meanings constructed by discourses are in fact created, used, and contested by all participants who are in different ways located in them. Even members of strongly marginalised groups are not simply passive recipients of a dominant discursive meaning about them. In fact, queer challenges the story of marginalisation as a weak trope even if it produces a story of struggle and oppression itself. Queer theory moves instead into the central production site of cultures and asserts centrality for the queer subject.

However, this does not mean that all individuals have the same access to influencing the establishment of meanings that become dominant. For gays, lesbians, bisexuals, and transgendered people it is crucial to understand that, while we actively participate in the constitution of discursive meaning, the organisation of social relations extends beyond individuals. Therefore, while, for example, white women are actively involved in relations and practices, their interpretation of events has not got the same power of influence for creating dominant meaning as white men's. And further, the discrepancies in access to social space and power do not always provide the possibilities for creating non-dominant interpretations in the first place. This understanding is based, yet again, on the Foucaldian concept of power. According to David Evans, Foucault's concept of power is

an all pervasive, normative, and positive presence, internalised by and thus creating, the subject. Indeed, the subject seems not to exist outside of immanent patterns of normative knowledge derived from language, objects and practices, i.e. discourses. 'Subjectivity' in the Foucaldian sense is always discursive, it refers to general subject positions, conceived as empty spaces or functions occupied by particular individuals in the pronouncement of specific statements. We are what we learn, internalise and reproduce as knowledge and the language through which it is understood. We are subjects of the power immanently installed in that knowledge.[20]

[19] J. Scott, *Gender and the Politics of History* (New York Columbia University Press 1988) at 254.
[20] D. Evans, *Sexual Citizenship: The Material Construction of Sexualities* (London Routledge 1993) at 11.

As Michel Foucault elaborated extensively in his *History of Sexuality, The Archaeology of Knowledge,* and *Discipline and Punish,* his theory of power was simultaneously a definition of how the subject comes into being as, foremost, a sexual subject, who considers sexuality the most essential, but hidden secret of its being. According to Foucault, European history shows how the sexual subject of modern societies was constructed out of an obsessive pursuit of ever greater knowledge about the subject's innermost selves—its bio-power—a secret to be discovered everywhere.[21] Gender and sexuality became the most pervasive form of identification in modern regimes, a fact which—ironically— apparently evades discursive interpretation through its stringent claim to eternal truth. The history of sexuality, in consequence, became a subject of academic research, largely through the circulation of Foucault's work by feminists and gay and lesbian authors.[22] It is the insight into the centrality of sexuality for the creation of subjectivity that makes queer theory challenge 'the regime of sexuality itself, that is, the knowledges that construct the self as sexual and that assume heterosexuality and homosexuality as categories marking the truth of sexual selves.'[23] The same insight is the reason why 'queer theory aspires to transform homosexual theory into a general social theory or one standpoint from which to analyze social dynamics'.[24]

This aspiration is intended as a critical intervention into heteronormativity. Heteronormativity is a central term within queer theory. It is based upon understanding sexuality as more than just the effect of cultural or discursive practice or merely the product of ideology or institutions. Rather sexuality is 'a regulatory apparatus that spans the organisation of social life in the modern world and that works in concert with other social totalities—capitalism, patriarchy, colonialism'.[25] As a regulatory apparatus, sexuality is not universal and equally valued in all its expressions, but it functionalises heterosexuality to occupy the centre of human sexuality and gender relations. Through thematising heteronormativity rather than heterosexuality, queer theory uncovers the institutional powers of certain discourses that organise more than just the sexual.[26] According to Corinna Genschel, queer analysis is directed against those systems of thought and those institutions which insist on the naturalness, the binding nature, and the pre-condition of heterosexuality, just as feminists have shown how terms such as morality, rationality or the public sphere are deeply dependent on gender. Thus, it is the normative ordering force of (hetero)sexuality which comes under critique, not practices of heterosexuality per se. This marks queer theory's distance from any notions of essential gayness or lesbianism.

---

[21] M. Foucault, *The History of Sexuality vol. I: An Introduction* (New York Vintage 1980) at 54.
[22] Duggan, *supra* n. 13 at 22.
[23] S. Seidman (ed.) *Queer Theory/Sociology* (Cambridge Mass. Blackwell 1996) at 12.
[24] Seidman, *supra* n. 27 at 13.
[25] R. Hennessy, 'Queer Visibility in Commodity Culture' (1995) 94/95 *Cultural Critique* at 31–76, 70.
[26] C. Genschel, 'Fear of a Queer Planet: Dimensionen lesbisch-schwuler Gesellschaftskritik' (1996) 216 *Das Argument* at 525–538, 528–529.

Some of the best research in gender and sexuality has demonstrated how normative discourses interpellate individuals into hegemonic social orders that produce the subjects of gender and the trajectory of their desire. These studies show how socially mediated discursive technologies inlay into psyche and corporeal reality the structures of corporeal rules—such as proper and improper gender identity—and the linguistic features that form a social register, which often presents the only social space for speech. The rules and features of human identity—foremost gender, sexuality, and race—compose the personal grammar that every subject has, and this grammar, unperceived, migrates with persons as they enter and transgress public and intimate spheres, orienting their expectations and demands. Rights struggles are a form of public demand in which the rules of gender and sexuality are prominent and easily traceable. Hence, the examination of competing political discourses and of particular individuals' and groups' participation in the creation, affirmation, or contestation of actual social and material relations on the official political stage, is an investigation into the very conditions of the social and the political per se. It is one of the reasons that traditional legal rights and lobby politics make such suitable material for tracing the conditions and the nature of the political (sexual) subject endowed with human rights in European democracies.

There is no high queer theory whose conditions remain stable while politics are analysed through it. Rather, the combination of the terms queer and theory in academia during the last ten years expresses a clear will to academic power, renders central what is deemed marginal and questions the stability of knowledge productions that are contained in the normative binary gender order. That project includes normal business in what counts as academic theory.[27] Thus, queer theory cannot remain aloof from that which it observes. The sovereign epistemic agent, ie the theorist, cannot assume an autonomous position as a master of the social, cultural, economic, or political relations theoretically analysed. Queer theory cannot be thought without a connection to the world outside of theory—theory and the political form an inseparable bond. Therefore, queer theory has specific consequences in different cultural contexts as well as in different academic disciplines and modes of inquiry. A queer approach to critical legal studies is, thus, a specific endeavour that cannot ignore the tradition of legal analysis nor the language of the law.

3. QUEER LAW

The law is an important site of struggle in activism for rights. Yet, it is also a site to which political participation and rights have often been reduced and which, in turn, presents a nearly hegemonic signifier of what is understood to be liberation, progress, and success in the history of lesbian and gay rights struggles.

---

[27] Warner, *supra* n. 12 at 18.

Law is more than the texts of treaties, directives and codes. Through its reference to the juridical it includes the discursive logic of ordering social, economical and political relations and of what subjects and societies *are* before the law. The question of how the juridical maintains its hegemonic position in the field of civil and individual rights, and how dominant forms of political practices are so inextricably interwoven with the juridical are questions I explored above. Here I will introduce the direction legal studies have taken and ought to take in the future to incorporate the insights of queer theory and legal politics as the production sites of gendered and sexual meaning.

Critical and feminist jurisprudence has placed race, gender, and sexuality at the centre of defining legal discourses, the constitution of the law, and practices in court rooms. Adding to this analysis, queer legal theorists have contributed another critical observation: the legal realm has been described as fundamentally heterosexual in that it is based on heteronormative discourses that essentialise sexual identities.[28] According to many queer legal theorists, the legal realm essentialises homosexuality, creates the subjects it needs to govern and is, thus, a major force in maintaining the privilege of heterosexuality.[29] Nevertheless, while the law plays a role in the regulation of sexuality, the processes of courtrooms can also inadvertently produce ungovernable pluralities.[30] The legal realm is not simply seen as the site of dominant and exclusionary regulation, but can potentially produce an entry point of challenge and change.

Thus, the complex political significance of the legal realm as a major site of rights movements needs to be investigated alongside the double-edged possibilities that realm contains. This means that the importance of legal battles is not denied from a queer theoretical perspective, but rather specifically and locally examined for the dilemma legal politics produce: a dilemma whose tensions are simultaneously irresolvable and productive. Both those aspects are part of most legal proceedings, which I have shown in specific examples from the European Court of Justice elsewhere.[31] The regulations of gender and sexuality and their hegemonic dominance present an irresolvable tension in the achievement of real equality. But when equality is legally negotiated there are always culturally productive elements at play that depend on how much the fundamental connections of gender and sexuality can be rendered legally understandable.

Legislation that regulates gender and/or sexuality does not generally attempt to offer any real definition of sex, man or woman. Yet, any effective functioning of legislation depends on them having a clear meaning. The mapping of the law rests on two assumptions: there are two types of human bodies, and two distinct

---

[28] J. Halley, 'The Construction of Heterosexuality' in Warner (ed.) *Fear of a Queer Planet: Queer Politics and Social Theory* (Minneapolis University of Minnesota Press 1993) at 82–104, 97.

[29] W. Morgan, 'Queer Law: Identity, Culture, Diversity, Law' (1995) 5 *Australian Gay and Lesbian Law Journal* at 1–41, 10.

[30] C. Stychin, *Law's Desire: Sexuality and the Limits of Justice* (London Routledge 1995) at 140.

[31] N. J. Beger, 'Queer Readings of Europe: Gender Identity, Sexual Orientation and the (Im)potency of Rights Politics at the European Court of Justice' (2000) 9 *Social & Legal Studies* at 251–272.

sets of gendered behaviour—including sexual object choice—follow from this alleged natural fact. The existence of sexual orientation as a marker of difference, for example, arises out of the construction of sex and gender. Most courts in Europe today follow a distinction that feminist studies brought to the fore thirty years ago: sex is defined as the biologically fixed and basically value-free difference between men and women, their chromosomal and visible bodily difference. Gender is then used to emphasise the social construct of roles ascribed to men and women, institutionalising a hierarchy that structurally disadvantages women. This distinction has gained a certain dominance in the perception of sexual difference in legal studies and often counts as the modern, new approach to gender inequality.[32] Queer law specifically focuses on the destabilisation of this distinction.

The distinction between sex and gender is one of the reasons for the lack of alliances between homosexual and transgendered rights movements since the advent of identity based fights for liberation in Europe in the late 1960s. The struggles for inclusion of lesbian and gay concerns in the transgender movement and vice versa are bound to the consequences the sex/gender divide bears on the distinctions between gender identity and sexual orientation. Both movements have long struggled to explain that lesbians and gay men are still *real* women and men and that transsexuals are primarily concerned with changing their outer appearance to mirror their *inner true sex*. Matters of sexual object choice are only of secondary concern.[33] This explanation is a historical product of the dominant gender order, not an invented choice of the movements. Yet, it does lead once again to the belief in the biological essence of sex and the social construction of gender. This belief, in turn, produced politics based on the fact that sexual orientation and gender identity are two distinct and unconnected parts of human identity. Thus, while the separation is not an issue of false consciousness, these politics do continuously veil the intrinsic link between a normalised binary gender system and the exclusion of homosexuality from the pantheon of naturally, socially, and morally promotable choices. These politics also obscure the fundamental connections of transgender and homosexual or bisexual issues which would turn the alliances of those movements into more than a sympathy towards other oppressed people. The division of the apparently clearly distinguishable categories of sexual orientation and gender identity more often than not produces a subordination of one category under the other. According to Antke Engel, even recent innovative suggestions for a 'Bill of Gender Rights' do not escape this logic of subordination.[34]

---

[32] This is also true for language contexts, such as German, that do not know such linguistic distinctions. In these contexts words like gender role (Geschlechterrolle) became the substitute for the English term gender and gender (Geschlecht) remained the equivalent of sex.

[33] P. Currah, 'Defending Genders: Sex and Gender Non-Conformity in the Civil Rights Strategies of Sexual Minorities' (1997) 48 *Hastings Law Journal* at 1363–1385, 1380.

[34] A. Engel, 'Differenz (der) Rechte—Sexuelle Politiken und der Menschenrechtsdiskurs' in *Quaestio* (Beger, Hark, Engel, Genschel, Schäfer) (eds.) *Queering Demokratie. Sexuelle Politiken* (Berlin Querverlag 2000) at 157–175, 163–165.

Any legal proceeding concerned with questions of homosexual, transgendered, or women's rights contributes to the definition of the relationship between sex and gender. Through the predominantly heteronormative foundation of Western law, sexual identity becomes the conflation of anatomical sex, socially constructed gender, and sexuality: in that logic, penis equals male and male equals sex with female. This rule has a long historical tradition. According to Ernst van Alphen, sexuality used to be understood as derived from the gendered soul: 'first we have a gendered identity, next, in its wake, a sexual orientation. When the gendered mind is incarnated in the corresponding body it results in authentic, that is heterosexual, sexuality.'[35] At the same time, however, an advanced modern European law insists on being able to distinguish between natural fact and social behaviour. Katherine Franke maintains that 'by accepting these biological differences equality jurisprudence reifies as foundational *fact* that which is really an *effect* of normative gender ideology.'[36] In other words an enlightened post-women's liberation law in Europe rests on an understanding of sex difference—as biological difference—accounting for the social construct of gender. This social construct might at times be acknowledged as discriminatory; but the fact of an existing gender difference that faithfully mirrors sex and biological difference is not really questioned. Within a queer approach, however, this constitutes an exchange of fact and effect. The social and cultural construct of gender is here proclaimed to be (re)productive of biological difference.

Besides disrupting the legal distinction between sex and gender, queer law also focuses on two other decisive aspects of legal practice that it seeks to disrupt: Firstly, the meanings of gender and sexuality are simultaneously individualised *and* totalised in court rooms. Wayne Morgan, a queer legal theorist, identifies simultaneous individualisation and totalisation of the subject as a fundamental procedure of disciplinary power of modern states.[37] On the one hand, identifying individuals as part of either one sex or the other, and subsequently of clear gender categories—even if those categories can be changed in the case of transsexuals—is part of exercising power in the direction of ordering and defining. Gender is acknowledged as changeable, sex—as biological and chromosomal foundation—is not.[38] The individual subject can only ever be part of one or the other gender; a transition period is only temporarily acceptable and often constitutes the fundamental problem for the social and employment environment of individuals. The law cannot know its subject if it cannot define it

---

[35] E. van Alphen, 'Introduction. The Gender of Homosexuality' (1995) 2 *Thamyris* at 3–10, 3.

[36] K. Franke, 'The Central Mistake of Sex Discrimination Law: The Disaggregation of Sex from Gender' (1995) 144 *University of Pennsylvania Law Review* at 1–99, 2.

[37] Morgan, *supra* n. 33 at 22.

[38] R. Wintemute, 'Recognising New Kinds of Direct Sex Discrimination: Transsexualism, Sexual Orientation and Dress Codes' (1997) 60 *The Modern Law Review* at 334–359, 335. Wintemute—a legal theorist who writes on lgbt rights—for example, painstakingly attempts to delineate a still existent chromosomal sex underneath all gender reassignment, and, thus, shows the deep difficulty some legal analysis has with a collapse or a final deconstruction of the sex/gender divide.

clearly in mutually dependent gender and sex categories. The individual is granted legal help to solve individually—for example an instance of discrimination—what is in fact only solvable on a broader social level on which we can ask for the reasons why discrimination occurs and is constitutive of certain social orders in the first place. In consequence, the embodied difference of those who are granted protection from discrimination must be retained. The discriminated subject remains discriminated even if legal protection is granted. The history of discrimination becomes once again the only significant marker of that identity.

Secondly, the law cannot afford to disrupt the belief in a clear and truthful biology, ie the body as the fundamental, transparent marker of difference. Law needs markers of difference to support any concept of equality at all. In short, difference is needed to conceptualise equality. Equality looms large in the argumentation brought to the European Courts on matters of transgender and homosexuality. Equality—on a par with the fundamental human rights dimension—is a right that is taken as evident, without the need for further argument. It rests on the presumption that sex is an objective, coherent, and stable difference, while the law has now reached the point of allowing gender to be a changeable concept. The hope of equality litigation is that sex/gender and sexual orientation will one day be no more significant than being left handed. The significance of discrimination against gays, lesbians, bisexuals, and transgendered people is reduced to the belief that an irrational prejudice must simply be abolished. However, neither gender nor sexuality is a natural difference that can be treated by equality: each remains inevitably a discourse with a history of subordination, norms and hierarchies. Equality discourse necessitates a comparison: equal to whom? Legal comparison needs a reasonable average, a majority that has a certain right which is occasionally denied to others and functions as the comparator for establishing the fact of discrimination. Equality more often than not is a comparison to a norm(ality) and the right of definition that rests in every norm(ality) is never questioned.

Claiming legal equality certainly remains a strategy that can be successful from a practical perspective, reducing the everyday hardship and cruelty many lesbians, gay men, bisexuals, and transgendered people experience. Yet, it will not actually deliver what it promises, namely fundamental equality and social justice. As soon as rights are demanded in areas that are central to the institutionalisation of heterosexuality, mainly the family, political practices in legal equality will necessarily fail. The explicit exclusion of adoption and custody of children in almost all gay and lesbian partnership legislation in Europe—apart from the Netherlands—is a good example in this respect.

For many writers in queer theory the legal arena is one of the places where deviant subjects are produced. This is indeed a process to which we should turn our analytical attention. The legal arena cannot operate without the logic of identity, yet subjects of the law do not exist prior to their negotiation in the legal processes. The power of the law lies in representing something as real, as the only possible representation of the real. So while subjects in court rooms are real people, they can only ever be represented partially in their diversities. The legal subject can only present itself *as subject* in the discursive logic of the juridical. Other possible truths and realities exist, but the reality that can be heard by the legal interpretation is hegemonic and dominant. Thus, the power of law is its acclamation of one reality as the most true reality, the most important reality.[39]

This approach de-mythologises legal rights and destroys the sometimes illusionary hope for true justice. At the same time it acknowledges the epistemological authority of the law: not as an all-powerful discourse, but as an important site for the constitution, consolidation, and regulation of sexuality.[40] Certain activist discourses on legal rights as fulfilment of equality are surely ripe for ontological and epistemological doubt. However emancipatory the political and legal actors, texts, and regulations try to be, they somehow have to remain within the logic of a heteronormative binary gender system. This makes the whole process of staging l/g/b/t legal politics at least a complicated and at times a very critical project. The rhetoric of the liberated future whose approach we are apparently witnessing is marked by a romanticised fascination with equality before the law while gayness, bisexuality, and (trans)gender deviance continue to cross boundaries of cultural norms.

In spite of this, institutionalised legal battles are not only a site of normative regulation and the production of deviant subjects. They can never undo the cultural markers that create, cement, institutionalise and change the meaning of difference and identity. That can only be done by social movements in a historical process of discursive challenge. Yet, they are potentially a battle field on which cultural markers could be rendered visible and where human diversity can at least be spoken. The great majority of those involved in fighting for legal rights do surely not pretend that the implications of rights argumentation are entirely unproblematic. However, so far the complexities of the discursive spaces available in legal politics have not been turned into a political practice in themselves. Political practices that engage the law frequently invest in a logic that incorporates diversity into the norm(ality), but rarely invest in a logic that questions the gender identities and sexuality of that norm(ality). Much depends on how and where gay men, lesbians, bisexuals, and transgender people want to constitute themselves as governable minorities to claim legal rights and where the coherence of sex, gender identity and sexuality can be disrupted. It is important to identify how legal arguments can be used to disrupt normative assumptions and how they can re-negotiate the conditions for the constitution of the legal and political subject.

---

[39] Herman, *supra* n. 4 at 6.
[40] Carl Stychin, *supra* n. 35, 156.

10

The Power of the Legal Field: Pierre Bourdieu and the Law

MIKAEL R. MADSEN and YVES DEZALAY

Pierre Bourdieu's encounter with law is marked by the sociologist, anthropologist and philosopher's approach to legal phenomena in the sense that he places law, its institutions and agents, in the broader context of law's interrelationship with other social forces than those immediately at stake only in the microcosm of law. By situating law in this larger theoretical scheme, he facilitates a study of the law informed by a theory of agency/structure, thus potentially importing one of the central debates of modern social theory into socio-legal studies. Applying this theoretical framework also enables the study of law in society to avoid becoming too law-centred or legally biased. As we shall see below, Bourdieu argues that the legal field has a structural homology to other social fields, as well as a historically specific relation with the state.

Like most social theorists, Pierre Bourdieu does not primarily deal with law, and yet addresses law, legal logic and the legal profession as central elements in contemporary society. As a consequence, Bourdieu's treatment of law cannot be introduced as a mere *sociology of law* and instead has to be presented in the broader social scientific context within which it has been developed. He is concerned, firstly, with law as an historical and social construction produced by legal agents; and, secondly, with law as a discourse of power, which is part of the construction of the state as it contributes to its legitimacy. Bourdieu's sociology of law is, therefore, a sociology of law, legal power, lawyers and legal culture and is developed in a variety of his empirical studies covering vast areas of social life. His theoretical understanding of law has been formed by a continuous interrelationship over the years between empirical studies and theoretical reflections and analyses.[1] Essentially, this follows a very basic claim that is apparent throughout Bourdieu's oeuvre, namely that it is *in between* conflicting positions that social practices are to be found and scientifically revealed. This is

---

[1] As an example of these dialectics, we would like to emphasise our attempts to develop a sociology of the international field as a way of *also* explaining the national and local battles in their interdependence with continuous struggles to construct new global universals (see below).

both true for the empirical studies and the more pure philosophical investigations, and is the foundation of his *reflexive* approach to sociology.[2]

Following the inherent logic of Bourdieu's sociology, this chapter will begin by introducing his epistemological position and some key theoretical concepts and will then relate these to his writings on law, legal power and the legal profession. The main theme will be the historical bonds between law and state power and how this relationship takes different forms in culturally different settings, for instance the US and Europe. The final section focuses on the international dimension of legal processes and seeks thereby to develop Bourdieu's theory beyond the specific national context in which it was originally constructed.

1. EPISTEMOLOGICAL PRELIMINARIES: REFLEXIVITY AND PRACTICE

The sociology of Bourdieu is equipped with an analytical apparatus which facilitates the study of legal practices in individual and overlapping social fields. On a general level, the theory is constructed around a series of inter-related and fairly open-ended concepts, enabling a complex assessment of the different dimensions of law such as the state, the legal profession and legal language. The theory supplies a number of analytical 'tools' which are now widely used by many sociologists. These include the notions of *field*, *symbolic power* and *cultural capital*. However, applying these notions de-contextually might lead to misrepresenting Bourdieu's objective as a scientist. We should, therefore, begin by introducing the 'predispositions'—or underlying assumptions—of the theory before reviewing its main concepts. Bourdieu's epistemological premises can best be understood by considering how he uses the concepts of *reflexivity* and *practice*.

Bourdieu's understanding of *reflexivity* differs from the ones developed by other contemporary sociologists, including Anthony Giddens and Ulrich Beck. For Bourdieu, reflexivity signifies the scientific process of uncovering the agents' orientations, and the predispositions shaping their habits and practices.[3] Clearly, the notion of reflexivity has great epistemological implications. In his early writings, Bourdieu argues that all scientific knowledge is constructed. Consequently, the initial shaping and demarcation of the scientific object becomes a crucial step in the research process. Already in 1968, in cooperation with Jean-Claude Passeron and Jean-Claude Chamboredon, he emphasized the need to avoid drawing on common sense understanding when posing sociological questions,

---

[2] See P. Bourdieu, *Raisons pratiques: Sur la théorie de l'action* (Paris Éditions du Seuil 1994) 10, and P. Bourdieu and L. Wacquant, *An Invitation to Reflexive Sociology* (Chicago University of Chicago Press 1992) at 26f.

[3] S. Lash in U. Beck, A. Giddens and S. Lash (eds) *Reflexive Modernization: Politics, Tradition and Aesthetics in the Modern Social Order* (Cambridge Polity Press 1994) 154–155. P. Bourdieu and L. Wacquant, op. cit., *supra* n. 2, part I.

and instead develop an autonomous subject area of systematic and theoretical foundations.[4] In practice, they suggest a double rupture: On the one hand, they propose a conscious break with the pre-constructions that dominate a given subject area in order to reconstruct the social processes that have formed leading ideas and which in effect allocate social positions in that specific particular area. On the other hand, they suggest a break with the sociologist's own assumptions, including the application of too rigid distinctions between the sciences—anthropology, sociology, ethnology, law, etc—when pursuing sociological work.[5] The double rupture as a continuous consideration throughout the research projects can be seen as a practical way of conducting reflexive sociology.[6] In the context of sociology of law, the researcher has to be self-critically aware of the role of her discipline as both an opponent and protagonist of legal discourse, while at the same time trying to break free from the dominance of the black letter law and its guardians.

In his book *Sociologies de la modernité*, Danilo Martuccelli roughly categorises Bourdieusian sociology as belonging to the 'differentiation thesis' formulated by Émile Durkheim and Talcott Parsons.[7] Notwithstanding its theoretical origins, Bourdieu's position nevertheless differs substantially from the more classical theories.[8] Throughout his works, there is a constant *transhistorical* concern; the assumed social *change* brought about by the shift from traditional to modern society is seen more as a process of *repositions* and *modifications* from a 'less' to a 'more' differentiated society.[9] Assessing Bourdieu's concern with what he calls the false opposition between objectivism and subjectivism can further illuminate this critical relationship with classical sociology. Throughout his oeuvre, we find him searching for ways to avoid the 'tyranny of dichotomies' through which classical theories often present the modern world. However, rather than abolishing the ideas of the objective and subjective, Bourdieu incorporates objective structures and subjective phenomena in a dialectical relationship in his field theory or theory of practice. The outcome of this dialectical process is *practice*, which means patterns that are neither solely subjectively determined nor derived from objective structures.[10] This enables him to deploy an analysis informed by both the objective structures and the way actors perceive, think about and construct the structures in a more complete way. The most central concepts in this analytical approach—but not exclusively—are the concepts of *field* and *habitus*, which we shall analyse in the following sections.

---

[4] P. Bourdieu, J. C. Chamboredon and J. C. Passeron, *The Craft of Sociology. Epistemological Preliminaries* (Berlin Walter de Gruyter 1991).

[5] See on *total science* P. Bourdieu and L. Wacquant, *supra* n. 2, 26f.

[6] See R. Lenoir 'Objet sociologique et problème sociale' in Patrick Champagne et coll (eds.) *Initiation à la pratique sociologique* (Paris Dunod 1999) 51–100.

[7] D. Martuccelli, *Sociologies de la modernité. L'itinéraire du XXe siècle* (Paris Gallimard 1999).

[8] *Ibid.*, 109.

[9] P. Bourdieu and L. Wacquant op.cit., *supra* n. 2, 78.

[10] This has also been termed *praxeology*. P. Bourdieu, *Outline of a Theory of Practice* (Cambridge Cambridge University Press 1977).

2. KEY CONCEPTS IN REFLEXIVE SOCIOLOGY

The *field* is a place for struggle between different agents, a sort of marketplace where different positions are held due to the amount of capital (economic, cultural, social and symbolic) that agents possess and which determine their potential influence on the functioning of the field.[11] Bourdieu defines the field as:

> A network, or a configuration, of objective relations between positions. These positions are objectively defined, in their existence and in the determinations they impose upon their occupants, agents or institutions, by their present and potential situation (situs) in the structure of the distribution of species of power (or capital) whose possession commands access to the specific profits that are at stake in the field, as well as by their objective relation to other positions (domination, subordination, homology, etc).[12]

It is important to note that the field is a network of objective relations between 'agents' or 'players' which exist apart from individual consciousness and will.[13] The field is an arena where struggle takes place. This struggle is centred on the valuation of the capitals possessed by the agents. Hence, capitals are relative and corresponding to a particular configuration of the field. Capital awards power in the field:

> [. . .] over the materialised or embodied instruments of production or reproduction whose distribution constitutes the very structure of the field, and over the regularities and the rules which define the ordinary functioning of the field, and thereby over the profits engendered in it.[14]

This struggle or conflict is what gives the field its dynamism, but also maintains it as a field. The agents are therefore challenging each other, but generally not the field as such—a fact attributable to the *habitus* of the agents in the field.[15]

The *habitus* is the shared set of dispositions that orient the agents in a particular field. The dispositions derive from the competition for the field—internal conflict—and with other social fields—external conflict.[16] Habitus can be defined as:

> the habitual, patterned ways of understanding, judging, and acting which arise from our particular position as members of one or several social fields, and from our particular trajectory in the social structure (e.g. whether our group is emerging or declining, whether our own position within it is becoming stronger or weaker).[17]

[11] Bourdieu and Wacquant, *supra* n. 2, 101.
[12] *Ibid*, 97.
[13] *Ibid*.
[14] *Ibid*, 101.
[15] D. M. Trubek, Y. Dezalay, R. Buchanan and J. R. Davis, 'Global Restructuring and the Law: Studies of the Internationalization of Legal Fields and the Creation of Transnational Arenas', (1994) 44 *Case Western Reserve Law Review*, 407–456, at 414.
[16] *Ibid*.
[17] R. Terdiman in P. Bourdieu, 'The Force of Law: Toward a Sociology of the Juridical Field', (1987) 38 *Hastings Law Journal*, at 811.

Habitus is, therefore, the internalised scheme which guides the players' behaviour. This internalisation, in turn, takes place by a dialectical process. The habitus both produces and is produced by the social world. On the one hand, habitus is a *structuring structure*; on the other, it is a *structured structure*. The notion of habitus is a significant step away from individualism towards a greater understanding of how the human mind is socially structured. Bourdieu notes: 'The individual is always, whether he likes it or not, trapped . . . within the limits of the system of categories he owes to his upbringing and training'.[18] Thus, habitus is neither due to a mechanical reaction to external constraint nor to a subjective, conscious, intention on the part of the agent. It is a practical sense— a socially founded *sense of the game*—which is constructed throughout the agent's particular and individual trajectory.[19]

Bourdieu's conceptualisation of the field and habitus raises the more practical sociological question of how fields change. Dynamically, the abstract hierarchy among different agents in the field expresses an incessant reason for some agents' interests to advance themselves while others protect the conditioning of the value of capital. The transformation of a field has, therefore, to be partly located in the *dynamism* of the field itself. Depending on the actual degree of autonomy of the field, competition in the field will always, to some extent, be aimed at the field itself, simply because of the very symbolic existence of the field as a structure of objective relations guiding the behaviour and strategies of the players towards it. However, the logics of bordering fields tend also to have a continuous potential influence. Therefore, from both an empirical and theoretical standpoint, what is crucial to discover are the forces that define the various fields, those *trying* to redefine them, and thereby also the boundaries of the field.

It is self-evident that there cannot be an a priori answer to how to identify these forces due to the continuous dynamism of the field. *The field is that space where the effect of the field is exercised*. This definition is obviously a tautology. Nevertheless, it emphasises the fact that the boundaries of the field are always at stake in the process of defining the field. Thus, the field is essentially a potential open space with dynamic borders and, consequently, there are no systems and subsystems, but rather an open interface with other fields.[20] This conceptualisation leads Bourdieu to take a critical stance against thinking in terms of systems, including professional systems, as we shall see below.

As a general strategy, the sociologist should, therefore, aim to approach the fields by looking at this process of competition between agents, drawing on their different resources and positions. His notion of *symbolic power* becomes a crucial tool for understanding and analysing the competition and exchange between capitals in the structuring of the field. Symbolic power is the power to transform the world: '[B]y transforming the words for naming it, by producing

---

[18] Bourdieu and Wacquant, *supra* n. 2, at 126.
[19] Bourdieu, *supra* n. 10.
[20] *Ibid.*, at 104.

new categories of perception and judgment, and by dictating a new vision of social divisions and distributions'.[21] This particular insight enables us to approach any scientific object, such as the legal field, as the social product it is and analyse it in the light of its historical process of construction.[22] Basically, any opening of a *field* functions both internally and externally as a way of questioning and redefining social hierarchies and power. This can more concretely be identified in the social mechanisms that produce nomenclatures, *métiers*, modes of education and generally other paths to power. In studying a field, the sociologist should view it as an open fluid space constituted by a mixture of loosely connected symbolic practices occupying different and changing positions within the particular social space but with a reference to a larger field of power as well as other fields.

3. THE GENESIS OF THE STATE, LAW AND LEGAL AGENTS

Against the background of this preliminary presentation of Bourdieu's theory, we can now explore the central points of reference in the legal *field*: the state, the legal profession and the power of modern law. But as Bourdieu writes:

> To start thinking about the state, is to expose oneself to and adopt the reasoning of the state, to apply the state categories of thought produced and guaranteed by the state and, thereby, risk to fail to recognise and appreciate the most fundamental truth of the state' [translation by authors].[23]

Bourdieu defines the state as a political entity that successfully claims the monopoly of legitimate physical and symbolic violence on a determined territory and its population.[24] Clearly, this takes its starting point in Weberian sociology but, importantly, adds the concept of *symbolic violence*. Not unlike the closely connected concept of *symbolic power*, it is defined as the power to construct and impose mental structures, categories of perception and thought, which become institutionalised in social and mental structures, and so present themselves as a matter of fact or even *natural*. Studying the state is entering this sphere of extreme symbolic dominance.[25] This insight should not be seen as limited to a narrow understanding of the state, but rather applicable to other areas of society, including the legal field. The analysis of the legal field should seek to break with the categories that are produced and guaranteed by law (and in the shadow of the state) as natural and given, and, thereby, reveal how law is constructed in interaction and competition between different fields.

---

[21] Bourdieu, *supra* n. 17, 839
[22] See Y. Dezalay and B. Garth, *Dealing with Virtue. International Commercial Arbitration and the Construction of a Transnational Legal Order* (Chicago University of Chicago Press 1996) at 31.
[23] Bourdieu, *supra* n. 2, at 101.
[24] *Ibid.*, at 107.
[25] *Ibid*

The state is not where we tend to look for it, as Loïc Wacquant notes in his forward to the English version of Bourdieu's *La Noblesse d'État*.[26] This is a central claim in this magnum opus on state nobility and throughout many of Bourdieu's other works, where we find a mere preoccupation with the state, or more precisely with the *field of power*, which is his 'translation', or indeed sociological reconstruction, of the dominating principles and forces in a given society. The state is not simply a 'ruling class' or a set of institutions but an arena of struggle concerning the *dominant principle of domination* and the *legitimate principle of legitimation*.[27] The outcome of this struggle has societally widespread consequences since it literally grants the 'right' to exercise *symbolic violence*, in addition to the exercise of more 'legitimate forms of power'.[28]

> The field of power is a field of forces structurally determined by the state of the relations of power among forms of power, or different forms of capital. It is also, and inseparably, a field of power struggles among the holders of different forms of power, a gaming space in which those agents and institutions possessing enough specific capital (economic or cultural capital in particular) to be able to occupy the dominant positions within their respective fields confront each other using strategies aimed at preserving or transforming these relations of power.[29]

Bourdieu is not offering a theory of the state, but rather producing an explanatory sociological framework concerned with the *particular* power deriving from the practices in the field of power. Hence, the state can be seen as:

> [T]he central bank of symbolic credit which endorses all acts of *nomination* whereby social divisions and dignities are assigned and proclaimed, that is, promulgated as universally valid within the purview of a given territory and population.[30]

On the basis of this abstract conceptualisation of the state, we shall track down the genesis of the legal profession in its interrelationship with the state in order to elaborate the close relationship between state, jurists and law.[31] We will aim at providing a general explanatory framework, but will also focus on the currently dominant forms of European and American law given their importance for the rest of the world.[32]

---

[26] L. Wacquant in P. Bourdieu, *The State Nobility: Elite Schools in the Field of Power* (Cambridge, Polity Press, 1996) xvii. Loïc Wacquant's remark is particularly true about the American state, where the boundaries between public and private are more blurred. See also Y. Dezalay and B. Garth, 'From Notables of the Foreign Policy Establishment to the International market of Professionals of Philanthropy and Human Rights: Strategies of Power and the Construction of a New Field of Expertise' (1999), *American Bar Foundation Working Paper 9818*.

[27] Bourdieu, *supra* n. 26, at 265.

[28] Bourdieu clearly draws on some of the classics of sociology, ranging from Weber and Norbert Elias to Charles Tilly.

[29] Bourdieu, *supra* n. 26, at 264–265.

[30] See L. Wacquant in Bourdieu, ibid, at xvii–xviii.

[31] See Bourdieu, *supra* n. 2, at 99f, and generally 'Science de l'État' (2000) 133, *Actes de la Recherche en Sciences Sociales*.

[32] Clearly, the relative weight of the 'the rule of law' in concrete legal fields has to be determined historically and empirically, taking into account other institutions and forms of expertise.

Institutionally, the modern (European) state evolved around a few central departments—the police, the justice system and the departments of finance and tax. The 'science d'État' developed at the same time in universities, and trained specialists to work in these departments. In this process of *institutionalisation* as well as *justification*, the development of modern law and the emergence of a fairly coherent group of *jurists* as central agents in the administration of an increasingly *abstract* state are of key importance. Moreover, as a by-product of this role in the early genesis of the state, the creation of a certain form of capital in relation to the state took place. As a particular form of objectified and codified symbolic capital constructed throughout the history of the state, this *juridical capital* became a significant resource of power.[33] Historically, we find quite a number of legal notions as central instruments in forming the modern state. The notion of *appeals* was, for example, clearly instrumental in eighteenth century France in helping to centralise the power of the state. The building up of independent, professionalised bureaucracy was to some extent linked to this centralisation process as the value of internal protocols and doctrines became crucial for controlling the more decentralised part of the administration. In many ways, bureaucratisation did not restrain the power of the state, but rather provided the foundation for the expansion of its powers.[34] In addition, *les sciences de l'État*, the very production of intellectual knowledge of the state (and for the state), which was presented as a mere *savoir bureaucratique* of practical application, became an important engine in justifying and extending state power.

The increasingly *autonomous* law faculties, based on the production and distribution of *modern legal science*, soon made up the central institutions in this general development.[35] Situated close to the state with the role of training and reproducing the state elite, as well as being delegated the concrete power to hand out the diplomas for significant public positions, the law faculty found in the scientific formalisation of its enterprise a powerful means of making itself indispensable as well as self-sustainable. Those 'oracles of law', based in academia or in the highest levels of the court-system could climb to the top of the legal field's hierarchy, sheltered from the actual 'realities' of law. Scientific formalism, which was closely associated with a certain degree of universalism, was not only instrumental in masking the close relationship with the state, but it also played a key role in teaching the new recruits the importance of conforming to the values of the legal profession. However, the division of labour within the field was constructed around a series of distinctions that essentially underscored the historical ambiguity of law and lawyers as, on the one hand

---

[33] See on the notion of *codification*, P. Bourdieu, 'Habitus, code et codification', (1986) 64, *Actes de la recherche en sciences sociales*, at 40–44.

[34] P. Bourdieu, O. Christin and P.-É. Will, 'Sur la science de l'État' (2000) *Actes de la Recherche en Science Sociales*, No. 133, at 8. See also Bourdieu, *supra* n. 2.

[35] The 'modern' law faculty was first constructed in Germany and then throughout Europe. R. Dahrendorf, 'Law Faculties and the German Upper Class' in V. Aubert (ed.) *The Sociology of Law* (London Penguin 1969).

guardians of tradition and order, and on the other, advocates of post-revolutionary liberalism.[36] This contrast between 'modernity' and 'tradition', which among those aspiring to join the profession often corresponded to a similar clash between scholarly capital and social capital, paradoxically allowed the field to present itself as a microcosm of social diversity.[37] The concrete allocation of power and prestige in the field was closely linked to this broad representation. Basically, the differentiation of legal commodities seemed to follow a parallel one to social class hierarchies within the field. This allowed the more privileged agents, such as the *grands professeurs* in France and Germany or the barristers in the UK to play more roles within this complex division of labour. On a general level, the 'freedom of movement' of the European jurists was, however, relatively limited given their close association with the state.

In the United States the institutional boundaries between the law and the state were much less explicit. The American legal field did not have the same need to distinguish itself from the state, and allowed its agents to act as politicians, businessmen or even advocates of civic morals. As a consequence of the key roles played by American lawyers in the forming of the American state, the legal field became a source of legitimacy for the state rather than drawing its legitimacy from the state as in Europe. While the European field has always focused on state affairs, the key feature of the modern American legal field is the institutional alliance between Wall Street law firms and Ivy League law schools.[38] This alliance effectively controls the top of the legal hierarchy, allowing the players to blend economic, social and scholarly capital. Hence, the main characteristic of the US model is a more flexible division of labour, materialised in more fluid and open hierarchies, which allows a certain number of learned 'cadets' to enter in addition to the usual *héritiers*. As the US field has developed with less ties to the state, there has been a greater need for it to develop stronger professional values. One can see this in the way that *pro bono* work on behalf of the poor and oppressed and the exposure of the close links between big business and elite law firms have gone hand in hand. Thus, like American business in general, the US legal field has found its legitimacy in a conscious investment in civic morals alongside big business, making it much less dependent on the state than in Europe.

Converting these fragmented observations on the development of legal fields into a more systematic sociology of legal agents and their self-institutionalisation as a profession requires more theoretical work. Bourdieu takes a critical stand against the branch of sociology generally known as the sociology of professions. This, however, does not imply a complete disagreement with the findings of all studies done in this area and its derivates (professionalism, professionalisation)

---

[36] C. Charle, 'Pour une Historie sociale des professions juridiques à l'époque contemporaine: Note pour une recherché' (1989) 76–77 *Actes de la recherche en sciences sociales*, 117–119.

[37] See V. Karady, 'Une nation de juristes', (1991) 86–87 *Actes de la recherche en sciences sociales* 106–115.

[38] Trubek et. al. *supra* n. 15, at 423.

but consists of a critique of the epistemological assumptions of some of these studies.[39]

> *Profession* is a folk concept which has been uncritically smuggled into scientific language and which imports into a whole social unconscious. It is the *social product* of a historical work of construction of a group and of a *representation* of groups that has surreptitiously slipped into the science of this very group. This is why this 'concept' works so well, or too well in a way [. . .][40]

Bourdieu and Wacquant argue that there are real dangers involved in using the common sense notion of 'profession' for scientific purposes since it commits the sociologist to the whole historical social construction pursued by the group of agents represented by the category. In other words, to study professions as an idealised representation of a homogenous group performing tasks beyond their class and general social origin is only to amplify the symbolic violence exercised by the profession itself. Instead, Bourdieu argues, such studies of processes of 'group formation' can benefit from being analysed from the point of view of reflexive sociology. This makes it possible to see how social fields are not closed but, rather, have a competitive and interdependent relationship with other social fields. In the case of the legal field this requires an awareness of the division of juridical labour and its ties to the field of power, as well as how this, as both a set of mental and social structures, influences the agents in their continuous battle over defining and dividing the terrain of law, taking place behind the symbolic smoke-screen of professionalism that is publicly presented.

Paradoxically, the force of law, the pull of legal reasoning, formalisation and other features of the legal field, is most strongly felt within the legal field in the constant battle over the authoritative interpretation of the *corpus juris*. To some extent, lawyers and jurists themselves are the first victims of their own trade. In their incessant endeavours to 'professionalise' as well as justify their monopoly, and to perpetuate their common symbolic capital, they are compelled to believe in, and defend, the symbols of law in their day-to-day experience.[41] Even legal interpretation is influenced by these constraints. In a similar way to theology, legal interpretation is a structurally limited exercise due to the institutional and social hierarchies of the field, influencing the application of norms and other sources of law.[42] These characteristics are closely related. Professionalisation, which is also a kind of 'disciplinarisation' of the habitus of legal agents, takes place alongside the scholarly production of legal knowledge, which together help to bring about social closure of the legal field. This *social construction* of law, engineered by legal agents as a matter of pure law, seeks on the one hand

---

[39] See the first section of this chapter on 'epistemological preliminaries'.

[40] Bourdieu and Wacquant, *supra* n. 2, at 242–243

[41] See P. Bourdieu, 'Les juristes, gardiens de l'hypocrisie collective' in F. Chazel and J. Comaille (eds.) *Norms juridiques et régulation sociale* (Paris LGDJ 1991) at 95–99. See also the F. Ocqueteau and F. Soubiran-Paillet 'Champ juridique, juristes et règles de droit' (1996) 32 *Droit et Société*, 9–26.

[42] See P. Bourdieu, 'Genèse et structure du champ religieux' (1971) 12, 3 *Revue française de sociologie*, 294–334.

to secure the autonomy of the field vis-à-vis the field of state power, and on the other to control the boundary between law and other fields of knowledge as a means of reinforcing its own hierarchies.

Notwithstanding the field's logic of constructing *universality* and social closure, the application of law by definition consists of mediation between facts and norms, thus involving other social fields. The legal field is by no means closed and the force of law is partly created by legal language's linguistic capacity to bridge such a highly specialised universe with the social issues that happen to be covered by law. Bourdieu captures this 'interaction' by underscoring the *appropriation effect* of legal language; the ways which it transforms elements of common language into specialised legal terms.[43] By doing so, legal language produces a rhetoric of universality and neutrality. The *universalisation effect* is created by the way in which legal language expresses the generality of the law by referring to trans-subjective values presupposing the existence of an ethical consensus and by using formulas that leave little room for individual variation. In parallel, the *neutralisation effect* is obtained through the use of passive and impersonal grammatical constructions, helping normative utterances to appear neutral.[44] Although law presents itself as an autonomous area of social life, with its own sources of legitimacy, Bourdieu's analysis reveals its dependence on the state, and also how it draws on exchanges with other fields.[45] It is not, therefore, the power of the legal discourse *per se* which should be the research subject for Bourdieusian sociology of law, but how law borrows from adjacent areas, such as science or morality, and reconstructs these as legal. Moreover, the sociology of law should not see itself as immune from the power of law, but, on the contrary, adopt a critical stance towards its own role producing references and justifications for the legal field.

4. THE EMERGENCE OF AN INTERNATIONAL LEGAL ARENA

Due to the emergence of modern law as a part of the genesis of the state, lawyers have inherently been agents of state expertise, generally playing key roles in the international import/export market of state knowledge and institutions. More recently, as the development of the legal field in the US has particularly shown, lawyers have also established themselves as experts of business and other forms of supportive knowledge, making them even more attractive knowledge-brokers. These expertises in significant areas of the modern political economy have placed lawyers in central positions in the process of global restructuring, as double agents of both the new liberal economic imperialism and human

[43] See Bourdieu, *supra* n. 17, at 819–820.
[44] *Ibid.*, at 820.
[45] See, on the power of legal language, M. R. Madsen, 'Hacia la paz y la democracia en Guatemala: Estrategias legales *suaves* en derechos humanos y contrainsurgencia constitucional', (2000) 88III *Revista de Ciencias Sociales*.

rights politics.[46] This role as literally both hired guns of global finance and crusaders of new universals—from liberal democracy to financial transparency—seems to correspond more to the US mode of producing law than the European one, which Bourdieu tends to take as his starting point.[47] Consequently, the final section of this chapter will outline a *Bourdieusian* sociology of the international legal field in order, on the one hand, to study the emergence of a global hybrid legal culture in the interrelated arenas existing between national and international levels and, on the other hand, to further develop the theory beyond the specific national context in which it was originally constructed.[48]

Although international interaction has intensified over the last decades, it is hardly a new phenomenon. Around the classic cosmopolitan centres, inhabited by equally cosmopolitan agents, competition between different nations through their foreign services and leading businesses in the market of ideology and knowledge have taken place for centuries. In addition to the more obvious exchanges—the import/export of commercial goods and commodities—an arena of *state interaction* has long been in place as a virtual forum to meet and speak the business of nations.[49] However, international 'interaction' should not be viewed as simply the practices of diplomatic services, but as the competition between nation states through strategies of imperialism.[50] The international arena, dominated by the old European empires until the mid 20th century, seems to take the form of an international *field* by being defined by the oppositions between different national and imperialist visions, which together form a network of objective relations.[51] In abstract terms, national fields are defined in opposition to each other, making the international field the space where different national fields both compete and borrow from each other, concurrently structuring the international field in a way that is homologous to the dominant national fields. Thus, rather than proclaiming the end of the state, the logic of fields suggests that the mode of production of national fields extends—in

---

[46] See Y. Dezalay and B. Garth, *Global Palace Wars: Lawyers, Economists and the Creative Destruction of the State* (Chicago Chicago University Press in press).

[47] See F. Ocqueteau and F. Soubiran-Paillet, *supra* n. 41, at 23.

[48] One might consider talking about *arenas* rather than *fields* with respect to international 'fields'. See for instance Trubek et. al., *supra* n. 15, and M. R. Madsen, 'Exploring International Fields with Bourdieu in the Suitcase: An Essay on the Applicability of Bourdieusian Sociology to the Study of Transnational *Fields*' (Paper presented at the European Sociological Association's Conference, Helsinki, August 2000). Moreover, the application of Bourdieusian sociology outside its original empirical terrain calls for some attention. See P. Bourdieu, *Distinction: A Social Critique of the Judgement of Taste* (Cambridge Mass. Harvard University Press 1984) xi–xiv, and Bourdieu, *supra* n. 2, 14f. See also D. Robbins, 'Bourdieu's Philosophy of Social Science and the Cross-Cultural Transfer of Social Science Concepts' (Paper presented at the European Sociological Association's Conference, Helsinki, August 2001).

[49] B. Badie, *L'état importé* (Paris Fayard 1993).

[50] See C. Charle, 'Des sciences pour un empire culturel: Note sur deux établissements scientifiques francais à l'étranger' (2000) 133, *Actes de la Recherche en Sciences Sociales*, at 90.

[51] See C. Charle, *La crise des sociétés impériales: Allemagne, France, Grande-Bretagne (1900–1940)* (Paris Éditions du Seuil 2001). The area of international commercial arbitration can be understood in a similar fashion. See Dezalay and Garth, *supra* n. 22.

slightly different forms, and by drawing on different resources—to the building up of the international, as it becomes an arena of national self-definition.

This conceptualisation provides a basic framework for analysing legal agents in the international field. As already noted, due to their specific history, lawyers have historically been well positioned in the international arena as mediators of both the internationalisation and the reproduction of national fields of power. In the more traditional Euro-imperialist configuration of the international arena, international lawyers, holding significant social, economic and political capitals, shared the business of international relations with an equally exclusive group of cosmopolitan notables trading in state expertise. Made up of nationals from a series of countries, this cosmopolitan elite shared the common symbolic capital of not only belonging to a national upper class but an international one. Strategies of internationalisation most often corresponded with national class hierarchies to the extent that such strategies aimed at a revalorisation of the capitals of not only the national, but also the cosmopolitan elite, as a way of reproducing itself. This, however, should not only be thought of as a thing of the past. In an almost grotesque fashion, strategies of internationalisation magnify the effect of the social hierarchies since such strategies tend to aim at a construction of the international field in a manner inspired by the 'original' international configuration dominated by diplomats.

The 'original' mode of production should not be confused with the very logic of the international field, but rather be seen as important empirical evidence of the, until recently, dominant mode of production of the *international* field. The intensification of exchanges marking globalisation both reinforce and challenge this configuration: it valorises the social capital of the old generation of 'cosmocrats', just as it at the same time challenges the 'family' mode of production of this cosmopolitan aristocracy. While the international field formerly was a closed, exclusive club of state experts, who adopted a dilettante approach to their international activities or viewed them as a matter of *noblesse oblige*, the acceleration of both economic and symbolic trading has led to a significant investment in international institutions. What simply used to be the hobby of these 'notables-generalists' has become a full-time vocation for a whole array of professional specialists, competitively trying to construct new international arenas configured around their own specific expertises and values. With the rapid growth of multinational corporations and new international institutions, the competition between nations has *also* developed into a turf battle between global entrepreneurs promoting their specific knowledge or values as universals, as a means to impose their domination on this 'new frontier' and in their own image. This exacerbated competition between multiple players, all claiming to be the true bearers of global markets, global regulation or global civil society, functions as a sort of self-fulfilling prophecy, accelerating the process of globalisation. As a consequence, the researcher should be cautious when applying grand theories of globalisation, as well as the alternative discourses seeking to challenge them, as they both are instrumentalised in the global strategies of internationalisation.[52] Instead, as a bottom-up approach and, in order to gain access to the *process* of globalisation, the researcher ought to select some of these battlegrounds and analyse the strategies of the various competitors and the resources mobilised by them.

Fighting on many terrains, law and lawyers—or more precisely American lawyers and the American mode of production of law—are key players in these global battles of expanding foreign trade and constructing international institutions. As the large law firms are the close advisers of the Wall Street financial institutions imposing the globalisation of financial markets, this hardly comes as a surprise. Moreover, the Wall Street legal elite happened to be at the core of the US Foreign Policy Establishment, which helped shape the new international order in the post WW II period by building an international alliance of professional elites, trained in American knowledge and values.[53] The considerable and continuous investment made by philanthropic institutions, such as the Ford Foundation, has greatly contributed to the restructuring of the international field in a fashion that has made it more open to new players as well as more competitive. Based on an anti-colonial and anti-aristocratic ideology, this new symbolic imperialism differs from the old European colonial model even though it borrows some of its logic.

In these global battles, the elite of American lawyers have been (and are) able to build on organisational resources which have been accumulated and constructed as a part of their own particular national history. At the turn of the century, when working as 'hired guns' to open a continental market and invent the institutions necessary to sustain it, they carefully diverted parts of the financial resources, as well as part of their own profits, to build professional institutions that could reproduce the legitimacy of the law and thereby distance it from the powerful and unscrupulous patrons paying their legal fees. It is by looking closer at these institutions at the forefront of this imperialistic strategy—the Wall Street law firms and the elite law schools—that we can both analyse and explain the lead taken by American lawyers.

In close dependency, the leading law schools continue to attract and select the most talented students worldwide and, thus, create a huge network of alumni familiar with—or at least well disposed to—the American model of producing law, while, simultaneously, the Wall Street and D.C. law firms build on this source of talent, enabling them to position themselves in the most glamorous and profitable parts of these new international markets, causing a second tier of European clones—like the City law firms in London or the 'Big Five'—to deal

---

[52] Y. Dezalay and B. Garth (eds.) *Global Prescriptions: The Production, Exportation and Importation of a New Legal Orthodoxy* (Ann Arbor University of Michigan Press forthcoming 2002).

[53] Y. Dezalay and B. Garth, 'Le Washington Consensus': contribution à une sociologie de l'hégémonie du néolibéralisme' 3–22 and 'Droits de l'homme et philanthropie hégémonique' (1998) *Actes de la Recherche en Sciences Sociales* 23–41.

with the more routine work.[54] The tactical advantage of this institutional alliance derives from the different resources and the complementary or, even at times, opposing strategies they allow to be combined. This mixture of expertise and aggressive marketing can be illustrated through one US law firm which concurrently boasts of being the patron of one of the leading think-tanks of the anti-globalisation movement, and also gives legal advice to multinational corporations. Indeed, the institutionalisation of this symbolic division of labour represents a great asset in complex global battles where the system of positions is often shifting or at least uncertain. Moreover, the loose structure of the American field of power, open to entrepreneurs and particularly to Wall Street professionals through the 'spoil-system', has served American elite lawyers well in the global game. The accepted approach of moving in, out and around the state, allowing them to at times embody the power of the US state or keep their distance depending on their clients or their own interests has been useful when playing the multiple roles essential for succeeding in the emerging international arena. This advantage has only been emphasised by the European lawyers' inability to play such multiple roles. Thus, handicapped by their own tradition and habitus with respect to the distance between business and state politics, European clones of the American law firm have only managed to achieve a lower profile in the international politics of globalisation and remain second rank players in this new emerging field of practice.

5. CONCLUSION

As a general outline of a Bourdieusian sociology of law, we have attempted to show how law can be studied on the basis of broader sociological concepts than those conventionally applied in the field. The epistemological concerns sketched out in the initial part of the chapter, as well as the theory itself, point in a direction which has consequences for the concrete construction of the research object in socio-legal research. In a way, this sociological approach provides the analytical 'tools' for the study of symbolic fields: a starting point for an analysis of adversarial practices as complementary strategies influenced by the positions and resources of the various players within diversified social spaces with bonds to law and legal agents. Consequently, as a sociological framework capable, to some extent, of bridging the gap between 'micro' and 'macro' levels of analysis that has dogged great parts of contemporary sociology, this particular theory offers more than an antidote to the *canon* of sociology of law. It critiques both the sociology of professions and the usual conceptualisation of the legal order as a *system*. Instead it offers a more general sociological framework which protects

---

[54] Y. Dezalay and B. Garth, 'The Big Five Versus Big law: Confrontational Rhetoric in the Service of Legitimating Shifting Relationships between Business and Law' in J. Drolshammer and M. Pfeifer (eds) *The Internationalization of the Practice of Law* (den Haag Kluwer 2001).

socio-legal analysis from the continuous danger of being too law-centred or biased. A central argument is that, notwithstanding its unique character, the legal field, like any other social field, should be understood as something that is constructed through a historical interaction with other fields. Moreover, the latter part of this chapter, on the emergence of the international field, equally shows how law and lawyers are both the instrument and effect of international competition: how one can only understand law by taking into account its role in an international game of competing symbolic imperialisms that essentially influence legal practices all the way down to the national and local levels.

Section 4

Interpretive Approaches

REZA BANAKAR and MAX TRAVERS

THE TERM 'INTERPRETIVE sociology' originates with Max Weber who argues at the start of *Economy and Society* that sociology as an academic discipline had to be concerned with the meaningful character of human group life. In contrast to Durkheim (the founder of systems theory), he was insistent that society was no more than a collection of interacting individuals:

> Interpretative sociology considers the individual and his action as the basic unit, as its 'atom'—if the disputable comparison for once may be permitted. In this approach, the individual is also the upper limit and the sole carrier of meaningful conduct . . . In general, for sociology, such concepts as 'state', 'association', 'feudalism', and the like, designate certain categories of human interaction. Hence, it is the task of sociology to reduce these concepts to 'understandable' action, that is, without exception, to the actions of participating individual men.[1]

Weber believed that meaning was impossible to study with the precision of natural science (like other interpretive thinkers he viewed physics as an inappropriate model for sociology), but it was possible to write generally about the world using the device of the 'ideal-type'. This is how he can talk about what we might call 'macro-phenomena', such as 'capitalism', 'bureaucracy' and 'law', and how these develop through history. This was, however, the closest one could get to addressing meaning on the ground: what people understand they are doing in any area of social life.

In the decade after Weber's death in 1920, a group of American researchers at the University of Chicago developed what we now understand as qualitative methods of investigation in sociology. Students were sent out into 'the field' as urban anthropologists, or to collect data by interviewing informants. As Max Travers' chapter demonstrates, this was also a theoretically-driven programme of research informed by George Herbert Mead's view of society as an interpretive process, and by a commitment to naturalistic observation as a scientific method. It became known as symbolic interactionism, and has resulted in many studies about law and legal institutions.

The largest body of research about law by symbolic interactionists was conducted in the 1950s and 1960s. This became known as the labelling tradition and

---

[1] H. Gerth and C.W. Mills (eds.) *From Max Weber: Essays in Sociology* (London Routledge 1991) at 55.

examined how criminal laws were made and enforced. It had a political thrust, in that many of the doctoral students studying with Everett Hughes and Herbert Blumer at the University of Chicago in the 1950s deliberately set out to debunk established institutions by showing how decisions by the police and courts were actually made (and the chapter discusses some of the similarities and differences between symbolic interactionism and the jurisprudential tradition of legal realism).

However, Travers also argues that there is no requirement for symbolic interactionists to take sides in the way suggested by Howard Becker during this period. In fact, the scientific programme of addressing different social worlds, as conceptualised by Blumer, could equally support a study that looks sympathetically at the perspective of 'powerful' or elite groups such as judges or politicians. He complains that too few researchers in law schools have taken up this agenda: so there is a 'missing interactionist literature' in the field of law and society studies which one does not find in the sociologies of education or medicine.

Ethnomethdology is another interpretive tradition developed in the 1940s and 1950s by Harold Garfinkel, a doctoral student of Parsons who became interested in the ideas of the phenomenological philosopher Alfred Schutz. The theoretical basis of symbolic interactionism is, in some respects, similar to Weber in that meaning is conceptualised as residing in the head, so one has to engage in an act of empathetic understanding (what Weber called 'verstehen' and Mead called 'taking the role of the other') to understand what was in someone else's mind. Alfred Schutz criticised Weber for not thinking deeply enough about the problem. Since we recognise objects for what they are, without this elaborate mental procedure, meaning must have a public, inter-subjective character. We acquire a common stock of knowledge (shared 'typifications') from being socialised into a common culture, and learning a common language.

Schutz retained the central idea from Weber that society consists of individuals who are constantly interpreting and making sense of the world around them. Garfinkel turned this into an empirical programme that addressed the interpretive and communicative methods used in social life: how people make sense of events and activities in the world around them, and how they present their own actions as being rational and reasonable.

The studies reviewed in Robert Dingwall's chapter are all concerned with the methods used in legal settings. These include Garfinkel's early study of jurors, based on access to tape-recordings of deliberations. Through listening to the tapes, he became interested in how jurors employed common-sense knowledge about the characteristics of vehicles, road junctions and drivers in determining whether there had been negligence. The study also revealed how they disregarded instructions from the judge, but tried to conceal this when they were later interviewed by researchers. One can see from this summary how ethnomethodology can contribute to a realist agenda in legal theory, in the same way as symbolic interactionism, through examining what actually happens, as opposed to what is meant to happen according to legal manuals.

Dingwall also considers studies which examine the methods used by coroners in deciding cause of death and the methods used in teaching law students how to think like lawyers. The most productive programme of research has, however, been based on the analysis of tape-recordings of legal hearings. He presents data from two studies, and explicates the skills used by lawyers to construct sequences of questions in cross-examining witnesses. The objective is to persuade 'the overhearers—judge and jury—to reach a conclusion by virtue of their own reasoning rather than by being told the answer'. Conversation analytic studies address the methods through which this is achieved, and so might even be useful in training advocates.

Dingwall contrasts the inductive character of conversation analytic research, where the analyst looks for patterns and regularity in a stretch of talk as a preliminary step towards constructing an analysis, with the theoretically-driven interests that motivate the critical discourse analyst. In his view, 'the cause of social criticism is furthered more by firmly grounded analysis of the specifics of a situation . . . than by superficial readings evaluated by reference to their ideological fluency'. This is, of course, one of those sociological debates that cannot easily be resolved, since researchers collect and analyse data with different epistemological and political assumptions. He is reacting here, as an interpretivist, against politically-motivated researchers who are too ready to read their own concerns and theoretical interests into a piece of talk than address how the participants understand their own actions.

Dingwall believes that interpretive approaches are informed by hidden liberal assumptions about the relationship between law and society, and that it is this, as much as their commitment to careful, inductive investigation, that makes it 'difficult to couple them to a "critical" agenda'. Whether or not one agrees with this political reading, symbolic interactionism and ethnomethodology deserve, in our view, to be taken rather more seriously in law schools than being dismissed as 'micro' or 'individualistic' approaches. They provide concrete accounts of what lawyers do, and how they understand their activities which can be contrasted to the largely abstract and idealised view of law one finds in other sociological literatures.

11

Symbolic Interactionism and Law

MAX TRAVERS

THE TERM 'SYMBOLIC interactionism' was coined by the American sociologist Herbert Blumer in 1937, although the intellectual origins of the approach lie in the writings of the nineteenth century pragmatist philosopher George Herbert Mead, and the tradition of urban ethnography established at the University of Chicago in the 1920s under the direction of Robert Park. The best-known studies were produced by the students who were taught by Blumer and Everett Hughes, at the University of Chicago between about 1947 and 1965 in what became known as the Second Chicago School.[1]

A number of other traditions have emerged as interactionists have engaged with developments in mainstream sociology, or created their own styles of analysis, such as grounded theory, dramaturgical analysis, and postmodern ethnography.[2] My focus in this chapter will, however, mainly be on the Chicago School tradition, represented by Blumer and Hughes, and how you can use analytic resources from this core tradition in researching legal settings.

1. INTELLECTUAL ORIGINS

Symbolic interactionism is one of the oldest traditions in American sociology, and can be traced back to the reaction of nineteenth century pragmatist philosophers such as William James, Charles Cooley and John Dewey to the economic and social problems created by industrialisation in the late nineteenth century. One way of attacking the conservatism of the upper-classes at the time was to critique what they viewed as an excess of determinism and abstraction in the European social theories taught at American universities.[3] The pragmatists argued that the grand theoretical schemes of thinkers such as Hegel, Kant or

---

[1] Blumer moved to the University of California at Berkeley in 1952, but his ideas continued to influence graduate students at Chicago during the 1960s. For more detail on the history of symbolic interactionism as a research tradition, see R. Prus *Symbolic Interaction and Ethnographic Research* (New York State University of New York Press 1996); M. Bulmer *The Chicago School of Sociology* (Chicago University of Chicago Press 1984) and G. Fine (ed.) *A Second Chicago School? The Development of a Post-war American Sociology* (Chicago University of Chicago Press 1995).

[2] For an introduction to these traditions, see M. Travers *Qualitative Research Through Case Studies* (London Sage 2001), chapters 3 and 8.

[3] J. Alexander, *Sociological Theory Since 1945* (London Hutchinson 1987), at 202.

Spencer left little scope for individual or collective action that might promote institutional change. They also did not address the world one encountered in everyday experience: there was a gap between the formal and static treatment of social institutions such as the economy or political system in academic texts, and how they actually evolved and changed.

George Herbert Mead developed a theory of society which was informed by this philosophical viewpoint. It was based on the idea that human beings differed from the animals in having an evolved capacity for communication through symbols, particularly language, and in their ability to reflect internally upon their actions. Whereas two dogs circling each other, and making aggressive noises before a fight were responding to biological stimuli, two human being in the same circumstances were interpreting meaningful symbols, such as an insult or a raised fist, and weighing up the likely consequences of their actions. Mead's theory addressed how we acquire a shared set of concepts and values in the course of socialisation through 'taking the role of the other'. A key stage is when a child participates in a team-game, which requires learning how to see yourself from the perspective of a set of players with different perspectives and roles, what Mead calls the 'generalised other'. This results in a view of society in which individuals are shaped by collective attitudes and sentiments, but also have the capacity for individuality and free-will in choosing different role models and reference groups. It is also a society which is in a constant state of evolution and flux, and has an emergent character. One can see, therefore, how Mead was advancing a liberal political viewpoint as well as providing the basis for what later became a programme of scientific investigation into the various institutions and groups that make up American society.[4]

At the same time as Mead was delivering his lectures on Mind, Self and Society at the University of Chicago, another reform-oriented intellectual movement influenced by pragmatism was developing a following in American law schools. This became known as legal realism, and involved turning away from abstract philosophies of law, in favour of examining how judges made decisions. Oliver Wendell Holmes observed in 1881 that 'the life of the law has not been logic but experience'.[5] Jurists working in this tradition, like Frank and Llewellyn, took issue with the view that case-law developed rationally through judges considering previous precedent. Instead, they emphasised the practical, and often political character of decision-making and the way in which judges use legal rules creatively to reach just outcomes. This justified political intervention into the judicial process, for example to protect victims of the Great Depression through agencies set up by Roosevelt's New Deal during the 1930s.[6]

---

[4] For a summary and discussion of Mead's ideas, see J. Baldwin, *G. H. Mead: A Unifying Theory for Sociology* (London Sage 1986).

[5] O. W. Holmes, *The Common Law* (Boston Little Brown 1948).

[6] For an introduction to the realist tradition, see A. Hunt, *The Sociological Movement in Law* (London Macmillan 1978), chapter 3.

Although they shared common philosophical roots, it is interesting to note that symbolic interactionism and legal realism had little else in common. The realists drew on a behaviourist or positivist model of social science which involved looking for hidden factors (such as the social background of judges) to explain legal outcomes, or examining the effect of laws on behaviour. The methods they adopted were the attitude scales employed by psychologists to measure different types of legal personality, and the analysis of official statistics.

By way of contrast, George Herbert Mead was a critic of radical behaviourism in psychology, and argued that the human sciences had to address the meaningful character of human group life, and the central importance of language.[7] Although Mead was a philosopher, he recognised the importance of naturalistic observation as a basis of science. This became the central method employed by symbolic interactionists in the first and second Chicago Schools, and resulted in a very different way of studying legal settings.

2. HERBERT BLUMER ON SYMBOLIC INTERACTIONISM

The central assumptions or methodological principles of symbolic interactionism are set out in a paper by Herbert Blumer published in 1969.[8] This explains and elaborates Mead's view of society as an interpretive process, and argues that sociologists should engage in exploratory, naturalistic research of different social worlds.

Society As an Interpretive Process

Blumer begins by suggesting that symbolic interactionism as a sociological perspective 'rests on three simple premises':

> The first premise is that human beings act towards things on the basis of the meanings that the things have for them. The second premise is that the meaning of such things is derived from, or arises out of, the social interaction that one has with one's fellows. The third premise is that these meanings are handled in, and modified through, an interpretive process used by the person in dealing with the things he encounters.[9]

It is worth thinking about this passage in relation to the different kinds of objects that you encounter in the course of everyday life. Blumer is suggesting that the meaning of any object, whether it is a physical object like a table, or another human being, or an institution like a college or university, or a technical document used in ordering human affairs like a statute or law report, does

---

[7] He described himself as a 'social behaviourist'.

[8] H. Blumer, 'The Methodological Position of Symbolic Interactionism' in his *Symbolic Interactionism: Perspective and Method* (Berkeley University of California Press 1969), at 1.

[9] Blumer, *ibid.*, p. 2.

not arise from the 'intrinsic nature of the thing', but from a 'process of inter-action between people'. Some objects, such as tables, have acquired relatively stable meanings, but there are many objects which mean different things to dif-ferent groups of people, or where the meaning of the object changes over time. Blumer suggests that this is because:

> The meaning of a thing for a person grows out of the way in which other persons act towards the person with regard to the thing. Their actions operate to define that thing for the person. Thus, symbolic interactionism sees meanings as social products, as cre-ations that are formed in and through the defining activities of people as they inter-act.[10]

One of the strengths of symbolic interactionism as a theory is that this way of conceptualising the creation of meaning can be applied to small groups of people interacting inside a particular institution over a short period, but also to the way in which collective institutions, and whole societies, change over time. Blumer notes that the large-scale objects that sociologists study, such as 'insti-tutions, stratification arrangements, class systems, divisions of labour, large-scale corporate units and other big forms of societal organization' should be understood not as 'entities operating in their own right',[11] but as 'arrangements of people' who are engaged in interpreting and defining each others' actions:

> The point of view of symbolic interactionism is that large-scale organization has to be seen, studied and explained in terms of the process of interpretation engaged in by the acting participants as they handle the situations at their respective positions in the organization . . . A knowledge of large-scale organisations and complexly organized areas is to be sought in the examination of the life of such organisations and areas as represented by what the participants do.[12]

Finally, it is worth noting that there is nothing individualist or subjectivist about this way of understanding the social world (a charge that is sometimes made against interpretive sociologies) despite the emphasis placed on the processual nature of social life. Mead and Blumer recognised the force of soci-ety (what Mead called 'the generalised other') and the power of organised groups and institutions in shaping the attitudes and actions of individuals. They do, however, differ from structural traditions in sociology in recognising how individuals, organisations and whole societies are continually changing, and that new meanings for objects emerge in the course of interaction. This is one reason why the concept of 'career' has enjoyed such popularity among symbolic interactionists, both as a way of studying individuals, but also collective phe-nomena such as race riots, moral panics, political movements and cultural trends such as consumer or artistic fashions.

---

[10] Blumer, 'The Methodological Position of Symbolic Interactionism' in his *Symbolic Interactionism Perspective and Method* (Berkeley University of California Press 1969) p. 5.
[11] Blumer, *ibid.*, p. 57.
[12] Blumer, *ibid.*, p. 59.

A Preference for Naturalistic Enquiry

The main method employed by sociologists and psychologists during the 1950s was to collect survey data and analyse this using techniques modelled on natural science, such as testing hypotheses, or finding causal connections between variables. Blumer was highly critical of research studies which employed this conception of scientific method in a mechanical fashion without investigating what was actually happening in a given area of social life.

Instead, Blumer proposes that the sociologist should always attempt to develop a 'first hand acquaintance' with different 'social worlds'. Here he draws attention to the fact that human beings 'have a persistent tendency to build up separate worlds, marked by an operating milieu of different life situations and by the possession of different beliefs and conceptions for handling these situations'.[13] This is a basic feature of human societies:

> One merely has to think of the different worlds in the case of a military elite, the clergy of a church, modern city prostitutes, a peasant revolutionary body, professional politicians, slum dwellers, the directing management of a large industrial corporation, a gambling syndicate, a university faculty, and so on endlessly.[14]

This is another key concept which has been elaborated by subsequent interactionists. Howard Becker has, for example, used the term 'art world' to refer to the whole set of people engaged in producing works of art, which includes the artist, the critics and art-dealers who define what is recognised as art, but also the various craft industries and trades that support artistic work.[15]

Although Blumer does not suggest a specific method that interactionists should employ in investigating a social world, most researchers favour spending a long period of time observing a particular group at first hand.[16] There are now all kinds of manuals you can consult on how to do fieldwork,[17] and it is easy to get the impression that it is a specialised skill that you need to learn from a qualified practitioner. In fact, both Robert Park and Everett Hughes had an uncomplicated understanding of what was required. They simply wanted their students to get out into society, and report about what was happening in different social worlds.

Hughes developed a particular interest in work, and encouraged his students to draw on their own backgrounds and life-experiences in choosing a topic to

---

[13] Blumer, *ibid.*, at 38.
[14] Blumer, *ibid.*, at 38–9.
[15] H. Becker, *Art Worlds* (Berkeley University of California Press 1982).
[16] This is known as doing fieldwork, although it is also commonly described as ethnography, or participant observation.
[17] See, for example, J. Lofland and L. Lofland, *Analysing Social Settings: A Guide to Qualitative Observation and Analysis* (Belmont CA Wadsworth 1995).

investigate.[18] He later acknowledged some of the obvious emotional and political difficulties that could arise, not least being refused access to a setting, but
noted that 'most people can be studied, and most can do more fieldwork than
they believe'.[19]

A cheaper, and less emotionally-demanding, alternative to fieldwork is the
research interview which has become a standard part of methods training in the
social sciences. One problem here is that you may only obtain idealised or interested accounts of what happens in an institution: but the best studies provide a
considerable insight into different social worlds.[20] To give one example,
Howard Becker's doctoral thesis, supervised by Hughes, was based on interviews with sixty high school teachers in Chicago.

3. SYMBOLIC INTERACTIONISM, LABELLING AND CRIMINAL JUSTICE

Most symbolic interactionist research about law was conducted during the
1960s, as part of a wider programme investigating social responses to deviance
which has become known as the labelling tradition.[21] This literature mainly
focuses on the interpretive processes involved in joining a deviant group, and the
psychological effects of being labelled. However, there are also a few studies
which look at the activities of 'moral entrepreneurs' and pressure groups in campaigning for new laws, and there is a larger body of ethnographic research about
the criminal justice process.

Labelling Theory

The usual way of viewing deviance, whether this is drug-taking, homosexuality
or organised crime, is to assume that there must be some psychological or social
cause, or that an individual is inherently evil or wicked in the case of child-

---

[18] See E. Hughes, 'Mistakes at Work' in L. Coser (ed.) *On Work, Race and the Sociological
Imagination* (Chicago University of Chicago Press 1995). Hughes was committed to the value of
comparative analysis, and argued that one could 'learn about doctors by studying plumbers: and
about prostitutes by studying psychiatrists'. Lawyers arguably have something in common with
doctors and plumbers, in that they 'practice esoteric techniques for the benefit of people in distress'.
They also have something in common with prostitutes and psychiatrists in that they need to maintain a professional distance in dealing with 'rather intimate problems' (*ibid.* at 79).

[19] E. Hughes, 'The Place of Fieldwork in Social Science' in *The Sociological Eye* (New Brunswick
Transaction 1993) at 496.

[20] For a discussion of the advantages of ethnography over interview studies, see H. Becker and
B. Geer, 'Participant Observation and Interviewing: A Comparison' in J. Manis and B. Meltzer,
(eds.) *Symbolic Interaction* (Boston Allyn and Bacon 1967) at 109.

[21] For some programmatic statements, see J. Kitsuse, 'Societal Reaction to Deviant Behavior:
Problems of Theory and Method' (1962) 9 *Social Problems* 247–56; E. Lemert, *Human Deviance,
Social Problems and Social Control* (Englewood-Cliffs New Jersey Prentice-Hall 1972); D. Matza,
Becoming Deviant (Englewood-Cliffs New Jersey Prentice-Hall 1969); E. Schur, 'Reactions to
Deviance: A Critical Assessment' (1969) 75 *American Journal of Sociology* 309–22; and H. Becker,
Outsiders (New York The Free Press 1973; first published in 1963).

abusers and paedophiles. In either case, a law may be required to prevent people acting in this way. Labelling theorists, on the other hand, argue that the real relationship between criminal law and deviance is exactly the opposite: deviance is created by how we respond to it. According to Howard Becker,

> . . . social groups create deviance by making the rules whose infraction constitutes deviance, and by applying those rules to particular people and labelling them as out-siders. From this point of view, deviance is not a quality of the act the person commits, but rather a consequence of the application by others of rules and sanctions to an 'offender'. The deviant is one to whom that label has successfully been applied; deviant behavior is behavior that people so label.[22]

From this perspective, drug-taking, homosexuality, organised crime, mental illness, and even paedophilia are not in themselves deviant activities. They have to be labelled as such by the moral, and political, responses of other members of society. This is evident from the fact that if one takes an historical perspective, many acts that we now view as wicked and anti-social, were once morally acceptable.

The largest body of literature in the labelling tradition are ethnographic studies of different deviant groups. These either reveal the social and interpretive processes, and 'career contingencies', involved in becoming a member (thereby undermining the view that there are social or psychological causes), or demonstrate how labelling can increase or 'amplify' deviant behaviour by creating groups of outsiders who are committed to a deviant identity.[23]

This theoretical perspective also results in a distinctive way of conceptualising criminal law. Structural-functionalists had portrayed this as representing the shared values of society, and praised groups like lawyers, the police, and also teachers and social workers, for promoting these values and combating deviance. Labelling theorists, on the other hand, are truer to Durkheim in recognising that deviance is necessary for society, since it strengthens our shared moral values, and that it is constantly necessary to create new deviant groups. They go further, however, in examining how laws get made through campaigns and political lobbying by 'moral entrepreneurs'.

There are not many empirical studies in this literature, although there has been a revival of this approach to the legislative process, and the construction of social problems more generally since the late 1980s.[24] A central theme is again the contingent and emergent nature of law-making as a process: how the success of a campaign depends on recruiting key politicians or newspaper editors to join the cause; or how bureaucracies sometimes have an interest in creating a moral panic through feeding stories to the mass media.[25]

---

[22] Becker, *ibid.*, at 9.

[23] For a classic study, see Becker *op.cit.*, chapters 3 and 4, on the career of the marijuana smoker.

[24] See M. Spector and J. Kitsuse, *Constructing Social Problems* (New York Aldine de Gruyter 1987) and D. Loseke, *Thinking about Social Problems* (New York Aldine de Gruyter 1999).

[25] These themes are developed in Becker, *supra* n. 21, chapter 7 which looks at the role of moral entrepreneurs in securing the enactment of the 1937 Marijuana Tax Act, and in the critique by D. Dickson, 'Bureaucracy Morality: An Organisational Perspective on a Moral Crusade' (1968) 16

Ethnographic Studies of the Criminal Justice Process

Although the programme of naturalistic enquiry promoted by Blumer and Hughes does not necessarily have to be critical of established institutions, one can see how it can easily develop a subversive or de-bunking character simply by describing what is usually hidden from the general public. It would also be fair to say that many of the doctoral students they supervised deliberately set out to be subversive, by exposing the arbitrary and unfair character of criminal justice institutions.

Jennifer Hunt's hard-hitting study of how police officers use force is a relatively recent contribution to this literature.[26] Hunt focused on how officers understood the distinction between using 'legal' or 'normal' force. Legal force was the force necessary to subdue a suspect, while normal force was justified to save face or re-establish control, or 'as a morally appropriate response to certain categories of crime and criminals'.[27] She gives the following graphic account of how normal force was used against a seventeen year old youth who had raped a nun:

> When the police apprehended the suspect, he was severely beaten and his penis put in an electrical outlet to teach him a lesson. The story of the event was told to me by a police officer who, despite the fact that he rarely supported the use of extralegal force, depicted this treatment as legitimate. Indeed, when I asked if he would have participated had he been present, he responded 'I'm Catholic. I would have participated'.[28]

Another theme in this literature is the extent to which the police and defence lawyers develop practices to make their lives easier. Jerome Skolnick showed, for example, how the police arrested only a small proportion of offenders since they did not want to overwhelm the courts with 'trivial' cases.[29] Abraham Blumberg described how the defence lawyers he worked with helped the court in persuading clients to plead guilty, rather than contesting the prosecution case.[30]

Although these studies convey a cynical view of criminal justice, they also provide a sympathetic insight into the worldview and practical concerns of

---

Social Problems 143–56 which looks at the help they received from the Federal Bureau of Narcotics. See also J. Gusfield, *Symbolic Crusade* (Urbana University of Illinois Press 1966) which adopts a broader structural approach in explaining the campaigns that resulted in Prohibition. For a critical discussion of this literature, see I. Taylor , 'Moral Enterprise, Moral Panic and Law-and-Order Campaigns' in M. Rosenberg, R. Stebbins and A. Turowetz, (eds.) *The Sociology of Deviance* (New York St. Martin's Press 1982) 123–49.

[26] J. Hunt, 'Normal Force' in E. Rubington and M. Weinberg, (eds.) *Deviance* 5th edition (New York Macmillan 1987).

[27] Hunt, *ibid.*, at 136.

[28] Hunt *ibid.*, at 138.

[29] J. Skolnick, *Justice Without Trial: Law Enforcement in Democratic Society* (New York John Wiley 1966).

[30] A. Blumberg, 'The Practice of Law as a Confidence Game' in (1967) 1 *Law and Society Review* 15–39.

occupational groups like the police and defence lawyers. There are also many studies that do not portray official agencies and institutions in a bad light, but simply describe the routine activities in these settings. A good example is Robert Emerson's ethnography of a juvenile court.[31] This looks systematically at how defence lawyers employed excuses and justifications in representing their clients, drawing on the interest many symbolic interactionists have shown in 'accounts' as a means of influencing how you come to be viewed by other people.[32] Irrespective of the political motivation behind many of these studies, they can also be viewed as a scientific programme that reveals a great deal about occupational careers and working practices in the American criminal justice system.[33]

4. SYMBOLIC INTERACTIONISM AND THE LEGAL PROFESSION

Symbolic interactionists have not conducted much research on law outside the criminal justice process, although there have been a few interesting ethnographies about different areas of legal practice. My favourite studies include the following:

Jerome Carlin on Sole-Practitioners in Chicago

Carlin was a student of Hughes, and this book reflects his interest in the stratified nature of occupations, and how every profession requires some people to engage in shady practices that are concealed from the public.[34] Based largely on interviews, it contains a lot of detail about the career histories of lawyers who could not get jobs in larger firms (monopolised by graduates from elite universities), and the day-to-day practice of law at the 'bottom end' of the profession. It is particularly revealing about the methods firms employed to obtain clients (including poaching and ambulance chasing). Ethics are portrayed as a luxury enjoyed by high-status firms.

John Flood on Barrister's Clerks

This study is a rare example of an ethnographic study conducted about the English bar, although we see this from the perspective of the clerks who act as

---

[31] R. Emerson, *Judging Delinquents: Context and Process in Juvenile Court* (Chicago Aldine 1969).

[32] See S. Lyman and S. Scott, 'Accounts, Deviance and Social Order' in J. Douglas (ed.) *Deviance and Respectability* (New York Basic Books 1970) 89–119.

[33] For a fuller review of this literature, see S. Hester and P. Eglin, *A Sociology of Crime* (London Routledge 1992).

[34] J. Carlin, *Lawyers on Their Own* (New Jersey Rutgers University Press 1962).

'middlemen' between solicitors and barristers.[35] It contains a lot of detail on what clerks expect from their barristers, and how they manage their careers. We also learn how clerks obtain and refuse work from solicitors, and the problems that arise in substituting briefs.

Alan Paterson on the Law Lords

This is an even rarer example of a study based on interviewing senior judges (the 'Law Lords' who sit in the British House of Lords), but also on observing 'the interaction between the Law Lords and counsel in a variety of appeals in the years 1972 and 1973'.[36] From this data, and documentary sources such as judicial biographies and reported cases, Paterson looked at some of the considerations involved in reaching decisions, and how they were influenced by their perception of how different 'reference groups', including other Law Lords, academics or parliament might react.[37]

5. CAREERS AND IDENTITY IN THE LEGAL PROFESSION: A CASE STUDY

All these ethnographies are concerned with identity, a key theme in symbolic interactionist work. These ideas can be explored in greater depth by looking at a piece of research I conducted based on thirty interviews with trainee and qualified solicitors. This also illustrates what is practically involved in doing a symbolic interactionist study, and how ideas and concepts from this tradition can be employed in collecting and analysing qualitative data.

Developing A Research Question

There is a large sociological literature about the legal profession. Structural-functionalists see lawyers as custodians of a cultural tradition which benefits society. Marxists see them as representing the interests of dominant economic groups. Weberians see the profession itself as an organised conspiracy against the public, which has secured a privileged market position, based on restricting access to legal services.

From a symbolic interactionist perspective, these global accounts do not provide an adequate way of addressing the complex set of organisations and social

[35] J. Flood, *Barristers' Clerks: The Law's Middlemen* (Manchester Manchester University Press 1983).

[36] A. Paterson *The Law Lords* (London Macmillan 1982) at 4.

[37] Paterson and Flood each draw on concepts from symbolic interactionism, such as those of 'career' and 'reference group' (see, for example, T. Shibutani, *Society and Personality* (Englewood Cliffs New Jersey Prentice-Hall 1961)), although there is little explicit discussion of theory in either text.

worlds that form a profession. This is because they do not address 'meanings as social products, as creations that are formed in and through the defining activities of people as they interact'.[38] They do not address the 'process of interpretation' that takes place at all levels of organisations, or the way in which they are continually changing.

My goal in this project was to examine some of this definitional work, which I hoped would become visible from the interviews. Blumer argues that it is important to view data-collection as an exploratory, inductive process. I went into the interviews with an open mind, hoping that I would be able to employ generalising concepts from the symbolic interactionist literature on work and careers, and that other themes would emerge naturally from the data.

Status and Career Choice

Although professional associations still like to present themselves as representing homogeneous occupational groups, there has always been a tremendous gulf between large law firms, and the smaller practices that provide services to low-income clients. Heinz and Laumann have produced a detailed picture of how law-firms are stratified in Chicago drawing on survey data about number of partners, annual income, types of client and other indicators.[39] What symbolic interactionists want to know, however, is how these distinctions are understood by people working in the profession. The following extract is from an interview with a first year Articled Clerk (legal trainee) in a large commercial firm of solicitors in Manchester. She is explaining the reasons why she applied to this firm as against either a larger commercial firm in London (a City firm) or a smaller firm dealing with legal aid work:

> . . . the reason why I didn't apply twelve months before the normal time is that I wasn't quite sure what sort of firm I wanted to go to . . . in that it seemed that at university the only people that have any information about firms have information only about large London City firms and it seemed that at university you had to apply to those and if you didn't get Articles with those . . . you were a nobody . . . you were a nothing . . . And it seemed, well to me anyway, that I thought 'Well, I should try for that', but deep down I knew that it wasn't what I really wanted, and didn't even bother applying. And it struck me that a lot of people are now saddled with Articles in those firms, and they're there because it's what they think you should do.

She had applied to firms in Manchester 'with a commercial department, a good litigation department [but] not so much legal aid type firms'. She did not wish to get 'involved in all that side of things' for the following reasons:

[38] Blumer, *supra* n.8, at 5.
[39] J. Heinz and E. Lauman, *Chicago Lawyers: The Professions of the Bar* (Chicago American Bar Foundation 1978).

I perceived that side of things as not as lucrative as this side of things and I also perceived it as . . . I don't really like getting involved in sort of the seedier side of life . . .
you know, and having ethical problems, and having to defend persons and things like
that, it's um . . . I'm not on a social crusade um so I thought that I would leave those
sort of firms and not bother applying to them.

This interviewee was highly conscious of the stratified nature of the profession, and this was also apparent in many of the other interviews.[40] Clearly, she
regarded her decision to do Articles in the provinces rather than in London as
being an 'accountable' matter.[41] The explanation which she gave seemed
designed to counter and down-grade the views of those who might think that
she was a 'nothing' or a 'nobody' because she was not in a 'London city firm'.

Hughes's observation that a 'man's work is one of the things by which he is
judged, and certainly one of the more significant things by which he judges himself' seems very appropriate here. Hughes argues that holding a given office
often carries with it what he terms a 'master-status', so that the job you do can
convey a powerful message about the sort of person you are. He has also noted
that 'the very demand for highly scrupulous and respectable lawyers depends in
various ways upon the availability of less scrupulous people to attend to the less
respectable legal problems of even the best people'. While this interviewee is not
making exactly this point, she certainly seems to be aware that, if you are placed
in a position where you are involved in doing 'dirty' work—having 'ethical
problems' and 'having to defend persons' and the like—there is a good chance
that you will come to be regarded as being a 'dirty' sort of person.[42]

This interviewee is not supplying an objective or disinterested account of the
nature of divisions within the profession. Instead, she presents herself as being
a particular type of person: one who is neither a 'social crusader' nor the sort of
person who applies to the biggest firms 'because it's what they think you should
do'. There is a great deal of judgmental and definitional work taking place to
produce and maintain status divisions in the legal profession.

The Distinction Between 'Doing' and 'Being'

Another way of studying identity in the legal profession is to consider how individuals see themselves in relation to their jobs. Here Erving Goffman has argued
that one can make a distinction between people who believe in the role they are
playing, and those who become cynical or disillusioned in the course of an occupational career.[43]

---

[40] Another example can be found in a remark made by an assistant solicitor who was moving
from one commercial firm to another. She was quick to point out that 'although it's not one of the
top five firms, it is still in the top ten'.

[41] Lyman and Scott, *supra* n. 32.

[42] E. Hughes, *Men and Their Work* (Glencoe The Free Press 1958), at 1, 42 and 71.

[43] See, for example, E. Goffman, *The Presentation of Self in Everyday Life* (New York Doubleday
1959) at 17–19.

Most people I interviewed did not experience a gap between 'doing' and 'being'. Individuals, in learning to 'do' law, at the same time came to see themselves as 'being lawyers' through the eyes of different others such as other lawyers and their clients. This can be illustrated by the following extract from an interview with an articled clerk in a general practice firm who described the way he looked at himself when he was advising a client:

> . . . I hope that when I see a client, the main thing in my mind is that for that particular time, half-an-hour or whatever, you treat your client as if they're the most important thing in your life. If you don't, they'll know it.

Later in the interview, he described himself as going through a 'metamorphosis' when he was asked to advise friends outside work:

> I switch to listening to everything they say . . . You listen more carefully. You may ask them questions which from your own experience may give you more information . . . But I do believe that, as opposed to just having a chat with someone and giving someone advice, even though you know them you are slightly different people.

It would seem from these extracts that giving advice to a client does not merely involve the exercise of a set of technical or presentational skills, but at the same time involves the Articled Clerk in seeing him or herself as 'being' more of a solicitor.

For some of the interviewees, acquiring an occupational identity was a more problematic matter. One individual had originally applied for Articles in a high street firm because he had an interest in civil liberties law and helping working class clients, but had since transferred to a commercial firm in Manchester city centre. Although he had admired the dedication of his colleagues, he soon became disillusioned with legal aid work. He described this in the following way:

> . . . it was just a bit wearying that, as I say, you know, you're going through a hell of a lot of work . . . and, as I thought, one way of putting it . . . doing legal aid work, you're regarded as more as um as sort of a social worker for the legal aid fund. You spend all your time on the phone sorting things out. You're not really doing a great deal of law in it, just chasing up legal aid applicants . . . filling this in, doing that . . . [ ] So that's what I thought, 'That's not good enough for me' . . . Anyone can acquire this sort of experience just by dint of being there . . . If you're in that sort of practice you will pick it up um . . . I thought I needed more out of my articles . . . or else all I could be was a high street lawyer.

One interesting feature of this extract is that this interviewee did not see legal aid firms as offering a career for 'second-rate solicitors' when he chose to work in that segment of the profession. It is not a view held by most legal aid lawyers but arises from the way he came to see himself in relation to his work. In fact, he only applied for a transfer after he became aware that people from his law degree (whom he regarded as academically beneath him) were now earning considerably more money and enjoying more status in commercial firms despite the fact that he was doing a more responsible and demanding job.

Moving to a larger firm did not fully resolve matters, however. Although he now had a higher salary, he still felt ambivalent about working there. He was very much conscious that, in the eyes of his old friends (who had encouraged him to become a legal aid lawyer) he had 'sold out'. During the interview, he told me that he agreed with this assessment. He would, for example, have liked to attend meetings of the Haldane Society of Socialist Lawyers, but felt that he would not be accepted in view of the fact he was working in a commercial firm.

Identity and Change in the Legal Profession

The value of interviewing even a few lawyers in this way is that one starts to see how the profession is produced over time, through the actions and interpretations of individuals responding to other individuals and groups. One can also see how professions are always changing, and developing new segments or specialisms.[44] Although these processes have been most extensively investigated in fields like science or medicine, there is scope for further research on changes inside the legal profession.

6. TAKING SYMBOLIC INTERACTIONISM SERIOUSLY

Symbolic interactionism has always been something of a marginal approach in sociology, and only really thrived in Chicago under the intellectual leadership of scholars like Robert Park, Herbert Blumer and Everett Hughes. Most American sociology departments still have a strong bias in favour of quantitative methods, and interactionists usually end up working in smaller colleges and universities.

There is a more positive story in that symbolic interactionist ideas and methods have effectively been absorbed by the mainstream discipline. The complaint made by Blumer that fieldwork methods were not taken seriously by the discipline in the 1950s remains true today in that relatively few postgraduates are encouraged or get the opportunity to spend several months doing ethnographic research. On the other hand, qualitative methods are now widely taught at both undergraduate and postgraduate levels in departments of sociology, as well as in inter-disciplinary fields such as media studies and criminology. A related development is that, partly as a result of the critique of quantitative sociology mounted by Blumer and other interactionists, every major social theorist recognises the importance of both what is theorised as the 'micro' level of society, and qualitative research methods. Anthony Giddens and Pierre Bourdieu have, for example, each engaged sympathetically with the interpretive tradition.[45]

---

[44] R. Bucher and A. Strauss, 'Professions in Process' (1961) 66 *American Journal of Sociology* 325–34.

[45] See, for example, P. Bourdieu, *Outline of a Theory of Practice* (Cambridge Cambridge University Press 1977) and A. Giddens, *New Rules of Sociological Method: A Positive Critique of Interpretivist Sociologies* (London Hutchinson 1976).

At the same time as macro-theory has been moving towards symbolic inter-actionism, many interactionist researchers have been keen to rejoin the socio-logical mainstream. This is true, to a certain extent, of the grounded theory movement founded by Barney Glaser and Anselm Strauss.[46] It is particularly clear in the case of Norman Denzin who has advocated a theoretical synthesis between interactionism and post-Marxist cultural studies.[47]

A plea for symbolic interactionism to be taken seriously means that it has to be taught, and appreciated, as a sociological approach in its own right, rather than as a way of doing critical theory, or a method that can complement quan-titative analysis. I now want to return to what is distinctive about the approach, through reviewing some common criticisms. I will also consider three topics that you could address in taking up this sociological approach to law.

Some Common Criticisms

Sociology is a subject constituted by argument and debate, and one can argue that the quality and interest of empirical studies during the 1960s and early 1970s lies partly in the fact that there were clear divisions between consensus, conflict and interactionist traditions which have become blurred in recent years. Interactionist sociologists wrote about deviant groups with such energy and bite during 1960s because they really did want to attack structural-functionalism. They believed that it was wrong on scientific grounds, and also because it spoke for the political establishment.

Interactionism was also fiercely criticised from the late 1960s by sociologists in the conflict tradition such as Alvin Gouldner in America, and by critical crim-inologists associated with the National Deviancy Conferences organised in England by, among others, Laurie Taylor, Stan Cohen, Ian Taylor, Paul Walton and Jock Young.[48] Their criticisms of symbolic interactionism have tended to stick, and become part of what is standardly taught to students in textbooks, even though conflict theory has itself been overtaken by political events, and is no longer such a vigorous or productive intellectual movement.

Symbolic interactionism, and interpretive sociology more generally, was defended in a number of books and articles, and it is worth consulting these to get a taste of the lively character of sociological debate during this period.[49] Two common criticisms were that the approach only deals with individuals, and that it is unscientific.

[46] B. Glaser and A.Strauss, *The Discovery of Grounded Theory* (Chicago Aldine 1967).

[47] N. Denzin, *Symbolic Interactionism and Cultural Studies* (Oxford Blackwell 1992).

[48] See, for example, A. Gouldner, 'The Sociologist as Partisan: Sociology and the Welfare State' (1968) *The American Sociologist* 103–16; I. Taylor, P. Walton and J. Young, *The New Criminology* (London Routledge 1973); and I. Taylor, *supra* n. 25.

[49] See, for example, D. Downes and P. Rock, *Deviant Interpretations* (Oxford Martin Roberstson 1979); J. M. Atkinson, 'Versions of Deviance' (1974) 22 *Sociological Review* 616–25; and J. Coulter, 'What's Wrong with the New Criminology' (1974) 22 *Sociological Review* 119–35.

The charge of individualism

One sometimes finds at the end of undergraduate essays the charge that symbolic interactionism only deals with individuals, or that it cannot address 'macro' or structural phenomena. It should be apparent from my summary of Mead and Blumer that this is not the case, but nevertheless it would be difficult to deny that much interactionist research attempts to understand and document the activities in different social worlds, rather than writing about the relationship between different institutions across a whole society.

Taylor, Walton and Young in *The New Criminology* criticised the interactionist literature on labelling for only addressing the role of moral entrepreneurs in campaigning for new laws. They complained that interactionists had a liberal or pluralist view of society, and so could not recognise 'the structured inequalities in power and interest which underpin the processes whereby . . . laws are created and enforced (the processes referred to in individualistic fashion by Becker in his discussion of moral enterprise)'.[50]

This criticism of labelling theory is slightly unfair since Becker never suggested that every criminal law results from a campaign (which would be absurd). They are correct, however, that interactionists are not interested in producing a global political critique of society. Instead, they are content in mapping out the different social worlds that constitute the criminal justice system, and focusing on how the people there understand their own activities. One might also add, from an ethnomethodological perspective, that people spend a lot of time inside organisations like law firms talking about the behaviour and personality of colleagues, clients, judges and the like. Once you start to think about this, the fact that sociology pays so little attention to individuals seems a startling omission.

The charge of being unscientific

Another charge made against symbolic interactionism during the 1950s was that it was unscientific. One sometimes hears this today when a grant application is turned down on the grounds that the proposed methodology is too 'impressionistic' or 'anecdotal'. Symbolic interactionists have responded to this by developing more elaborate methods to collect and analyse qualitative data, such as grounded theory, and becoming more self-conscious about method.

It should be remembered that Blumer defended exploratory naturalistic research as the only scientifically valid way to investigate social settings, and was highly critical of research based on statistical techniques. More generally, one can argue that a formal research design, whether it employs grounded

---

[50] Taylor, Walton and Young, *ibid.*, at 168.

theory, or some model or procedure based on natural science, will not necessarily result in a more insightful analysis, and from a symbolic interactionist perspective may actually prevent you from seeing or reporting what is happening in a particular social setting.

The fact that this charge can be made illustrates the fact that social scientists differ considerably in their understanding of science. The objective of most traditions is still, after all, to produce a scientific understanding of society that can be contrasted to the flawed or incomplete viewpoint of the people they are studying. Interactionists, on the other hand, believe that society consists of the definitional and interpretive work of people going about their practical tasks in different social settings.

This also explains the objection that interactionists have to ethnographies informed by critical theory. A number of powerful, and superbly crafted ethnographies about law have been written by critical sociologists. These include Pat Carlen's *Magistrates' Justice* which employs concepts from Erving Goffman within a Marxist structural framework,[51] and the work of ethnographers, and anthropologists associated with the Amherst school.[52] A good example is the excellent paper in this volume by Jennifer Pierce (chapter 8) which makes a political point about racism in the legal profession based on interviews with black Americans who have moved from large firms to become sole-practitioners.

From a symbolic interactionist perspective, these studies supply a considerable insight into different social worlds, but they do not go far enough in addressing the perspectives of different individuals and groups. Here there is admittedly a tension within the tradition between those who believe that the ethnographer must take sides,[53] and the view that all sides need to be addressed or at least acknowledged in studying a given institutional setting.[54] It will be apparent in reading Pierce that she has more sympathy for the perspectives of subordinate groups like African-Americans or women, than the legal establishment.

Symbolic Interactionist Research on Law: Three Topics

There are all kinds of topics relating to the legal system that have not been studied using ethnographic methods. One I am particularly familiar with is immigration control in the United Kingdom. It is interesting that before my own study there had been no observational research on immigration appeals

[51] P. Carlen, *Magistrates' Justice* (Oxford Martin Robertson 1976).

[52] See, for example, S. Merry, *Getting Justice and Getting Even: Legal Consciousness among Working-Class Americans* (Chicago University of Chicago Press 1990).

[53] H. Becker , 'Whose Side Are We On?' (1961) 14 *Social Problems* 239–47.

[54] See, for example, R. Dingwall, ' "Don't Mind Him—He's from Barcelona": Qualitative Methods in Health Studies' in J. Daly, I. MacDonald and E. Willis, (eds.) *Researching Health Care* (London Routledge 1992) 161–75.

tribunals.[55] More generally, however, there has been almost no research about the work or perspectives of the civil servants who administer the tribunals system, the various agencies who give legal advice to appellants, the work of immigration officers, the private companies who run detention centres, and the appellants themselves. I would argue, along symbolic interactionist lines, that they can be viewed as a set of overlapping 'social worlds': and that it would be interesting to conduct more research on a number of these different groups, and particularly on the perspective and experiences of the appellants.[56]

A second topic it might be interesting to pursue would be to gain access to the group of lawyers and judges concerned with a particular area of law, and try to document how it develops and changes in response to new situations. This kind of sociological study has never been done, and might offer a way of reviving the realist tradition in legal theory, which lost its way, partly because it employed quantitative methods in looking for hidden causes, rather than adopting the approach recommended by Blumer.

A third topic one might want to investigate is the nature of the law-school itself. There have been a few studies about socialisation in the legal profession, and Stacy Burns has provided a close ethnomethodological description of how students were taught in Yale Law School.[57] One does not, however, get a sense from this literature of how any law school operates and changes as an institution, or the perspectives of faculty and students.

Once you begin to think about these topics, it becomes apparent that large areas of the legal profession have never been investigated using ethnographic methods. What is particularly interesting is that much more interactionist research has been done in educational and medical settings, simply because more sociologists have been employed in these professional fields. There is what might be termed 'a missing interactionist literature' on law, certainly after the early 1970s, so that there are relatively few studies that address legal professional practice in much depth. There are, of course, good institutional reasons why this has not so far happened, but it would be good to see a few more doctoral students in law departments doing ethnographic research, and engaging more seriously with symbolic interactionism as a theoretical tradition.

---

[55] M. Travers, *The British Immigration Courts: A Study of Law and Politics* (Bristol The Policy Press 1999).

[56] My study of immigration tribunals was partly influenced by the work of the British interactionist Paul Rock. He has conducted ethnographic research about different occupational perspectives in a Crown Court (*The Social World of an English Crown Court: Witness and Professionals in the Crown Court Centre at Wood Green* (Oxford Clarendon Press 1986)), and the work of civil servants in Britain and Canada (*A View From the Shadows: The Ministry of the Solicitor-General of Canada and the Making of the Justice for Victims of Crime Initiative* (Oxford Clarendon Press 1986)).

[57] S. Burns, 'Practising Law: A Study of Pedagogic Interchange in a Law School Classroom' in M. Travers and J. Manzo, (eds.) *Law in Action: Ethnomethodological and Conversation Analytic Approaches to Law* (Aldershot Ashgate 1997) 265–89.

12

Ethnomethodology and Law

ROBERT DINGWALL

THIS CHAPTER INTRODUCES ethnomethodology and conversation analysis
(CA) and explains their relevance to the study of law and society.[1] In the
transcript of the *Proceedings of the Purdue Symposium on Ethnomethodology*,
Garfinkel describes how he devised the term as a result of work with covert
recordings of jury-room deliberations on five civil cases in Wichita, Kansas, as
part of the Chicago Jury Project.[2] He noticed the way in which the jurors
debated the cases and their concern for issues about the methodology of argument—what was an adequate account; what was an adequate description; what
was adequate evidence? He recalled the headings of the Human Relations Area
Files, compiled at Yale since 1949. These are a database of anthropological studies of traditional societies around the world, summarised in a standard format
and indexed according to the institutions and behaviours which they document.[3] One set of index headings relates to the indigenous knowledge of these
societies about the natural world—ethnobotany, ethnophysiology, ethno-
physics and so on. Ethno-methodology, then, would refer to the study of the
ways in which ordinary members of a society dealt with issues concerning the
status of their knowledge about the world. How did they make the world appear
a more or less organised and orderly place? This broke down into two further
questions. How did people go about their everyday business, while showing to
others that their behaviour was reasonable and rational in the context where it
occurred? Conversely, how did people make sense of the activities of others
around them or in interaction with them? Language was the most important
medium for performing these tasks—'talk is a "constituent feature of the same

---

[1] Because these are, above all, empirical traditions of scholarship, the chapter frequently cross-
refers to a collection of papers which apply these approaches to the study of issues in law and society: M. Travers and J. Manzo, (eds.) *Law in Action: Ethnomethodological and Conversation
Analytic Approaches to Law* (Aldershot Ashgate 1997). However, the chapter is also intended to be
fully intelligible on its own for readers who do not have access to that collection.

[2] R. J. Hill and K. S. Critenden, (eds.) *Proceedings on the Purdue Symposium on
Ethnomethodology* (Institute for the Study of Social Change Purdue University Institute
Monograph Series No.1 1968). The findings of the Chicago jury project are reported in H. Kalven
and H. Zeisel with the collaboration of T. Callahan and P. Ennis, *The American Jury* (Boston Little
Brown 1966). Work from the covert recordings was banned and not published, although Garfinkel
refers to it in *Studies in Ethnomethodology*, *infra* n. 6, without quoting from the original data.

[3] Further information can be found at /www.yale.edu/hraf/.

setting that it is used to talk about" '.[4] In other words, as we talk about something, we also talk into existence a set of social relations between speaker and hearer(s) which make sense of talking about that thing in that way at that time and in that place.

The research programme represented by *Studies in Ethnomethodology* develops this agenda.[5] The first chapter continues the attempt to define ethnomethodology through reference to a study of the Los Angeles Suicide Prevention Center (SPC).[6] Garfinkel shows his concern with the practical construction of order. In everyday activity, we are not troubled by the philosophical problems of producing exhaustive descriptions of the world. When we talk about an event, we necessarily provide incomplete accounts, which we expect our audience to accept on the implicit basis that we could, if requested, provide additional detail that will 'make sense' of what we have been saying. In practice, however, hearers normally wait to see if the significance of what we are saying becomes clearer as we continue. As a result, the placement of an item within a sequence is likely to have implications for the way hearers respond to it. The work of the SPC, in collaboration with the LA Coroner's Office, began with uncertainties about the cause of a death. Its investigators were tasked with resolving these uncertainties in a way that would be officially recognized as adequate and reasonable. This was done by fitting them into a legal classification of causes. The classification provided a framework for making connections between the available data. Ideally, the result would be a unique reading of each item that fitted it into an apparently logical sequence of events leading ineluctably to whatever category was adopted. By making *these* data into *these* facts which could only be understood as going together by virtue of their sequential organization in *this* account, SPC investigators were able to demonstrate the adequacy of their inquiries and conclusions to people who might be entitled to review their work or motivated to construct a different account. Both investigators and reviewers, however, were engaged in essentially the same task using essentially the same ethno-methods.[7]

A number of early ethnomethodological studies focussed on these issues of classification. Garfinkel himself devoted a substantial part of *Studies in Ethnomethodology* to the problems of coding records for research purposes and the difficulty of reconciling data compiled for organizational purposes with the concerns of social research.[8] Whatever the intentions of their authors, the looseness of language left records open to a range of different future readings depending on who was reading them for what purposes. Confronted with this open texture, social scientists found they could not write exhaustive rules for coding any more than lawyers can write exhaustive laws for classifying deaths.

[4] Garfinkel, quoted in R. Turner, (ed.) *Ethnomethodology* (Harmondsworth Penguin 1974) at 17.
[5] H. Garfinkel, *Studies in Ethnomethodology* (Englewood-Cliffs New Jersey Prentice-Hall 1967).
[6] Reprinted in Travers and Manzo from a different source, *supra* n. 1.
[7] See also J. M. Atkinson, *Discovering Suicide* (London Macmillan 1978).
[8] Garfinkel, *supra* n. 6, at 18–24, 186–207.

The statistical data used in research and policy were produced by the ad hoc work of coders bridging the gap between the coding rules and the records they were being applied to. In deciding 'what the rules really meant', the coders relied on their ethnomethodological skills, their folk knowledge of what would be considered plausible. As a result, they wrote into the coding features that would later be discovered as findings, for example that automobile crashes were a rare cause of suicide. This work was the foundation of a series of studies of the social construction of official statistics and, indeed, the social construction of all quantitative data used by social scientists.[9]

Heritage points out that Garfinkel did not present his observations as the kind of nihilistic critique of quantitative methods sometimes attributed to him or put forward by others.[10] Nevertheless, these studies were perceived as an attack on much post-war social science and on the statistical apparatus of the modern state and its policy delivery systems in areas like law enforcement. Many powerful enemies were created and the work was widely dismissed. However, many of its questions remain effectively unanswered. What is the point of elaborate modelling exercises on crime rates if the basic data are the result of the discretionary decision-making of patrol officers operating within particular organisational environments? How do we actually study that process? How can we use such research to improve our understanding of what the numbers represent, which would make a non-trivial contribution to both theory and practice in crime control?

Although early ethnomethodological research was often regarded as indistinguishable from other qualitative or micro-sociologies, particularly symbolic interactionism or Goffman's dramaturgical sociology, the contrasts gradually became apparent. In some ways, qualitative practice was challenged just as sharply as quantitative.[11] Ethnomethodology, and later CA, set themselves apart from other traditions particularly through their caution in dealing with the mental processes of actors.

[9] For example, M. Bloor, 'Bishop Berkeley and the Adeno-Tonsillectomy Enigma: An exploration of variations in the social construction of medical disposals' (1976) 10 *Sociology* 273–87; M. Bloor, 'A minor office: The variable and constructed nature of death certification in a Scottish city' (1991) 32 *Journal of Health and Social Behavior* 273–87; A. Cicourel, *Method and Measurement in Sociology* (New York Free Press 1964); A. Cicourel, *The Social Organization of Juvenile Justice* (New York Wiley 1967); A. Cicourel, *Theory and Method in Argentinian Fertility* (New York Wiley-Interscience 1974); A. Cicourel and J. Kitsuse, *The Educational Decision-Makers* (Indianapolis Bobbs-Merrill 1963); J. Douglas, *The Social Meanings of Suicide* (Princeton Princeton University Press 1967); J. Kitsuse and A. Cicourel, 'A Note on the Use of Official Statistics' (1963) 11 *Social Problems* 131–39; L. Prior, *The Social Organisation of Death* (Basingstoke Macmillan 1989); D. Sudnow, *Passing On: The Social Organization of Dying* (Englewood-Cliffs New Jersey Prentice-Hall 1967); and J. Meehan, 'Record keeping practices in the policing of juveniles' in Travers and Manzo *supra* n. 1.

[10] J. Heritage, *Garfinkel and Ethnomethodology* (Cambridge Polity Pres, 1984) at 136. Indeed, the penultimate chapter of *Studies in Ethnomethodology* is a detailed discussion of the implications of case selection criteria and their operationalization for outcome prediction in a psychiatric service.

[11] Cicourel, (1967) *supra* n. 9, at 39–72.

Ethnomethodologists distrust the qualitative researcher's traditional foundation of truth claims in the intuitive or empathic abilities of the observer or inter-
viewer. As Garfinkel is fond of observing, if you want to know what goes on
inside people's heads, you should become a brain surgeon rather than a sociologist. Few sociologists seem previously to have thought that the understanding
of other people's minds was a serious methodological problem. This conclusion
was reached by two slightly different routes. One was Weber's classic exposition of *verstehen*, the notion that we could understand why someone else acted
as they did by an act of empathic understanding, which derived from the
hermeneutic tradition in German philosophy. The other was associated particularly with Cooley and Mead, and is summed up in the notion of 'taking the role
of the other', again an essentially imaginative act, that, if placed in your situation, this is how I would think and feel. The problems with this assumption
began to be explored during the 1930s by Alfred Schutz, an Austrian philosopher.[12] Schutz is best described as a *social* phenomenologist: in contrast to con-
temporaries like Husserl, Heidegger and Merleau-Ponty, he insisted that the
mediation of private experience through language meant that experience was
necessarily socialised.

Schutz argued on theoretical grounds that the stability of everyday life rested
upon every member's knowledge of typical situations, typical actors, typical
motives, typical lines of action, etc. and the constant renewal of confidence in
these by their repeated confirmation in interaction. Garfinkel asked what would
happen if this confidence were systematically breached.[13] His 'breaching experiments' showed, for example, how anger and confusion resulted from sustained
attempts to probe the meaning of statements, indicating the practical limitation
of uncertainty, or from the instruction to one family member to behave like a
lodger and ask permission every time before doing anything in their home, indicating the assumptions about appropriate behaviour for people in a particular
kind of relationship with one another. Another experiment involved telling students that they were going to experience a new form of counselling where the
counsellor would be hidden by a screen and would only give 'Yes' or 'No'
answers. In fact the answers were given at random but the students' behaviour
as they talked aloud about the responses showed that they were treating them as
minded actions and looking for the intent behind them.

Harvey Sacks's paper in the Travers and Manzo collection discusses the work
of lawyers as repairers of failures of confidence in everyday life. The lawyer's
job is to envision points of breakdown and to prepare strategies for minimising

[12] For example, A. Schutz, *The Phenomenology of the Social World* (London Heinemann 1972; first published 1932).

[13] H. Garfinkel, 'Common-sense knowledge of social structures: The documentary method of interpretation' in J. Scher, (ed.) *Theories of the Mind* (New York Free Press 1962), H. Garfinkel, 'Studies of the routine grounds of everyday activities' (1964) 11 *Social Problems* 225–50; Garfinkel, *supra* n. 5, at 35–103; see also P. McHugh, *Defining the Situation: The Organisation of Meaning in Social Interaction* (Indianapolis Bobbs-Merrill 1968).

these (contracts, trusts, wills, conveyances, etc.) or to offer patches to prevent order unravelling by supplying certainty. From the advice of lawyers to the decisions of courts, practical closure is brought to disputes or uncertainty over the meaning of legal statements and continuity restored to social relations. In doing so, however, the lawyer at work inhabits a kind of meta-world which is ordered and stabilised in parallel to the world of everyday life but relies on the same devices, such as the practical limitation of questioning, respect for the motives of others and so on. In his introduction to Sacks's collected lectures, Schegloff recalls a story that Sacks used to tell about a law school class discussing the recovery of damages for the overflight of property by an aeroplane.[14] It was agreed that no damages could be collected if the plane were being flown in a 'proper' manner and the discussion then turned to what height would be 'proper'—2,000 feet? 1,000 feet? 250 feet? 5 feet? Sacks reported that the last of these proposals was treated as frivolous and outside the bounds of common sense. This led him to wonder how this boundary had been crossed and why the same response had not been elicited by the penultimate term in the list. He had precipitated an unintended breaching experiment. Legal reasoning was clearly constrained by 'common sense' in exactly the same way as everyday reasoning, although in this case it was the 'common sense' of lawyers that the students were learning. This paper is not, however, typical of Sacks's work.

While *Studies in Ethnomethodology* had questioned many of the foundational assumptions of sociological methodology, it had not established an alternative: a striking feature of the book is the paucity of data—ad hoc observations from the Suicide Prevention Center, students' reports on breaching experiments they had been asked to carry out, descriptions and quotes from clinical and research interviews with the would-be transsexual, Agnes. The data are used to illustrate the theoretical argument rather than examined as topics in their own right. Sacks's achievement was to develop a way to use ethnomethodological thinking to understand specific things about the world. According to Schegloff, Sacks did not set out to study language or conversation but to discover how ordinary things got done in a recognisably consistent and orderly fashion.[15] Conversation simply happened to be an ordinary thing that could be recorded and reproduced for examination on an indefinite number of future occasions in order to reflect on how the participants had done it. Schegloff recalls Sacks talking in the winter of 1964 about a telephone call to the Suicide Prevention Center as an example of a common problem, the caller's withholding of their name at the beginning of the call. How had they succeeded in doing this without making an issue of it? The opening of conversations became the subject of the first lectures that Sacks gave in the 1964–5 academic session. Over the next ten years, until Sacks's death in 1975, Sacks and Schegloff, together with Gail Jefferson who transcribed Sacks's lectures before becoming an analyst in her own right

---

[14] H. Sacks, *Lectures on Conversation* (Oxford Blackwell 1992: volume I) at xiii.
[15] Sacks, *ibid.*, vol. i: xvi–xvii.

and the originator of the standard notation for CA data, developed a generic programme for the study of talk as co-ordinated action, productive of social order. As others became interested, the programme widened into what is now known as 'institutional talk', using the ideas and methods of CA to explore the production of particular local orders.[16] The increasing availability of light-weight video cameras has also made it possible to achieve some other parts of Sacks's original goals of studying how ordinary things happen by looking at gesture and movement, both independently and in co-ordination with talk.[17] The features of this history relevant to law can be brought out from the papers collected by Travers and Manzo.[18]

The papers which stand in a most direct line of descent from Sacks's work are those by Drew, Watson, Matoesian, Maynard, and Manzo and Komter.[19] Drew, Matoesian and Komter examine aspects of courtroom behaviour, Watson's data are from police interrogations and Maynard and Manzo use the unedited videotape of a jury deliberation recorded for a Public Television documentary. I shall concentrate on the Drew and Matoesian chapters, which both deal with rape trials.

Neither directly addresses the commonest argument about the legal system's treatment of rape, namely the feminist claim that it demonstrates law's embedded patriarchy. The institutional response has included reforms of courtroom examination designed to restrict certain lines of questioning, particularly the investigation of the complainant's previous sexual history. However, many women feel that these reforms have been ineffective in preventing a double victimization—by the original assault and by their treatment in court. By focussing on how cross-examination works, rather than beginning from a critical point, Drew and Matoesian show both why this reform is relatively ineffective and why the problem is so intractable.

Drew's paper focusses on the ways in which witnesses manage the potential implications of questions which they have been asked. In the Anglo-American adversarial tradition, justice is thought to be the outcome of a competition between attorneys to test the veracity or credibility of each other's witnesses.

---

[16] P. Drew and J. Heritage, *Talk at Work* (Cambridge Cambridge University Press 1992), D. Boden and D. Zimmerman, *Talk and Social Structure* (Cambridge Polity Press 1991).

[17] C. Heath, *Body Movement and Speech in Medical Interaction* (Cambridge Cambridge University Press 1986).

[18] Conversation analysis has not been well-served by secondary texts. However, the recent books by D. Silverman, *Harvey Sacks: Social Science and Conversation Analysis* (Cambridge Polity Press 1998) and P. ten Have, *Doing Conversation Analysis: A Practical Guide* (London Sage 1999) can be recommended.

[19] All page references are from Travers and Manzo, *supra* n. 1: P. Drew, 'Contested evidence in courtroom cross-examination' (first published 1992) 51–76, R. Watson, 'The presentation of victim and motive in discourse: The case of police interrogations and interviews' (first published 1983) 77–98; G. Matoesian, ' "I'm sorry we had to meet under these circumstances": Verbal artistry in the Kennedy Smith Rape Trial' 137–82; D. Maynard and J. Manzo, 'Justice as a phenomenon of order: Notes on the organization of a jury deliberation' (first published 1993) 209–38; and M. Komter, 'Remorse, redress and reform: Blame-taking in the courtroom' 239–264.

Examination-in-chief is interactionally designed to maximise credibility and cross-examination to discredit witnesses where possible. Under cross-examination, we can see witnesses attending to the intentions believed to lie behind questions and constructing their answers accordingly. The following extract is taken from a sequence analysed by Drew:

```
14: W:  I don't remember what he said to me that night.
15: (1.2)
16: A:  Well yuh had some uh (p) (.) uh fairly lengthy
17:      conversations with thu defendant uh:didn' you?
18: (0.7)
19: A:  On that evening uv February fourteenth?
20: (1.0)
21: W:  We:ll we were all talkin.
22: (0.8)
23: A:  Well you kne:w at that t:ime that the
24:      defendant was (.) in:terested (.) in you (.)
25:      did'n you?
26: (1.3)
27: W:  He: asked me how I'(d) bin: en
28: (1.1)
29: W:  J-just stuff like that
30: A:  Just asked yuh how (0.5) yud bi:n (0.3) but
31:      he kissed yuh goodnigh:t (0.5) izzat righ:t.=
```

This extract shows three features which are important for understanding the methodology of conversation analysis. The first is the three-turn sequence which is fundamental to the organisation of social interaction.[20] This is most obvious in question and answer sequences like cross-examination but occurs everywhere. It works like this: I say something, you respond to it and I am then positioned to decide whether your response is adequate and adequately connected to what I said first. In that third position, I can either decide to move on or rework (repair) my first turn and hope you will respond more satisfactorily or ask you to explain (account for) your failure to link your turn in second position to mine in first. Look at lines 16–26 in this extract. Lines 16–17, which are in first position for this example, also stand as third position in relation to line 14. The witness says she doesn't remember what the alleged rapist said to her. The attorney makes this the basis of a question about the lengthy conversations she is supposed to have had with him on a specific night, 14 February. This both looks back to the adequacy of her response, that she has not remembered anything from long conversations on a particular evening, memorable both in relation to the alleged rape and to the cultural significance of St Valentine's Day, and forward to the possibility that she can give a more precise answer in the next

---

[20] This is something of a simplification: other parts may be inserted in the sequence and the third turn may be left blank if the first party does not choose to comment on the second party's display of understanding or the design of their response.

turn. At line 21, however, the witness comes up with another rather general response. The attorney comments on the adequacy of this turn at lines 23–25 by again asking for a more specific answer, (notice the way in which all three turns are further linked by the poetic structure 'Well *pronoun* . . .').

Both here and in the longer sequence from which it is taken, we can also see the way in which both parties are showing their orientation to the implications of their turns. The witness's repeated production of answers which the attorney finds unsatisfactory indicates her attention to his intentions in asking the questions. Conversely, his repetition of the questions in the absence of satisfactory answers indicates a hearing of those answers as motivated, that the witness has not failed to satisfy him by accident or misunderstanding but as an act of will. Remember that this talk is being produced for a judge and jury to 'overhear'. Having continued long enough for the attorney to judge that the witness's evasiveness is established, he closes in at lines 30–31 by posing a contrast between her picture of an evening spent in unmemorable and uninvolving conversation with the defendant and earlier testimony that he had kissed her goodnight. Notice the way it is set up as a puzzle—such uses of contrasts are very common and seem to be a device for involving and persuading the overhearers—judge and jury—to reach a conclusion by virtue of their own reasoning rather than by being told the answer.

Drew's analysis is, of course, somewhat more complex and tightly argued. However, this illustration provides a basis for looking at Matoesian's work on a 'celebrity trial' and, in particular, his attempt to explain why the defence attorney's cross-examination of the alleged victim's friend, whom she had called to drive her home from the Kennedy estate after the incident, was hailed as a professional triumph. Matoesian quotes the full 4 minutes and 21 seconds of the critical passage which is 266 lines of transcript. This is a brief extract:

```
43: DA:  ( )That's not my question miss Mercer,
44:       you understand my question? (.) my question
45:       is did you meet this man (.) who your friend says
46:       is the alleged rapist?
47:       (0.6)
48: AM: Yes.
49: DA:  In this dark hallway is that right.
50:       (1.4)
51: AM: Yes
52:       (.)
53: DA:  And you ask him to help him— (.) help— (.)
54:       You ask the rapist to help you find her shoes
55:       (0.6) is that correct?
56:       (2.3)
57: AM: Yes.
58:       (0.5)
59: DA:  And he turns around and goes with you:: (1.5)
60:       uh::::: out of the house is that right?
61:       (0.8)
```

62: AM: Yes.
63:      (0.7)
64: DA: Through the dining room (.) to begin with (.) is
65:      that correct.
66:      (1.8)
67: AM: Yes
68 DA: It's dark in that house (.) right.
69:      (0.5)
70: AM: Yes.
71:      (.)
72: DA: You're walking through the dining room with this
73:      man (0.5) is that correct?
74:      (.)
75: AM: Yes.
76: DA: The man who's allegedly a rapist right?

We can see the three-turn structure used here in a rather different way. The attorney (DA) takes the witness (AM) through her story in very small steps and is happy to elicit a brief agreement to each of these. In the turn just before the extract, the witness seems to have picked up the intent of the strategy—to question the consistency between her friend's characterisation of Kennedy Smith as a rapist and her own behaviour walking through an empty and darkened house with him to look for a pair of shoes. However, her attempt to avoid answering a direct question has been challenged by the attorney (lines 43–46) and he then frames almost every question for the next three minutes or so as answerable by 'yes' or some equivalent. The distribution of pauses before these responses suggests that the witness understands what is being implied but cannot find a way out of it. The attorney is entitled to insist on his specific questions being answered specifically, and receives the judge's assistance in this at a later point. Notice again the way in which the overhearers are invited to solve a puzzle which is posed repeatedly as the sequence unfolds and the attorney takes the witness through the dining room, onto the patio, across the lawn, down an unlit stairway, through a gate onto the beach and back, all in the dark and all in the company of a man who she says is a rapist.

In these simple examples, we can identify two of the reasons why conversation analysis is so important for law and society scholars. The first is its contribution to an understanding of the practical skills of a legal system that depends heavily on orality. If you want to train counsel, witnesses, judges or interrogators to do their job more efficiently and effectively, then an understanding of the institutional talk of courtrooms, interrogation suites and law offices will make a vital contribution. Unlike other qualitative approaches or, indeed, many other ways of studying language, CA gets to a level of detail and precision that makes it replicable and reproducible. The exact circumstances of the trials dissected by Drew and Matoesian may not re-occur: an understanding of what made these cross-examinations so effective is fundamental to the improvisational skills of being an attorney or, for that matter, of being a witness. The second reason is to do with the consequences of orality itself and the question of the extent to which many of the complaints of would-be reformers are grounded in things which are actually reformable. If the issue of credibility is central to trials, then cross-examination will always turn on it, whatever restrictions may be placed on its substantive content. A lawyer who is discharging his, or her, professional responsibility to a defendant will always test the credibility of a witness for the prosecution. Since there are rarely third parties present in crimes like rape, and a critical issue is likely to be that of the consent of the participants to intercourse, the alleged victim will almost always have to give evidence. As these extracts show, a competent attorney does not need to ask a woman prurient questions about sexual history to attack the credibility of her story. The sense of being raped twice over may be inescapable in a legal system that expects evidence to be tested in public.

Garfinkel's own research developed in rather different ways represented by the 'ethnomethodological studies of work'.[21] This emerged in parallel with CA and has often been critical of it. In particular, it has suggested that CA has become mechanistic and lost the focus on the active use of language as a tool by actors. Where CA has become increasingly interested in fundamental dimensions of interaction, which are either common to all occasions where joint action occurs or whose systematic variation constitutes a basis for the classification of such occasions, 'studies of work' have tried to remain closer to Garfinkel's original vision of a social science which would understand the uniqueness of activities, the qualities that made something happen in this particular way on this particular occasion.[22]

In practice, this has been a very difficult goal to achieve and there is some dispute over the extent to which published work differs from ethnomethodologically-influenced ethnography of the kind currently being undertaken by people like Emerson, Miller and Holstein, on the one hand, or CA, on the other.[23] The two papers discussed here reflect this tension. Lynch's paper reports on judges' work in Toronto, based mainly on reconstruction of talk from field notes, and Burns analyses a videotaped sequence from a law school classroom.

The opening of Lynch's paper is as clear a methodological statement as one can find. His interest is in the production of the judge as a participant in courtroom

[21] For example, H. Garfinkel, *Ethnomethodological Studies of Work* (London Routledge 1986), and in Travers and Manzo, *supra* n. 1: M. Lynch, 'Preliminary notes on judges' work: The judge as a constituent of courtroom "hearings"' 99–132 and S. Burns, 'Practising law: A study of pedagogic interchange in a law school classroom' 265–88.

[22] H. Garfinkel, 'Ethnomethodology's program' (1996) 59 *Social Psychology Quarterly* 5–21.

[23] R. Emerson, 'Constructing serious violence and its victims: Processing a domestic violence restraining order' in G. Miller and J. Holstein, (eds.) *Perspectives on Social Problems* 6 (Greenwood Ct. JAI Press 1994) 3–28; G. Miller, *Enforcing the Work Ethic: Rhetoric and Everyday Life in a Work Incentive Program* (Albany Suny Press 1991); G. Miller, *Becoming Miracle Workers: Language and Meaning in Brief Therapy* (New York Aldine de Gruyter,1997) and J. Holstein, *Court-Ordered Insanity: Interpretive Practice and Involuntary Commitment* (New York Aldine de Gruyter 1993).

interaction. There is no judge *prior* to this interaction who has some kind of secret or invisible motivation to which the analyst has a privileged access. This distinguishes it from, for example, symbolic interactionist studies which assume that it is possible to make inferences about the judge's state of mind from his or her verbal or non-verbal actions or from interviews, to find out what is 'really going on' in the judge's head during courtroom interaction. The object of Lynch's paper is to describe how the participants in court proceedings collectively produce the judge as a fact, observable to them and to any other competent watcher. Here it differs from dramaturgical analyses, where the focus is on an actor's performance of a role. Lynch argues that a role is the creation of the speeches and actions of all the participants and of the hearings or 'overhearings' which those speeches and actions create or project. The judge does not necessarily have to be signalled as an audience or, indeed, even physically hear what is being said: it is enough that the other parties talk to each other in a way that orients to the judge's shadow. Lynch looks first at the judge as a virtual presence in taped plea bargaining exchanges and then at the court hearing itself and the ways in which the judge's physical presence is oriented to as a feature of the interaction between counsel, witnesses and other participants. At the end of the hearing, the judge's summing up produces the rational order of the hearing and finds 'the truth' behind the array of data and motivational possibilities which have been entered in evidence. The judge speaks for the public, who are a silent audience for the oral work of trial, and formulates what is to be regarded as an adequate conclusion or set of inferences from the talk and events that have gone on.

Lynch's paper can usefully be read in the light of Atkinson's discussion of formality in court proceedings.[24] Atkinson points to the way in which many of the features of hearings which are conventionally read off as 'oppressive' are actually intrinsic to the interactional organisation of the event. Maintaining order and a shared focus of attention in a complex multi-party interaction is a non-trivial organisational problem. The physical arrangements of courts, the distinctive clothing of various participants, the turn-taking rules for examination and cross-examination, the rules of relevance specifying what is admissible and inadmissible and so on may be the necessary conditions for doing the job at all. In a similar fashion, Lynch's analysis brings out the way in which orientation to the judge and the design of interaction to sustain the attention and involvement of the judge holds together the process of court work. Just as our collective preference for an adversarial system of justice entails the possibility of cross-examination and the destructive testing of the credibility of witnesses in rape trials, so the public and oral nature of proceedings has implications for the construction of judges as figures towards whom certain kinds of verbal and other behaviour is required. Atkinson suggests that there may be some elements of overdetermination which survive from a past when offenders, witnesses and

---

[24] J. M. Atkinson, 'Understanding formality' (1983) 33 *British Journal of Sociology* 86–117; see also R. Dingwall and D. Greatbatch, 'The virtues of formality' in J. Eekelaar and M. MacLean, (eds.) *A Reader on Family Law* (Oxford Oxford University Press 1994) 391–99.

other members of the public might be less familiar with courtrooms as inter-actional locales than is the case in an age where television and films have made some version of courts a familiar experience. However, the necessity of doing the work may be an important constraint on what can be changed, unless we fundamentally change the job itself.

Garfinkel has placed considerable emphasis in the studies of work pro-gramme on collaborations with people who have a native competence in doing the work being studied—leading to partnerships with mathematicians and architects, among others. How, he challenges them, specifically, do you do it—whatever 'it' is. Again, it is important to stress that these people are not being used as native informants to provide an ironic commentary on 'what is really going on': they are, rather, native practitioners who can work in a way that is recognized as competent by others and can be encouraged to specify the skills involved. Burns's paper is an example. She records how Garfinkel encouraged her to go to law school after undergraduate studies in sociology and to make the process of instruction into a research topic. The sequence examined in the paper shows a distinguished law professor teaching students how to argue a point in court. Actually, as Burns demonstrates, there is very little ostensive teaching, where students are told what to do. The classroom mimics the law court with a confrontation between students and teacher where the students are required to talk as if they were counsel and where the teacher switches between responding in the manner of a difficult judge and giving a situated commentary on the ade-quacy of the students' talk. Success occurs where students can do 'being a lawyer', talking through their point in the way that a practitioner would. The public nature of this confrontation, often described by students as humiliating, mimics the public accountability of the courtroom. This goes right down to the listening demanded of other students who may be called on without notice to take up the point and which anticipates the listening demanded of opposing counsel, monitoring examinations for objectionable practices.

Burns brackets questions about the substantive content of the laws which are being taught in favour of her focus on the practice of law. The fit between her paper and Lynch's is striking in the integration of the experiences of law school and law practice. It raises equally difficult questions about the potential for reform projects. Law school is a hard, stressful and often painful experience, which may be very uncomfortable for students from milieux where the kind of public accountability enforced by the pedagogic practices described by Burns is rarely experienced or valued. At the same time, it is a close proxy for the public experience of trial in an oral and adversarial system. It does not seem that the one is easily reformable without changing the other in rather fundamental ways—which leads to some very basic normative questions.[25]

---

[25] There is a separate question about how well this kind of law teaching prepares students for the non-confrontational work that makes up a large element of legal practice or, indeed, for the rather cursory nature of trial in many lower courts.

On the whole, ethno/CA writers have not been interested in such questions. Sacks seemed to envision his work as a natural science of society and once remarked that a lot of revolutions could go on without ever changing everyday life very much. Garfinkel's interest in the specificity and 'just-whatness' of actions brackets normative issues in favour of 'how does this work' questions about local social order. The phenomena described by ethno/CA are neither good nor bad: they just are. Judging them is not a scientific matter, except that a scientific understanding of the practices may point to their evolutionary adaptiveness as a matter to be confronted by would-be reformers: as Atkinson showed, some courtroom practices probably could be changed without compromising the public process of adversarial justice. Beyond a certain point, however, we would no longer have such a process and we would need to weigh the consequent gains and losses very carefully.

The modest restatement of what is in effect the classic Weberian distinction between the vocations of science and politics is a difficult position to hold in the face of competition from critical analysts with a different kind of motivation. Conley and O'Barr, for example, in a widely used introductory text on law and language, announce their intention of exposing the limitations of the law and of its alleged use to perpetuate certain distributions of power.

> The particular body of work that is our focus here introduces another important variable into the law-language equation: power. This research looks at the law's language in order to understand the law's power . . . The dominant element in [most people's encounters with the law] is language. To the extent that power is realized, exercised, abused or challenged in such events, the means are primarily linguistic. This book is a search for those linguistic means.[26]

This is a manifesto for the integration of the study of the organisation of interaction and the dynamics of power. By examining language and social interaction, we will be able to discover answers to some of the puzzling questions of law and society research. This has documented the law's failure to deliver equal treatment but has often been less successful at exposing the mechanisms by which inequality is produced. The study of interaction will allow the sources of injustice to be discovered. We can see the differences in the way Conley and O'Barr discuss Matoesian's research on hearings of rape cases.

They begin by considering the 'legal, political and scholarly discourse about rape' and its analysis of the extent to which this crime is an expression of male power and domination. They then move to connect these abstract ideas with the real use of language in courtrooms 'to understand how discourse practices reflect, ratify and sometimes challenge social hierarchies'. The sequence is important: power and domination come first and the language is inspected for its expression of them. Various extracts from Matoesian's data are first introduced

---

[26] J. Conley and W. M. O'Barr, *Just Words: Law, Language and Power* (Chicago University of Chicago Press 1998) at 2.

as exemplifying 'linguistic features of the rape trial that may contribute to the process of revictimization'. These cover 'five features that lawyers manipulate to control witnesses: silence, question form, topic management, evaluative commentary and challenges to the witness's capacity for knowledge . . . [these are] important strategies whereby cross-examining lawyers can dominate witnesses'. If we take silence as an example, then we have already seen in the earlier extract from the Kennedy Smith trial how silence may take on significance from its place in a sequence of utterances. The witness, AM, is taken through a series of questions which imply a disjuncture between her characterisation of Kennedy Smith as a rapist and her actual behaviour on the night in question. Her silence is not a matter of comment at any point in the sequence but may be heard as showing her understanding of where the cross-examination is leading and the inferences that the judge and jury are being invited to draw. This is somewhat more subtle than the examples which Conley and O'Barr take from Matoesian's earlier work where lawyers call hearers' attention to silence by repeating questions, commenting on delay in responding or exaggerating the space before they produce their next turn.[27] Conley and O'Barr acknowledge that many of these phenomena do have the kind of functional basis sketched earlier: Although the particular concern with the politics of rape may lead them to be seen as uniquely gendered, in fact, they are generic to cross-examination as it deals with competing assessments of the credibility of evidence, of the evaluation of witnesses' honesty or dishonesty, their consistency or inconsistency and so on. However, drawing on another paper by Matoesian,[28] Conley and O'Barr go on to argue that conversation analysis reveals two other phenomena which are distinctively gendered: the 'sexual double bind' and the covert exploitation of the witness's prior sexual history.

The 'sexual double bind' refers to a woman's difficulty in an acquaintance rape case of explaining how an ordinary social encounter turned into a criminal act. If she presents herself as emotional, the lawyer may depict her as irrational, taking revenge for a bad experience when she had at the time consented. If she presents herself as cool, the lawyer may question her account of having been dominated: indeed she may even be portrayed as rationally motivated by some improper intent towards the alleged rapist, looking to be bought off, perhaps. The point about sexual history relates to the way in which most US states, and the UK, have banned general questions about a rape victim's prior sexual experience, so that the issue of consent on *this* occasion cannot be coloured by evidence of consent on other occasions with other men—or indeed by evidence of innocence or virginity. A skilled attorney may, though, find ways of evading the spirit of these prohibitions, even while observing their letter.

---

[27] G. Matoesian, *Reproducing Rape: Domination through Talk in the Courtroom* (Cambridge Polity Press 1993).

[28] G. Matoesian, 'Language, law and society: Policy implications of the Kennedy Smith rape trial' (1995) 29 *Law and Society Review* 669–702.

An important difficulty in evaluating these arguments is the lack of detail in the transcripts. Although Conley and O'Barr criticise the CA notation system as a barrier to non-specialist readers, its design is not random. In several of the extracts, for example, the location of pauses and overlaps is potentially important for analysing their hearing. Take this sequence from the prosecutor's cross examination of Kennedy Smith:

1. P So you have this conversation___, well you had this act, then you
2. ejaculate and then you say, 'Well I'm going into the water and take a
3. swim now.'
4. W Yes
5. P That sounds not too romantic, Mr Smith.
6. W I don't know how to respond to that.

Line 6 is presented as evidence of the emotional indifference of Kennedy Smith. However, two crucial features are missing from this transcript. The first is any indication of what is going on between lines 5 and 6: how is Kennedy Smith's response positioned in relation to the question? Is there an overlap? Is there a pause? Moreover, the prosecutor's turn at line 5 is not syntactically a question. The relation between lines 5 and 6 could sustain an account of a man who is embarrassed or ashamed about his behaviour, of casual sex with a stranger but not necessarily of coerced sex. Indeed, it is even arguable that line 6 is simply a response to the prosecutor's failure to formulate a question at line 5. She has simply made a comment and left it hanging. The second critical absence is the prosecutor's next turn: what happens in the third position following her utterance in line 5? How does she hear line 6 or, perhaps better, how does she invite the judge and jury to hear line 6? Is this actually a noticeable line in the context at all?

The sequence which is most visibly gendered, where Conley and O'Barr reproduce a section of cross-examination from the Kennedy Smith trial focussing on the point at which the alleged victim removed her pantyhose, directly parallels the repetitive questioning sequence discussed earlier. Conley and O'Barr assert that her failure to recall precisely when she removed this item of clothing plays on its equivocal status as underwear or outerwear. Their male students typically assume that decent people do not lose track of their underwear; however, their female students draw a distinction between pantyhose and more intimate garments. It would be as legitimate to remove them to walk on the beach as to do so as a precursor to voluntary sexual intercourse, and consent to the latter cannot be inferred from the former. Again the transcript lacks critical details about pausing and the relative placement of utterances. However, it is arguable that the pantyhose are really marginal to the central issue of the quality of the witness's memory of events on the evening in question. Whether their removal is a prelude to a walk on the beach or sexual intercourse is less critical than the fact that their removal is the kind of event which a witness might reasonably be expected to recall, whenever it happened, and that a failure to recall it invites adverse inferences about the reliability of her testimony. Although the repetition may be held to have a prurient character, there is no evidence that it is heard this way in the context in which it is produced.

This is the key difference between CA and critical discourse analysis. Critical discourse analysts know in advance that rape courtrooms are sites for power and domination: conversation analysts insist that we must first understand what is happening as a local phenomenon before considering whether other variables may be relevant.

The argument has been most clearly laid out by Schegloff in two papers which review the programme of institutional talk research within CA and of critical discourse analysis.[29] He contrasts the positions of those who would begin by stipulating the existence and relevance of power and status within and between social formations such as classes, ethnic groups, genders, age grades and occupations and those who are actually producing the observable social order through their moment-to-moment orientations to whatever matters are locally relevant at the time of production. The first of these, of which Conley and O'Barr might reasonably be regarded as an exemplar:

> . . . allows students, investigators, or external observers to deploy the terms which pre-occupy *them* in describing, explaining, critiqueing, etc. the events and texts to which they turn their attention. There is no guaranteed place for the endogenous orientations of the participants in those events; there is no principled method for establishing those orientations; there is no commitment to be constrained by those orientations. However well-intentioned and well-disposed towards the participants—indeed, often enough the whole rationale of the critical stance is the championing of what are taken to be authentic, indigenous perspectives—there is a kind of theoretical imperialism involved here, a kind of hegemony of the intellectuals, of the literati, of the academics, of the critics whose theoretical apparatus gets to stipulate the terms by reference to which the world is be understood—when there has already *been* a set of terms by which the world was understood—by those endogenously involved in its very coming to pass.[30]

Schegloff concludes with the stinging comparison of critical discourse analysis to those who speak of Columbus 'discovering' America as if there were not indigenous people already there. In the same way, he implies sociologists are prone to 'uncover' or 'reveal' features in everyday life as if ordinary people were not already doing it quite adequately without any identifiable reference to these features. The task is not 'to privilege sociology's concerns under the rubric 'social structure' but to discover them in the members' worlds, if they are indeed there.[31] The cause of social criticism is furthered more by firmly grounded analysis of the specifics of a situation, in this case of language or text, than by superficial readings, evaluated by reference to their ideological fluency.

[29] E. Schegloff, 'Reflections on talk and social structure' in D. Boden and D. Zimmerman, (eds.) *Talk and Social Structure* (Cambridge Polity Press 1991) 44–70; E. Schegloff, 'Whose text? Whose context?' (1997) 8 *Discourse and Society* 165–88. See also the exchange between Schegloff and Billig, in (1999) 10 *Discourse and Society* which continues the debate.

[30] Schegloff, *ibid.*, (1997) at 167.

[31] Schegloff, (1991) *supra* n. 29 at 66.

This may, though, misrepresent the tradition of social and political theory in which the major microsociologies of our time—symbolic interactionism as well as CA and ethnomethodology—are embedded. Most contemporary macro-sociologies still see the foundations of social order either in terms of contract or consensus. The first, which goes back in its essentials to Hobbes and Locke, proposes that, confronted with the perils of disorder, human beings created institutions to restrain their passions, particularly in the form of some kind of sovereign power—a monarch or a constitution—with the legitimate authority to regulate human conduct. Social order is the product of human design. The second owes something to Rousseau but a great deal more to Freud and some readings of Parsons. Order is a matter of human nature—we are just born that way—or of invisible internalisation of rules, norms, conventions, etc.

A third possibility, however, which sociologists have now largely abdicated to economics, considers social order as the spontaneous product of the local pursuit of self-interest. Gamble outlines the main features in a discussion of Hayek's work.[32] Hayek contrasts *taxis* and *cosmos* as two different types of order. Taxis is order that results from the exercise of human will and intention, which might be represented by the writing of statutes and the design of enforcement systems. Cosmos is order which no-one has consciously created. It is the unintended consequence of human agents using the local knowledge available to them to pursue their interests within a framework of very general rules of proper conduct, like the features of practical reasoning identified as ethnomethodology. Knowledge is imperfect, fragmented and local. No one knows the outcome of any particular action or its impact on aggregate outcomes. Nevertheless, as long as everyone adheres to the rules of proper conduct, the pursuit of self-interest will produce an order that is maximally beneficial to all participants.

If contemporary microsociologies are indeed set within this context, it becomes clearer why it is so difficult to couple them to a 'critical' agenda. Adopting Schegloff's Weberian position does not resolve the problem but merely avoids it by refusing to go where the intellectual direction leads. In fact, there remains a perfectly respectable moral result: a spontaneous liberal order must rest on the moral action of individuals. Self-interest is maximised by self-restraint. If we are concerned about various kinds of oppression and injustice, then much more may be achieved by a focus on our individual responsibilities to deal properly with each other rather than by reactive measures directed at sweeping changes. Consider, for example, the extent to which affirmative action has become part of the middle class welfare state and perpetuated the social exclusion of poor people of all ethnic groups, genders, sexual orientations or whatever. Will it be more effective if I am required to conduct a job search in particular ways by law or because I believe that it is the right way to do it?

---

[32] A. Gamble, *Hayek: The Iron Cage of Liberty* (Cambridge Polity Press 1996) at 36–40.

Ethnomethodology and conversation analysis may, then, not simply be a resource for analysing the linguistic technology of law or the character of legal work. At least implicitly, they may contain the basis of a very deep questioning of the role of law in relation to social order, of the extent to which law does indeed penetrate everyday life and of the degree to which it can be a vehicle for achieving reformist goals. Considered in their full context, ethnomethodology and conversation analysis may indeed be what their founders claimed them to be: not merely new research technologies but new ways of thinking about sociology and its core intellectual project. As such, they necessarily challenge some of the currently hegemonic assumptions of law and society studies about both the positive and the normative aspects of its research agenda. Are we really trying to find out how law works or to find illustrations for an *a priori* critique?

Section 5

Postmodernism

REZA BANAKAR and MAX TRAVERS

'POSTMODERNISM' IS AN intellectual movement that became popular during the 1970s and 1980s. It was originally used to describe a trend within art, architecture and literature, but it soon grew into an entire world-view, which broke radically with, and urged its followers to move beyond, the totalising constraints of the 'metanarrative' of Reason constitutive of classical modernism.[1] In this sense, postmodernism can be described as an anti-foundationalist movement pitched against the dominant philosophical traditions, assumptions and endeavours to attain an ultimate knowledge, reality or truth. This also means that an understanding of postmodernism, but also poststructuralism which was one of the main sources of the postmodern movements' initial intellectual inspirations, requires revisiting the notion of modernity. We, therefore, start this section with a brief overview that explains the relationship between 'modernism', 'postmodernism' and 'poststructuralism', and assumes less knowledge than the two chapters that follow by Gary Wickham and Shaun McVeigh.

The postmodernists' main argument is that the modern world, as conceptualised by Marx, has ended; we are now living in 'postmodernity' or a 'postmodern world', although some theorists prefer to use the term 'late-capitalism' or 'late-modernity'. This is partly a claim about the many changes that have taken place in industrialised societies since the nineteenth century. It is also often a philosophical claim that is similar to the doubts expressed by nineteenth century Romantic thinkers about the benefits of reason and science. Poststructuralist thinkers do not always use the term 'postmodern', or argue that we are entering a new era of human history. They do, however, challenge the central 'modernist' assumption that one can arrive at 'the truth' through the exercise of reason, and construct a better world.

In our view, poststructuralism is best understood as making a philosophical point about modernity. It does not ask us to give up science, and return to the middle-ages (although one can detect a certain nostalgia for a pre-industrialised past in Shaun McVeigh's chapter). Nor does it argue that sociology, as an empirical discipline, is no longer possible, or should be abandoned as an attempt to

---

[1] Some proponents of postmodernism are also known as deconstructivists. Deconstructionism is a 'subversive' approach to literary criticism based on the denial of interpretative primacy attributed to the author as the source of meaning.

produce a better society. Nor does it even have any political implications, since one can hold liberal or conservative views as a poststructuralist (and, in this respect, it is similar to the nineteenth century Romantic movement). What one can say, however, is that the philosophical objective of someone like Derrida is to make us question the received ideas that we take for granted from the Enlightenment. The fact that Marx now appears as both naive and ethnocentric, whereas even his political opponents would not have advanced this criticism in the 1960s and 1970s, indicates the extent to which this critique has been successful in universities.

The poststructuralist philosopher who has had the greatest impact on social science is undoubtedly Michel Foucault. Before his death from AIDS in 1984, Foucault advanced a sustained critique of the Enlightenment through a series of historical studies. *Discipline and Punish* was, for example, intended to show that modern rational methods of punishment, such as imprisonment, are not necessarily morally superior to the tortures inflicted on criminals in the middle-ages.[2] This book has a Weberian theme: the use of reason has resulted in a soulless world, in which governments classify populations using statistical methods, and we have given up our freedom to experts like doctors, social workers and psychiatrists.

Gary Wickham starts by acknowledging that Foucault 'rarely wrote at any length about law' (the same observation used to be made of Marx). He has, however, still managed to find a number of characteristically provocative comments and asides made by Foucault about the relationship between law and the 'disciplines' that 'characterize, classify [and] specialize' human populations.[3] In most of these comments, law is portrayed as a surface or secondary phenomenon that prevents us from understanding the real nature of power. He observes, for example, that the 'system of rights' that was 'egalitarian in principle' created by the nineteenth century bourgeoisie was 'supported by all those systems of micro-power that are essentially non-egalitatarian . . . that we call the disciplines'.[4]

Similarly, when Foucault developed an interest in 'governmentality' in the 1970s, he was not primarily interested in law, but rather in the 'rational forms' and 'technical procedures' through which governments exercise power over populations, or encourage them to govern themselves.[5]

How then can one employ a Foucauldian approach in studying law? Wickham suggests that one way would be to employ an 'archeological' and 'genealogical' approach in investigating how law features in any area of society, such as gambling, and how this is implicated in relations of power. It should be clear from this section that Wickham is not interested in making a political point

---

[2] M. Foucault, *Discipline and Punish: The Birth of the Prison* (London Allen Lane 1977).
[3] M. Foucault *ibid.*, at 223.
[4] M. Foucault *ibid.*, at 222.
[5] M. Foucault, *The Foucault Reader* edited by P. Rabinow (New York Pantheon 1984), at 337–8.

about gambling, and instead presents it, in almost neutral terms, as a set of discourses and practices. A critical theorist like Herbert Marcuse would have viewed this as a device used by economically-dominant groups to control and pacify the masses, along with horoscopes, and television soaps.[6] What Foucault himself would have made of this topic must remain a matter for conjecture, although he would probably have used it to say something provocative about modernity, with his usual philosophical bite.

Shaun McVeigh is a legal philosopher, rather than a social scientist, and so his chapter, like most of the papers published in journals such as *Social and Legal Studies* or *Law and Critique*, is not concerned with collecting and analysing empirical data. Instead, it advances a philosophical position in relation to the common law, through considering the ideas of different poststructuralist thinkers, including Lyotard, Deleuze, Guattari, Baudrillard, Derrida, Irigaray and Lacan. The central, by now familiar, argument is that human beings have lost their freedom in a postmodern world dominated by 'technology' and 'capital' to the point where there is no possibility of resistance.

According to the traditional metanarratives of legal theory, law embodies the prevailing values and aspirations of the majority of people of a society. Thus, it constitutes the society through the imposition of an order, which is the essence of the rule of law and which lies in line with the will of the majority. This rule of law brings continuity, uniformity, and predictability to the process of legal decision-making, facilitating social organisation and cooperation in society. Postmodernists challenge this account of the rule of law by arguing that social behaviour and organisation is not governed by the law, because the study and transmission of law requires texts, which must be interpreted before they can be enforced. Since there are different ways of interpreting laws, it is not the laws but their interpretations that are the real rulers. Hence, because of its dependency on text and documentation, and the fact that law is founded on layers of 'interpretable and transformable textual strata', modern law is open to deconstruction.[7]

The deconstructibility of law is hampered by the dominant legal discourse, which in its search for the truth of the law reduces the meanings interpreted in a text and conceals the open-ended nature of legal texts. Legal science contains techniques of interpretation used to yield the meaning of the laws, ie reveal the law's 'truth'. However, not everyone is granted the privilege of interpretation; and justice becomes a rhetorical tool which serves the interest of the powerful. By contrast, as McVeigh explains, the question of justice for Derrida was about responding to 'the singularity of the other' and addressing the other in 'the language of the other'.

We notice here the affinity of postmodernism with critical legal studies, legal pluralism and the feminist critique of the law. Postmodernism too rejects the

---

[6] H. Marcuse, *One Dimensional Man* (London Routledge 1974).
[7] S. Ahmed 'Towards a Feminist Theory of Legal Rights' (1995) 4 *Social and Legal Studies* 56–73, at 61

idea that the state is the only source of law and argues that 'people operate in several spheres simultaneously—in the market, at work, in the family, as consumers: hence there is an uneven and unstable, nonsynchronic mixing of types of rules, some of which may be empowering, others oppressive'.[8] While legal pluralists find much in common with the approach of postmodernists to the state and the law, a part of the feminist movement finds support for their cause in the postmodernist's urge to subvert and defy the domination of political and legal communities, which monopolise the right of interpretation. The discourses of these dominant interpretive communities are intrinsically gendered reconstructing the maleness of the law and politics. Hence, it is hardly surprising if many feminist scholars find the postmodernist's 'subversive' approach to law, which aims to defy the law's objectivity, abstraction and foundational claims, appealing.

There are, however, considerable differences, and points of contention and debate, between critical legal studies and postmodernism. It should be apparent from McVeigh's chapter, despite the abstract and difficult nature of the language, that he ultimately recommends postmodern jurisprudence as a progressive movement that allows us to ask critical questions about authority and injustice. Some readers may, however, find that his arguments are, apparently, self-contradictory. One might, for example, want to question how one can criticise state power if there really are no firm foundations for obtaining knowledge or making ethical judgements. And what exactly is meant by the suggestion in the last sentence that 'a postmodern jurisprudence engages in ways to dispute and judge on grounds that are not altogether there'? This deliberately unclear, not to say paradoxical, statement is typical of post-structuralism as a philosophical movement. One can, however, see how some critics doubt its transformative abilities, since it cannot 'come up with an alternative vision, a vision of the economy and the polity that will complement its vision of community'.[9]

---

[8] J. F. Handler, 'Postmodernism, Protest, and the New Social Movements' (1992) 26 *Law and Society Review* 697–731, at 705.

[9] Handler *ibid.*, p. 727.

13

Foucault and Law

GARY WICKHAM

T HIS CHAPTER HAS three main aims—to offer a summary and discussion of what Foucault had to say about law, to offer an introduction to some of Foucault's methods for those interested in learning to use Foucault as a resource for the study of law in society and to offer a discussion of what Foucault's notion of governmentality might mean for this study.

The first section deals with the fact that Foucault had little directly to say about law and suggests he thought the category less useful than those of discipline and norms. The second section provides a brief introduction to the tools of archaeology, genealogy, discourse and power-knowledge and indicates how they may be employed in the study of law in society. The third section extends this methodological discussion such that it covers the later notion of governmentality, which has spawned a new and distinct approach within the world of Foucault scholarship.

1. FOUCAULT, LAW, DISCIPLINE AND NORMS[1]

Foucault rarely wrote at any length about law. Admittedly, in *Discipline and Punish*[2] and in a lecture published (at least in English) as the second of 'Two Lectures'[3] there are extensive discussions and in the first volume of the *History of Sexuality*[4] project, law occasionally features, as it does in a number of his

---

[1] Much of the shape and content of this section relies on A. Hunt and G. Wickham, *Foucault and Law: Towards a Sociology of Law as Governance* (London Pluto Press 1994) at 39–40; and on A. Hunt, 'Foucault's expulsion of law: toward a retrieval', (1992) 17 *Law and Social Inquiry* 1. It should be noted that the argument, expressed in these places, that Foucault concentrates on the notions of disciplines and norms at the expense of law, an argument followed, at least to some extent, here, has been challenged by some scholars. The most detailed counter-argument is provided by V. Tadros, 'Between Governance and Discipline—The Law and Michel Foucault', (1998) 18 *Oxford Journal of Legal Studies* 75; but see also R. Mackie, 'Review of A. Hunt and G. Wickham *Foucault and Law: Towards a Sociology of Law as Governance* and D. Caudill and S. Gold (eds) *Radical Philosophy of Law*', (1997) 2 *Newcastle Law Review* 121; N. Rose and M. Valverde 'Governed by Law?', (1997) 7 *Social and Legal Studies* 541.

[2] M. Foucault, *Discipline and Punish: The Birth of the Prison* (London Allen Lane 1977).

[3] M. Foucault, 'Two Lectures' in C. Gordon (ed.), *Michel Foucault. Power/Knowledge: Selected Interviews and Other Writings 1972–1977* (Brighton Harvester 1980).

[4] M. Foucault, *The History of Sexuality Volume I: An Introduction* (New York Pantheon 1978).

interviews,[5] especially those given after 1975. However, there is not much more; no one would ever seriously apply to Foucault any label such as legal scholar, legal theorist, sociologist of law, or critical legal thinker. In this sense, then, it is hardly surprising that the worlds of legal and socio-legal scholarship have been slow to recognise the potential of his insights and remain somewhat wary of the speculation necessary to draw them out.

At the centre of Foucault's treatment of law lies his treatment of power. Indeed, it might be said that Foucault is only interested in law to the point that it helps him propose his very particular understanding of power. 'Instead of seeking the explanation in a general conception of the Law, in the evolving modes of industrial production . . . it seemed to me far wiser to look at the workings of Power'.[6]

For Foucault, while law is crucially about power, the power of law is very limited, very one-sided (simultaneously 'complex and partial'). This is perhaps why he spends so little time on law. He tries throughout much of his work (as I discuss in more detail in the next section) to study power as a positive as well as a negative phenomenon—power as productive, as producing social relations, producing subjects and institutions. If we view power only as a negative force—that is, as a force that says 'no, thou shalt not', that works by prohibitions—Foucault believes we will miss much, even most, of what power does. For Foucault, law seems to be largely about negative power, sometimes only about sovereignty and its capacity to guarantee truth, and he is keen to change this, to move law aside in favour of a broader conception of power:

> In short, it is a question of orienting ourselves to a conception of power that replaces the privilege of the law with the viewpoint of the objective, the privilege of prohibition with the viewpoint of tactical efficacy, the privilege of sovereignty with the analysis of a multiple and mobile field of force relations, wherein far-reaching, but never completely stable, effects of domination are produced. The strategical model rather than the model based on law.[7]

During the nineteenth century, Foucault proposes, the 'psy' sciences (psychiatry, psychology, etc.) added another dimension to the law's capacity to guarantee truth. In this way, the law, both supported by and under the influence of these sciences, turned particularly towards a certain sort of individual. The law here is still about negative power, but its focus is more particular. The negative control of individuals and society expresses itself through the category of 'the dangerous individual':

> by bringing to the fore not only the criminal as author of the act, but also the dangerous individual as potential source of acts, does one not give society rights over the individual

---

[5] See especially C. Gordon (ed.), *supra* n. 3; and L. Kritzman (ed.) *Michel Foucault. Politics, Philosophy, Culture: Interviews and Other Writings of Michel Foucault, 1977–1984* (New York Routledge 1988).

[6] M. Foucault, P. Rabinow (ed.) *The Foucault Reader* (New York Pantheon 1984) at 337–8.

[7] Foucault, 'Two Lectures', *supra* n. 3, at 102.

based on what he is? [—] a foreboding of the dreadful dangers inherent in authorizing the law to intervene against individuals because of what they are; a horrifying society could emerge from that.[8]

Returning to law-as-sovereignty, Foucault insists that this form of law became 'the monarchic system's mode of manifestation', its very way of ruling, in other words, not simply a tool it used:

> Law was not simply a weapon skilfully wielded by monarchs: it was the monarchic system's mode of manifestation and the form of its acceptability. In Western societies since the Middle Ages, the exercise of power has always been formulated in terms of law.[9]

For Foucault, this way of thinking about power—monarchy as negative law and negative truth—has been so persistent, and so persistently problematic, that he minted a dramatic metaphor to try to breach its dominance:

> At bottom, despite the differences in epochs and objectives, the representation of power has remained under the spell of monarchy. In political thought and analysis we still have not cut off the head of the king.[10]

Foucault's treatment of law-as-sovereignty leads him to a particular treatment of rights. For Foucault, 'right'—that is, the sovereign right of the king to command—slides easily into 'rights', such that the rights that are at the heart of modern legal and political discourse are simply another means for negative power to operate.[11] In making this move, Foucault subtly introduces the notion of the subject into the picture. The subjects that emerge are definitely negative—subjects in the sense of being subjected, subjected to power—but they are subjects nonetheless. They are the vehicles by which law as negative power operates. Crudely put, subjects have rights, but they only have rights so that negative power can operate through law and they are only subjects inasmuch as this negative power operates. Seen in this bleak way, Foucault's account of law and rights is not a long way from some Marxist accounts. As Foucault notoriously opposed Marxist accounts, we should not be surprised that at this point he wants to move away from law and rights and introduce the more subtle notions of disciplines and norms:

> The problem for me is how to avoid this question, central to the theme of right, regarding sovereignty and the obedience of individual subjects in order that I may substitute the problem of domination and subjugation for that of sovereignty and obedience.[12]

Foucault says disciplines are 'to be found on the underside of law', as they make their way from prisons and asylums to factories, schools, hospitals and

---

[8] M. Foucault, 'The Dangerous Individual', in Kritzman, *supra* n. 3, at 151.
[9] Foucault, *The History of Sexuality Volume I, supra* n. 4, at 87.
[10] *Ibid.*, at 88–9.
[11] Foucault, 'Two Lectures', *supra* n. 3, at 95–6.
[12] *Ibid.*, at 96.

other modern institutions. Indeed, disciplines are the characteristic forms of modern power:

> disciplines characterize, classify, specialize . . . effect[ing] a suspension of the law that is never total . . . Regular and institutional as it may be, the discipline, in its mechanism, is a 'counter-law'.[13]

This suggests that while he sometimes contrasts law and discipline, more fundamentally Foucault sees them as interdependent—law is 'colonised' by the disciplines.[14]

> Historically, the process by which the bourgeoisie became in the course of the eighteenth century the politically dominant class was masked by the establishment of an explicit, coded and formally egalitarian juridical framework, made possible by the organization of a parliamentary, representative regime. But the development and generalization of disciplinary mechanisms constituted the other, dark side of these processes. The general juridical form that guaranteed a system of rights that were egalitarian in principle was supported by these tiny, everyday, physical mechanisms, by all those systems of micro-power that are essentially non-egalitarian and asymmetrical that we call the disciplines . . . The real, corporal disciplines constituted the foundation of the formal, juridical liberties.[15]

While this has the disciplines dominating law, it is slightly misleading. It is not all one-way traffic, by any means. Law tries to recode disciplines as a form of itself and has some success. Many aspects of the daily work of the disciplines in the modern institutions upon which Foucault concentrates (the prisons, hospitals, asylums, schools, factories, etc.) are given a quasi-legal form.

Even when we turn to what Foucault considers the core of disciplinary power—techniques of surveillance (Foucault's provocative histories of some of these techniques of surveillance at work in the asylum, the prison, the hospital, and so on, are now almost legendary)—we see law and disciplines weaving an intricate web. The asylum, for instance, Foucault tells us, was a 'juridical microcosm':

> The asylum as a juridical instance recognized no other. It judged immediately and without appeal. It possessed its own instruments of punishment, and used them as it saw fit.[16]

As I have indicated, this already complex picture is made more complex by Foucault's insistence on a separate role for norms. The law/discipline nexus outlined above, this is to say, has an even more particular operational character. While quasi-legal forms of discipline may be the order of the day, the limits to the law's role mean that very little reaches the stage of formal legal proceedings,

---

[13] Foucault, *Discipline and Punish*, *supra* n. 2, at 223.
[14] *Ibid.*, at 170.
[15] *Ibid.*, at 222.
[16] M. Foucault, *Madness and Civilization: A History of Insanity in the Age of Reason* (New York Harper and Row 1965) at 265–6.

of offences actually being prosecuted. Far more commonplace is the use of norms or standards. He even speaks of the 'growing importance assumed by the action of the norm, at the expense of the juridical system of the law'.[17] Foucault's treatment of 'normalisation' involves, as is to be expected, his very particular understanding of power.

In the everyday work of the disciplines (more correctly the discipline/norm nexus) power functions more as a power 'whose task is to take charge of life needs continuous regulatory and corrective mechanisms . . . to qualify, measure, appraise, and hierarchise, rather than display itself in its murderous splendor'.[18] In other words, power-through-disciplines/norms is more positive, more productive, than power-through-law-alone.

In marking out some differences between law, on the one hand, and disciplines and norms, on the other, Foucault discusses the expansion of the reach of judges and judging, arguing that we have moved 'from an age of "inquisitorial" justice to an age of "examinatory justice"':

[J]udging has increased precisely to the extent that the normalising power has spread . . . The judges of normality are present everywhere. We are in the society of the teacher-judge, the doctor-judge, the educator-judge, the 'social worker'-judge.[19]

Crucially Foucault eventually shifts his focus from both the law/discipline nexus and the discipline/norms nexus to the relationship between law and governmentality. We return to this matter in a later section, after our introduction of some of Foucault's methodological tools.

2. FOUCAULT'S TOOLS AND THE STUDY OF LAW IN SOCIETY[20]

As noted in the introduction, this section considers archaeology, genealogy, discourse and power-knowledge—four research tools (perhaps 'philosophical tools' is not too strong a term) Foucault developed. He developed them in ways that mark them out very much as 'Foucaultian' tools, but this is not to say, of course, that he invented them, as if in a vacuum. Far from it; they are, taken as a group or singly, the products of his diligent study of the work of the many thinkers who influenced him. For now, it is enough to mention just a handful: negatively, he was strongly influenced by his desire to rid himself (and his followers) of the effects of phenomenology (particularly as espoused by Sartre) and a certain type of hermeneutics, on the one hand, and of Marxism, on the other (in the 1950s in France these two poles seemed to define the outer limits of what was possible); in achieving this, among his positive influences were the French

---

[17] Foucault, *The History of Sexuality Volume I*, *supra* n. 4, at 144.
[18] *Ibid.*
[19] Foucault, *Discipline and Punish*, *supra* n. 2, at 304–5.
[20] Much of the shape and content of this section relies on G. Kendall and G. Wickham, *Using Foucault's Methods* (London Sage 1999) at 24–56.

historians of sciences around Canguilhem, the German philosophers Nietzsche and Heidegger, and some French thinkers who straddled literature and philosophy, like Blanchot and Bataille.[21] I offer a brief summary of the main features of each of these four tools in turn before offering an example to demonstrate how, together, they might be used in socio-legal studies.

Archaeology

Archaeology's main task is to describe statements in the archive,[22] statements covering the sayable and the visible (as, for example, in the invention and maintenance of prisons). This is no simple matter. Even if we understand 'statement' in its most basic sense, accept Foucault's basic definition of 'archive'—'the general system of the formation and transformation of statements'[23]—and allow that his concern to develop a particular type of French history as a defence against 'totalisation'—'the archaeological description of discourses is deployed in the dimension of a general history'[24]—is not necessarily relevant to our present task, we still must come to grips with the complexities of what is involved in the task of description. To give some idea of these complexities, consider the following facts about archaeology:

—archaeology describes regularities of statements in a non-interpretive manner (content to remain at the level of appearances, eschewing any quest to go 'beyond' this level to find 'deeper meanings');
—archaeology describes statements in a non-anthropological manner, as a means of avoiding the search for authors (again remaining at the level of appearances—the appearances of statements—to avoid the habit of seeking to source meaning in human beings);
—archaeology describes the relation between one statement and other statements;
—archaeology describes 'surfaces of emergence'—or places within which objects are made objects in discourse;
—archaeology describes the institutions that acquire authority and provide limits within which discursive objects may act;
—archaeology describes the 'forms of specification' in which discursive objects are targeted.

In performing these complex tasks of description, it must also be said that archaeology formulates rules for the repeatability of statements—that which

---

[21] M. Gane 'Introduction: Michel Foucault' in M. Gane (ed.), *Towards a Critique of Foucault* (London Routledge & Kegan Paul 1986).
[22] M. Foucault *The Archaeology of Knowledge* (London Tavistock 1972) at 131.
[23] *Ibid.*, at 130.
[24] *Ibid.*, at 164.

allows certain statements to recur—and analyses the positions that are established between subjects in regard to statements.[25]

Genealogy

Foucault developed the tool of genealogy well after he had developed that of archaeology, as he realised the importance of the notion of power to his thinking (archaeology in the 1960s, genealogy mainly in the 1970s; he seems to have borrowed the term 'genealogy' from Nietzsche, but, as always with Foucault, used it in his own special way). I suggest the two are complementary, inasmuch as genealogy still concentrates on statements in the archive. As Foucault puts it:

> If we were to characterise it in two terms, then 'archaeology' would be the appropriate methodology of this analysis of local discursivities, and 'genealogy' would be the tactics whereby, on the basis of the descriptions of these local discursivities, the subjected knowledges which were thus released would be brought into play.[26]

Indeed, I see no evidence against supposing that Foucault meant all the tools in his tool-kit to be used alongside one another.[27] It is this spirit that I add four to our list of summary points about the methodological tools of Foucault:

—genealogy describes statements but with an emphasis on power;
—genealogy introduces power through a 'history of the present', concerned with 'disreputable origins and unpalatable functions';[28] for example, with regard to psychiatry, Foucault says, 'Couldn't the interweaving of effects of power and knowledge be grasped with greater certainty in the case of a science as "dubious" as psychiatry?';[29]
—genealogy describes statements, as an ongoing process, rather than as a snapshot of the web of discourse;[30]
—in this way, genealogy concentrates on the strategic use of archaeology to answer problems about the present.

---

[25] For more on the complexities of archaeology, see especially: P. Bevis, M. Cohen and G. Kendall 'Archaeologizing genealogy: Michel Foucault and the economy of austerity', (1989) 18 *Economy and Society* 323; B. Brown and M. Cousins 'The linguistic fault: the case of Foucault's archaeology' in M. Gane (ed.), *Towards a Critique of Foucault, supra* n. 23.

[26] Foucault, 'Two Lectures', *supra* n. 3, at 85.

[27] I am grateful to Gavin Kendall for this point.

[28] N. Rose 'The Formation of the Psychology of the Individual in England 1870–1939' (London Unpublished PhD thesis University of London 1984).

[29] Foucault, 'Two Lectures', *supra* n. 3, at 109.

[30] M. Foucault, 'The Order of Discourse' in R. Young (ed.) *Untying the Text: A Post-Structuralist Reader* (London Routledge & Kegan Paul 1981) at 70–1.

Discourse

This term should be marked 'Danger'. The tool of discourse is undoubtedly crucial in Foucault's work, but it is crucial in ways that are in fact not necessarily related to, indeed sometimes opposed to, what is, perhaps, the standard meaning of the term in English. Where the English word suggests the dominance of the linguistic, Foucault means language as only one component among several. We might add English words like 'institution', 'procedure', and 'practice', perhaps among others, into the mix, were we to try to pin down Foucault's 'discourse' in this way. But better, I think, to tackle the problem of how to make wise use of this multi-faceted tool by first offering some examples of Foucault's own use of it, showing in doing so that he never meant it as a totalising tool, and by grasping as its two key features that it has no 'inside' and no 'outside'.

In Foucault's hands, a discourse is primarily about production. In this way, certain discourses on sex produce sexuality and types of person like 'homosexual', 'heterosexual', 'deviant', etc., certain medical discourses produce asylums and mental patients and certain penological discourses produce prisons and prisoners. This does not mean, of course, that Foucault is proposing that before the existence of these discourses none of these things existed.

For example, the discourses on sexuality on which he focuses his attention emerged in the eighteenth and nineteenth centuries not out of thin air, but as more and less dramatic refinements of certain kinship ties, certain Christian 'sins of the flesh', certain ancient but long-lasting techniques of 'self-mastery', etc.[31] However, care is also needed at the other end of this dilemma—Foucault is certainly not suggesting, therefore, that sex 'itself' exists in some 'pure' non-discursive space and time. While we might reasonably think of the 'raw materials' of Foucault's discourses—bodies, sex, death, etc.—as non-discursive, we must not think we can gain access to this realm without discourse.

Foucault weaves an intricate web here, but it is one that would be familiar to many philosophers, especially those concerned with epistemology. The relationship of the discursive to the non-discursive is pretty much that portrayed in those sophisticated philosophical accounts of knowledge that recognise the dangers of both extreme scepticism and extreme dogmatism (that is, those that are aware that we cannot successfully argue that knowledge of the external world is impossible or that it is straightforwardly possible either—knowledge is something in between). Exponents of various forms of this position—best known as mitigated or constructive scepticism—include Mersenne and Gassendi in the seventeenth century, Hume and perhaps Kant in the eighteenth, Quine, Wittgenstein and Davidson in the twentieth.[32] To flesh out just one aspect of just one of these

---

[31] Foucault, *The History of Sexuality Volume I*, *supra* n. 4.
[32] See especially R. J. Hankinson, *The Sceptics* (London Routledge 1994); C. Hookway, *Scepticism* (London Routledge 1990); J. Malpas, *Place and Experience: A Philosophical*

thinker's work in the area, consider Quine's use of Neurath's Ship metaphor. This suggests that producing knowledge is not at all the same as building a wooden ship under perfect conditions, perhaps in a dry dock (new materials, good tools, plenty of time, etc.). Rather, it is like repairing such a ship at sea: one has to work a plank or two at a time, often in difficult conditions and with whatever tools one has to hand and, crucially, the other planks must remain in place while one is working.[33] Such is Foucault's way of handling the relationship between the discursive and the non-discursive: the non-discursive might be thought of as the 'pure' sailing space within the ship, but the operation of discourses—the planks working together as a ship—define it, such that while we know its existence is important, this existence is dubious or even meaningless without the ship; and we can only ever deal with the ship a few planks at a time.

By insisting that discourses have 'no inside',[34] Foucault is insisting that there is no hidden mechanism that makes discourses work, nothing we should be digging for beyond or behind the use of words and symbols that make their use possible. What we need for Foucaultian discourse analysis is there in front of us. Remembering that when Foucault was invited to name his Chair at the College de France he chose 'Professor of the History of Systems of Thought', we should be especially keen to understand discourses in terms of visible 'systems of thought'. This involves being vigilant against the possibility that 'thought' is seen as something special, as the product of some higher order called 'thinking'. For Foucault, it is much better to understand 'thought' as simply the name given to 'surfaces of appearance' involved in the operation of various institutions, procedures, apparatuses, etc., all of them quite public and visible. So, to give a preview of the example which is to conclude this section, the legal discourses involved in the regulation of gambling involve much thought, but we do not and should not look for the 'source' of the thinking 'inside' some head or heads. We are presented with the surfaces of appearance of this thinking in written judgements and regulations, in the design of casinos and other gambling venues, in the comportment and conversations of the gamblers and the staff at the venues, in policing arrangements and practices, and so on. This is discourse—quotidian not mysterious.

By saying that discourses have no 'outside', Foucault is, in an important sense, simply expanding his argument that discourses have no 'inside'. In accepting that surfaces are what we have to work with and that we need no more—there is nothing 'inside' or 'behind' discourses making them 'tick'—we are accepting that there is, neither, nothing 'outside' them, nothing that somehow guarantees their existence and operation. This is to say, we should not trouble ourselves by trying to

---

Topography (Cambridge Cambridge University Press 1999); R. H. Popkin, *The History of Scepticism from Erasmus to Descartes* (New York Harper Torchbooks 1968).

[33] Hookway, *ibid.*, at 222–4.

[34] I owe much of the discussion of the relationship between Foucault's discourse and its 'inside' and 'outside' to I. Hunter, 'Michel Foucault: Discourse versus Language' (Unpublished MS Brisbane Griffith University 1984).

anchor discourses to 'the world', or some other such supposedly fixed point of reference. Points of reference for Foucault are never fixed, they are always fragmented. Before attempting to cement this point in place by expanding the above example, I should stress that we are again on the ground of mitigated or constructive scepticism. Inasmuch as we cannot say either that knowledge of the external world is impossible or that it is straightforwardly possible, we must recognise that both extremes of the 'inside' and 'outside' positions—'pure thinking' and the 'independent world'—are wrapped up in the same package. There is no way to separate either or both of them such that it or they function as some sort of bedrock on which our investigations might rest when needed.

The legal discourses involved in the regulation of gambling involve many references to things supposedly 'outside' gambling. But we do not and should not look for the 'source' of the things in some supposedly fixed 'world' or other external 'reality'. Again I must stress that we are presented with the surfaces of appearance of these things—in written judgements and regulations, in the design of casinos and other gambling venues, in the comportment and conversations of the gamblers and the staff at the venues, in policing arrangements and practices, and so on. Discourses do not produce the 'external world', in some crude sense, just as they do not crudely produce thoughts, but it is not possible to separate 'internal thinking', 'external world' and discourses from one another; in Foucault's discourse analysis, they are all parts of the one package and cannot meaningfully be taken as separate entities, just as 'ship', 'space inside ship' and 'sailing' cannot meaningfully be taken as separate entities when one analyses a sailing ship at sea.

A final note about the tool of discourse is called for, to deal briefly with the notion of episteme. The simplest way to understand this notion—and this is simple without being simplistic—is to think of an episteme as a large loose collection of discourses built up over time and space. Epistemes are not in any way determinate of discourses, rather the term is used by Foucault to allow us to occasionally consider the vaguely co-ordinated (co-ordinated without a co-ordinator, of course) operation of discourses over certain time periods and certain spaces. As McHoul and Grace put it:

> Sometimes he treats the discourses separately; at other times, he looks at their contribution to the possibility of each period having an overall view of the world (which he calls 'the Western episteme').[35]

Power-Knowledge

I introduced Foucault's treatment of power in the previous section. I have so far said nothing directly about its complex relationship with knowledge. I will

[35] A. McHoul and W. Grace, *A Foucault Primer: Discourse, power and the subject* (Melbourne Melbourne University Press 1992) at 32.

allow my discussion of this relationship to emerge from the following summary of power-knowledge. It almost goes without saying that Foucault uses the tool of power-knowledge alongside the others I have been at pains to outline. It is definitely one tool in his tool-kit, not a super-tool that might be used in place of the others. Bearing this in mind, the main points about power-knowledge are:

- —power-knowledge helps in the use of the tools of archaeology, genealogy, and discourse, as part of Foucault's approach to history;
- —power-knowledge starts with discourse—discursive relations are power relations, connecting the visible and the sayable, but remember, Foucault does not want us to conflate power and discourse;
- —'power', in Foucault's 'power-knowledge' formulation, is best thought of in technical terms, in the mundane sense of making things work;
- —'power', in Foucault's 'power-knowledge' formulation, is a strategy focusing on relations between the visible and the sayable, one that prevents the exhaustion of the visible. Remember, for Foucault, power is productive, not repressive and not a possession;
- —'power', in Foucault's 'power-knowledge' formulation, involves resistance to power, but this too is a technical component of power, part of the way it operates;
- —'power', in Foucault's 'power-knowledge' formulation, is a relation of forces while knowledge is a relation of forms, yet the two relate to each other as different—power is non-stratified, local, unstable and flexible, while knowledge is stratified, stable and segmented;
- —'power', in Foucault's 'power-knowledge' formulation, is 'microphysical', inasmuch as Foucault positions it in the relationship with knowledge as having a slight primacy;
- —this is to say that 'power', in Foucault's 'power-knowledge' formulation, would exist without knowledge, but knowledge could not exist without power;
- —in other words, knowledge supports power in action;
- —'power', in Foucault's 'power-knowledge' formulation, produces subjects;
- —these subjects are not the same as individuals, in the way they are commonly understood;
- —for Foucault, the category of individuals is an invented category, not a natural one;
- —'power', in Foucault's 'power-knowledge' formulation, is involved in subjectivity, via discourse, so we can say that subjects form some of the conditions for knowledge.

A detailed example

Our example, introduced already, concerns the regulation of gambling. It will be remembered that discourses of gambling regulation have no 'inside' and no 'outside', but this does not tell us much about how a Foucaultian analysis of these discourses would work in full. First stop is archaeology.

An archaeology of gambling regulation would describe regularities of statements concerned with gambling and its regulation—formal documents produced by governments, courts, lobby groups, etc. and informal statements that might find their way into an archive, like newspaper reports and transcripts or copies of broadcasts—in a non-interpretive manner. Such descriptions would not, this is to say, go 'beyond' these archival traces in a bid to find 'deeper meanings'. As well, such descriptions would be 'non-anthropological'—not looking for the authors of the statements (even if the name of some leading politician or judge of the time and place is prominent among the statements; Foucaultian analysis does not, of course, completely eschew reference to the names of prominent authors of statements, rather, it does not grant them special status). In this way, Foucaultian analysis seeks to avoid the supposed need to determine some 'human meaning' in statements, in favour of remaining at the level of appearances (it should be clear by now that this is one of the keys to good Foucaultian analysis).

In doing all this, an archaeology of gambling regulation would also describe the relation between one statement and other statements. For instance, it would describe the ways in which statements about the need for fewer gambling outlets must, at least in most jurisdictions in the Western world, confront statements about the attractions of gambling as a source of taxation revenue (though it would remain silent on the political morality battles involved, unless of course such battles surface as statements of their own; its silence covers only supposedly implicit meanings).

As well, an archaeology of the regulation of gambling would describe the institutions which acquire authority and provide limits within which discursive objects may act and would describe the 'forms of specification' in which these discursive objects are targeted. By this I mean such an analysis would describe courts, police, casinos, legal and illegal betting operations—in short, any institutions actively involved in defining the discursive objects of gambling and its regulation in any given jurisdiction—and describe the ways in which such institutions limit what is to count as gambling and its regulation (by legislation, commercial competition, police operational procedures, possibly even organised criminal violence and intimidation, etc.). And it would, in doing this, describe the exact nature of such legislation, competition, procedures, violence, etc., as the forms of specification in which gambling and its regulation are targeted.

The tool of genealogy would enhance the descriptive work of archaeology by describing the 'disreputable origins and unpalatable functions' of the ways gambling and its regulation are conducted—undermining any attempts to hide the sordid aspects behind the cloak of any formal 'scientific' studies of the industries involved. In this way, the genealogical component seeks to add an ongoing strategic dimension to the snapshot picture made available through archaeology.

Having said enough above about the use of discourse concerning this example, I move straight on to power-knowledge.

The discursive relations involved in this example are power relations, connecting the visible and the sayable—the visible of casinos, legal and illegal betting shops, police officers and their uniforms, etc. and the sayable of politicians, judges, gambling advocates and opponents, etc. and prevents the exhaustion of the visible. Of course, inasmuch as Foucault does not want us to conflate power and discourse, we must not think that the power involved in these discourses is the only power involved in the regulation of gambling. Power is also involved in the mundane sense of making the acts of gambling and its regulation work— power produces the types of person to be investigated here (gamblers, judges, officials, police officers, criminals, etc.) and the institutions to be investigated (casinos, courts, even the law, etc.), power is productive, not repressive and not a possession. Sure there is resistance to the power here, but this is part of the way it operates—the resistance (formal organised opposition to gambling, attempts by operators to bribe or coerce regulators, even the sheer grinding nature of the legislative and bureaucratic procedure, etc.) is much more a part of the operation of power than it is a threat to its existence.

These power relations are relations of forces, but of course, in being discursive relations they also involve knowledge, as a relation of forms. Power and knowledge relate to each other in the following manner: the power that produces the gambling persons and institutions is non-stratified, local, unstable and flexible (the judges, courts, gambling houses, laws, gambling, criminals, families, money, governments, taxes, and so on form a jumble of shifting alliances and hierarchies, the reach of which varies and the effects of which are never certain), while knowledge is stratified, stable and segmented (the knowledge of gambling and its regulation, whether formal or informal, is slower to shift in these ways and hence provides the continuity to this particular power-knowledge relationship). Yet it must be remembered that this gambling and regulation 'power jumble' has a slight primacy—it would exist without the gambling-regulation knowledge, but the knowledge could not exist without it. The gambling-regulation knowledge supports the gambling-regulation power in action (and here we can see that the production of particular types of subjects through power forms some of the conditions for knowledge).

3. GOVERNMENTALITY AND LAW[36]

The word 'governmentality', a neologism of Foucault's, is an amalgam of 'government' and 'mentality' (literally, mentalities of government). A useful way to begin to think about what Foucault means by it is to see it as a development of his various tools examined above. In this way, governmentality, too, is not a

---

[36] Some of the shape and content of this section relies on Hunt and Wickham, *supra* n. 1.

radical departure for Foucault, it is another stage in his long-term project to understand and analyse the complexities of the relationship between power and knowledge, a project that includes his development of the tools archaeology, genealogy and discourse. Nonetheless, it is certainly the case that Foucault's thinking about governmentality appears to have accelerated in the late 1970s and it is at this time that he wrote his suggestive essay 'On Governmentality'.[37] I return to this essay shortly, after some necessary definitional discussion.

Mitchell Dean says Foucault's 'study of governmentality is continuous with' at least some approaches to the study of the state—it, like these approaches, 'regards the exercise of power and authority as anything but self-evident'.[38] Differences between the two, Dean argues, emerge at the point where Foucault breaks with 'the characteristic assumptions of theories of the state' in order to think about government as the 'the conduct of conduct'.[39] Dean then offers two related definitions of 'governmentality'. By the first,

> It deals with how we think about governing, with the different mentalities of government . . . The notions of collective mentalities and the idea of a history of mentalities have long been used by sociologists (such as Emile Durkheim and Marcel Mauss) and by the *Annales* school of history in France . . . For such thinkers, a mentality is a collective, relatively bounded unity, and is not readily examined by those who inhabit it . . . The idea of mentalities of government, then, emphasizes the way in which the thought involved in practices of government is collective and relatively taken for granted . . . the way we think about exercising authority draws upon the theories, ideas, philosophies and forms of knowledge that are part of our social and cultural products.[40]

By Dean's second definition,

> 'governmentality' marks the emergence of a distinctly new form of thinking about and exercising of power in certain societies . . . bound up with the discovery of a new reality, the economy, and concerned with a new object, the population. Governmentality emerges in Western European societies in the 'early modern period' when the art of government of the state becomes a distinct activity, and when the forms and knowledge and techniques of the human and social sciences become integral to it.[41]

Pat O'Malley, writing for a socio-legal audience speaks of governmentality as a distinctive 'approach':

> There is a considerable literature exploring and developing this approach . . . influenced strongly by the thinking of Michel Foucault . . . but . . . advanced primarily in recent years by British and Australian scholars. The journal *Economy and Society* has been a principal site for the development of this approach, which is frequently referred to as the 'governmentality' literature. While 'governmentality' refers to a particular

---

[37] M. Foucault, 'On Governmentality', 6 *Ideology and Consciousness* 5.
[38] M. Dean, *Governmentality* (London Sage 1999) at 9.
[39] *Ibid.*, at 10–16.
[40] *Ibid.*, at 16.
[41] *Ibid.*, at 19.

technology of government that emerges in the eighteenth century, the term is more generally used to refer to the approach adopted in its study. The approach is characterized by two primary characteristics. The first is a stress on the dispersal of 'government,' that is, on the idea that government is not a preserve of 'the state' but is carried out at all level and sites in societies—including the self government of individuals . . . The second is the deployment of an analytic stance that favors 'how' questions over 'why' questions. In other words it favors accounts in terms of how government of a certain kind becomes possible: in what manner it is thought up by planners, using what concepts; how it is intended to be translated into practice, using what combination of means? Only secondarily is it concerned with accounts that seek to *explain* government—in the sense of understanding the nature of government as the effect of other events.[42]

These two definitions, taken together, not only capture many features of Foucault's treatment of governmentality (I deal with still other features as this section progresses), they also show the ways in which this treatment builds on his earlier tools and makes use of them, as well as tools developed by others.

In considering how we might think about law in terms of this particular tool, I suggest that governmentality understands law as another means of, and another location for the exercise of, government. Law is not a special 'external force'. As for other objects treated as falling within the ambit of governmentality, legal objects are discrete practices of government: 'Practices of government . . . do not form those types of totalities in which the parts are expressions or instances of the whole. Rather, they should be approached as composed of heterogeneous elements having diverse historical trajectories'.[43]

In thinking about law and governmentality we might think of Foucault making something of a shift—from discipline to government.

It was a matter not of studying the theory of penal law in itself, or the evolution of such and such penal institution, but of analyzing the formation of a certain 'punitive rationality' . . . Instead of seeking the explanation in a general conception of the Law, or in the evolving modes of industrial production . . . it seemed to me far wiser to look at . . . the refinement, the elaboration and installation since the seventeenth century, of techniques of 'governing' individuals—that is, for 'guiding their conduct'—in domains as different as the school, the army, and the workshop. Accordingly, the analysis does not revolve around the general principle of Law or the myth of Power, but concerns itself with the complex and multiple practices of a 'governmentality'

---

[42] P. O'Malley, 'Imagining Insurance Risk, Thrift and Industrial Life Insurance in Britain', (1988–89) 5 *Connecticut Insurance Law Journal* 676 at 679 n. 7. For more on the complexities of the governmentality approach, see also A. Barry, T. Osborne and N. Rose (eds), *Foucault and Political Reason: Liberalism, Neo-Liberalism and Rationalities of Government* (London UCL Press 1996); G. Burchell, C. Gordon and P. Miller (eds) *The Foucault Effect: Studies in Governmentality* (Brighton Harvester Wheatsheaf 1991); M. Dean and B. Hindess (eds) *Governing Australia* (Melbourne Cambridge University Press 1998); P. Miller and N. Rose, 'Governing Economic Life', (1990) 19 *Economy and Society* 1; N. Rose, *Governing the Soul* (London Routledge 1989); N. Rose and P. Miller, 'Political Power Beyond the State: Problematics of Government', (1992) 43 *British Journal of Sociology* 173.

[43] Dean, *supra* n. 37 at 29.

which presupposes, on the one hand, rational forms, technical procedures, instrumentations through which to operate and, on the other hand, strategic games which subject the power relations they are supposed to guarantee to instability and reversal.[44]

The term 'government' in Foucault's hands is, as we have already seen, different from its usual use to describe a combination of legislatures and bureaucracies. In thinking of government as the 'conduct of conduct' Foucault is, again as we have seen, effectively shifting the focus of the study of government away from the notion of the state. In doing so, he is thereby shifting the focus of socio-legal studies away from the nexus between law and state. For Foucault, government is, as it were, a domain of the socio-legal that is much more than law. This means Foucault is, at least in a sense, on the side of socio-legal scholars in their long-running disagreement with 'black letter' lawyers as to the proper scope of the study of the law. Indeed, in the 'On Governmentality' essay referred to earlier, he goes so far as to say that government is,

> not a matter of imposing laws on men, but rather of disposing things, that is to say to employ tactics rather than laws, and if need be to use the laws themselves as tactics . . . the instruments of government, instead of being laws, now come to be a range of multiform tactics. Within the perspective of government, law is not what is important.[45]

In this essay, Foucault spells out the historical version of the governmentality theme. This features, from roughly the end of the eighteenth century, the emergence of what he calls the concern with 'security', which may be better understood in English by the word 'welfare'. In this period, and well into the twentieth century (and arguably into the twenty-first; see Rose for an argument that this type of 'government of the social' died off in the late twentieth century), a liberal model of government developed that characterised and promoted individuals in a particular way, as bundles of 'interests'. Law's role under this type of liberalism is no longer so negative in Foucault's eyes (though it has to be said that he is oblique here too and I rely on one of his main English interpreters, Colin Gordon, in making this point). Law now becomes a means of setting and regulating the bounds in which individuals can pursue their 'interests', especially, but not exclusively, their economic interests. It is in this context that Foucault discusses the increasing importance of rights. As Gordon puts it: 'disrespect of liberty is not simply an illegitimate violation of rights, but an ignorance of how to govern'.[46]

In wrapping up this section, it might be said that this later governmentality work by Foucault suggests a slightly stronger role for law than that suggested by the material considered in the first section. It might be said, but as his discussion of law in the governmentality work is no less oblique than in the earlier work, even such a claim, qualified by the term 'suggests', is, I believe, too strong.

---

[44] Foucault, *The Foucault Reader*, *supra* n. 6, at 337–8.
[45] Foucault, 'On Governmentality', *supra* n. 36, at 13.
[46] C. Gordon, 'Governmental Rationality: An Introduction' in Burchell et al (eds), *supra* n. 41 at 20.

4. CONCLUSION

I have argued that law, for Foucault, is about power, albeit mainly negative power. Law, for Foucault, is about sovereignty and this law-as-sovereignty guarantees a certain truth—the truth of negative power. Law, for Foucault, is about a means of domination. Law, for Foucault, needs to be supported by (or possibly supplanted by) the more subtle notions of disciplines and norms, which he employs to describe institutions which, crucially, do most of the judging in modern societies. In analysing law in society (or, more accurately, the limits of law and the role of disciplines and norms) Foucault makes full use of his tool-kit of analysis, featuring archaeology, genealogy, discourse and of course power-knowledge, and anyone studying law who seeks to follow him would do well to come to grips with his use of these tools. The notion of governmentality Foucault developed quite late in his life adds an extra dimension to his approach to law. Inasmuch as this notion is simultaneously a new tool in his tool-kit and a more sophisticated description of important aspects of the operation of power from the eighteenth century onwards, it is rich with possibilities for the study of law in society.

I have argued all this, yet I have done so very much on the basis of the concession that when describing Foucault's treatment of law, we largely find ourselves raking through the fallen leaves of his work and picking up a hint here and a suggestion there. It is a somewhat unsatisfactory situation, no doubt, but unavoidable. Foucault simply did not say enough directly about law and its role to allow more than this. At very least it is fertile ground for argument. As I hinted above, the 'governmentality approach' seems to me to be the Foucaultian approach most involved in overcoming this limitation, by running hard with what little there is and building what almost amounts to its own 'Foucault and law'.[47] Perhaps this is the best that can be done.

---

[47] For just some examples, see: D. Garland, ' "Governmentality" and the Problem of Crime: Foucault, Criminology, Sociology', (1996) 1 *Theoretical Criminology* 173; B. Hudson, 'Punishment and Governance', (1998) 7 *Social and Legal Studies* 553; D. Ivison, 'The Technical and the Political: Discourses of Race, Reasons of State', (1998) 7 *Social and Legal Studies* 561; O'Malley, *supra* n. 42; P. O'Malley, 'Governmentality and the risk society', (1999) 28 *Economy and Society* 138; P. O'Malley, 'Uncertain subjects. Risks, liberalism and contract', (2000) 29 *Economy and Society* 459; G. Pavlich and G. Wickham (eds) *Rethinking Law, Society and Governance: Foucault's Bequest* (Oxford Hart 2001); F. Pearce and S. Tombs, 'Foucault, Governmentality, Marxism', (1998) 7 *Social and Legal Studies* 567; Rose and Valverde, *supra* n. 1; L. Weir, 'Recent developments in the government of pregnancy', (1996) 25 *Economy and Society* 372.

14

Postmodernism and Common Law

SHAUN McVEIGH

THE POSTMODERN AS a genre and as a topic within the academy might be considered a part of a long polemic concerning both the status of 'the new' and the attributes of enlightenment. At issue, for some, is the status of 'Western reason' and 'secular modernity'. For others it is more a question of learning to live without belief in redemption or even very much belief in this world. In relation to law, postmodernism might be taken as exploring the representations and relations between authority and injustice in the face of the technologies of law and technological domination.

The situations in which the postmodern has been invoked have been diffuse. It is a term that has been attached to interventions in architecture, art, cultural and social theory as well as the social and natural sciences.[1] It is not clearly the case that the accounts of the postmodern that emerge are assimilable to one overarching theory or theme. The postmodern, then, might be considered as persisting with the polemical accounts of postmodern theory (postmodernism); the elaboration of the processes of postmodernisation; and of the categorisation of the temporal epoch of postmodernity. As such, accounts of the postmodern are more readily approached through the discursive and institutional limits of polemical intervention. Accordingly to label something as postmodern is to enter a polemic rather than to determine a substantive concept.

Polemics have their time and place. The burst of political radicalism and the re-definition of intellectual and academic roles that marked postmodernism in the 1970s and 1980s has given way to a more nuanced response to, and responsibility towards, the ends and ending of 'our' modernity. This chapter presents a relatively restricted range of issues in an attempt to jostle postmodernism into relation with common law jurisprudence. The first limit is established by social theory. Topically, social theory might be considered a discourse on the modes of criticism of the social. Here, it is given an even more restricted sense as the criticism of forms of enlightenment (Which enlightenment? Which relationship to truth?). A second limit ties the question of enlightenment to those of modernism and postmodernism. This has been interpreted here as linking enlightenment to questions of technology. A third, more or less strategic, limit has been to address these issues primarily to questions of jurisprudence and justice. These

---

[1] T. Woods, *Beginning Postmodernism* (Manchester Manchester University Press 1999).

limits, of course, do little to diminish the extent of the question. By way of elaboration this chapter moves, more or less, from postmodernism towards jurisprudence. The postmodern it examines is largely generated by the reception of 'French theory' into 'Anglophone legal theory'. The exposition here is not determinedly polemical, but takes up a series of disputes to delimit a domain.

1. A POSTMODERN CONDITION

If only by virtue of a title, Jean-Francois Lyotard's *The Postmodern Condition* (1979, 1984) provides one well worn path into the discursive elaboration of relations between the modern and postmodern.[2] Two themes shaped Lyotard's account of postmodern knowledge: the authority of reason and the ethos of those who use it. At issue was the struggle of how to live with and against technological nihilism.

Postmodernism, for Lyotard, was a particular mode of engagement with the modern and with questions of enlightenment. It begins with a loss of a sense of authority, a pervasive incredulity towards the metanarratives of modernity: emancipation, science, wealth and justice.[3] The postmodern was not simply the modern at its end, it was an event that will also have been there at its inception.[4] It marked that which cannot be incorporated into the order of the modern, but, at the same time, it was that which allowed the modern to emerge. As such postmodernism operates to re-inscribe, in affect and form, the event of modernity. As a question of social theory, postmodernism might be thought of as engaging in a criticism of what counts as enlightenment pitched against the modern rather than nature, superstition, the ancients or barbarians.

The modern condition that has most concerned the postmoderns can be considered in terms of technology and technicity.[5] At a level of great generality, many postmoderns have disputed the way in which human beings inhabit the world. Drawing on the work of Heidegger and Nietzsche, it is the instrumental will to dominate nature and the world that is taken as characteristic of modernity.[6] This 'will to mastery' (or technicity) can also be seen in the rationalisation that destroys traditional knowledge and wisdom, as well as the faith in progress that characterised liberalism and the industrial logic of nineteenth century capitalism and colonialism.[7] The problem of technicity encompasses all reason and all metaphysics. For Heidegger technicity results in a primordial turn away from

---

[2] J.-F. Lyotard, *The Postmodern Condition: A Report on Knowledge* (Minneapolis University of Minnesota Press 1984).

[3] *Ibid.*, xxiv.

[4] *Ibid.*, at 79–81, 'What is Postmodernism?'.

[5] *Techne* in Greek equates several terms of order and norm.

[6] M. Heidegger, 'The Question Concerning Technology' in M. Heidgegger *The Question Concerning Technology and Other Essays* (New York Harper & Row 1977).

[7] E. Wyschogrod, *Spirit in Ashes: Hegel, Heidegger, and Man-Made Mass Death* (New Haven Yale University Press 1985).

Being. This was made apparent with the emergence of Greek philosophy and has since then tainted all of Western philosophy. In this light modernity is but the latest torsion in the process, albeit the one that has revealed most starkly the injustice of our understanding of being and subjectivity. In 'our' present condition technicity and technology can no longer be considered as outside of us; we are, fatally, its subject.[8]

These concerns can also be found at the core of natural law legal theory in the consideration of the relation between nature and technology (often re-staged in disputes between natural law and positivism).

The dangers of technicity can also be understood in relation to the institution of technology. Where existence is not simply being threatened, existence threatens to become an aesthetisiced effect of technology in which nature and subjectivity mutate into an indifferent order of chance, desire and language. It is a situation in which technology and capital have come to incorporate and thrive on points of resistance.[9] Or one in which reality is to be viewed virtually as but a temporary effect of media technology.[10]

2. REASON

The French postmodern response to this situation has not been so much to produce a genealogy of modern technology but to provide a demonstration of the consequences of technology for the thinking of subjectivity.[11] Where once a response to the threat of meaningless existence brought on by rampant technology might have been found in the ethical guidance of human life, there is no longer a position that can readily be taken outside of the horizon of technicity.

Typically French postmodern theory has generated responses to this condition on two registers: one the displacement or overcoming of metaphysics; and the other the elaboration of new conceptual personae, or conducts of life, through which to inhabit the postmodern form of life. The questioning of the philosophical tradition of metaphysics has proceeded by insisting on the 'radical finitude' of metaphysics: a displacement of the way in which metaphysics has produced a closed order of time and place and of the subject.[12] In particular,

---

[8] This formulation points to one of the ways in which questions of gender, race and class are given subordinate status within postmodernism.

[9] J.-F. Lyotard, *Libidinal Economy* (London Athlone Press1993).

[10] J. Baudrillard, *The Perfect Crime* (London Verso 1996).

[11] V. Descombes, *Modern French Philosophy* (Cambridge Cambridge University Press 1980).

[12] The metaphysics that is disputed emerges from Hegelian attempts to merge identity and being. Hegel proposed a global interpretation of history in which rationality as spirit progressively invested the world. From this point everything can be disputed from within reason (as opposed to religion). The development of spirit and the manner of its investment proceeded through institutionalised forms. Rationality is fully achieved in the ultimate institution, the Hegelian State. History then comes to an end because reason has become absolute. Attempts to retrieve history and reason from this end have drawn on a variety of philosophical traditions. In relation to questions of law, ethics, and justice the influence of Kantianism has been extensive. Contesting the influence of Hegel and

postmodernism has paid attention to the excess of the system, or what remains as excluded, as other, in the formation of systems, metaphysical and physical. In various ways what exceeds the metaphysical system has been found in the materiality of discourse and things. In an ethical and theological register this has been characterised in terms of the recognition of the singularity or otherness of the other. In an aesthetic register it has been figured as the unassimilable, the unrepresentable or the sublime that characterises the eventfulness of the event. In law, the unassimilable can be related both to an aboriginal injustice unmeasured by law and untouched by restitution, and to a justice 'yet to come'.

For the French postmoderns it is necessary to reason against the tyranny of reason in order to escape from both technological nihilism (rationalism) and irrational activism (decisionism). To do this postmodernism has pursued a series of hetero-logical and utopian paths through reason. The pitch, and affirmative tone, of much of the discourse of postmodernism might be characterised in terms of the celebration and loss of a form of reason and modernity. The risk, as many counter-polemicists claim, is simply that the postmoderns succumb, with due irony and cynicism, to what they seek to escape or displace.[13]

3. ETHOS

The displacement of metaphysics has been accompanied by the shaping of new ethical personalities. In order to flourish in a postmodern condition, it is claimed, it is necessary to re-fashion existing conducts and forms of life.[14] What is striking in this regard is the anti-humanistic humanism that these conducts of life take. In the more apocalyptic strains of postmodernism the subject is no longer attached to the Law (order of being); life is no longer instituted in terms of an enduring institutional substrate that links conscience, humanity, and history. Instead the subject is instantiated in relation to a variety of technical networks: of desire, of power, of language, of media images and so forth. It is in relation to these scapes that the new conceptual personae emerge and conduct themselves.

For example, in *Libidinal Economy*, Lyotard developed the persona (person, mask) of the pagan.[15] The pagan inhabits an economy of libidinal intensities and seeks to affirm life through an 'active passivity'.[16] In contrast to the orders of judgement where every act is used, pagan existence affirms the intensity of every event. The pagan for Lyotard practices a sort of unconventional conventionalism

Kant has been that of Heidegger and Nietszche. See I. Ward, *Kantianism, Postmodernism and Critical Legal Thought* (Amsterdam Kluwer Academic Publishers 1997).

[13] J. Habermas, *Philosophical Discourse of Modernity* (Cambridge Polity 1987).

[14] W. Hennis, *Max Weber, Essays in Reconstruction* (London Allen & Unwin 1988). See also the chapter on identity in this book.

[15] J.-F. Lyotard, *Libidinal Economy* (London Athlone Press 1993).

[16] J. Williams, *Lyotard and the Political* (London Routledge 2000).

fighting against the terror of the 'true' and of mechanical instrumentalism. The pagan conducts his or her life by the liberating power of intensities (even ones of cruelty and violence). In later work, more influenced by Kant, Lyotard elaborated a paganism: the art of judging without the criteria of anthropology or prescriptions (knowledge, obligation and community). Such judgement is ethical in the 'honouring of the name' of the other and in bearing witness to the terror of living in the world. It is political in seeking an ungrounded practice of justice based on the recognition of the agonistic 'incommensurability' of discourses. It resists the improper totalisation of discourses of, say, politics and law in the name of humanity.[17] In this conduct of life, judgment becomes a form of politics.

Gilles Deleuze and Felix Guattari have elaborated the figure of the nomad in order to negotiate the multiple planes and territories of existence with corporeal acts of flight and becoming.[18] For Foucault the problem is not so much the technologies of science as that of the governmental relations of power and knowledge. His later work on the formations of the self used aesthetics as a form of self-discipline to shape a persona capable of resisting the indifferent freedoms of rationality.[19] Thematically these postmoderns have attempted to confront technology with personae capable of resisting technicity by exceeding it through pragmatic cultural resistance and by dwelling in the imaginary, heterotopic, zone beyond 'the law'.[20] They have contracted an unnatural naturalism.

With more extravagant melancholy, Jean Baudrillard has revealed the capacity of contemporary technologies of sign systems to overcome the real through the endless simulation of the media-scape. In return he has proposed a persona impelled by ecstatic mimicry, to seduce sign systems into revealing the history of the end of history. Roland Barthes has described power in terms of a rhetoric machine, and responded with the fatalistic reduction of the self to rhetorical points of remembrance. In one account, the personae of Barthes and Baudrillard are skeptical, melancholic and pessimistic; in another, they are stoical. There is no escape from their visions of technology.[21] They conduct themselves in a situation fully exteriorised as technicity and desire.

In a less apocalyptic tone Jacques Derrida, Luce Irigaray, and Jacques Lacan have informed us that the possibilities and impossibilities of full presence—'sensuate' and 'sexuate' being— and subjectivity have been with us for some time. For these writers the postmodern condition is best approached through the aporiae or perplexities of thought; and through re-thinking the linkages of law to those of authority and ethics. The personae developed through these lines of thought are less recognisably postmodern. Lacan deployed the whole range of

---

[17] J.-F. Lyotard, *The Differend* (Manchester Manchester University Press 1988) at 128–150. Questions of authority and the dangers of injustice are not avoided by these means.

[18] G. Deleuze and F Guattari, *What is Philosophy?* (London Verso 1994) Chs. 3 and 4.

[19] See the preceding chapter by Gary Wickham.

[20] The pragmatic need not be equated in an obvious way with common sense, since this is precisely what is at issue.

[21] A. Kroker, *The Possessed Individual* (London Macmillan 1992).

pyschoanalytical personae, and has also developed an account of the subject positions through which it is possible to act.[22] Irigaray has sought to realise the possibility of women within the sphere of civil government.[23] Derrida has mimed and redefined many of the personae of philosophy into the figures of the double and the host.[24] For Derrida they point to the duplicitous role that must be performed in order to deconstruct and survive metaphysics.

These conducts of life can be contrasted to those that conform to the condition of the modern (figures thrown up by the forms of life appropriate to State and Church) and the postmodern (figures of the consumption of capital). In the restricted context of postmodernism presented here the personae of the French postmoderns might initially be taken as performing the tasks of philosophy in the absence of a universal subject. They are figures turned to the other: often delirious, tracing the limits of reason, and the edges of empire.[25]

4. MODERN AND POSTMODERN IN THE COMMON LAW

Translating from one idiom and genre to another is not without its effects. The results of bringing a postmodern question of technology into relation with common law are of a distinctly hybrid character. Here they are explored by examining the links between the sites of dispute, the conducts of life and the limits of reason of the personae of postmodernism and law.

One way of understanding the polemics concerning the epochal distinctions between modernity and postmodernity is as a judgment about what is capable of generating the most intense political and legal conflict. The wager of postmodernism has been that where once the site of central political and legal questions was religion, it is now one of technology.[26] This claim is neither fully historical nor sociological, but it will miss its mark if it fails to address some existential reality, or the sense of its loss. Some way also needs to be found to demonstrate that these concerns touch the institutional form of the common law and its modes of inscription and transmission. Finally, for present purposes, some connection needs to be made between these issues and the forms and conducts of life presented by postmoderns. These questions can be given shape through two key inscriptions of modernity in law: the first fixing the political-legal order of modernity and the second, its modern technology.

A first moment of the modern in law has been associated with the formation of the modern state in Western Europe in the sixteenth and seventeenth centuries. In political-legal terms this modernity was established through the system

---

[22] D. Milovanovic *Postmodern Law and Disorder* (Liverpool Deborah Charles Publications 1992).

[23] L. Irigaray, *Je, Tu, Nous* (London Routledge 1993) and *I love to you* (London Routledge 1996).

[24] J. Derrida, *Aporias*, (Stanford Stanford University Press 1993).

[25] See the section coming on Justice: Judgement.

[26] C. Schmitt, 'Age of Neutralisations and Depoliticisations' (1993) 96 *Telos*.

of European Public Law (*jus publicum Europaeum*) and marked by a contrast between a secular political-legal order and one that was religious-moral (Christian). In juridical terms this political–legal modernity was associated with the development of the concept of sovereignty. The attendant civil and natural law jurisprudence gave form both to the sovereign state and the duties and rights of its citizens. It also established new distinctions between the religious and secular domains, and the social and cultural spheres. The immediate impetus to this development was the need to remove sectarian religious bodies, and their disputes about religious truth, from the political sphere—and so to displace two centuries of sectarian religious war in Europe.[27] In England and Wales the political task of pacification was achieved by subordinating the church to the State. It can also be recalled that part of this process of pacification was geo-political. The *jus publicum Europaeum* not only established a regime of rival nation states within Europe but also left the rest of the world free for colonisation.[28]

A second inscription of modernity concentrates on the technology of law. One beginning might be made with the reception and rediscovery of Roman law in Europe in the twelfth century, when the 'revolution of interpreters' began a modern delimitation of the methods of law. Disputes over the status of the modernity and truth of law have been tied both to the interpretative techniques of jurists and to the technologies of government. These polemics have encompassed the full range of theological and philosophical disputes concerning the elaboration of relation between truth and justice, as well as those over the licit representation of images of God, the Sovereign, and the legal person.[29] However for many twentieth century critics, Lyotard and Jurgen Habermas included, it is the 'arts of government' developed in the eighteenth and nineteenth centuries that have done most to undermine the promise of rational enlightenment. Central to this development was the social science of statistics. [30]

The legal state of early modern Europe was primarily adjudicative in form. The truth of law, so to speak, was individual and based on face-to-face encounters in the courtroom. Its modes of adjudication and knowledge were established through direct knowledge, experience of human affairs, and testimony—all bound by oath. In short it was through law that the social order was represented and judged. Crudely it can be claimed that this form of government was displaced by the development of the 'aggregative' (empirical) knowledge of the social sciences. Statistics created a new domain of 'positivities' through new methods of calculation. It created a new field of objects, not restricted to population alone, that function 'as if' they were real.[31] By these means a new configuration of the modern came into disputation. For many critics it is the

---

[27] D. Saunders, *Anti-Lawyers Religion and the Critics of Law and State* (London Routledge 1997) Ch. 1.

[28] R. Young, *Postcolonial History* (Oxford Blackwell 2001).

[29] P. Goodrich, *Oedipus Lex* (Berkeley University of California Press 1995) Chs. 3 and 4.

[30] T. Murphy, *The Oldest Social Science* (Oxford Oxford University Press 1998).

[31] *Ibid.*, at 119.

'aggregative' knowledges that have destroyed the classical (legal) subject and turned a transcendental order of law (natural law) into a 'positivity' or 'virtuality'. Philosophical reason, it was claimed, could no longer stand in opposition to power.

A number of points of departure can now be developed to highlight postmodern accounts of the site or ground of law.

The first relates to Sovereignty and the nation state. If the concept of competing national sovereign states took shape against confessional religion in the early modern period then such concepts have been in decline since 1945. The United Nations Declaration of Human Rights 1948 bears the marks of the emergence of one sort of enlightenment project—a new moral order—and decline of another: the *jus publicum Europaeum*, the competing political order of nation states. One, not entirely plausible, claim has been that 'globalisation' and the development of 'economic-political' spheres of influence mark the transformation, and imminent redundancy of sovereignty as the keystone of modern political and legal thought. A new global order has a new global value: human rights. A less dramatic claim points to the complexity of networks and relations in these spheres. These networks, it is claimed, have displaced the sovereign nation state as the focal point of the government of institutions, ideas and passions. The authority of state law stands at risk and with it an order of responsibility for injustice and justice.

Another point of departure lies with the links between sovereignty, territory and law. The regime of technologies elaborated since the middle of the nineteenth century allows for the regulation of a fully de-materialised set of legal relations. The links between, say, law and a material substrate of things—or of personal relations of obligations, or even formal procedures of adjudication—have become increasingly tenuous. It is at least plausible to claim that the legal person is no longer the possessive individual of contract and property. Instead, or in addition, the legal person of social law might be viewed as an administrative object, subject to social laws. Second, the use of the knowledge generated through statistics is not readily represented in a domain of law dominated by command and obedience, or the direct observation of events and judgment, or the transcendent reason of natural law and state positivism. Third, the legal rationality of statistics differentiates itself from ethics, aesthetics and science, without necessarily posing a new legal order beyond process. The dominance of the statistical domain might also be reflected in the proliferation of substantive-procedural criteria such as reasonableness, good faith and non-discrimination in all areas of law, since these terms, even with their ethical resonance must be understood aggregatively.

The account presented here has emphasised that law has changed the means and objects of its regulation. Regulation through law no longer proceeds according to a principle of limited unity marked by distinctions between public and private spheres, State and civil society and so forth. Instead regulation proceeds according to a juridical saturation of social reality.

The attributes of legal order circulate around registration systems, standard forms, and compliance regimes and are performed through a wide range of media.[32] With or without nostalgia for earlier legal forms and legal subjectivities, these statistical regimes are now represented in terms of virtual systems of simulation.[33] All this, however, remains some distance from Baudrillard's diagnosis of the loss of reality (as if reality could altogether be there in a system of representation). Postmodern accounts of technology and technicity have pointed to the ways in which reason and technology do not have a static relation but one that is generative or libidinal. The immediate concern is with epistemic consequences of technological change. These concerns, no doubt, will involve the conduct of life in relation to the changing forms of representation and public presence of law.[34]

The most significant political aspect of the postmodern condition for thinking about law is the loss of sovereign authority, and of technical or institutional control. Thomas Hobbes' Leviathan is often taken to represent the emergence of political modernity with its depiction of the sovereign state establishing authority out of the chaos of war and measureless injustice. The sovereign establishes both authority and measure (techne) and law. In the postmodern condition measure and law have been characterised as a chaotic order beyond sovereign authority. Again it is possible to doubt the apocalyptic tone and recognise that relations of authority change both with force of arms and the ordering of ideas.

This section opened with a wager. Do the present disputes over technology and technicity represent a moment of existential reality in the manner that religion once did? Postmodernism has picked up on the sense of a technology no longer engaged in production but in endless consumption of aggregate equivalence. This situation would appear to be quite unlike the political disputes characterised by religion. There, salvation was at issue and sides must clearly be taken. One consequence of regimes of contemporary technology, it is claimed, is that this type of political response no longer makes sense. However, it might be more accurate to say that disputes over technology have not been framed in technological terms, if only, at present, because the polemics of technology demand it be a perfectly neutral instrument. They mimic other disputes.[35]

---

[32] These, of course, have not been the only developments in the technology of law. A fuller account would include developments in the expressive dimension of authority; the administrative re-organisation of the practice of law; the changes in the legal archive and legal memory effected by computer and expert systems; and the doctrinal and administrative changes necessary for impersonal government over mass populations.

[33] P. Goodrich, *Languages of Law* (London Weidenfeld & Nicolson 1990).

[34] Recollect the itinerant order of the common law circuit of judges travelling the country, seeking crime and business, satisfying the desire for justice, and enforcing the order of the Crown. Project a future for a world human rights court where subscribers act as jurors. The point is one of technological formation of desire.

[35] Is the present 'War on Terror' religious? Is the 'War on America' one of technology? Do wars of technology take on a religious form?

5. POSTMODERN ETHOS IN COMMON LAW

How might the personae of postmodernism and of law respond to the post-modern condition in law?

Two accounts of the 'orders of life' have dominated the interpretation of legal modernity. They roughly correspond to the two rival 'orders of life' and orders of domination that have flourished in Western Europe: one, secular and political, organised around administration and government; and the other, religious and ethical in origin, concerned with redemption and transformation.[36] In the early modern period these orders of life came into sharp conflict. One consequence of this was the formation of the modern state.

The conduct of life of the lawyer and the official was tied to the requirements of office and the state rather than religion. Ethical conduct was determined through reason of state and not directly by any higher ethics. To perform the roles of government it was necessary to practice a certain indifference, or bracketing off (*adiaphorism*), of ethical beliefs. By contrast, and often in dispute, the religious and ethical conduct of life has been more concerned with the delimitation of an ethically unified world, peopled with morally unified persons. The conduct of life of the religious order is designed to complete this ethical order.[37]

Reinhart Kosselleck has claimed that the contrasts in the conduct of the rival orders of life still shape our understanding of modernity. The religious order of life was not defeated in the seventeenth century, but displaced.[38] In their search to restore a fully ethical order, critics of the state and of secular modernity continued the transformative aspirations, and intellectual practices, of the enlighteners. They denounce the state as unethical and charge it with stunting the souls of its citizenry and annihilating their enemies in the name of indifference. State officials are capable only of remembering the past and not the possibilities of the future. In short the conduct of life of the state official refuses life.

The counter arguments and defences are equally polemical. Without the state and its law, it is argued, there could be no peace in which a civil society could flourish, and no place for enlightened thought. In ignoring this fact, the enlighteners re-commit their adherents to sectarian dispute with all its attendant dangers. The only difference now is that they are crusaders for atheism, republicanism, materialism and technocratic salvation.[39] Far from stunting the souls of its citizens, the

---

[36] The distinction made here does not stand entirely apart from a long dispute within the tradition of Western thought on the relative primacy of metaphysics and politics.

[37] D. Saunders, *Anti-Lawyers Religion and the Critics of Law and State* (London Routledge 1997) Ch. 3.

[38] R. Kosselleck, *Critique and Crisis: Enlightenment and the Pathogenesis of Modern Society* (Oxford Berg 1988).

[39] It is easy to overstate these distinctions. The political settlement of England did not result in either a sharp differentiation between church and state or their joining. Instead the orders were compressed in an Anglican settlement. In like manner the enlighteners of the eighteenth century British Isles were not, on the whole, dissenting revolutionaries. They actively defended the civil

conduct of life of the administrative-legal order provides a restricted ethics suitable for the many roles that officials, and citizens, are required to perform. It is not a question of such a conduct of life failing to develop a transcendent ethical personality. It is simply that such personalities, dispositions and enthusiasms have no particular part to play in administrative-legal government.[40] There may be no place for such a conduct of life at all.

If the polemic remains within the terms of this dispute, on their face, the French postmoderns, as heirs of the Enlightenment *philosophes*, and as practitioners of existential dissent, take up their roles within the religious order of life.[41] Postmodern personae have been more effective in re-inhabiting the sites of ethical or critical modernity, notably the University, than those of administrative legal modernity. In this respect the criticisms of law made by the postmoderns fall into the polemic of ethical natural law, albeit an unnatural law without nature. In this respect many of the disputes between modern and postmodern social theory remain internal to ethical natural law. Such polemics have their own unglorious histories of exclusion and persecution. At least one influential feature of postmodern thought has been precisely to resist repeating such polemics. For example, the fragmentary style of commentary, the endless deferral of the decision, the sedimentation of context and so forth have been associated with developing different ways of conducting academic and public discourse. On this rests a debate about the style and fashion of postmodern discourse. In conducting life in relation to law, attention must always be paid to the dignity of law and its reasons.[42]

For all that French postmodern ethoi have been aimed at the heart of administrative-legal order they have remained outside the central concerns of government. Postmodernism has not sought to function as a formal critique, or as an alternative to government, but to produce a series of counter practices. The pagans, nomads, and seducers of postmodernism have not on the whole sought judicial preferment. Although there is no reason why such accounts cannot be developed.[43] In this context postmodernism could be viewed as celebrating antinomian romanticism. That is, in celebrating an existence defined in terms of the escape from institutional limits of the State and the redemption of unity of feeling and action.

---

and political rights of the 1688 'revolution' by promoting a civil society in opposition to sectarian enthusiasms. See R Porter *The creation of the modern world: the untold story of the British enlightenment* (New York Norton 2000).

[40] I. Hunter, *Rival Enlightenments* (Cambridge Cambridge University Press 2001).

[41] It is certainly the case that most of the polemics over the status of the moderns and postmoderns have proceeded within the genre of religious dispute. There is an equally important polemic conducted between reason and rhetoric, philosophy and poetry, history and philosophy, where the true grounds of representation are disputed. P. Goodrich, 'Europe in America: Grammatology, Legal Studies, and the Politics of Transmission' (2001) 101 *Columbia Law Review* 2033.

[42] *Ibid.*, at 2056–2057.

[43] J. Minson, 'Ethos in the Service of the State' in M Dean and B Hindess (eds), *Governing Australia* (Cambridge Cambridge University Press 1998) Ch. 3.

However, it is precisely the claim of postmoderns that the polemic has moved on. The development of new technologies of government has blurred, if not destroyed, the modern orders of life. Hence the agitation for new conducts of legal life.[44] Postmodernism, it could be claimed, responds to these transformations rather than repeats, without more, the institution of modernity. In which case the personae of postmodernism might be viewed, however partially, as developing conducts of life to respond to that new order. How this encounter with legal technology is understood depends on the delimitation and complication of the relations of authority and justice, and of reasons of state and ethical reason.

6. DELIMITATIONS OF LAW AND FORCE

Postmodern interventions in the reason of law have steered an uneasy course between showing law as a cynical exercise of power and in contemplating ways of living well before the law. In the latter context postmoderns have sought ways to inscribe another place or scene of law and to relate this to the status of the other within law. Here, following the thematisation of technology and technicity, attention is paid to two delimitations of reason: one in relation to force and authority, and the other, in the relation of law to justice (Derrida) and injustice (Lyotard).

Within the polemic of modern and postmodern, the jurisprudence of modernity has been characterised in terms of determining what is proper to law: giving it its internal order and external authority. This ordering has frequently been associated with the attempt to justify technicity and the destructive force of reason. In postmodern jurisprudence one strategy of displacing the effects thought has been that of re-inscribing such totalities within networks of difference.[45] Deconstruction, associated with the work of Jacques Derrida, has been strategically put to work in this respect. Deconstruction more or less seeks to demonstrate the ways in which the hierarchies of legal order are maintained by an incessant valorisation of oppositions. It shows how such valorisation is anything but unequivocal in its operation. This is so to the extent that, under analysis, the oppositions are shown to be barely oppositional at all. They continuously invoke another scene, or double logic, that both allows and prevents the legal order from performing according to its orders (some of these oppositions can be listed: voice over writing, soul over body, spirit over letter, man over woman, force over violence, domiciled over stranger, justice over injustice, and proper over improper).

---

[44] P. Schlagg, *The Enchantment of Reason* (Durham Duke University Press 1998). Consider the emergence of new personae within the common law: the victim; the asylum seeker; the senseless sufferer; the conscientious consumer; the entrepreneurial academic; the depressed and bored legal official who has lost his or her vocation; and so on.
[45] D. Cornell, *The Philosophy of the Limit* (New York Routledge 1991).

Much of the work of postmodern theory in United States of America has dis-puted modern jurisprudence in the field of epistemology. It has been concerned to work towards a jurisprudence that recognises, and respects, equality in dif-ference.[46] Here rather than proceed by way of a summary of this diverse body of work, the delimitation of law will be worked through the body of the text of Herbert Hart's *The Concept of Law*.[47] Hart's work stands at the end of a tradi-tion of legal positivism, inaugurated by Hobbes, that grounds law and legal authority in force. Law, in this tradition, is a counter-force of the violence of chaos. It raises most starkly the difficulties in establishing the authority of law as anything other than undifferentiated violence.

Despite its strikingly different tone, *The Concept of Law* comes close to many to the concerns of postmodernism in the attention it pays to pragmatics, the vagaries of conventional meaning, and the phenomenological practices of law. In *The Concept of Law*, Hart suggested, following Wittgenstein, that law be considered a distinct language game or practice. It is to be one where a 'rule of recognition' determines the validity of what can be recognised as law. The appropriate source of recognition was to be identified through the acceptance of the officials of law. This was so both as a matter of institutional fact and prag-matic order. The insistence of the conventional and the pragmatic seems to leave little room for internal dispute. Law is either ordered according to the rules of the practice of law, or it is not. If it is not then little more can sensibly be said of it in relation to law.[48]

Deconstruction has generally followed the errant workings of the devices that allow the construction of the system as a total system. It demonstrates the lim-its to totalisation by elaborating the ways in which the legal order is held in place by a series of equivocal differences, dislocations, paradoxes, impossible necessities—aporiae. One such aporia or point of equivocation can be found with Hart's legal officials. The officials of law find themselves caught in a para-dox. They must identify themselves as bearers of the law before they have recog-nised the law itself. They can only recognise themselves as officials of the law if

---

[46] G. Minda, *Postmodern Legal Movements* (New York New York University Press 1995). For Minda, postmodern jurisprudence emerges as a composite of critical legal studies, critical race theory, feminism, identity jurisprudence, intersectional jurisprudence, law and literature and narra-tive jurisprudence. Postmodernism is, or is the site of, a 'multiculturalism' of jurisprudence. Its themes have been disputed under the topics of anti-foundationalism, anti-essentialism, social con-struction, and legal transformation.

[47] H. L. A. Hart, *Concept of Law* Revised edition (Oxford Clarendon 1994).

[48] Lyotard, who also loosely adopted Wittgenstein's account of the practice of rules, raises the stakes in his account of language games. For Lyotard, the practice is not to be considered at the level of the institutional system, but at the level of the sentence (phrase). Whenever someone's experience cannot be phrased in its own terms, that person suffers the wrong of a differend. This differend can-not be recognised or reconciled within the domain of the addressors language. Where Hart writes jurisprudence for the administration of law, Lyotard takes on the role of the witness to the differ-end or of an absolute difference between two sides of a conflict. One seeks to minimise dispute in the name of other, the other to maximise its recognition in the name of injustice. J.-F. Lyotard *The Differend* (Manchester Manchester University Press 1988) at 3–31.

the law is in place. Yet the law cannot be in place without officials to perform the act of recognition. This temporal confusion affects all of Hart's attempts to delimit the legal from the non-legal (the violent, the ethical, and the political), since it cannot be determined in advance what is inside and what is outside the law, or what is factual and what is normative.

The mark or trait that makes law, turns out both to be absolutely legal and non-legal. At some point, that can never be established by convention, the law must be somewhere recognised as being there beyond convention. Typically this perplexity is held in place by the figure of the sovereign; a figure, like that of the law, that can be neither fully legal nor non-legal. The sovereign and the official must authorise themselves to recognise a law that they are in the process of creating.[49] What is authorised, however, is no longer simply law in opposition to non-law.

This problem can be pursued further. For the law to be recognised as conventional it must be repeatable. Yet this repetition does not repeat purely conventionally. It creates an interior space of law, one contaminated by the violence of non-law. This is so because what is recognised as law is the aporia of law, the network of law and non-law elaborated by the impossible temporal positioning of the legal official. What is mis-recognised in this account is the force of law. In *The Concept of Law* this spacing produces a number of effects that double the conventional divisions and horizons of the text.

For example, Hart inscribes a thematic of evolutionary genetics and a violent legal therapeutics and obstetrics in order to establish the primacy of secondary rules of recognition.[50] He also develops an energetics of statics.[51] Such effects can be examined in terms of the ways in which the material supports and relays of law disseminate meaning; or, more simply, in the way in which such texts create contexts. It is, perhaps, an accident of a quite determined kind that the authoritative inscriptions of Hart's concept are transmitted in terms of pathological engagement with the paternity, or legitimacy, of the law. It is inscribed against an order of genesis, gender, or the maternity of law; and against colonial government.

It is worth noting that this double commentary on law is not simply aberrant. It is necessary to control and enact the temporal logic of the text. Without this doubling, the secondary rules of change, adjudication and recognition that characterise civilised legal systems will not be able to supplement and unify the primitive systems of law based on force. This, of course, is the 'union' that Hart desires. The trace of the material and maternal body of law provides

---

[49] J. Derrida, 'Laws of Genre' in D Attridge (ed), *Acts of Literature* (London Routledge 1992).

[50] H. L. A. Hart, *The Concept of Law* (Oxford Clarendon Press 1961; 2nd Edn 1994): for the heart of the legal system (*ibid.*, at 98); for embryonic form (*ibid.*, at 95); the evolutionary history of the legal family (*ibid.*, at 112); for the pathology and embryology of legal system (*ibid.*, at 117–123) including forced Ceasarians (*ibid.*, at 120))

[51] *Ibid.*, at 95.

an account of change, development and spacing as an internal horizon of law that cannot be distinguished in advance from the attempt to bring together force and reason.

A deconstruction of Hart's account of recognition does not destroy the law, or even allow the claim that it is wrong because it mis-recognises what is proper to law. It addresses what follows from deciding on what is undecidable: that distinguishing legitimate force from non-legal violence is indeed only a matter of conventional recognition. The complexities of institution also infect attempts to contextualise *The Concept of Law* in historical, ideological and sociological terms, since they too will remain within its order of representation. To explain *The Concept of Law* as in part justifying and repeating the ways of colonial administration; or as endorsing a patriarchal understanding of the fraternal rule of law; or as the end point of modern rationality, does not exhaust the logic of the text. Such explanations are themselves, in a sense, a product of a tradition of texts that treat law as the institution of rationality. Part of the wager of post-moderns is that this possibility is necessary to thought.

The delimitation of reason that postmodern deconstructions have been most concerned with have been those that have asserted a certain completion of the project of universal rationality. In its place deconstruction insists that, while some versions of reason and history have indeed reached an end, this has not exhausted, totally, history and reason.[52] The same could be said of law. The consequences of this type of demonstration lead in two directions. First, reason alone does not constitute the identity of law or its subjects. Second, deconstruction attempts a displacement and re-inscription of such systems. Hart's accounts of conventions and practices of law might be re-inscribed within a more general account of the authorisation of violence.

7. JUSTICE: JUDGMENT

Postmodern interventions in law have increasingly returned to questions of judgment and ethics as a privileged site from which to consider the responsibilities of law. The importance of questions of judgment to postmodernism is no great surprise. If the modernity that postmodern jurisprudence resists is primarily the technicity of instrumental aggregation, then the site of judgment— and the incalculable aspects of the decision—become the point of openness or attentiveness to the relationship with the other, and with justice.

Within postmodern legal theory the relationship to the other has been used to re-cast much of the basic ordering of ethics and justice. It has done so by displacing the claim that reason is sufficient to reach the truth.[53] Central to this

---

[52] As a corollary, there is no end to deconstruction, but this does not mean it has no point.

[53] It is the displacement of this nexus that opens postmodernism to charges of both scepticism and fideism.

understanding of ethics has been the work of Emmanuel Levinas.[54] In the Kantian tradition, ethics acts as the horizon and precondition of the political, just as justice is the horizon and precondition of the law.[55] The preconditions of law might be thought, in terms of particular judgments of justice. For Levinas the relation to the other is prior to all reason and law. It is an other who constitutes me as an ethical being: I discover my responsibility through responding to the other. The maxim of formal justice—*audi alteram parte*—hear the other side, becomes 'recognise the absolute responsibility to the other'.[56] For Levinas this command and response is ethical.

In his essay 'Force of Law', Derrida situates the responsibility to the other in relation to justice.[57] In so doing justice is cast as an aporia of judgment rather than in terms of meaning and power. For Derrida the question of justice is one of how to respond to the singularity of the other, as wholly other. This response is both necessary and infinite. It is necessary, as Levinas relates it, as the ethical condition of existence. It is infinite because it is an absolute responsibility. To meet this responsibility requires the movement 'beyond law'; beyond the presumed unities of legitimate action, and of regulatory, calculable, ideals of justice. Justice in this sense is quite singular—for example, in response to the pain and suffering of an other. It arises without reason and justification.

Responsibility to the other is also impossible and unpresentable. I cannot, but must, address the other in the language of the other. Responsibility for the workings of justice within the (symbolic) order of representation, and within the domain of the calculable (right), requires calculation in relation to a third. The judgment of justice in law must respond to both all the other others, and to the demand of justice itself. As such it must also deal with force—with the calculation of claims and with enforcement and subjugation.

For Derrida, to judge at all it is necessary to experience this impossible (undecidable, indeterminable) necessity—this is the aporia of judgment. A just judgment must respond both to the infinite demand of justice and the finite calculation of law. It must neither expel the phenomenality of violence; nor the demand of justice from the symbolic order of law; nor permit the termination of justice in the calculability of law. Judgment depends on this sense of undecidability. It is this that makes it necessary to decide. In practising judgment in relation to that which is beyond measure, there is always the risk of irresponsibility. This is so both in the sense of not responding, and of the just being in proximity with the worst.[58]

---

[54] S. Critchley, *The Ethics of Deconstruction* 2nd edn (Cambridge Polity 1999).

[55] C. Douzinas and R. Warrington, *Justice Miscarried* (Hemel Hempstead Harvester Wheatsheaf 1994), chapter 4.

[56] The linking of the Kantian themes of freedom and responsibility to judgment is central to Heidegger. See P. Schalow, *The Renewal of the Heidegger-Kant Dialogue* (Albany SUNY 1992).

[57] J. Derrida, 'Force of Law: The "Mystical Foundation of Authority"' in D. Cornell et al. (eds) *Deconstruction and the Possibility of Justice* (New York Routledge 1992).

[58] *Ibid.*, at 63–66.

Derrida's account of justice can be recast a little to conform to the theme of this chapter. First, although Derrida refuses the terminology of character, he does elaborate something of the kind, in delimiting the impossible, or exorbitant, receptivity of responsible judgment. Being just requires an openness to what is to come, a passivity sufficient to receive the other as other.[59] Secondly, Derrida insists in situating the obligation of judgment within its institutional frame. The question of authority and of order is not lost to that of responsibility to the other. At the same time, the question of authority is not determined, or answered, by invoking a responsibility to the other. There is no possibility of simply moving beyond the law. Thirdly, much of the force of Derrida's demonstration of the impossibility of justice and the possibility of injustice lies in welcoming what is beyond the law. In part justice is re-cast in messianic form. The future is not yet present, but there is an opening towards it. In so far as there is the possibility of a future, a context is always open. Justice as the experience of the obligation to the other takes on the structure of this promise. It remains undetermined, yet to come—and singular.

The task here is not to assign injustice to the technology of law and then to await a justice yet to come. The claims of justice and injustice both circulate in relation to the law. The technologies of law are based on injustice: authority, as measure, is instituted on the memory of injustice. To forget suffering, even as a means to end violence, repeats injustice. How, then, is it possible to respond to the challenge: without measure, what if the best were really the worst?

8. POSTMODERN JURISPRUDENCE

Prudence, perhaps, might be the last word to be associated with the postmodern encounter with technology and technicity; with authority; with injustice; and with the relation to the other. Prudence names that which enables one to judge, administer and submit to the authority of the law. The conceit of this chapter has been that postmodern interventions in law are aimed at transformation. A postmodern jurisprudence might be imagined in terms of how to respond to our present condition, including the immemorial injustice of reason as measure, and the technologies of the transmission, inheritance and representation of law. In this aspect jurisprudence is a melancholy science, and judgment a work of mourning.

In sum, it has been suggested that a postmodern jurisprudence engages in ways to dispute and judge on grounds that are not altogether there.

---

[59] It might be contained in the politeness 'after you', or in the declaration 'welcome'.

Section 6

Pluralism and Globalisation

REZA BANAKAR and MAX TRAVERS

THIS SECTION PROVIDES an introduction to studies of law which are conducted with an awareness of the socio-cultural plurality of modern societies. Not surprisingly, we also find considerable theoretical diversity across these approaches themselves. In the first of the three chapters presented in this section, Anne Griffiths explores the diversity characterising legal pluralism by demonstrating how it cuts across a number of issues ranging from indigenous and customary law to globalisation. John Flood follows up this discussion in his chapter on law and globalisation by focusing on the interaction between legal and global structures created by the expansion of markets. Finally, David Nelken draws attention to the sociological complexity of the concept of legal culture, while at the same time wondering 'how far it is appropriate to continue to focus on variation in national legal cultures at a time of globalisation'.

If with legal pluralism we mean 'a situation in which two or more legal systems coexist in the same social field',[1] then its underlying idea is as old as the sociology of law itself. Although, Eugen Ehrlich and Georges Gurvitch did not use the concept of legal pluralism, they nonetheless recognised through their work the significance of socio-cultural diversity of their contemporary societies and dismissed the privileged status conferred on state law by legal positivism.[2] A similar approach to law also grew out of legal anthropology's preoccupation with social control and how the imposition of centralised colonial laws were received and experienced by the indigenous people of the colonised countries. Sociologists, such as Ehrlich, and social anthropologists, such as Malinowski, who were amongst the first scholars to develop pluralistic theories of law, did so for different reasons. Yet, due to their broadly conceived understanding of law and the legal system—which not only included the traditional legal institutions, but also the 'non-legal forms of normative ordering'—their overall approach came to bear some basic similarities.[3]

Owing to the work of scholars such as John Griffiths, Masaji Chiba and Sally Falk Moore, legal pluralism was brought to the forefront of socio-legal research in the 1980s. There were many reasons for the popularity of this approach. It contained, for example, assumptions backed by empirical observations, which

---

[1] S. E. Merry, 'Legal Pluralism,' (1988) 22 *Law & Society* 869–901, at 870.
[2] See chapter 2.
[3] *Ibid.*

could be called upon to critique 'legal instrumentalism' and challenge the conception of law as a universal instrument of social and economic planning, change and reform.[4] More importantly, legal pluralism was one of the few approaches capable of recognising the cultural diversity of modern societies. It proved, therefore, a useful vantage point for viewing the culturally heterogeneous make-up of modern societies and deconstructing the universal claims of positive law.

The deconstructive potential of legal pluralism also appealed to a new generation of theorists, who developed a postmodern understanding of the concept. For Boaventura de Sousa Santos, for example, legal pluralism is

> not the legal pluralism of traditional legal anthropology in which the different legal orders are conceived as separate entities coexisting in the same political space, but rather the conception of different legal spaces superimposed, interpenetrated and mixed in our minds as much as in our actions, in occasions of qualitative leaps or sweeping crisis in our life trajectories as well as in the dull routine of eventless everyday life.[5]

This second wave of legal pluralism, which is mapped out by Anne Griffiths, received a new impetus in the 1990s with the rise of globalisation. The realisation that local and the global were no longer 'necessarily predicated upon territorial boundaries and geographic space' necessitated a new conception of societal processes and a new understanding of social and cultural identity. A global transformation of the world economy, from production based on local and national markets to a global marketplace (i.e. to a global network of 'local' marketplaces), could only be realised by employing the social, political, cultural and legal structures at the national level. However, the highly complex interaction between the global and the local forces brought about a transformation of national social structures out of which emerged a new concept of 'local' that was independent of geographic proximity. Culture, cultural identity, geographic space and territoriality no longer necessarily coincided. This transformation manifested itself in various ways reflecting the tension between the local and the global. Some institutions, such as large legal firms, learned to recognise and 'embrace' the diversity of the global order, while others turned themselves into pockets of resistance against the supranational forces of globalisation. An example of the latter is found in the resurgence of extreme nationalistic political parties and anti-capitalist movements.

John Flood's chapter demonstrates the primacy of economic forces and their influence on the global development of law, legal practice, legal education and, ultimately, on the formation of legal profession. His study of legal education is

---

[4] 'Legal instrumentalism' understands the law as an independent instrument of social control and social change. R. Cotterrell, *Law's Community: Legal Theory in Sociological Perspective* (Oxford Clarendon Press 1995) at 44.

[5] B. de S. Santos, *Toward a New Common Sense: Law, Science and Politics in The Paradigmatic Transition* (London Routledge 1995), at 472–473.

the story of the legal profession's attempts to cope with the demands of the new global market economy.

There is little doubt as to the significance of law and lawyering for the creation and reproduction of the global business order. The development of mega-law firms, the growth in number of international chambers of commerce world-wide and the spread of international commercial arbitration and the increasing application of *lex mercatoria* as the vehicle for attaining international justice illustrates the degree to which law and global forces are interwoven. This development has promoted the vision of a rising 'third culture', i.e. a more or less autonomous legal culture necessitated, created and reproduced above all by the global economic forces at meta-national level.

One of the thought provoking points made in John Flood's chapter is that although the new *lex mercatoria* might function as the law of globalisation, nevertheless 'of all the legal regimes in the world only two are of consequence in transnational work, namely, English law and New York state law'. This is in line with other evidence of the Americanisation of international commercial arbitration recorded in the mid 1990s.[6] Does it mean that 'the third culture' is in fact but an internationalised version of the Anglo-American legal culture? And what does such a development potentially mean for the future of national legal orders?

The revival of legal pluralism in the 1980s and the debate on globalisation during the 1990s gave a boost to cultural studies of the law. Yet, comparative studies of legal cultures, which is clearly of methodological and theoretical importance to legal pluralism and globalisation studies, is in fact part of a much less trendy theoretical preoccupation which goes back to Max Weber's comparative sociology of law. As David Nelken demonstrates in his chapter, comparing legal cultures is a method for developing comparative sociology of law.

The notion of 'legal culture' pinpoints the intersection of a number of multi-faceted concepts such as culture, law, legal institutions, perceptions, attitudes and behaviour, thus creating a theoretically and methodologically challenging field of research. *Comparative* studies of legal cultures introduce, however, one extra challenge into this already complicated field by drawing attention to the impact of the researchers' own cultures of origin, previous cultural experiences and expectations on how they view and understand the other (legal) cultures which they happen to study. In *Contrasting Criminal Justice* Nelken explains the complexity of the epistemological issues raised through comparative works by asking:

> How can we be sure that we are comparing 'like with like' both in terms of the distinctive elements of the criminal process and its place in the larger culture? How far does the idea of treating criminal justice as a series of decision stages which can, and should, be studied empirically, reflect Anglo-American assumption and practices?[7]

---

[6] Y. Dezalay and B. Garth, 'Merchants of Law as Moral Entrepreneurs' (1995) 29 *Law and Society Review* 27–64.

[7] D. Nelken (ed.) *Contrasting Criminal Justice: Getting from here to there* (Aldershot Ashgate 2000) at 4.

Can we do comparative sociological research without the first hand experience of the culture(s) we are studying; without, for example, being able to speak the language of, and see the world, at least momentarily, from the point of view of those we are investigating? What are the advantages and disadvantages of long-term engagement with the cultures we are studying? Such questions, which should ultimately be discussed in the light of the cultures of origin of the researchers, lie at the heart of comparative sociology of law. It also means that comparative sociology of law places the issue of methodology and its intimate relationship with theory at the centre of research. By doing this it makes a valuable contribution to the field of socio-legal studies, where it is relatively rare to find discussion of methodological issues.

15

Legal Pluralism

ANNE GRIFFITHS

L EGAL PLURALISM HAS generated a great debate about the meaning and scope of the concept of 'law' within the fields of sociology, anthropology, and legal theory. The term and the concepts it encompasses cover diverse and often contested perspectives on law, ranging from the recognition of differing legal orders within the nation-state, to a more far reaching and open-ended concept of law that does not necessarily depend on state recognition for its validity. This latter concept of law may come into being wherever two or more legal systems exist in the same social field. The two perspectives range along a continuum, which varies according to the degree of centrality that is accorded to state law. On the one hand, state law defines the conditions under which legal pluralism is said to exist. On the other, its centrality is displaced by the recognition that state law may be only one of a number of elements that give rise to a situation of legal pluralism. These differences in the scale and projection of legal pluralism derive from differing standpoints that to some extent depend upon the purposes for which its concepts are being invoked. In some instances, it is called upon to deal with ideological assertions about law; in others, it is used to promote a more social-scientific and descriptive theory of law based on empirical data, one of the hallmarks of which has been the production of a large, diverse, and rich ethnography that has developed out of fieldwork. To a degree these two approaches represent the product of differing historical, economic, and political factors that have conjoined to create different sites for study over time and space. Whatever the focus, legal pluralism raises important questions about power—where it is located, how it is constituted, what forms it takes—in ways that promote a more finely tuned and sophisticated analysis of continuity, transformation, and change in society. These are questions that have claimed and continue to claim the attention of both lawyers and social scientists. They are especially pertinent given the challenges presented by globalisation and the place of local communities within it when dealing with 'the accelerated flows of various commodities, people, capital, technologies, communications, images, and knowledge across national frontiers'.[1]

---

[1] N. Long, 'Globalization and localization: new challenges to rural research' in H. L. Moore (ed.) *The Future of Anthropological Knowledge* (London and New York Routledge 1996) 37–59 at 37.

In this chapter, it is not possible to present a comprehensive account of legal pluralism with its many permutations; instead, it will highlight some of the main approaches that have generated so much debate about the meaning and scope of the concept.[2] The term, legal pluralism, is of relatively recent origin, generally attributed to a collection of papers published by Gilissen in 1971 titled *Le Pluralisme Juridique*. Since then John Griffiths[3] has mobilised debate around what he views as two different approaches to legal pluralism, one engaging with 'weak', 'juristic' or 'classic' pluralism (that he associates with a lawyers' view of legal pluralism), and the other with a form of 'strong', 'deep' or 'new' legal pluralism, (associated with a social science view of law). For John Griffiths, whose interest lies in establishing 'a descriptive conception of legal pluralism'[4] for comparative purposes, it is the social science perspective that embraces law as an empirical state of affairs that is key. This leads him to define legal pluralism as 'that state of affairs, for any social field, in which behaviour pursuant to more than one legal order occurs'.[5]

1. WEAK, JURISTIC OR CLASSIC LEGAL PLURALISM

Much of the earlier work associated with the weak, juristic or classic legal pluralism deals with indigenous law represented as a counterpoint to European or

---

[2] For an overview of the field see J. Vanderlinden, 'Le pluralisme juridique: Essai de Synthèse' in J. Gilissen (ed.) *Le pluralisme juridique* (Bruxelles Bruxelles Presses del'Université 1970), 'Return to Legal Pluralism: Twenty Years Later' (1989) 28 *Journal of Legal Pluralism and Unofficial Law* at 149–157; M. Galanter, 'Justice in Many Rooms: Courts, Private Ordering and Indigenous Law (1981) 19 *Journal of Legal Pluralism and Unofficial Law* at 1–47; J. Griffiths, 'What is Legal Pluralism?' (1986) 24 *Journal of Legal Pluralism and Unofficial Law* at 1–55; A. Griffiths, *In The Shadow of Marriage: Gender and Justice in an African Community* (Chicago Chicago University Press 1997) at 28–38 and 211–240; S. E. Merry, 'Legal Pluralism' (1988) 22(5) *Law & Society Review* at 869–896; F. von Benda-Beckmann, 'Comment on Merry' (1988) 22(5) *Law & Society Review* at 897–901; K. von Benda-Beckmann and F. Strijbosch (eds) *Anthropology of Law in the Netherlands* (Dordrecht and Cinnaminson Foris Publications 1986); A. Allott and G. Woodman (eds) *People's Law and State Law: The Bellagio Papers* (Dordrecht and Cinnaminson Foris Publications 1985); C. Greenhouse, 'Legal Pluralism and Cultural Difference What Is the Difference? A Response to Professor Woodman' (1998) 42 *Journal of Legal Pluralism and Unofficial Law* at 61–71; C. Greenhouse and F. Strijbosch (eds) 'Legal Pluralism in Industrialized Societies', (1993) 33 *Journal of Legal Pluralism and Unofficial Law*; G. Woodman, 'Customary law, State courts, and the Notion of Institutionalization of Norms in Ghana and Nigeria' in A. Allott and G. Woodman (eds) *People's Law and State Law: The Bellagio Papers* (Holland and Cinnaminson Foris Publications 1985), 'Ideological Combat and Social Observations: Recent Debate about Legal Pluralism' (1998) 42 *Journal of Legal Pluralism and Unofficial Law* at 21–59; N. Rouland, *Legal Anthropology* (trans. Phippe G. Planel London Athlone Press 1994); J. Belley 'Pluralimse juridique' in A. Arnaud (dir) *Dictionnaire encyclopédique de théorie et de sociologie du droit* 2nd edn (Paris Librairie Générale de Droit et de Jurisprudence 1993); W. Tie, *Legal Pluralism: Toward a multicultural conception of law* (Aldershot and Brookfield Dartmouth Ashgate 1999); L. Sheleff, *The Future of Tradition: Customary Law, Common Law and Legal Pluralism* (London and Portland Frank Cass 2000).

[3] J. Griffiths, *supra* n. 2.

[4] J. Griffiths, *supra* n. 2 at 1.

[5] J. Griffiths, *supra* n. 2 at 2.

Western-style law.[6] An interest in this subject developed out of a combination of intellectual and pragmatic pursuits. Out of the Enlightenment came an interest in tracing the evolution of human development in which law played a key role because it was viewed as representing rationality over other forms of order, created, for example, out of self-interest or force. Thus, law became the index of a 'civilized' society, marking a transition for humanity and society from an irrational to a rational state of being. In charting this progress, which was conceived in universal terms, law became key because it provided the predominant feature which would distinguish so-called primitive from more civilised societies. Given the evolutionary and universal hypotheses underlying such an account of human development, it was necessary to engage in comparative research, to look at law in other societies. Both lawyers and anthropologists rose to the challenge—none more so than Sir Henry Maine,[7] credited as the key exemplar and impetus behind this universal search for law.

At the same time the development and growth of nation-states in Europe was reaching its zenith, marked by the acquisition of colonies and colonial subjects that required to be governed. Whether under direct or indirect rule, regulation took the form of law which, as Chanock,[8] among others has noted, was the cutting edge of colonialism in its attempt to control and govern its colonial subjects while bringing about their transformation and that of the societies in which they lived. In this context, while European or Western law was imposed on colonial subjects, it was also recognised that such law was inappropriate in certain cases, for example, in governing the family life of subrogated persons and that regulation of such matters should be left to the local, customary, or indigenous law of that group. It therefore became necessary to make a study of these forms of law to provide for its incorporation within the framework of the colonial state. In this way local, customary, or indigenous law was viewed as something 'other' than Western law, as a separate and distinct form of law. Under this model of legal pluralism, the state defines the parameters that mark the territories of legal systems within its domain, such as customary and Islamic law, in ways that depict them as separate and autonomous spheres. A prime example of this type of pluralism is provided by Hooker[9] who surveys plural legal systems in Asia, Africa, and the Middle East and who defines legal pluralism as circumstances 'in

---

[6] What to call law other than state law has generated a great deal of discussion. Terms such as local, folk, customary, informal, people's law and indigenous law have all been mooted, but the point has been made that there is no characterization which consistently follows any supposed distinction between state and folk law. For discussion of this issue refer to A. Allott and G. Woodman (eds) *supra* n. 2 at 13–20

[7] Sir H. Maine, *Ancient law: Its Connections with the Early History of Society and Its Relations to Modern Ideas*, 1st edn (London J. Murray Reprinted as no. 734 in Everyman's Library, London, J. M. Dent and Sons 1965).

[8] M. Chanock, *Law, Custom and Social Order: The Colonial Experience in Malawi and Zambia* (Cambridge Cambridge University Press 1985) at 4.

[9] M. Hooker, *Legal Pluralism: An Introduction to Colonial and Neo-Colonial Laws* (Oxford Oxford University Press 1975).

the contemporary world which have resulted from the transfer of whole legal systems across cultural boundaries'.[10]

2. CRITIQUES OF THIS MODEL

Many scholars have rejected the above model of legal pluralism because it reflects a legal centralist or formalist model of law. It is too statist in its conception of law, which has consequences for the ways in which we perceive law. Under this model authority became centralised in the form of the state, represented through government, the most visible manifestation of which is the legislature. Law formed part of this process of government but was set apart from other government agencies, having its own specific institutions, such as courts and legal personnel who required specialist training. Law was conceived as gaining its authority from the state, and, increasing it by becoming part of the process of government. This authority, at its most basic level, was upheld through the power to impose or enforce sanctions.

While associated with government, law was at the same time able to develop relative autonomy both from the state and from society through the existence of its own institutions, which dealt exclusively with legal matters. Legal activity became set apart from other forms of social and religious activity, not just in terms of institutions, but also through the language that accompanied this development, which reinforced the need for specialist personnel. In this way law became established as a self-validating system, a system whose validity, authority, and legitimacy rely no longer on any external source such as morality or religion, but rather on internal sources which are self-referential for its regulation and perpetuation. These sources include written texts embodied in statutes and cases. They acquire recognition and derive authority through the institutional domains that give rise to them, namely, legislatures and courts, as well as through the personnel, judges and lawyers, who are instrumental in their creation.

The rules generated from these sources are 'legal' rules which are set apart from those rules created from other sources—for example moral or religious rules (which may be drawn from society at large)—and within the legal domain not only acquire precedence over other such rules, but are also used to define the parameters of discussion and to determine outcomes. To sum up, the characteristics of this model are that it promotes a uniform view of law and its relationship to the state,[11] one which places law at the center of the social universe and which endorses normative prescriptions for interpreting society. In this model legal norms are set apart from, and privileged over, social norms[12] and

---

[10]   M. Hooker, *supra* n. 9 at 1.

[11]   J. Griffiths, *supra* n. 2 at 3.

[12]   S. A. Roberts, *Order and Dispute* (New York St Martin's Press 1979) at 25; M. Galanter, *supra* n. 2 at 20.

used to determine outcomes where conflict arises.[13] Thus 'law' is confined to a particular framework, one that sets it apart from social life and which promotes an image of autonomy that is used to maintain its power and authority over social relations in general, thereby sustaining a notion of hierarchy while at the same time maintaining an image of neutrality and equality within its own domain. The pervasive power of this legal centralist or formalist model of law is such that it may be said that all legal studies stand it its shadow.[14]

Nonetheless this model of law has been highly contested. It raises particular issues for the study of legal pluralism, many of which form part of debates that have taken place over the ages concerning the very meaning of law itself. Some specific critiques are discussed below.

Law as universal across time and space

Under this model law is decontextualised in that it is presented as universal across time and space. Thus, it not only purports to account for law over time but also to mark its presence across the globe at particular moments in history. Such an approach is essentialist or reductionist in nature for it elevates a particular model of law that developed out of a particular period in history to the status of the governing paradigm that is to provide the framework for locating law at all times and in all places. Subject to critique within its own domain (see discussion of strong legal pluralism below), it becomes more problematic when used for comparative purposes for it exercises the authority to determine what counts as law to the exclusion of those accounts that fail to meet its criteria.

State power over the recognition, legitimacy, and validity of law

This exclusionary power of classification led Evans-Pritchard,[15] who worked among the Nuer in southern Sudan, to observe that judged in these terms the Nuer did not have law. Dissatisfaction with branding those societies that did not conform to the centralist model, as primitive or lawless, prompted many scholars including Gluckman,[16] Bohannan,[17] and Pospisil[18] to shift their focus to the

[13] S. A. Roberts, *supra* n. 12 at 20; J. L. Comaroff and S. A. Roberts, *Rules and Processes: The Cultural Logic of Dispute in an African Context* (Chicago and London University of Chicago Press 1981) at 5.

[14] M. Galanter, *supra* n. 2 at 1; J. Griffiths, *supra* n. 2.

[15] Sir E. E. Pritchard, *The Nuer: A Description of the Modes of Livelihood and Political Institutions of Nilotic People* (Oxford Oxford University Press 1940) at 162.

[16] M. Gluckman, *The Judicial Process among the Barotse of Northern Rhodesia (Zambia)* 2nd ed (Manchester Manchester University Press 1955), *Custom and Conflict in Africa* (Glencoe Ill. and Oxford Free Press and Blackwell 1955).

[17] P. Bohannan, *Justice and Judgment among the Tiv* (London Oxford University Press for the International African institute 1957; 2nd ed with new preface 1968).

[18] L. Pospisil, *Kapauku Papuans and Their Law* (New Haven Yale University Publications in Anthropology n. 54, Yale University Press 1958).

study of disputes. The advantage in making this shift was that it immediately expanded the field of inquiry, for, by focusing on disputes, scholars no longer had to locate their legal studies in particular sources and institutions. What became important was to define law, not in terms of form, but of substance, which represented the means by which order is established and maintained within society. This was reflected through a society's handling of conflict in disputes. Concerns over trying to define law cross-culturally also led a number of scholars at a later stage to make the case for rejecting use of the term law, because of its parochial and ethnocentric connotations, in favour of using disputing and processes of order as the frame for comparative analysis.[19] Many of these studies adopted a methodological approach based on ethnography, involving intensive fieldwork, which focused on local, specific, micro-studies in order to provide, what Clifford Geertz has referred to as the 'thick description' of analysis.[20] As such they provided a counterpoint to analyses of law based on abstract legal theory and gave voice to the multiple ways in which people dealt with positions of dominance and subordination, exclusion from formal legal arenas, or negotiations surrounding their access to, and use of, law. They also marked a move away more generally, in the study of law, from the study of rules and institutional frameworks to more actor-oriented perspectives and the study of dynamic processes.[21]

This study of disputes with its more inclusive approach, which dominated much of legal anthropology through several decades was not, however, without its problems. It also engendered critique on the grounds of

(a) the ahistorical nature and presentation of many disputing studies,[22] the need to expand the concept of dispute settlement to embrace dispute processing and the extended case study method,[23]

(b) the need to study troubleless as well as trouble cases,[24] and thus the need to combine a study of order or everyday life along with the study of

---

[19] R. L. Abel, 'A Comparative Theory of Dispute Institutions in Society' (1973) 8 *Law & Society Review* at 217–347; S. A. Roberts, *supra* n. 12; J. L. Comaroff and S. A. Roberts, *supra* n. 13.

[20] C. Geertz, *The Interpretation of Culture: Selected Essays* (New York Basic Books 1973).

[21] L. Nader and B. Yngvesson, 'On Studying Ethnography of Law and its Consequences' in J.J. Honigmann ed. *Handbook of Social Cultural Anthropology* (Rand Mcnally Chicago 1973); J. L. Comaroff and S. A. Roberts, *supra* n. 12; A. Griffiths, *supra* n. 2.

[22] F. G. Snyder, 'Anthropology, Dispute Processes and Law: A Critical Introduction ' (1981) 8(2) *British Journal of Law & Society*, 141–180 at 143; M. Cain and K. Kulcsar, 'Thinking Disputes: An Essay on the Origins of the Dispute Industry (1982) 16(3) *Law & Society Review* 375–402 at 326.

[23] P. H. Gulliver, *Social Control in an African Society* (London Routledge and Kegan Paul 1963); J. Van Velsen, 'The Extended Case method and Situational Analysis' in A. L. Epstein (ed.) *The Craft of Social Anthropology* (Tavistock London and New York 1967), 129–149; M. Gluckman 'Limitations of the Case-method in the Study of Tribal Law' (1973) 7 *Law & Society Review* at 611–641; R. Abel, 'Reply to Max Gluckman' (1973) 8 *Law & Society Review* at 157–159; L. Nader and H. F. Todd (eds) *The Disputing Process—Law in Ten Societies* (New York Columbia Press 1978).

[24] K. N. Llewellyn and E. A. Hoebel, *The Cheyenne Way: Conflict and Case Law in Primitive Jurisprudence* (Norman University of Oklahoma Press 1941); J. F. Holleman, 'Trouble Cases and Troubless Cases in the Study of Customary Law and Legal Reform' (1973) 7 *Law & Society Review* at 585–586.

disputes.[25] This ultimately led a number of scholars to discover the limitations of the case method study and thus to a reorientation of their work towards the significance of legal rules and institutions outside processes of dispute/conflict management,

(c) neglect in many disputing studies until the early 1970s of the fact that many of the societies under investigation had been influenced by and become part of colonial states and a wider economy,[26] the problems associated with uncritically adopting dispute as a unit of analysis; merely substituting the study of disputes for the study of law 'simply replaces one problem with another',[27]

(d) the problematic role of ethnography in the production of knowledge.

One reason for adopting an ethnographic approach to law was to provide a counterpoint to analyses of law based on abstract legal theory by engaging in the study of people's specific, concrete, lived-experiences of law. But while ethnography may provide another perspective on law which differs from those that are based on abstract legal theory it has also been subject to critique about its claims to knowledge and representation. Clifford and Marcus[28] and Marcus and Fischer[29] among others, have challenged the ways in which anthropologists have constructed anthropological texts to establish 'ethnographic authority'. Wilmsen has criticised the practice of ethnography as removing selected parts of social context from its social formation resulting too often in a form of cultural essentialism.[30] Feminist scholars have challenged what they perceive as the dominance of male authority in the construction of knowledge, while feminist legal scholars have long been critical of the ways in which mainstream legal discourse fails to take adequate, if any, account of women's voices, practices, and experiences in its analysis of law.[31]

[25] S. A. Roberts, *supra* n. 12; J. L. Comaroff and S. A. Roberts, *supra* n. 13.

[26] F. G. Snyder, *supra* n. 22, and 'Law and Development in the Light of Dependency Theory' (1980) 14 *Law & Society Review* at 723–804; *Capitalism and Legal Change: An African Transformation* (New York and London Academic Press 1981); P. Fitzpatrick, 'Traditionalism and Traditional Law' (1984) 28 *Journal of African Law*, 20–27, 'Law and Societies' (1984) 22 *Osgoode Hall Law Journal*, 115–138, 'Review Article: Is it Simple to be a Marxist in Legal Anthropology ?' (1985) 48 *Modern Law Review*, 472–485.

[27] M. Cain and K. Kulcsar, *supra* n. 22 at 397; A. Griffiths *supra* n. 2 at 32.

[28] J. Clifford and G. Marcus, *Writing Culture* (Berkeley University of California Press 1986).

[29] G. Marcus and M. Fisher (eds) *Anthropology as Cultural Critique* (Chicago University of Chicago Press 1989).

[30] E. N. Wilmsen, *Land Filled with Flies: A Political Economy of the Kalahari* (Chicago and London University of Chicago Press 1989).

[31] N. Lacey, 'From Individual to Group?' in B. Hepple and E. Szyszczak (eds) *Discrimination: The Limits of Law* (London Mansell 1992); C. Smart, *Feminism and the Power of Law* (London Routledge 1989), 'The Woman of Legal Discourse' (1992) 1(1) *Social & Legal Studies* at 29–44, *Law, Crime and Sexuality: Essays in Feminism* (London Sage 1995); C. MacKinnon, 'Feminism, Marxism, Method and the State: An Agenda for Theory' (1983) 8(2) *Signs* at 635–658; *Feminism Unmodified: Discourses on Life and Law* (Cambridge Mass. Harvard University Press 1987); M. A. Fineman, 'Implementing Equality: Ideology, Contradiction and Social Change: A Study of Rhetoric and Results in the Regulation of the Consequences of Divorce' (1983) 4 *Wisconsin Law Review* at 789–886, 'Introduction' in M. A. Fineman and N. S. Thomsadsen (eds) *At the Boundaries*

All the problems associated with the weak, juristic or classic form of legal pluralism come back to the question of power, that is, power to define law, to apply it and to use it. In other words, to accord authority, legitimacy, and validity to the claims made by the members of a society (or the converse). Collier and Starr reject the concept of legal pluralism because, in their eyes, it fails to take adequate account of the power relations that pertain to legal systems and their relationships with one another, treating them as having equal weight when in reality this is rarely the case.[32] While this charge may be laid against the weak, juristic or classic form of legal pluralism, it is not necessarily valid for the strong, deep or new legal pluralism discussed later below.

State law's claims to integrity, coherence, and uniformity

In promoting the view that only state law is law and excluding other forms of normative ordering from falling within the definition of law, the legal centralist/formalist model makes assertions about the integrity, coherence, and uniformity of state law. While legal pluralists have challenged its ideological assertions as to the exclusivity of state law this has mainly been achieved, as Woodman points out, by references to the existence and characteristics of non-state law.[33] He argues that by focusing on the challenges raised by non-state law scholars have tended to implicitly accept the integrity of state law and the claims made for it (other than that of exclusivity). Yet he argues that 'There is strong evidence that state laws are (a) not internally self-consistent, logical systems, and (b) not clearly bounded and distinct from other social normative orders'.[34] Nonetheless he underlines Merry's observation that the ways in which other normative orders shape state law are 'particularly unstudied'.[35]

He argues for recognition of state legal pluralism, pointing to research carried out by scholars under the heading of *Polycentricity of Law*,[36] which is concerned with studying the use of sources of law in different sectors of state administration in several Nordic countries. This kind of research, by acknowledging use of differing sources of law, allows for the possibility of conflict between different state sectors as to the degree of authority that is accorded to the different sources. Not only that, but it allows for the possibility of incompatibility.

of Law: Feminism and Legal Theory (Routledge London 1991) at xi–xvi; L. E. White, 'Subordination, Rhetorical Survival Skills, and Sunday Shies: Notes on the Hearing of Mrs G' in M. A. Fineman and N. S. Thomadsen (eds) *At the Boundaries of Law: Feminism and Legal Theory* (London Routledge 1991) at 40–58; M. Minow, 'Consider the Consequences' (1986) 84 *Michigan Law Review* at 900–918.

[32] J. F. Collier and J. Starr (eds) *History and Power in the Study of Law: New Directions in Legal Anthropology* (Ithaca and London Cornell University Press 1989)

[33] G. Woodman, 'Ideological Combat', *supra* n. 2 at 51.

[34] G. Woodman, 'Ideological Combat', *supra* n. 2 at 51.

[35] S. E. Merry, *supra* n. 2 at 884.

[36] H. Petersen and H. Zahle (eds) *Legal Polycentricity: Consequences of Pluralism in Law* (Aldershot Dartmouth 1995).

However, as Woodman[37] notes, it is not clear whether this research 'has revealed incompatible contradictions between the observance of sources of law, or between norms claiming to regulate social behaviour'.

For Woodman, the study of legal pluralism must include state law pluralism within its remit. He makes the case for an ethnography of state law that would examine its plurality and diversity within legal fields, taking account of variation in ways which may promote a better understanding of how law works, for example by showing how a term like customary law may vary in its content and application according to whether it is applied by local people, as part of their 'living' law, as distinguished from what is recognised as customary law by lawyers and courts.[38] For John Griffiths, however, the notion of state law pluralism is an impossibility. Thus, the kind of legal pluralism depicted by Hooker, is for him an expression of legal doctrine forming part of the state's ideological assertions about law. He argues that Hooker's categories of state law are based on a conceptual analysis of law, derived from documentary evidence of the formal rules of state law, rather than on the empirical or social facts that provide the foundation for his theory of legal pluralism. For John Griffiths, given that the law of the state represents a single legal order, legal pluralism can only be said to exist where non-state law and state law coexist, for his definition of legal pluralism is centred on the recognition of non-state law. What others refer to as state law pluralism he views simply as instances of legal diversity or of lack of uniformity of law within a single legal order.

Woodman, however, highlights an important aspect of state law that John Griffiths ignores, that is, its salience and power as a social fact. Woodman makes the point that state law need not be categorised as doctrine alone, but may be viewed as having a reality in the social world that it inhabits. Thus rules contained in an operative state law are social facts as well as doctrine. This aspect of state law is comparable with non-state law and can be used to provide the kind of insight that would be denied under a centralist/formalist model of law and that can, for example, account for the differences between folk law and lawyers' customary law.[39] Such an approach, that treats state law as a social fact, has the advantage of undermining the ideological power of the centralist/formalist model, by blurring the boundaries between state and non-state law on which such a model depends. While John Griffiths also seeks to undermine the power of this model he does so in the context of maintaining a clear separation between state and non-state law which raises questions about whether there is a fundamental difference between state law and non-state law and between non-state law and other elements of social ordering. These issues will be addressed in the section on strong legal pluralism below.

[37] G. Woodman, 'Ideological Combat', *supra* n. 2 at 47.
[38] G. Woodman, 'Customary Law', *supra* n. 2.
[39] G. Woodman, 'Customary Law', *supra* n. 2 at 35.

3. RECONCEIVING LAW: TRANSNATIONAL AND GLOBAL PERSPECTIVES

Taking the state as the central vantage or standpoint from which to analyse law is also problematic in an age where law and legal institutions now cross local, regional and national boundaries and in which the 'local' is embedded in and shaped by regional, national, and international networks of power and information. These intersecting, cross-cutting and dialectical relationships may be seen as the product of globalisation, defined by Twining as 'those processes which tend to create and consolidate a unified world economy, a single ecological system, and a complex network of communications that covers the whole globe, even if it does not penetrate to every part of it'.[40] In this context, the power of transnational forms of law and ordering derived from such diverse sources as the European Union, the European Convention on Human Rights, the World Trade Organisation, the World Bank, the International Monetary Fund, and religious movements, is one that is either ignored or inadequately accounted for under a statist/centralist conception of law.

One arena where complex networks of communication have had an impact on state governance is in the field of human rights. As Merry observes 'indigenous groups often define themselves in terms being developed by the global movement of indigenous peoples' human rights and the provisions of state law'.[41] Such groups, in making claims to retain their land and/or water rights, are forced by law to assert their cultural distinctiveness (regardless of whether that is a dominant feature for the group itself) if such claims are to be successful. In this way 'the legal provisions of the nation in which an indigenous community lives as well as those of the international order affect how a particular indigenous community presents itself and the kinds of identities it assumes'.[42] This perspective is important, for it belies one that would simply treat such groups as 'traditional', in favour of acknowledging 'recent accommodations to the shifting global and national frameworks of power and meaning in which the community lives'.[43]

Women's groups within nation states have also managed to mobilise around international conventions, such as the UN Convention on the Elimination of All Forms of Discrimination Against Women, in order to challenge state laws that have had an adverse impact on them and their children. For example, the case of Unity Dow in Botswana who raised a constitutional challenge to the state's citizenship laws which prevented children born to Tswana women married to foreigners from acquiring citizenship, while at the same time granting citizen-

---

[40] W. Twining, *Globalisation and Legal Theory* (London Edinburgh Dublin Butterworths 2000) at 4.
[41] S. E. Merry, 'Crossing Boundaries: Ethnography in the Twenty-First Century' (2000) 23(2) *PoLAR* 127–133 at 127.
[42] S. E. Merry, *ibid*. at 127.
[43] S. E. Merry, *ibid*. 41 at 127.

ship to the children of Tswana men married to foreigners, and those of unmarried Tswana women whose fathers were non-citizens. In bringing this case Unity Dow had strong support from certain feminist groups within the country, such as Emang Basadi (Stand Up Women), as well as from other international human rights networks, such as the Urban Morgan Institute for Human Rights, University of Cincinnati College of Law, that lodged an Amicus Brief with the High Court in Botswana on her behalf.[44]

With regard to economic development and international aid, there has been a shift in policy from providing direct aid to governments on the part of multilateral agencies and donor states and a corresponding redirection of investment and development funds to private sector organisations. An important consequence of this policy has been the proliferation of non-governmental organisations (NGOs) that provide an array of services including education, healthcare, voter literacy, small business development, resource management, and monitoring of human rights. These NGOs represent a diverse array of organizations from multi-million pound organisations that operate on several continents to agencies that represent commercial interests, grass roots alliances, or village based religious or cultural groups. While they vary greatly in terms of size, organisational components, sources of funding, and their relationship with the state, it is clear that whatever their particular composition,

> Local and transnational NGO's may also operate on a global level, forming alliances with private companies or other NGO's to facilitate the exchange of ideas and information, mediation between commercial interests and humanitarian concerns, and lobbying organizations like the UN on issues such as women's empowerment and environmental preservation.[45]

What is clear is that the role of the state must be re-examined in the context of this intersection of development, transnational capital, civil society, non-governmental actors, and states. Thus nation-states can no longer be treated as discrete legal entities that can be studied in isolation either internally or externally.

For some scholars these transnational forms of order mark a 'disengagement of law and state',[46] while for others, like Sassen,[47] the focus is not so much on disengagement as on reconceiving the role of the state in ways that belie its adherence to notions of sovereignty and territoriality. This is necessary, for as Sassen observes, 'today's global economy poses a challenge because it simultaneously

---

[44] For details, see A. Griffiths, 'Gendering culture: towards a plural perspective on Kwena women's rights' in J. K. Cowan, M. Dembour and R. A. Wilson (eds) *Culture and Rights: Anthropological Perspectives* (Cambridge Cambridge University Press 2001) 102–126 at 117–119.

[45] L. Leve and L. Karim, 'Introduction Privatizing the State: Ethnography of Development, Transnational Capital, and NGO's' (2001) 24(1) *PoLAR* 53–58 at 53.

[46] W. Twining, *supra* n. 40 at 52; B. de Sousa Santos, *Toward a New Common Sense: Law, Science and Politics in the Paradigmatic Transition* (London Routledge 1995).

[47] S. Sassen, 'De-nationalization: Some Conceptual and Empirical Elements—APLA Distinguished Lecture' (1999) 22(2) *PoLAR* at 1–16.

transcends the authority of the national state, yet is at least partly implanted in national territories and institutions'.[48] The challenge exists because of methodological and conceptual frameworks employed by social scientists that tend to view the national and non-national as mutually exclusive zones and because of 'the explicit or implicit assumption about the nation-state as the container of social processes and the implied correspondence of national territory and national exclusive territoriality (the institutional encasement of that territory)'.[49] What is required is another perspective on the relationship between local, regional, national, and global domains and their relationship with law, one, which moves beyond an 'ossified notion of culture and the binaries that it underwrites'.[50]

Such a perspective involves an examination of how power operates in different places, how it gets transformed, and an exploration of the complex ways in which 'local forms of knowledge and organization are constantly being reworked in interaction with changing external conditions',[51] so that the knowledge produced is both simultaneously local and global, but not universal.[52] In this way there is a recognition of a reciprocal interaction between the global and the local in ways which do not essentialise either in terms of the 'other' but rather acknowledge the ways in which the global may constrain the local while at the same time also acknowledging the ways in which the local appropriates and transforms the global for its own needs.

The importance of this type of analysis is that it undermines any view of globalisation as a 'monolithic entity'[53] the effects of which are dictated 'by some supranational hegemonic power'[54] with uniform results, as this fails to capture 'global ordering in terms of a complex changing pattern of homogenization and diversity'.[55] Merry observes that just as 'local places cannot be studied in isolation, nor can the global be understood except as constituted by multiple locals clustered together at some local spot'.[56]

This also promotes an understanding of the relationship between local and global domains that is not necessarily predicated upon territorial boundaries and geographic space. For example, Sassen observes that the new international finance professionals and immigrant workers 'operate in contexts which are at the same time local and global'.[57] This is because finance professionals form

---

[48] S. Sassen, *ibid.* at 1.

[49] S. Sassen, *ibid.* at 1.

[50] L. Abu-Lughod, 'Introduction: Feminist Longing and Postcolonial Conditions' in L. Abu-Lughod (ed.) *Remaking Women: Feminism and Modernity in the Middle East* (Princeton Princeton University Press 1998) 3–31 at 17.

[51] N. Long, *supra* n. 1 at 50.

[52] H. L. Moore, 'Introduction' in H. L. Moore (ed.) *The Future of Anthropological Knowledge* (London and New York Routledge 1996) at 10.

[53] H. L. Moore, *ibid.* at 9.

[54] N. Long, *supra* n. 1 at 42.

[55] N. Long, *supra* n. 1 at 50.

[56] S. E. Merry, *supra* n. 41 at 129.

[57] S. Sassen, *supra* n. 47 at 3.

part of a network that cuts across the boundaries of nation states. Yet, at the same time, these professionals experience very particular working conditions (associated with international finance centers) that form 'part of an international yet very localized work sub-culture'.[58] Thus, what emerges is a global network of 'local' places that share specific features, but where the definition of 'local' has nothing to do with geographic proximity. In the same way, immigrants who enter new communities maintain cross border links with those left behind in their countries of origin. Such links promote an understanding of culture that may be viewed as 'local' because the immigrants and native compatriots share a common set of beliefs and practices, but which is not dependant upon territoriality for its existence.

A recognition that culture and geographic space and territoriality need not coincide is important because it highlights the fact that concepts of cultural identity, law, and difference, that gives rise to notions of the 'other', need not be mapped in terms of territoriality. Greenhouse[59] is critical of approaches to legal pluralism that treat it 'more or less as a synonym for cultural pluralism'. She argues that equating legal pluralism and social/cultural pluralism is highly problematic because such an equation makes law *a priori* and preeminently a sign of cultural identity, as if law's production could be separated from the social processes by which people self-identity or are identified by others as belonging together in a 'cultural group'.[60] She rejects the ways in which 'anthropological discussions on legal pluralism *have* tended to take an axiomatic corollary relationship between the organisation of *legal orders* and an on-the-ground schema of *cultural identity*—as if cultural identity has some axiomatic corollary in territory and legality'.[61] This approach, which is premised on the 'idea that law and cultural identity are each other's corollary' is, as she points out, 'fundamental to the cultural self-legitimations of the nation-state'.[62]

Yet the nation-state cannot be ignored. As Greenhouse acknowledges 'while the conceptual status of the nation-state is in doubt among social theorists' nonetheless as 'recent analyses of globalisation and transnational life make clear, current world conditions by no means remove the nation-state from the horizons of people's stake and aspirations'.[63] No more so than when considering citizenship, yet as Greenhouse notes,[64] this poses a conundrum for researchers for 'ethnography is circular if one posits in advance the nation-state as a cultural or social entity, yet ethnography's relevance depends to some extent on democratic institutions and the ways they do and do not work in and

---

[58] S. Sassen, *supra* n. 47 at 3.
[59] C. Greenhouse, *ibid.* at 64.
[60] C. Greenhouse, *ibid.* at 65.
[61] C. Greenhouse, *ibid.* at 65.
[62] C. Greenhouse, *ibid.* at 65.
[63] C. Greenhouse, 'Commentary' (1999) 22(2) *PoLAR* at 104–109 at 104.
[64] C. Greenhouse, *ibid.* at 104.

across states'.[65] What is required is re-engaging with the state in ways which allow for it to be factored into ethnographic research as *an* element for discussion but which does not focus on it as *the* primary point of reference from which such research commences.[66]

4. STRONG, DEEP OR NEW LEGAL PLURALISM

The strong, deep or new legal pluralism provides a mechanism for doing this. It recognises that legal pluralism exists in all societies, that is, that there are multiple forms of ordering that pertain to members of a society that are not necessarily dependent upon the state for recognition of their authority. This form of pluralism allows for an analysis of law that avoids the kind of critiques leveled against the weak, juristic or classic legal pluralism discussed above. It acknowledges (as the other pluralism does not) what Santos has termed 'porous legality' or 'legal porosity' that is 'the conception of different legal spaces superimposed, interpenetrated, and mixed in our minds, as much as in our actions [that constitutes] interlegality'.[67]

A number of scholars, such as Pospisil,[68] who wrote about different legal levels, and Smith who focused on corporations, have been associated with developing this new legal pluralism.[69] One of the most influential has been Sally Falk Moore, whose concept of the semi-autonomous social field has provided a framework for pursuing this type of pluralism (although Moore herself does not explicitly locate her work within a legal pluralist tradition). Moore addressed the problem of the contextual character of law in her comparison between the Chagga of Tanzania and the garment industry in New York.[70] She developed the term 'semi-autonomous social field' to indicate a social unit that generates and maintains its own norms. Thus, the semi-autonomous social field is one that

> can generate rules and customs and symbols internally, but that . . . is also vulnerable to rules and decisions and other forces emanating from the larger world by which it is surrounded. The semi-autonomous social field has rule-making capacities, and the means to induce or coerce compliance; but it is simultaneously set in a larger social

---

[65] See also C. Greenhouse and D. J. Greenwood, 'Introduction: The Ethnography of Democracy and Difference' in C. Greenhouse (ed.) *Democracy and Ethnography: Constructing Identities in Multicultural Liberal States* (Albany SUNY Press 1998) and C. Greenhouse, 'Legal Pluralism and Cultural Difference' *supra* n. 2 at 61–71.

[66] H. L. Moore, *supra* n. 52 at 12 argues that the focus should be on 'the impact of governmentality on ways of living and on social institutions, including the state'.

[67] B. de Sousa Santos, 'A Map of Misreading—Toward a Postmodern Conception of Law' (1987) 14(3) *Journal of Law & Society* at 279–302.

[68] L. Pospisil, *supra* n. 18, and *Anthropology of Law: A Comparative Theory* (New York Harper & Row 1971).

[69] M. G. Smith, 'Some Development in the Analytic Framework of Pluralism' in L. Kuper and M. G. Smith (eds) *Pluralism in Africa* (Berkeley University of California Press 1969), *Corporations and Society* (London Duckworth 1974).

[70] S. F. Moore, 'Law and Social Change: The Semi-Autonomous Social Field as an Appropriate Subject of Study' (1973) 7 *Law & Society Review* at 719–746.

matrix which can, and does, affect and invade it, sometimes at the invitation of persons inside it, sometimes at its own instance.[71]

She uses this concept to demonstrate how state regulation reaches the working floor of a factory through the filters of these social fields. Thus, legal pluralism is a social fact that is not characteristic of a specific type of society or of a given social field. These fields are not unaffected by state regulation, but neither are they fully subject to it. In providing an empirical account of these fields Moore makes no claims about the nature of the orders that pertain to them or about the nature and direction of influence between the normative orders. The fact that they are semi-autonomous undermines the hegemonic claim to universal validity and dominance for state law, as state law is acted upon by other normative orders. Thus semi-autonomous social fields highlight the gap between state assertions of legality and empirical reality.

The importance of this perspective is that it counteracts the predisposition to think of all legal ordering as rooted in state law. This is necessary, for the weak, juristic or classic legal pluralism cannot serve as the basis for an analytic and descriptive framework of pluralism because the relationship between the law of the state and other law is predefined.[72] Thus, in order to get away from legal centralism in formulating a descriptive conception of legal pluralism 'it is necessary to identify legal pluralism in the strong sense'.[73] Moore's model provides one means of doing so. Not only that, but it has been developed by scholars to provide an account of the dynamics of change and transformation in a society.

Fitzpatrick,[74] for example, has gone on to develop the concept of 'integral plurality' which focuses on the interaction between normative orders, based on the proposition that state law is integrally constituted in relation to a plurality of social forms. In doing so, he makes the shift from seeing the semi-autonomous social field as constituted by state law, to observing how state law is shaped by its constituent normative orders and vice versa. From this perspective 'Law is the unsettled resultant of relations with a plurality of social forms and in this law's identity is constantly and inherently subject to challenge and change'.[75] Building on this theory, Henry integrates the dimension of individual action.[76] By drawing on Giddens' analysis of structure and action, according to which action shapes structure and structures constrain and enable actions, he

---

[71] S. F. Moore, *ibid.* at 720.
[72] K. von Benda-Beckman, 'Legal Pluralism' (2001) Tai Culture VI/1 & 2 at 11–17.
[73] G. Woodman, 'Ideological Combat', *supra* n. 2 at 33.
[74] P. Fitzpatrick, 'Law and Societies' *supra* n. 26.
[75] P. Fitzpatrick, *ibid.* at 138.
[76] S. Henry, *Private Justice: Towards Integrated Theorising in the Sociology of Law* (London Routledge & Kegan Paul 1983); 'Community Justice, Capitalist Society, and Human Agency: The Dialectics of Collective Law in the Corporation' (1985) 19 *Law & Society Review* at 303–327, 'The Construction and Deconstruction of Social Control: Thoughts on the Discursive Production of State Law and Private Justice' in J. Lowman, R. Menzies and T. Palys (eds) *Transcarceration* (Gower Farnborough 1987).

creates a space which allows for human actions to have an impact, even where the persons who carry them out may be powerless.[77]

According to Merry, the new, strong or deep legal pluralism has reoriented, or may in the future reorient, legal analysis away from the ideology of legal centralism and from essential definition of law in a number of ways.[78] It can guide it to an historical understanding, embracing an examination of the cultural or ideological nature of law and legal systems, or towards a dialectical analysis of the relationship among normative orders that provides a framework of understanding the dynamics of the imposition of law and of resistance to it.

Working with gender

One arena where this type of analysis has proved emancipatory is in discussions concerning the gendered nature of law. As noted earlier, feminist scholars have long been critical of the ways in which mainstream legal discourse fails to take account of gender in its analysis of law. A legal pluralist perspective provides a means of giving recognition to those normative orders that impinge on women's lives and so factor them into analyses which can take account of the conditions under which women and men find themselves silenced or unable to negotiate with others in terms of day-to-day social life, or the converse, and how this shapes their perceptions, access to and, use of law. My own Kwena ethnography drawn from detailed life histories and extended case studies highlights the gendered world in which women and men live and how this affects women's differential access to law, empowering women in some contexts while constraining them in others.[79] In her study of how Swahili women pursue marital disputes in local Kadhi's (Islamic) courts, Hirsch offers a nuanced analysis of the ways in which women acquire power or are deprived of it in a setting where customary law, religious law, Western law, and social norms concerning male and female speech intersect and interact.[80] Hellum's work in Zimbabwe, which draws on the concept of the semi-autonomous social field in the framing of her research, reveals the ways in which norms regulating kinship, marriage and gender were upheld or generated in the process of resolving procreative problems.[81]

This type of analysis is especially pertinent for postcolonial societies where there is a tendency to analyse pluralism in terms of the weak, juristic, or classic model. The problem lies in the fact that, as Stewart observes:

[77] A. Giddens, *Central Problems in Social Theory: Action, Structure and Contradiction in Social Analysis* (Berkeley University of California Press 1979).

[78] S. E. Merry, *supra* n. 2 at 889–890.

[79] A. Griffiths, *supra* n. 2.

[80] S. Hirsch, *Pronouncing and Persevering: Gender and the Discourses of Disputing in an African Islamic Court* (Chicago University of Chicago Press 1998).

[81] A. Hellum, *Women's Human Rights and Legal Pluralism in Africa: Mixed Norms and Identities in Infertility Management in Zimbabwe* (Oslo and Harare Tano Aschehoug and Mond Books 1999).

Postcolonial legal doctrine has a centralist orientation—the task of contemporary legal scholars is seen as interpreting the customary law which evolved in the colonial state courts in the light of contemporary legislation and supreme court practice. It is not concerned with understanding the contemporary social contexts despite the fact that the people's customs and practices are constantly evolving outside of the framework of court decisions and interpretations.[82]

Such an approach ignores the dynamics of social change and transformation. For those engaged in women's law in Africa

Concepts such as [the strong] legal pluralism and the associated tool of the semi-autonomous social field open up new and crucial ways within which the interaction of law and life can be explored, thereby making it possible to obtain a more holistic picture of the factors that affect women's lived realities and the choices they make, or the decisions and directions that are forced upon them.[83]

Working with globalisation

Adopting a perspective on legal pluralism in the strong sense also meshes well with approaches to analysing globalisation and the place of the local within it. Given the uneven and diverse effects of globalisation Long stresses the need to study the processes of 'internalization' and 'relocalization' of global conditions in order to uncover 'the emergence of new identities, alliances and struggles for space and power within specific populations'.[84] In this enterprise actor-oriented perspectives are essential because they refuse to permit an analysis of the local as a sphere that is simply acted upon through the imposition of external institutions, interests, or market forces that derive from national, regional or international agencies brought to bear on its domain. Instead, these perspectives provide for an analysis that not only examines how the global shapes the local but how the local responds. Such an analysis promotes a more finely tuned account of the effects of globalisation and its interventions, one that acknowledges that these phenomena represent socially constructed and continually negotiated processes. This viewpoint not only allows for local agency but provides insights into local actors' strategies for dealing with such phenomena, involving their manipulation, appropriation or, even, subversion of such phenomena, in particular contexts. This in turn promotes an understanding of how these 'external' interventions become endowed with diverse and localised sets of meaning and practices.

In this way, social actors not only interact with globalisaton in terms of their own existing experiences and understandings of culture, but also acquire new

---

[82] A. Stewart 'The contribution of feminist legal scholarship' in A. Stewart (ed.) *Gender Law & Social Justice* (London Blackstone Press 2000) 3–18 at 11.

[83] A. S. Bentzon, A. Hellum, J. Stewart, W. Nucube and T. Agersnap, *Pursuing Grounded Theory in Law: South-North Experiences in Developing Women's Law* (Norway and Zimbabwe Tano Aschehoug and Mond Books 1998) at 46.

[84] N. Long, *supra* n. 1 at 43.

experiences and understandings which are generated in the course of this encounter, so that, as Long observes, these processes provide 'insights into the processes of social transformation'.[85] Thus a study of the concrete ways in which social actors negotiate their universe serves as an alternative form of analysis to that which is based on abstract and theoretical forms of discourse that seek to account for both continuity and change in social relations. The value of this type of analysis lies in the fact that actors' actions 'can in no way be seen as simply determined by planned intervention or by the exigencies of culture'.[86] It also, as Long has argued, provides 'new insights into the interpretation and analysis of neo-liberal policies, theories and practices that go beyond the common tendency to explore them solely from a macro-economic or macro-political angle'.[87]

5. CRITIQUES OF THIS MODEL

This more open-ended approach to pluralism has come under attack for being too vague and ill-defined, in danger of drawing no distinction between the differing normative orders, and thus, conflating them all under the rubric of law. For Tamanaha,[88] embracing a Malinowskian notion of law as 'all the rules concerned and acted upon as binding obligations'[89] is unworkable because it is so broad as to make the concept of legal pluralism neither definable or useful. For Teubner,[90] defining pluralism in terms of vague connections between social and legal terms that are interpenetrating and mutually constitutive merely creates a situation of 'ambiguity and confusion'.[91] Tamanaha maintains that lumping all normative orders together is unscientific because he argues that there is an empirical distinction between state law and other forms of normative ordering.[92] He views state law norms and non-state norms as being ontologically distinct because state law norms come into being through the institutional apparatus of the state, while non-state norms are social norms that exist by virtue of their being part of the social life of the group, rather than through institutional recognition. While acknowledging that non-state norms may become incorporated into state law (by virtue of their recognition by designated state officials), where this occurs they become transformed in such a way that they can no longer be identified as non-state norms. Thus, weak legal pluralism cannot exist.

---

85 N. Long, *ibid.* at 50.
86 N. Long, *ibid.* at 52.
87 N. Long, *ibid.* at 52.
88 B. Z. Tamanaha, 'The Folly of the "Social Scientific Concept" of Legal Pluralism' (1993) 20 *Journal of Law & Society* at 192–217.
89 B. Malinowski, *Crime and Custom in Savage Society* (London Kegan Paul 1926) at 55.
90 G. Teubner, 'The Two Faces of Janus: Rethinking Legal Pluralism' (1992) 13 *Cardozo law Review* 1443–1462 at 1444.
91 For this reason Teubner turns to systems theory to provide a definition of legal pluralism. For a critique of his approach see Twining, *supra* n. 40 at 87.
92 B. Z. Tamanaha, supra n 88 and *Realistic Socio-Legal Theory: Pragmatism and a Social Theory of Law* (Oxford Clarendon Press 1997).

The problem that legal pluralism presents for scholars such as Tamanaha is that legal orders or systems require to be clearly identified. The difficulty is that legal pluralism rejects a definition of state law which is limited to state law. Yet once non-state law is acknowledged it becomes impossible to define law precisely and any attempt to do so 'slides to the conclusion that all forms of social control are law',[93] Such a conclusion renders it impossible to define law in a way that can allow the concept of legal pluralism to be sustained. Tamanaha also rejects strong legal pluralism on the basis that it embraces an anti-state ideology, which presupposes that non-state or indigenous law is good, a bias that renders the concept inadequate as an analytical tool for legal analysis.

These arguments have been countered by claims that such an analysis fails to take account of the social scientific concept of law as a social fact, without any presumption about whether it is good or bad. From this perspective both state and non-state law are social facts and both embody aspects of control and particular forms of argumentation so that, for Woodman 'the distinction between state law as doctrine and non-state law as social ordering is no more than a distinction of relative emphasis on the sources of information most readily available, not an ontological divide'.[94] Woodman rejects Tamanaha's attempt to define law 'as a distinct form of social control which is clearly distinguishable from the others',[95] pointing out that attempts to do so have proved unsuccessful in this regard. He argues that if there is no empirically discoverable dividing line that may be applied to the field of social control 'we must simply accept that all social control is part of the subject matter of legal pluralism'.[96] To take for granted that such a dividing line exists, without empirical proof, is both 'irrational and unscientific'. Similarly, Tamanaha's argument that it is essential to distinguish state laws from other social norms because there is no other means of differentiating law 'is also not a valid social scientific argument'[97] Thus, while Tamanaha observes that 'strong legal pluralism is the product of social scientists'[98] his arguments operate at an ideological level and fail to engage with a social scientific perspective on law.[99]

While other scholars, such as Cotterell[100] espouse a more moderate view of legal pluralism, allowing for its possibility, they still give analytical primacy to state law. Even Merry in her approach to pluralism observes 'it is essential to see state law as fundamentally different [from other forms of ordering] in that it

---

[93] B.Z. Tamanaha, *supra* n. 88 at 193.
[94] G. Woodman, 'Ideological Combat', *supra* n. 2 at 43.
[95] G. Woodman, *ibid.* at 44.
[96] G. W. Woodman, *ibid.* at 45.
[97] G. W. Woodman, *ibid.* at 45.
[98] B. Z. Tamanaha, 1992 *supra* n. 88 at 202.
[99] More recently Tamanaha appears to have shifted his views as to what constitutes a core concept of law and to engage with legal pluralism in a different manner. See B. Z. Tamanaha, 'A nonessential version of legal pluralism' (2000) 27 *Journal of Law & Society* at 296–321 in which he appears to endorse what many scholars of legal pluralism have already espoused although he does not comment on either his earlier views or his reasons for conversion.
[100] R. Cotterell, *Law's Community: Legal Theory in Sociological Persepctive* (Oxford Oxford University Press 1995).

exercises the coercive power of the state and monopolizes the symbolic power associated with state authority'.[101] Yet F. von Benda-Beckmann takes issue with Merry on the grounds that she conflates ways in which the concept has been elaborated in empirical research with the issue of whether or not 'the concept as such can be useful as a theoretical possibility of pluralism'.[102] He makes the case for more rigorous attention to be paid to legal pluralism as an analytical concept. In developing this abstract concept he would adopt a plurality of normative orders in society as the point of departure for empirical research. The advantage of this approach is that it would take account of normative systems' ideologies, their claims to exclusive validity and to the monopoly of legitimate power as *empirical* phenomena. This means that such claims would form part of the object of study. They would not, therefore, be taken as the starting point from which research would commence that might lead to the exclusion of certain types of normative ordering from consideration on the basis of their lack of recognition by the dominant system (as is the case with a statist model of law). This is important for as K. von Benda-Beckmann has observed it is not only state law that lays claim to exclusive validity; religious and local laws also make such claims.[103]

Adopting such an approach would not mean that law would become indistinguishable from all other forms of social ordering as 'differences in the sources of rules and the sources of effective inducement and coercion can easily be clarified by indicating the dimensions along which manifestations of law vary'.[104] The strength of this analytical approach is that it 'provides a starting point for looking at similarities and differences in several dimensions of variation in a consistent way and therefore provides a much better perspective on differences in form and function than the state-connected concept'.[105] This is because it does not subscribe to any particular ideology of law and it also allows degrees of differentiation in state law to be documented, differences which are often obscured at present because of an implicit acceptance of the rhetoric concerning the homogeneity of state law.

Another challenge that has been leveled against this approach to legal pluralism is that it privileges 'the folk categories of Western law'[106] by imposing them on the normative orders of all peoples, however removed they may be from the culture that gave rise to them. In so far as other people's normative systems would be made to conform to Western categories this is an ethnocentric enter-

---

[101] S. E. Merry, *supra* n. 2 at 879.

[102] F. von Benda-Beckmann, 'Riding the Centaur—Reflections on the Identities of Legal Anthropology' (Unpublished paper given at the International Workshop on Anthropology of Law at the Max Planck Institute for Social Anthropology, Halle 22 Sept, 2001) at 8. See also F. von Benda-Beckmann, 'Citizens, strangers and indigenous peoples: Conceptual politics and legal pluralism in F. von Benda-Beckmann, K. von Benda-Beckmann and A. Hoekema (eds), Natural resources, environmental and legal pluralism. *Yearbook Law and Anthropology* 9 1–42 at 7–9.

[103] K. von Benda-Beckmann, *supra* n. 72.

[104] F. von Benda-Beckmann, *supra* n. 102 at 9 and at 20–21.

[105] F. von Benda-Beckmann, *ibid.* at 9.

[106] S. A. Roberts, 'Against Legal Pluralism: Some Reflections on the Contemporary Enlargement of the Legal Domain' (1998) 42 *Journal of Legal Pluralism and Unofficial Law* 95–106.

prise, one that seeks to enlarge the legal domain but on the basis of a parochial conception of law. For this reason it is an inadequate tool for the purposes of defining law cross-culturally and engaging in comparative analysis.

This critique of legal pluralism, however, raises two issues that it fails to address, namely:

a) the notion that *any* conception of law must necessarily be based on Western legal theory, and thus, a denial that a more adequate, less ethno-centric, theory of law can ever be developed for comparative purposes; and

b) that it leaves the ideology of state law intact, for it continues to define law in parochial terms that continue to exclude all those that are 'other' because they fail to conform to its remit.

6. MOVING FORWARD: DEVELOPING A RESEARCH AGENDA

These debates highlight the extent to which approaches to legal pluralism are dependant upon the ways in which law itself is constructed as a concept. Such construction marks ongoing processes of identification, negotiation, and con-testation reflecting a project that is always in the making as scholars search for continuity and transformation in their analyses of law over time. Three ways in which an actor-oriented, ethnographic study of law in the strong legal pluralist vein could make a contribution to these debates and to the development of a research agenda that more adequately takes account of the global and local dimensions of law would be to explore the following.

Law as a system of representation and meaning

This approach would analyse law in terms of a system of representation, one that creates meaning within a system of state power. Such an analysis would examine how law creates, produces and enforces meanings and relationships about civilization, rationality, equality, and due process. It would attend to the cultural significance of law through examining discourses concerned, for exam-ple, with development, democratisation, and the rule of law. However, it would also focus on the processes by which law comes to be a sign of cultural identity and the implications that this has for claims to citizenship and for the rights of various ethnic or minority groups, which would not be solely dependent upon states assertions as to territory or territoriality. Indeed, in this process it is not only the law of the state that constructs meaning but also religious law, local nor-mative orders and customary law that generate their own version of identity. Such research would provide a more detailed comprehension of the ways in which ethnonationalist movements work, as well as a more comprehensive under-standing of the factors underlying religious movements which cut across national boundaries and which, in some cases, form part of the opposition to the government of the day.

Mobilisation of law at a local, national and international level

This analysis would examine the ways in which indigenous or local people seek to mobilise the support of the international community by engaging with a human rights discourse of self-determination and cultural rights. Such research would look at what sources these actors draw on in the construction of their claims and the ways in which they utilise international or global networks to construct their cultural identity. It would also explore the extent to which their claims are constrained by state law, while at the same time rendering state law open to challenge. It would investigate what are the shifting global, national and local frameworks of power that make such claims possible. Such research would directly examine the ways law, power and solidarities cross-cut each other and would take account of the circulation and materialisations of power in the local construction of authority, identities, norms and strategies. Natural resource management and environmental protection presents one pressing area for research, where indigenous groups and their representatives are trying to develop 'indigenous' forms of management of tropical forests, land, and water by calling for recognition of local communal rights. The ways in which they formulate their claims, in terms of participation, self government, 'good governance' and sustainability, derived from the language of administration and international law, would make for a fruitful area of study.

State law as shaped by other normative orders

This approach would explore the ways in which other normative orders shape state law that would provide for detailed analyses of its plurality and diversity within legal fields. This would allow for a more systematic account of the conditions which give rise to variation in state law, including the degrees of its institutionalization and mandatoriness. Such an analysis would provide a more fully informed understanding of the ways in which state law works, one which allows for differing degrees of compatibility and/or incompatibility, thus empirically subjecting state law's claims to homogeneity to investigation. It would also examine the varying ways in which bureaucratic government agencies seek to administer the lives of those individuals and collectivities that are subject to them while at the same time taking account of the ways in which such persons and groups respond. Thus it would explore the multifarious ways in which the state, through its various development programmes and organizational structures attempts to control territory and people, and how this relates to non-state modes of control and regulation at both local and supranational levels. Part of this research would explore the ways in which state legal systems manage the differing ideological charters of its constituent populations and negotiate cultural meanings of difference. Such an approach would ensure that, in analysing difference, legal pluralism and cultural pluralism do not simply become equated with one another in ways that map the cultural self-legitimations of nation-states.

16

Globalisation and Law

JOHN FLOOD

IN AN ESSAY on the aftermath of the destruction of the World Trade Centre in New York City, the political scientist, David Held, wrote:

> In our world, it is not only the violent exception that links people together across borders; the very nature of everyday problems and processes joins people in multiple ways. From the movement of ideas and cultural artifacts to the fundamental issues raised by genetic engineering, from the conditions of financial stability to environmental degradation, the fate and fortunes of each of us are thoroughly intertwined.[1]

Four months later on 1 January 2002, the Euro became the common currency of most of Europe. Whether one was in Spain, Greece, Belgium or Germany, one would reach into one's wallet for the same money. Nearly 300 million people were using a currency that had replaced drachmas, francs, pesetas and marks.

Two events that are emotionally and materially quite distinct, yet their ramifications will be felt around the world for a long time. They encapsulate some of the positive and negative aspects of globalisation. A common currency provides for transparency in exchanges: differentials in the price of a Volkswagen Golf in Spain and the Netherlands become readily apparent. One no longer needs the *Economist's* Big Mac index to calculate relative affordability. Tourists do not have to wonder whether they are losing out on exchange rate conversion.

Although good things can flow from globalisation, the potential for suffering is omnipresent and rising. Transnational currencies such as the dollar, pound sterling or Euro give uncosted advantages to their host states, allowing them to inflate domestic debt at the expense of developing nations. Countries relying on primary resources such as minerals or agriculture are rarely able to set prices that embody *their* ideal value of the products. The futures and commodity exchanges in Chicago and London determine those for them. Only countries or national corporations with the power to form a monopoly (eg DeBeers and diamonds) or a cartel (eg OPEC and oil) that make possible a high margin of rent in their prices are safe from the vagaries of the world markets. The kinds of economic differences found between the US and Argentina or Mali are potentially serious stimuli to violence and other illegal activities like the drug trade, human trafficking and money laundering.

---

[1] D. Held, 'Violence and Justice in a Global Age' in *After Sep. 11: Perspectives from the Social Sciences* (http://www.ssrc.org/sept11/essays/held.htm, 2001).

Intergovernmental institutions designed to sponsor global economic harmony—the World Bank and the International Monetary Fund—have frequently promoted the liberalisation of economies without counting the social cost of diminishing their welfare states. Even the flurry of activity by the G8 countries to encourage debt reduction in poor countries, with the help of the Jubilee campaign, has stuttered to a standstill.

Globalisation is, therefore, a diverse set of processes including the economic, cultural, social and political. We cannot make it go away, nor can we drive it in a particular direction. Those commentators who argue that the 'Washington consensus' determines the fate of the world, even in the crudest of Marxist terms, are being over-deterministic. Globalisation can take us in unexpected directions as well as the obvious. Rich countries are as successful in importing alien diseases (eg Ebola) as they are in importing exotic cuisines. While it is difficult to pin down globalisation like a specimen insect, we can typify it in a number of ways. Following Held and his colleagues,[2] I will describe three variants: hyperglobalisers, sceptics, and transformationalists. I will then give three examples of global activity where globalisation is making a significant contribution. These are the development of capital markets work by international law firms and investment banks; the emergence of a global insolvency market; and the response of legal education to these phenomena. The examples will illustrate how law is implicated in globalisation. To understand this, however, my characterisation of law will be eclectic and pluralistic in that I will be considering state law at one extreme and social norms at the other.

1. THE CHARACTER OF GLOBALISATION

The hyperglobalisers are exemplified by the consultants McKinsey who advise governments and corporations on their strategic aims. Their Tokyo partner, Kenichi Ohmae, is the apostle of the borderless world where the nation-state is no longer relevant for the advance of corporate capitalism.[3] We can think of the automobile manufacturers (Ford, General Motors), Coca Cola, and McDonalds. The process of hyperglobalisation is progressive, unilinear and inexorable. Opponents of globalisation (sceptics) argue against this position, countering the hyperbole of globalisation with statistics demonstrating the failure of global economic integration, suggesting at best a move towards regionalisation has occurred and that globalisation is a myth.[4] Whereas hyperglobalisation postulates that its progressive agenda will lead to radical change for the benefit of all,

---

[2] D. Held et. al., *Global Transformations: Politics, Economics and Culture* (Cambridge Polity Press 1999).

[3] K. Ohmae, *The Borderless World* (London Fontana 1991) and *The End of the Nation State* (New York The Free Press 1995).

[4] P. Hirst and G. Thompson, *Globalisation in Question: The International Economy and the Possibilities of Governance* (Cambridge Polity Press 1996); and see J. Gray, 'The Era of Globalisation is Over' (Sep. 24, 2001) *New Statesman* at 25.

north and south, sceptism sees internationalisation accentuating the differences between north and south. The third perspective of globalisation, transformationalism, recognises the contingency of action and the historicity of structure as enabling and constraining globalisation.[5] While transformationalism accepts great change is taking place in the economy, politics and culture, the degree to which it is happening is yet unknown and the redistribution of resources in the world is still unequal with some getting richer and some areas becoming marginalised.[6] The nation state is able to continue claims to power and authority but they are limited more and more by the emergence of stronger supranational forms of governance, such as the European Union and the World Trade Organisation. Ultimately, the destination of globalisation—if one exists— is unknown. Whichever perspective is chosen, each represents a threat to homeostasis and each can be shown to function within very loose normative structures.

Globalisation is not entirely anarchic but nor is it tightly rule-bound. The law of globalisation is almost a new *lex mercatoria* only partially dependent on state authority for its legitimacy or its disputing systems.[7] Global law is derived from a number of sources, among the most popular is contract—private ordering— the drafting of agreements. Contract is able to enmesh states as parties to an agreement without the protection of sovereign immunity. Contract can transcend national boundaries more easily than international law is capable of doing. It is at the level of private ordering that difference is resolved into a document that circumvents the contingencies of jurisdictional conflict. Private ordering emerges away from the centre, as Teubner argues, '. . . *global law will grow mainly from the social peripheries, not from the political centres of nation-states and international institutions*'.[8] Global law is a *malleable law* made by professionals during the construction of deals.[9] Without this malleability, global law could hardly come into being: it would be brittle and weak, under constant disputation. Yet malleable law is remarkably successful in constituting the global legal order.[10]

[5] A. Giddens, *The Consequences of Modernity* (Cambridge Polity Press 1990).

[6] Held et. al., *supra* n. 2 at 8.

[7] Y. Dezalay and B. Garth, *Dealing in Virtue: International Commercial Arbitration and the Construction of a Transnational Legal Order*. (Chicago University of Chicago Press 1996); G. Teubner, ' "Global Bukowina": Legal Pluralism in the World Society' in Teubner, G. (ed) *Global Law Without A State* (Aldershot Dartmouth 1997).

[8] Teubner, *supra* n. 7 at 7. Note that social periphery here needs to be interpreted broadly, since the major international financial institutions are hardly peripheral.

[9] In some cases this is referred to as soft law, which it is not, as it depends on New York and English law for its legitimation. Soft law operates in contexts where there is no governing law. See, eg J. Flood and E. Skordaki, 'Normative Bricolage: Informal Rule-Making by Accountants and Lawyers in Mega-Insolvencies' in Teubner, *supra* n. 7, where soft law operates in international insolvency.

[10] The rule of law is usually held up as the defining element of civilised society. Under malleable law, however, the rule of law often has a harsher, more rugged character. The following anecdote demonstrates. During the closing of a major deal of an acquisition of a company by another, the documentation was continuously being changed and redrafted. The directors of the selling company

In the next part, an example of private ordering is portrayed. Capital markets is one of the fastest growing forms of financial activity in the world.[11]

2. CAPITAL MARKETS: RAISING MONEY AROUND THE WORLD

At the end of 1999, the managing directors (the former partners) of Goldman Sachs received remuneration packages to the order of about $10 million each.[12] Most of it was reward for being the top financial adviser and underwriter in the world, being in the biggest deals such as advising Vodafone in its takeover of Mannesman, producing a telecommunications company worth £225 billion.[13] Capital markets work is high value service with enormous premiums for those who do it.

The fifty years following World War II constituted a key expansion period for global capital. Foreign direct investment grew, the Eurodollar market increased global capital liquidity, and immense political change ushered in a wave of privatisations as states sloughed off their possessions—state industries, utilities and service providers. The market rather than the state was to reign.[14] The 1980s 'Big Bang' in the UK enabled the global banks, especially those in the US, to establish investment banks free from constricting regulation. For the American banks, the Glass-Steagall Act had corseted their activities by preventing the simultaneous engagement of commercial and investment banking.[15] Stock broking changed, as brokers and jobbers merged and the stock exchange rules were relaxed, outlawing cartels. Although the recession of the late 1980s and early 1990s constrained growth for some time, as shown by the rise in insolvency statistics, global investment rose inexorably, as demonstrated by the increases in foreign direct investment flows (FDI).[16] In the last 15 years of the twentieth century, the progress of the economy has altered, in that boom and slump can co-exist in different parts of the world. Thus, at the end of the century while the US was economically triumphant, the Asian tigers were limping

came to their lawyers' office in the City of London expecting to sign the documents, close the deal and depart celebrating their new riches. On arrival they were placed in a conference room and told they would have to wait while the last few wrinkles were ironed out. Seventy-two hours later they were released from their confinement when the documents were finally agreed between the lawyers. The lawyers couldn't let the directors leave the office because they knew they wouldn't return, so they held them until they could sign. There was nothing the directors could do but comply. They were under the force of the rule of law.

[11] B. de S. Santos, *Toward a New Common Sense: Law, Science and Politics in the Paradigmatic Transition* (New York Routledge 1995) at 275. Santos calls this type 'globalized localism' and 'localized globalism'.

[12] A. Garfield, 'High-flying Goldman Sees Wage Bill Double to $8.7bn' *The Independent* 22 Dec. 1999 at 13.

[13] D. Gow, 'Now Vodafone Wants Net Alliances' *The Guardian* 5 Feb. 2000 at 32.

[14] A. Gamble, *The Free Economy and the Strong State*, 2nd ed. (Basingstoke Macmillan 1994).

[15] S. Finch et. al., 'Replacing the Depression's Final Legacy' (2000) 9 *International Financial Law Review*.

[16] Held et. al., *supra* n. 2 at 249.

in a field of thorns. In order to recapture their ferocity, the Asian economies have begun to produce their own big bangs.[17] One other feature of this period ought to be mentioned and that is the growth in regulatory institutions in the global economy. The most assertive has been the Securities and Exchange Commission (SEC), which now appears to be seeking the role of global regulator. During the 1980s the SEC was dealing with various insider trading scandals, including the savings and loans industry and the manipulation of the junk bond market (high yield debt) created by Michael Milken and which subsequently crashed in 1989 causing the downfall of Drexel Burnham Lambert a year later.[18] During the 1990s the junk bond, now high-yield debt market, recovered and was legitimised.[19] The global economy, with the success of the GATT Uruguay Round, has now a transnational watchdog and dispute arbiter in the World Trade Organisation.

In other ways, the SEC has begun to reduce the barriers to American markets for foreign investors by easing its disclosure requirements.[20] Taking regulatory manoeuvres into account during the economic activity of the last 50 years, capital markets work has boomed. For example, 'the six largest mergers/acquisitions in 1998 totalled over $300 billion and were funded by a combination of equity and debt issues'.[21] Hodgart also notes that 'the six largest auto manufacturers [in 1999] are reported as having a "strategic acquisitions war chest" totalling in excess of $100 billion'.[22]

Capital markets work involves gaining access to finance in markets throughout the world. This may be through issues of stock, bonds, securitization of debt or loans,[23] depositary receipt programmes, initial public offerings (IPOs), or privatisations. The last 20 years have shown bankers' and lawyers' ingenuity in developing new forms of financing and means of packaging them. Demands for creativity have risen as the equities market globalised and diverse jurisdictions' requirements had to be co-ordinated in strategic ways. If we compare debt markets with equities markets the difference becomes apparent: trading in debt markets requires less research and availability of information, relies on high quality borrowers with less concern about the underlying credit, and therefore was able

---

[17] R. Mannix, 'Foreign Investors Snap Up Korean Bargains' (2000) 9 *International Financial Law Review* at 28–33 and N. Kinami, *The Japanese Big Bang* (London Freshfields 1998).

[18] J. B. Stewart, *Den of Thieves* (New York Simon & Schuster 1991). Drexel Burnham Lambert, and Milken, underwrote 60% of the junk bond market in the second half of the 1980s. See C. Sheldon and T. Abbondante, 'Great Expectations: HighYield Debt in European Leveraged Acquisition Finance' in *US Capital Markets Report* (London Euromoney 1999).

[19] Sheldon and Abbondante, *ibid.*

[20] E. Kamman and A. Covello, 'New SEC Disclosure Rules for Non US Companies' in *US Capital Markets Report* (London Euromoney 1999). See also H. Laurence, 'Spawning the SEC' in (1999) 6 *Indiana Journal of Global Legal Studies* at 647.

[21] A. Hodgart, 'Introduction' in *IFLR Review of the Year: Capital Markets Forum 1999* (London Euromoney 1999) at 6.

[22] *Ibid.*

[23] For example, see M. Lewis, *Liar's Poker* (London Coronet Books 1989) at 97 *passim*. In *Liar's Poker* Lewis describes the creation of the mortgage bond market by Salomon Brothers.

to internationalise more rapidly. This is where the reduction of mistrust plays a big role. Information deficits are greater in equities markets where borrowers are a more diverse group than in debt markets and the accuracy and integrity of legal drafting becomes paramount.[24] One final point should be made here: most of these transactions are undertaken in New York state law and/or English law as the primary overarching legal categories because this is where the money is. As a result these two legal systems have become de facto global legal systems (see also Globalising Legal Education below). However, much of the detailed work of capital markets has to take account of local conditions and is therefore done in local laws which could be Irish, French, Thai, etc. Therefore, we have a set of primary and secondary legal systems that have to be co-ordinated. This is performed by lawyers who employ the creativity of drafting—agreements, contracts, undertakings—to capture the myriad qualities of the global *lex mercatoria*.

The best way to illuminate capital markets work is through case studies of capital markets work in action. The example below shows law firms, investment banks and intergovernmental organisations working in concert.

3. CASE STUDY: TELELOMUNIKACJA POLSKA S.A.

TPSA, a Polish telecoms operator, was one of the largest privatisation initial public offerings (IPOs) undertaken in Central and Eastern Europe at $920 million, as the Polish government sold a 15 per cent share in this company. Because of the essentially risky nature of enterprises in Eastern Europe, the European Bank of Reconstruction and Development (EBRD) often takes a stake in the enterprise—in this case $75.5 million—to shore up confidence. The consortium that won the deal was a partnership of Goldman Sachs and Schroders, advised by Baker & McKenzie as lead counsel. Before the launch of the issue Goldman Sachs pulled out of the deal, arousing speculation that the deal was dead. It still went ahead and attracted $1.5 billion from international investors, that is, it was two and a half times oversubscribed. Baker & McKenzie prepared the offering and provided opinions for the securities regulators. All was done within a very tight timetable, but the task was anything but simple. For example, the due diligence was vast with the company spread all over Poland. Lawyers were sent to all parts of the company and country; the final report was over 4,000 pages long. Without a thorough due diligence—a type of intensive legal audit—a deal such as this would not be feasible. It requires lawyers to check inventory to ensure it is real, to check contracts actually exist. The lawyers have to pore over every document within the company that commits the business in any way. Only large law firms have the capacity to mount a due diligence campaign of this magnitude.

---

[24] F. Neate (ed). 'World-Wide Public Offerings of Securities: British Gas' in *The Developing Global Securities Market* (London Graham & Trotman 1987) at 8–15.

Seventy five per cent of the offer was in the form of global depositary receipts listed in London. The documentation required to complete an IPO of this sort runs into the thousands of pages, many of which must be signed and countersigned by the various parties at the appropriate times with the correct seals. The law firms not only have to draft the documents but ensure they are co-ordinated with the timing requirements of the regulators in the US, UK, Poland, etc. Moreover, the lawyers must synchronise the requirements of the different legal regimes, eg that legal and beneficial interests can actually be separated, that legal concepts subsisting in one legal jurisdiction (eg floating charge) can be interpreted in those where they do not exist. Nothing is worse, but it happens, for lawyers to discover that some documents have been erroneously prepared or that a security cannot be perfected after the money has begun to be drawn down. Retrospective repair tasks can mean financial and legal exposure for lawyers and clients alike with potentially irremediable prospects depending on local legal requirements.

The US law firm of White & Case advised the State Treasury of Poland, and TPSA was advised by the US law firm of Hunton & Williams. Even though the bulk of the issue was listed in London, the majority of the legal work was carried out by American law firms. The difference between TPSA and other privatizations in the region was that instead of finding an outside investor partner first, revising the finance and corporate governance, then moving to an IPO, TPSA went for the IPO first, and then sought a partner. Without the due diligence work by the lawyers for the consortium, the deal would have been impossible.

This case does demonstrate the importance of international institutions in enabling emerging markets to participate in global capital markets. Of interest though, is that the World Bank has been criticised for aiding countries that could themselves borrow funds in the capital markets. US Treasury Secretary, Lawrence Summers, said, 'Lending in (emerging market) countries should be confined to the areas where they can increase total financing capacity', adding that sometimes the bank's lending can 'crowd out private sector finance'.[25] However, these institutions are able to help develop legal and regulatory structures in emerging markets that facilitate the growth of free markets, the rule of law, and a linkage to capital markets. Indeed, the general counsel for the European Bank of Reconstruction and Development (EBRD) said:

> The EBRD's mandate is to foster the transition towards market economies in the countries of the Former Soviet Union and Central and Eastern Europe, and to promote private and entrepreneurial initiative . . . Recognising fully the importance to sustainable economic development of stable 'rules of the game' and the establishment and continued strengthening of law administration and enforcement institutions, the EBRD has embarked on the provision of legal technical assistance to its countries of operation that will foster the transition process.[26]

[25] Reuters, 'US Calls for World Bank Reform' (http://www.altavista.co.uk/content/reu_news_article jsp?category=business&id=0) 2000.
[26] J. Taylor, 'New Laws, New Lawyers and the EBRD' (1996) 24 *International Business Lawyer* at 98.

To reinforce its point, the EBRD has carried out legal audits on its constituent jurisdictions to determine the receptivity of the legal system to investment.

In the next section, we examine how insolvency, a paradigmatic local activity, has evolved into a globalised business. The rise of the multinational company has meant that global solutions are now being sought for transnational corporate meltdowns.

4. TRANSNATIONAL INSOLVENCY

Much insolvency or bankruptcy work is done informally, that is, without court intervention. This type of work is known as restructuring or 'turnarounds'. Companies usually do not want to signal to others—their investors, creditors, customers—that they are in financial trouble, so they go to great efforts to hide or to disguise the problems they encounter. The UK has had a long tradition of assisting companies on the verge of insolvency, a tradition known as the 'London Approach'. It is a prime example of where the global and local intersect.

The London Approach is a fairly arcane procedure,[27] which dates back mainly to the mid-1970s.[28] Kent calls it 'a means of reducing mistrust'.[29] Smith graphically describes the inception of the London Approach:

> The origins of the London Approach can be traced back to the recession of the mid-1970s. This was the first serious interruption to world economic growth since 1945. We at the Bank of England (at least those of us with as many grey hairs as me) remember it most for the secondary banks' crisis and for the launching by the Bank [of England] of the so-called lifeboat. This was the first bank support operation that the Bank of England had had to organize, but, in the context of the London Approach, it was an influential forerunner of the Bank's later involvement in workouts for non-financial companies.[30]

It was the switch from financial to non-financial contexts that set the Bank of England on a new path towards corporate rescue. But the path meandered among only the big, major corporates; it circumvented small and mid-sized companies. Smith explains how the Bank of England became involved:

> The mid-1970s saw an increasing number of non-financial companies encountering severe financial problems. Burmah Oil . . . was a notable example, highlighted by the suddenness with which the crisis blew up and the need for some very prompt action— on that occasion by the Bank of England itself. There was very little experience of organizing workouts in those days; we were not used to major companies coming to their bankers and saying that, unless they were given more liquidity immediately, they

---

[27] C. Bird, 'The London Approach' (1996) 12 *Insolvency Law & Practice* at 87–89.

[28] R. Floyd, 'Corporate Recovery: "The London Approach"' (1995) 11 *Insolvency Law & Practice* at 82.

[29] P. Kent, 'The London Approach: Lessons From Recent Years' (1994) Feb. *Insolvency Bulletin* at 7.

[30] M. Smith, 'The London Approach' (paper presented to Wilde Sapte Seminar London 1992) at 2.

would have to stop trading. In particular, we had hardly any experience of arranging support operations for companies which had obtained finance from a wide range of banks and other sources, a trend which had just taken hold in the early 1970s. These were the beginnings of what came to be called multi-bank support operations. My predecessors at the Bank in the late 1970s identified a need to co-ordinate discussions among the banks with loans outstanding to a company in difficulty. This usually meant the Bank taking the initiative in convening meetings of banks and, on occasions, other interested parties to help secure collective agreement to a refinancing package.[31]

The Bank of England thus had as its motive 'not want[ing] companies to be placed in receivership or liquidation unnecessarily for wider economic reasons; we wanted viable jobs and productive capacity to be preserved'.[32] During the recession of the late 1980s and early 1990s the Bank of England was involved in about 150 workouts.[33]

Its current incarnation stems from a circular the Bank of England helped to draft, which was distributed by the British Bankers Association in 1990. The London Approach has no formal status in law, nor does it constitute a set of rules. At best it is a set of principles which contains as its objective

> to provide a flexible framework whereby Banks can continue to extend support to companies in financial difficulty, pending agreement as to the way forward [which] may include the provision of additional short term liquidity.[34]

The London Approach only applies to major corporates. Or, as Pointon characterizes it:

> The final major flaw that I see is that the London Approach is only really appropriate for large situations, therefore the number of cases handled using this process is relatively small. Indeed, it has been said that only those who have borrowed vast sums receive the benefits of such treatment.[35]

The London Approach has four phases. First, there is a standstill covering all debt owed. All bank lenders must give unanimous support. In this stage the banks often have extremely limited information about the debtor's true financial position, thus emphasising the notion of trust as an essential component of rescue. Second, the banks send in investigating accountants who would not be the company's auditors. Third, the lead bank negotiates with the other banks— which can be as few as six or as many as 106—to provide a new facility for the company. This is a difficult and tense period. It is also one where the 'majority banks', ie those with the most exposure, may take decisions that will bind all banks. Pointon describes this phase:

---

[31] *Ibid.*, at 2–3.
[32] *Ibid.*, at 3.
[33] P. Kent, 'Trading And Investing In Distressed Debt' (paper presented to Euroforum Conference London 1994).
[34] F. Pointon, 'London Approach: A Look At Its Applications And Its Alternatives' (1994, March) *Insolvency Bulletin*. at 5.
[35] *Ibid.*, at 7–8.

To give an idea of the complexity of arrangements, many major groups have multinational subsidiaries in as many as 20 countries. Funding of these groups is frequently through syndicates with 30 or more banks who all need to agree with the proposed restructure. These banks are often in differing financial positions; some may be secured, for example, and may come from countries with different business cultures and differing perceptions of the ways in which situations should be dealt with. As a result of these complexities there has been one case where the legal documents needed to be redrafted 17 times. Problems such as this can make achievement of final agreement very expensive in legal terms.[36]

In the final phase, according to Pointon, 'the corporate has a new operating and financial structure which should allow it to prosper. Naturally, the Banks and their appointed accountants will, however, monitor on-going progress closely'.[37]

A key role in a London Approach workout is assigned to the lead bank. It will coordinate the rescue and have the task of bringing it to fruition. Smith remarks that a lead bank has:

> to perform a difficult balancing act; it must, for example, provide firm but not overbearing leadership. It must also be a good communicator; one of the most frequent complaints we receive at the Bank of England is that a lead bank has failed to provide banks with information which they regard as essential for the decisions that they are being asked to make. A lead bank is tempting disaster if it takes, albeit probably inadvertently, the views of banks for granted. It must, in other words, be sensitive to the circumstances of individual banks however small or where they come from. Above all, a lead bank needs to be flexible; it must be able to respond to the unexpected and know when to give ground in difficult discussions.[38]

The London Approach is expensive to implement. A successful workout could cost £6 million over its life. A banker put it this way:

> Let's, for example, take a small company, a typical mid-corporate, with three bankers, poor management, lousy at forecasting, with annual sales of £10 million, borrowings of £4.5 million, owns its own factory and some machinery, has a mortgage debenture to one and a charge to another. This wouldn't be any good for a London Approach. There's no meat on the bone, there's no value, nothing to play with, all the assets are secured.

There are two other factors that help make the London Approach unique. The whole process takes place outside the glare of publicity. One banker said the last thing he wanted to see was the unsecured creditors jumping out at the news. The cloak of secrecy also helps the banks work together rather than in competition with each other. This is especially so in the meetings where the workouts are structured. These meetings are delicately negotiated, contingent affairs rife with bluff and double bluff.

---

[36] F. Pointon, 'London Approach: A Look At Its Applications And Its Alternatives' (1994, March) *Insolvency Bulletin*. at 7.

[37] *Ibid*.

[38] Smith, *supra* n. 30 at 7–8.

The risk of rescue is also negotiated between the banks. A workout specialist said:

> Everyone must share the pain equally. Sometimes its not the same and we have various matrices we use to make it equitable. You sit around the table with the other banks and you say if we liquidate the business you will get fifty cents in the dollar. Is there anyone who wants to take that? Everyone says no, but one or two say we can't take this or that. They've said they don't want the fifty cents, so it's a matter of moving them to one of the other scenarios. You have to run different scenarios for restructuring plans—worst-case scenario, second worst case, best case, etcetera. You don't know if it'll work since it's all guesswork. We run the scenarios over one year, three years, 12 years to see what it will look like.

In difficult moments the Bank of England is able to step in to 'ease' the process. Kent declares:

> The Bank of England's role in workouts is part missionary, part peacemaker. As missionary, we advocate the London Approach as a basis for constructive cooperation regarding a customer's cash flow crisis. As peacemaker, we try to help banks resolve those differences which threaten to undermine an attempted workout.[39]

He has further followed that view: 'I have always made clear that our interest is not as a supervisor or "regulator" of the market'.[40] Another banker believed the Bank of England was useful:

> It is good for dealing with bank regulators in other countries. If you have seventy banks in a team and one, say, a Spanish bank, hasn't signed on then the Bank of England can talk to the Spanish bank regulator, and say we've got a major restructuring going on here and sixty nine banks have signed on but yours hasn't. Why not? And very often it's because the bank doesn't know about it. They might send a relatively junior official who has to pass recommendations up to his seniors and depending on how quickly they get passed, it can screw up or work well. The Bank of England can make it move up the hierarchy quickly. The Bank could also make rumbling noises about bank licence renewals, but they don't control foreign banks.

One official at the Bank of England commented that this was not how he viewed the role of the Bank:

> Our role is one of peacemaker, that is, not passive but quite active . . . We know the core group of bankers well and the main players are always in contact with each other. We are invited in. A bank calls me and says there may be a workout coming up, and that might be enough—that call—to bring everyone into line. We have no sanctions, although we have all sorts of relationships with banks and companies. Some companies are so big; they borrow in their own names. Indeed, they have better credit ratings than their banks. So we do have considerable authority. In a workout it may be worth going along with the majority because they will be in a similar situation again soon. If a bank is prepared to cooperate in a workout now, it will be to its advantage next time.

---

[39] Kent, *supra* n. 29 at 5.
[40] Kent, *supra* n. 33 at 5.

On the whole, bankers (and lawyers) are strongly opposed to the thought of a statutory basis for the London Approach.[41] It would run counter to its philosophy. Many thought that parliamentary draftsmen would be incapable of understanding the minutiae of the London Approach and so it was best left in the hands of those who knew how to do it.

To the bankers and lawyers involved in the London Approach its genius lies in the informality and the infinite flexibility with which it can be moulded and shaped.

In the final section of this chapter, we turn to legal education, something that has not typically been thought of in global terms. But with the global reach of the international law firms and the impact of the World Bank, legal education has to accept that a parochial outlook is insufficient.

5. GLOBALISING LEGAL EDUCATION

The relationship between globalisation and the field of law is reflexive: as the economy expands and integrates, its need for regulation also grows; the economy demands particular kinds of law and law thereby shapes the economy. The relatively small numbers of players in the global law field means that there is a paucity of formal educational skills at large, and so the result is that much of the craft of lawyering for the global order is learned through apprenticeship with elites rather than through academic routes, following Samuel Butler who wrote, 'An art can only be learned in the workshop of those who are winning their bread by it'. Formal educational institutions subsequently came late to these challenges. The first to do so were the major business schools in Europe and the US. Legal education has, however, been slow and inadequate in its response.[42]

Elite status is reinforced by the open recognition of many consumers of law and lawyers that of all the legal regimes in the world only two are of consequence in transnational work, namely, English law and New York state law (see Capital Markets above). Thus the number of potential law schools able to supply graduates capable of doing legal work at this level is small. Other jurisdictions are significant, of course, but they are dominated by this Western duopoly. I have shown elsewhere that international business lawyers often define themselves by three attributes:

a mastery of the English language, which is the common language of international business and finance; an ability to draft contracts, more in the prolix Anglo-Saxon style rather than in the concise continental way; and an understanding of private

---

[41] City of London Law Society 'Corporate Restructuring and the London Approach' (unpublished paper 1996) at 2.

[42] Cf. J. Flood, 'Megalawyering in the Global Order: The Cultural, Social and Economic Transformation of Global Legal Practice' (1996) 3 *International Journal of the Legal Profession* at 169–214.

dispute resolution systems, such as arbitration. On occasion a fourth requisite is claimed, namely, admission to another jurisdiction, notably the New York bar.[43]

The key here is that the prototypical international business lawyer can operate in any system of law provided the conditions above are met. This is reinforced by advertisements for lawyers in the major financial institutions. The European Bank for Reconstruction and Development, for example, advertised for counsel with the following characteristics:

> **Education:** graduate law degree from a leading university required; post-graduate degree from a leading university in another country desirable; **Work Experience:** at least four years international lending, investment or project/asset finance experience in a leading international law firm or the legal department of a leading international bank or other financial institution required; **Skills:** excellent legal drafting in English required; evidence of good negotiating skills desirable; **Languages:** excellent spoken communication in English required; fluency in a language other than English, preferably a central or eastern European language, desirable.[44]

Have certain dominant educational institutions become gatekeepers for a global corps of leaders? Let me give a taste of how this may be perceived by others. At the 1995 International Bar Conference in Paris during a session on the globalisation of the legal profession, an East African delegate remonstrated with the UK and US members who were talking of the dominance of their respective laws and professions in the global marketplace as synonymous with globalisation. The delegate resented bodies such as the International Monetary Fund coming to third world countries and issuing edicts on the appropriate measures to modernise their economies. What galled him particularly was the way in which the IMF ignored local professionals, preferring instead to work with UK and US law firms. The delegate warned that if such bodies refused to acknowledge the contributions that local professionals could make, then foreign advisers would find themselves excluded from practising in these countries. They had to learn to work in partnership with locals. This intervention was met with silence.

In an attempt to discern law schools' responses to globalisation I analysed the prospectuses of a set of the top law schools in the US and the UK. I was interested in the kind and quantity of international courses offered and, more importantly, whether there was an explicit embrace of globalisation within courses or elsewhere. As long ago as 1991 it was argued that law schools should not just introduce courses with international dimensions, but should in fact internationalize the entire curriculum because internationalisation/globalisation had begun to infuse all aspects of life. Business schools have already faced this. For example, Duke University's Fuqua School of Business offers an MBA via the internet and short residential classes in places as far apart as Salzburg, Shanghai and Sao Paulo. I adopted these indices as proxies for the law school response to a perceived need for legal development in the way that the EBRD general counsel was

[43] *Ibid.*, at 190.
[44] Source: *Economist*, 25 January 1997 at 129.

mentioning above. In comparing legal education in the US and UK it is essential to bear in mind that in the former law is a graduate degree whereas in the latter it is part of the undergraduate curriculum. To compensate for that I have mainly examined graduate prospectuses in the UK and ordinary American law school catalogues. I believe this can be justified by the fact that most international institutions, eg World Bank and EBRD, demand a graduate degree as the minimum qualification for entry. Many American law schools also offer the LL.M. degree, partly as a way of upgrading J.D. degrees from lower-rank schools for US students, and partly as a way of inducting foreign students into US law. Both American and British universities actively market their degrees to overseas students who bring in lucrative amounts of tuition fees.

In the UK the top law schools are clustered in the 'golden triangle' of Oxford, Cambridge and London. Each offers a taught one-year, self-contained, graduate degree, usually the LL.M. Of the three London is unusual in that six separate law schools combine their efforts to produce a London-wide programme of graduate study with many more courses than either Oxford or Cambridge. Table 1 shows the proportions of international courses.

TABLE 1
International Graduate Courses at Top UK Law Schools

Name and Degree	Total Graduate Courses	International Courses
Cambridge—LL.M.	28	8 (28%)
London—LL.M.	142	60 (42%)
Oxford—B.C.L.	24	6 (25%)

Oxford and Cambridge have not capitalised on the international/global market in a substantive way, although their brand names are recognised everywhere. International courses comprise about one quarter of their law courses. London, however, has close to a half of its LL.M. courses focussed on international themes.

The American situation is quite different. For purposes of comparison I selected the four top national law schools, namely, Harvard, Yale, Columbia, and Chicago, which offer the J.D. degree, and separated out the proportions of their international courses. See Table 2.

TABLE 2
International Courses at Top US Law Schools

Name and Degree	Total Courses	International Courses
Chicago—J.D	155	22 (14%)
Columbia—J.D.	265	37 (14%)
Harvard—J.D.	249	48 (19%)
Yale—J.D.	110	11 (10%)

In absolute terms the numbers of courses provided are greater than in the UK, with the exception of London. Despite the greater numbers, in percentage terms American schools offer fewer courses than their British counterparts. The real difference lies in the approach of the schools. Oxford and Cambridge offer a traditional array of courses along the lines of private and public international law, with perhaps alternative courses on international dispute resolution. London has internationalised a bigger range of courses; eg labour law, environmental law, energy law, investment law. The addition of SOAS to the London law schools also provides courses on topics, such as Chinese and Japanese law, African and Islamic law. While it is possible to concentrate on particular areas of study in the London LL.M., the courses are distributed quite widely through the London law schools.

In this respect the delivery of international courses in the US law schools is probably more highly developed, especially at Harvard and Columbia. For example, Columbia organises its courses under various rubrics—eg corporate and securities law, human rights, international, foreign and comparative law. Within the latter group there are courses on international economic law (GATT and WTO), Russia and the CIS, cross-border legal transactions, and specialist courses on aspects of Japanese, Korean, Latin-American and East European law. This is bolstered by centres that specialise in some of these areas, such as the Parker School of Foreign and Comparative Law, the Center for Japanese Legal Studies, and the Center for Chinese Legal Studies. Finally, the intellectual stature of these schools is underpinned by journals that produce and disseminate knowledge. Columbia, for example, has, out of a total of 11 in-house journals, at least four concerned with international matters, namely, the *American Journal of International Arbitration*, the *Columbia Journal of Transnational Law*, the *Journal of Chinese Law*, and the *Journal of East European Law*.

Reasons for the differences are not difficult to find. UK universities usually have highly bureaucratised systems of course delivery. Introducing a new course is a long-term project, often involving validation by others than the instructor. American law schools are largely autonomous units within the university structure and have a much more flexible response to the organisation of law courses. There is considerable room for experiment. For example, at Harvard the ongoing O.J. Simpson criminal trial became the basis for a criminal evidence course.

American law schools are, in a sense, terminal institutions. That is, the award of the J.D. degree permits the holder to sit the bar examination and begin practice. In the UK a law degree enables one to apply for a vocational law course, not to practise. Furthermore, American law professors are generally paid more than other professors in the university, which has the effect of enhancing their status. They also retain stronger links with key practitioners, often giving them adjunct faculty status. For example, in the international, foreign and comparative law curriculum at Columbia four courses are taught by adjunct faculty: three by attorneys with major New York law firms; one is jointly taught between a law firm partner and a senior counsel to the Chase Manhattan Bank; and one by the chief counsel to the World Bank.

Most law schools tackle the problems of globalisation by running courses or graduate degrees specialising in the area. One law school has attempted to mark itself as a global law school. New York University Law School has created a 'global law school program' which has been supported by $75 million in donations. It has three main aims: to create a global faculty of 20 law professors from around the world who will teach in conjunction with NYU faculty; to endow 20 full scholarships for overseas graduate students; and to support research through a centre on property and innovation in a global economy.[45] The visiting faculty are predominantly UK, German, and Japanese, representing the more powerful interests in the world. There is one from Egypt, representing both the Arab and African interests, although he teaches in Switzerland.

This is the most explicit form of merchandising yet by a law school, and one with imperial ambitions, when it says,

> As the processes of transformation and globalization unfold, law is playing and increasingly will play a critical role; indeed, the success of the emerging global community will depend in large part upon the integration and accommodation of disparate traditions through law. American law and its lawyers are playing a pivotal role: the United States has developed the world's most elaborate legal system; our Constitution is an obvious model for compacts governing the relationship of governments to their citizens; and American commercial law is providing the reference point as others develop their own legal regimes.[46]

Although this single instance cannot be taken as a general trend in legal education, it is, I believe, indicative of a burgeoning commercialisation of legal education. NYU has developed a 'super-niche' through co-opting globalisation as its motif (in contrast to its well-known niche tax LL.M. programme). Most others, whether British or American, have relied on the adjective international rather than global. It is a transition that business schools have already undergone.

The role of the global law school as presented here is one that will export American legal ideas and concepts throughout the world, especially in the emerging markets. In some ways it is a backwards step from what is already being done by law firms and other international institutions. For example, Gordon *et. al.* argue that a significant role of international institutions like the IMF is to offer 'technical assistance' by transplanting basic, so-called 'neutral' laws, eg tax and budget laws, to countries that either do not have them or possess inferior versions of them.[47] These are evidently not value-neutral exercises

---

[45] 'The Global Law School Program', *NYU: The Law School Magazine* (1995, Special Issue) at 5–6.

[46] *Ibid.*, at 5.

[47] R. Gordon, et. al. '"Technical Assistance" and the Globalization of Black Letter Law: the Good, the Bad, and the Ugly' (paper presented at the Law and Society Association Meeting Glasgow Scotland 1996).

in legal technical assistance; amongst other things, tax and budget laws exercise a considerable impact on social welfare programmes, which might have far-reaching consequences for a developing country. No account is taken of the adverse impact of Western values on such countries. This is evident in the IMF's own words when it writes:

> Much [technical legal] assistance was to members with economies in transition from central planning that are seeking advice to establish an appropriate legal framework for a sound fiscal structure, modern financial sector institutions, and market-oriented financial transactions. Often the assistance to these countries involved revision of legislation passed early in the transition period that has since proved inadequate . . . The department helped to build capacity among local officials both through the discussions involved in giving advice and by conducting courses and seminars. . . .[48]

This kind of development is being taken further as the United Nations attempts to establish a global accounting qualification through the intergovernmental working group on International Standards of Accounting and Reporting (ISAR), 'ISAR hopes a global qualification will provide a 'benchmark' which will be used by developing countries to reduce 'the education gap' with the developed world.

The stated purpose is to enhance local professionals and place them in fair competition with Western accountants. It is also a means of imposing a Western view on the manner in which accounts should be done.[49]

Perhaps the last point to be made here, although not insignificant, is that the elite law schools are key credentialing institutions that feed candidates to the major law firms, international NGOs and big corporations.

6. CONCLUSION

I have suggested the relationship between globalisation and the field of law is reflexive. Although transnational legal work deals with the 'big picture', it requires an intensive attention to detail in legal documentation. Lawyers, especially those in the large law firms have to develop facilities to feel comfortable in a number of legal regimes and either have their offices throughout the world or have a set of alliances that allows them to call on expertise whenever they need it. Global lawyering cannot be parochial: it has to evolve at both the local law level and the meta-law level, which attempts to integrate and to co-ordinate the localisms. But it is more than that. We are now seeing potential moves towards convergence with the push to global regulation, the adoption of model legal codes, eg UNCITRAL. The large law firms are in the vanguard and are the ones most likely to benefit from these moves. They have access to the widest spread of legal resources and expertise, they possess the largest amount of legal

---

[48] IMF, *Annual Report 1996*. (Washington DC International Monetary Fund 1997) at 150.
[49] 'UN to Develop International Qualifications' (1996, Sep.) 5921 *The Accountant*.

technology, they have strong connections with governments and international governmental organisations, and they can commandeer the greatest number of highly trained entrants from the elite law schools. The close ties that evolve in these contexts act as barriers to entry for many outside. How then do they prove their bona fides in order to join?

I believe this raises a number of questions that we are only just beginning to consider. Is globalisation a new name for modernisation with its imperialist connotations? Are we seeing domination through a particularly Western mode of law discourse, a deterritorialisation of law? Does globalisation mean that the global and local coexist or are the tensions too great? Can ideas of economy and justice co-exist or are they antagonistic to each other? Are the great international organisations promoting economic discourse at the expense of discourses on community, ethics and justice?

The examples provided in this chapter are meant to stimulate further thinking on globalisation and law—whether it be in the field of international business transactions, crime in the international arena or human rights. As lawyers we have an obligation to think about these issues and formulate the means, and the theories for dealing with them.

17

Comparative Sociology of Law

DAVID NELKEN

APPRECIATING HOW LAW works in other countries can be a matter of life and death. One well travelled colleague who teaches legal theory likes to tell a story of the way crossing the road when abroad requires good knowledge of the local customs. In England, let us assume, you are relatively safe on pedestrian crossings, but rather less secure if you try to cross elsewhere. In Italy, he argued, you need to show almost the same caution in both places; but at least motorists will do their best to avoid actually hitting you. In Germany, on the other hand, or so he alleged, you are totally safe on the zebra crossing. You don't even need to look out for traffic. But if you dare to cross elsewhere, you will simply not be seen . . . Whatever elements of truth this comparison may contain the example also illustrates the dangers of oversimplification and stereotyping that makes writing about and learning from other societies so complicated. In this chapter I shall first indicate the type of questions studied by comparative sociology of law and then describe some of the ways it can be pursued. I then introduce the concept of legal culture and consider the influence of starting points in grasping other cultures. Finally I ask how far it is appropriate to continue to focus on variation in national legal cultures at a time of globalisation.

1. RETHINKING COMPARATIVE SOCIOLOGY OF LAW

The sociological study of law from a comparative perspective can number such distinguished predecessors as Montesquieu, Maine or Weber. In attempting to throw light on how things are elsewhere empirical research on law in different societies can be extremely intellectually stimulating because it raises many of the most puzzling questions of the law and society relationship. Why do the UK and Denmark complain most about the imposition of European Union law but maintain the best records of implementation? And what does this tell us about the centrality of enforcement as an aspect of law in different societies? Why in the United States and the UK does it often take a sex scandal to create official interest in doing something about corruption, whereas in Latin countries it takes a major corruption scandal to excite interest in marital unfaithfulness? What does this tell us about the way culture conditions the boundaries of law and the way law helps shape those same boundaries?

Comparative sociology of law cannot go it alone. Progress in this field requires learning from and collaborating with many other disciplines including comparative law, history, international relations, political science, anthropology, cultural studies, comparative psychology and comparative economics. But, as is most obvious in the case of much comparative law scholarship, it may also be necessary to contest other approaches. There is much to be learned from the attention which comparative lawyers give to legal elites, to doctrine and to history. Such matters are often an essential element in explaining which legal ideas and institutions are adopted and the logic of their internal evolution. Comparative sociology of law, however, also aims to get to the parts that comparative law cannot reach. In part it does this by studying the 'law in action', alternatives to law and the avoidance of law, and the way legal developments interrelate with wider social and political trends. As a social science perspective, however, it also works with different categories: no longer merely rules, procedures and institutions, but disputes, 'trouble cases' and scandals, law as social control and social regulation, law as an aspect of social and cultural order, law as producer and product of social change and law as shaper and controller of cultural flows. Instead of focusing only on legal systems or legal traditions it is likely to employ unfamiliar concepts borrowed from social and political theory such as regimes of 'power-knowledge', the 'symbolic capital' of different professional groups, or the autopoiesis of legal systems under modern conditions of social system differentiation.

Within the social sciences, some argue that *all* sociological research is inherently comparative: the aim is always to explain variation.[1] But where data is drawn from foreign societies there are further complications of understanding other languages, practices and world views which make it more difficult to know whether we are comparing like with like (indeed often it is that which becomes the problem). Others claim that for these and other reasons comparative work is actually impossible. It faces the allegedly unavoidable dangers of Occidentalism, thinking that other societies are necessarily like ours, or Orientalism, assuming that they are inherently different from us.[2] In a period of globalisation, it has been suggested, the links between societies and individuals have been so extended that it makes little sense to look for independent legal cultures.[3] But comparisons continue to be made, and need to be made, and the extent to which societies and cultures have become homogenised is an empirical question.

Comparative sociology of law has a long way to go to realise its potential. Some work is too closely linked to the more practical questions raised by comparative lawyers, for example the much discussed problem of whether

[1] M. Feeley, 'Comparative Criminal Law: Comparison for what purpose?' in D. Nelken (ed.) *Comparing Legal Cultures* (Aldershot Dartmouth 1997) at 93–104.

[2] M. Cain, 'Orientalism, Occidentalism and the Sociology of Crime' (2000) 40 *British Journal of Criminology* at 239–260.

[3] R. J. Coombe, 'Contingent Articulations: a Critical Studies of Law' in A. Sarat and T. Kearns (eds) *Law in the Domains of Culture* (University of Michigan Press Ann Arbor 2000).

Continental legal systems control their police forces better than is done in Anglo-American systems.[4] Much of the more theoretical work in English is about Japan, and there is relatively little written, for example, about the countries of Continental Europe. It is particularly important not to ghettoise this type of work (as in the way comparative law leads a somewhat fugitive existence in the law schools). Comparative research should be seen as a way of testing any claims made by the sociology of law and as an essential means of helping this discipline fulfil its promise. By helping us appreciate the fit (or lack of fit) between law and society in different social contexts it brings into view those aspects of the relationship which are usually hidden from the scholar who is, after all, also part of his or her own society.[5]

2. DOING COMPARATIVE RESEARCH

All comparative work is demanding and difficult. We should not underestimate what is entailed merely in trying to describe carefully how similar processes, for example criminal procedures, actually work in other societies.[6] But we should beware of using the challenges of comparative research merely as occasions for 're-enacting' past theoretical battles such as those between positivists and interpretivists, or between the search for explanation and the enterprise of translation.[7] A wide range of theoretical approaches may all have something to contribute, even though, of course, our ideas as to what comparison is and can be about will condition what we look for and how we look for it. Likewise, our choice of empirical research methods will depend on and further our chosen theoretical approach. For example, different types of data are likely to be gathered through exercises in 'virtual comparison' which rely on collaboration between foreign scholars, the method of 'researching there' which entails short research visits, and the process of actually 'living there' associated with ethnography.[8]

Some current approaches, however, are unlikely to be productive. A common form of extensive collective comparative work proceeds on the basis of what we might describe as comparison 'by juxtaposition' of the sort 'this is how we do it in Denmark, how do you do it in your country?'. Usually this is policy driven research on the look out for new ideas, and almost always it fails to get to grips

---

[4] J. H. Langbein and L. L. Weinreb, 'Continental Criminal Procedure: 'Myth and Reality', (1978) 87 *Yale Law Journal* at 1549–1569.

[5] D. Nelken, 'The Meaning of Success in Transnational Legal Transfers' in (2001) 19 *Windsor Yearbook of Access to Justice* at 349–366; 'Comparing Legal Cultures' in A. Sarat (ed.) *The Blackwell Companion to Law and Society* (Oxford Blackwell forthcoming 2003).

[6] J. Feest, J. and M. Murayama, 'Protecting the Innocent through Criminal Justice: A case study from Spain virtually compared to Germany and Japan' in D. Nelken (ed.) *Contrasting Criminal Justice* (Aldershot Dartmouth 2000) at 49–76.

[7] D. Nelken, 'Whom Can You Trust? The Future of Comparative Criminology' in D. Nelken (ed.) *The Futures of Criminology* (London Sage 1994) at 220–244.

[8] D. Nelken, 'Virtually there, Researching There, Living there' in Nelken, *supra* n. 6 at 23–48.

with the questions of comparability which should be the object of any comparative exercise. What are we trying to understand? Why are *these* societies being compared? What needs to be made explicit is the theoretical justification for and point of any comparison. The number of countries being compared does not matter as such. Even one foreign society if examined with reference to a theoretical problem can furnish important findings. Thus Haley treats 'law as a window on Japan and Japan as a window on law', so as to show what happens in a society where the cultural ideal is to make legal enforcement depend to the maximum extent on existing social consensus.[9]

All comparative research involves the search for social, cultural and other similarities and differences. Whilst it is common to find entrenched arguments in favour of one or other of these strategies neither should be embraced dogmatically. Both are important and at the end of the day inseparable. Careful comparison requires avoiding the assumption of similarity at all costs whilst also taking care not to be deceived by what may turn out to be only apparent difference. Assuming as an universal that criminal behaviour is essentially associated with young men is simply ethnocentric presumption.[10] But setting out to demonstrate that all higher courts have an essential role in governmental social control becomes a provocative argument if the cultures surveyed are as different as Muslim, Chinese, French and British.[11] Arguing that 'legal epistemes' are incommensurable paralyses comparison.[12] But it can be very fruitful to try to explain patterned differences in legal ideas and behaviour, for example in attitudes to mediation in the penal system, against a background of otherwise similar social and economic political conditions.[13] In looking for similarities and differences we will need to examine both action and words, and their interrelationship. In the face of current immigration influxes towards the European Union some European countries have strong ideals about integration but weak social provisions for assistance with employment and housing; for others it is the reverse. In general, in many legal cultures what is of most importance may often be found more in words than in practice;[14] just because it does not (yet) have a place in the world of practice and hence represents an ideal of what the society would like to become.

The idea of 'functional equivalence', the claim that all societies face similar problems, even if they solve them in somewhat different ways, is a heuristic tool which should be handled with care. It may be the case that other societies meet

[9] J. Haley, *Authority without Power: Law and the Japanese Paradox* (New York Oxford University Press, 1991).

[10] M. Gottfredson, and T. Hirschi, *A General Theory of Crime* (Stanford Stanford University Press 1990).

[11] M. Shapiro, *Courts* (Chicago Chicago University Press 1981).

[12] P. Legrand, 'What Legal Transplants?' in D. Nelken and J. Feest (eds.) *Adapting Legal Cultures* (Oxford Hart Publishing 2001).

[13] A. Crawford, 'Contrasts in Victim-Offender Mediation and Appeals to Community in France and England' in Nelken, *supra* n. 6.

[14] D. Nelken (ed.) *Law as Communication* (Aldershot Dartmouth 1996).

a given social problem by using unfamiliar types of law and legal techniques.[15] But it will also be worth extending our analysis to the role of other legal and non-legal institutions, alternatives to law, competing professional expertises as well as other groupings within civil society such as the family or patron client network. There may also simply be no 'solution', especially if the 'problem' is not conceived as such. We should be prepared to find that cultures have the power to produce relatively circular definitions of what is worth fighting for and against and that institutions and practices express genuinely different histories and distinct priorities.

Societies construct the role, boundaries and meaning of law in very different ways. Sometimes even subtle differences can be important, for example whether diversion from criminal justice is seen as intrinsic to the criminal process, as in Holland, or somehow extrinsic to it, as in the UK.[16] The often unexpected social consequences of such definitions need to be examined empirically. Attempts in Italy to deny prosecutors any discretion actually ended up strengthening their hands against corrupt politicians.[17] Conversely, Weber's Muslim Kadi judges can make little of their apparently unlimited discretion because it has to be exercised in accordance with community norms.[18]

3. THE CONCEPT OF LEGAL CULTURE

There is a great dearth of concepts which can be deployed in comparative sociology of law. Apart from terms borrowed from theorising within the master social science disciplines something can and needs to be done to rework the categories used in comparative law. The idea of legal culture, in its more sociological versions[19] represents one such possible conceptual tool.[20] But it is not without its detractors. And the problems in employing it illustrate many of the disagreements about how to do comparative work which we have mentioned so far.

Legal culture points to differences in the way aspects of law are themselves embedded in larger frameworks of social structure and culture which constitute and reveal the place of law in society. These may concern the extent to which law is party or state directed (bottom up or top down). It has to do with the

---

[15] K. Zweigert, and H. Kotz, *An Introduction to Comparative Law* 2nd edn (Trans T. Weir) (Oxford Oxford University Press 1987).

[16] C. Brants, and S. Field, 'Legal Cultures, Political Cultures and Procedural Traditions' in Nelken *supra* n. 6 at 77–116.

[17] D. Nelken, 'Comparing Criminal Justice' in M. Maguire, R. Morgan and R. Reiner (eds.) *The Oxford Handbook of Criminology* 3rd edn. (Oxford Oxford University Press 2002) at 175–202.

[18] L. Rosen, *The Anthropology of Justice* (Cambridge Cambridge University Press 1989).

[19] Contrast V. Gessner et. al. (eds.) *European Legal Cultures* (Dartmouth Aldershot 1996) and C. Varga, ed. *Comparative Legal Cultures* (Aldershot Dartmouth 1992).

[20] D. Nelken, 'Understanding/Invoking Legal Culture' in D. Nelken (ed.) *Legal Culture, Diversity and Globalization* Special Issue of (1995) 4 *Social and Legal Studies* at 435–452.

number, role and power of courts and legal professions, the role and importance
of the judiciary, the nature of legal education and legal training. It draws attention to ideas of what is meant by 'law' (and what law is 'for'), of where and how
it is to be found (types of legal reasoning, the role of case law and precedent, of
general clauses as compared to detailed drafting, of the place of law and fact). It
can be found in different approaches to regulation, administration and dispute
resolution. There may be important contrasts in the degree to which given controversies are subject to law, the role of other expertises, the part played by
'alternatives' to law, including not only arbitration and mediation but also the
many 'infrastructural' ways of discouraging or resolving disputes.[21] Attention
must be given to the role of other religious or ethical norms and the ambit of the
informal. Accompanying and concretising such differences, explaining and
attempting to justify them, there are likely to be contrasting attitudes to the role
of law, formal and substantive ideas of legitimacy, or the need for public participation.

How then should legal culture be distinguished from other aspects of society
and culture? On this there is no unanimity. For different purposes, or in line
with competing approaches to social theory, legal culture can be seen as manifested through institutional behaviour, or as a factor shaping and shaped by differences in individual legal consciousness, as a pattern of ideas which lie behind
behaviour, or as another name for politico-legal discourse itself. Sometimes
legal culture is identified independently from political culture, at other times it
is categorised as an inseparable aspect of political culture. It may be sought in
'high culture' and 'low culture'. When treated as constitutive of cultural consciousness generally this may be examined through structured interviews about
the sense of justice,[22] contextualised as part of everyday narratives, as in the
work of the Amherst school, or distilled from the ideology behind legal doctrine,
as in the writings of American Critical legal scholars.

The diversity in ways of thinking about how to draw the line between legal
culture and other phenomena is not necessarily unproductive. It can be useful for
reminding us that in many societies there is a wide gulf between legal culture and
general culture, as where the criminal law purports to maintain principles of
impersonal equality before the law in societies where clientilistic and other par-
ticularistic practices are widespread. Indeed, there is need for more attention to
be given to the way past and present work in the sociology of law assumes and
mobilises a (local) vision of legal culture even (or even especially) where the
problem of legal culture is left unexplicated rather than being squarely
addressed. It forces the sociologist of law to confront the problem of reflexivity,
the way her framing of problems for discussion reproduces rather than questions

---

[21] E. Blankenburg, 'Civil Litigation Rates as Indicators for Legal Culture' in Nelken *supra* n. 1 at
41–68.
[22] V. Hamilton, and J. Sanders, *Everyday Justice: Responsibility and the Individual in Japan and
the United States* (New Haven Yale University Press 1992).

the taken for granted assumptions of her own legal—and academic—culture about the role and the rule of law.

But these ambiguities help us appreciate why there are lively disputes over the usefulness of this concept and of over how it should be studied. Lawrence Friedman, who has made extensive use of the term in his writings, introduced the useful distinction between the 'internal legal culture' of legal professionals and academics and the 'external legal culture' representing the opinions and pressures brought to bear by wider social groups. Roger Cotterrell criticises Friedman's broad brush use of the concept claiming that it is too vague and impressionistic.[23] He argues instead for the study of the way professionally managed legal ideology shapes wider consciousness. Friedman replies that even a vague concept can subsume other less vague and more measurable categories. Legal culture determines when, why and where people turn for help to law or to other institutions, or only 'lump it'. For example it would be a finding about legal culture if French but not Italian women were reluctant to call police to complain about sexual harassment. As a step in explanation, our accounts of legal culture serve to capture an essential intervening variable in influencing the type of legal changes which follow on large social transformations such as those following technological breakthroughs.[24]

In line with the different methodologies which compete in the social sciences there is an important divide between those scholars who look for 'indicators' of legal culture in the activity of courts and other legal institutions, and those who insist instead on the need to interpret cultural meaning. The first approach uses culture (or deliberately simplified aspects of it) to explain variation in levels and types of litigation or social control, the second approach seeks to use legal related behaviour by institutions or individuals as an 'index' of culture. The first strategy seeks a sort of socio-legal esperanto which abstracts from the language used by members of different cultures, preferring for example to talk of 'decision-making' rather than 'discretion'. The rival approach aims at providing 'thick descriptions of law as local knowledge';[25] it is concerned precisely with grasping linguistic nuance and cultural packaging and with the problems this poses of faithfully translating another system's ideas of fairness and justice and making proper sense of its web of meanings.

Some authors draw a contrast, not unrelated to Friedman's typology, between the factors conditioning the 'supply side' of law as embodied in the activities of legal and paralegal institutions, and the 'demand' side representing social patterns of use of legal institutions. In what he calls a sort of 'natural experiment' Erhard Blankenburg asks why Germany has one of the highest litigation rates in Europe and Holland one of the lowest when both countries are

---

[23] R. Cotterrell, 'The Concept of Legal Culture' in Nelken *supra* n. 1 at 13–32.

[24] L. Friedman, 'The Concept of Legal Culture: A Reply' in Nelken *supra* n. 1 at 34.

[25] C. Geertz, 'Thick Description: Towards an Interpretive Theory of Culture in C. Geertz *The Interpretation of Culture* (London Fontana 1973); C. Geertz, *Local Knowledge: Further Essays in Interpretive Anthropology* (New York Basic Books 1983).

socially and culturally so similar and economically interdependent. (In respect of our example of traffic accidents, Germany brings sixteen such cases per thousand population to court for every two brought to trial in Holland). His answer, carefully documented with respect to different types of legal controversy, is that in Holland there are a series of 'infrastructural' alternatives to litigation. This is said to demonstrate the determinant role played by the 'supply side' even where the 'demand' for law is assumed to be similar.

Blankenburg's argument is not free from the ambiguities identified by Cotterrell. It is not always clear whether his aim is to find a way of characterising differences in (national) legal cultures or instead to use the concept of legal culture itself as a tool for explaining the behaviour of legal institutions. Sometimes legal culture seems to be the explanation of the filters and alternatives which Blankenburg sees as characterising Dutch 'law in action', at other times only the name we give to such patterns of litigation and avoidance (in which case it would be tautologous to use this as part of any explanation). Any clear cut distinction between supply and demand is also questionable (are lawyers' strategies one or the other?). Demand is shaped by supply, and vice versa. Assumptions of 'functional equivalence' across cultures are always questionable; what counts as an alternative or 'supplement' is itself culturally contingent. We could just as well say that it is the different function of the courts in Holland which means that the ready availability of para-lawyers and other intermediaries leads to less litigation. *In another society (including Germany) the alternatives which Blankenburg uses to explain the low rate of litigation in Holland could easily lead to still greater litigation.*[26]

But the main drawback of such an approach is its insistence that rates of social behaviour can be understood independently of the meanings that actors themselves attach to them. Interpretative approaches, by contrast, try to grasp the secrets of culture by focusing on key local terms, which are sometimes admitted to be almost but not quite untranslatable. Blankenburg himself explores the meaning of the term 'beleid' in Holland which refers to the often explicit policy guidelines followed by government, criminal justice personnel and complex (public) organisations in general.[27] Other scholars have examined the idea of the state in common law and Continental countries and have sought to understand for example why litigation is seen as essentially democratic in the USA and as anti-democratic in France. They contrast the different meanings of the 'Rule of law', the 'Rechtstaat', or the 'Stato di diritto', the Italian term 'garantismo' versus 'due process', or 'law and order' as compared to the German 'innere sicherheit'; they unpack the meaning of 'lokale justiz' as compared to 'community crime control'.[28] This strategy explores how concepts both reflect and constitute culture; as in the changes undergone by the meaning

---

[26] D. Nelken, 'Puzzling out Legal Culture: A comment on Blankenburg' in *supra* n. 1 at 58–88.

[27] E. Blankenburg, and F. Bruinsma, *Dutch Legal Culture* 2nd edition (Deventer Kluwer 1994).

[28] L. Zedner, 'In pursuit of the Vernacular; Comparing Law and Order Discourse in Britain and Germany' (1995) 4 *Social and Legal Studies* at 517–534.

of 'contract' in a society where the individual is seen as necessarily embodied in wider relationships,[29] or the way that the Japanese ideogram for the new concept of 'rights' came to settle on a sign associated with 'self interest' rather than morality.[30]

4. WE AND THE OTHER

But who uses such terms, when and for what purposes? The besetting problem of the interpretative approach is deciding whose ideas we should be trying to understand. For different purposes we may be interested in the views and behaviour of politicians, legal officials, legal and other professionals, or legal scholars, in the powerful or the powerless. Is it safe to expect practitioners or academics necessarily to know the answers to our questions? Though we will always want to know what the natives think it does not follow that we actually want to think like a native. We may want to know more or less than they do and for certain purposes we may even come to know more. But if we do not look to them for corroboration of our ideas there is always the risk of imposing our own interpretations.

The ability to look at a culture with new eyes is the great strength of the outside scholar. But the observer's questions may often have more relevance to the country of origin than that under observation. Similarities and differences, for example, often come to life for an observer when they are exemplified by 'significant absences', such as the lack of any reference to 'community' in discourse about crime prevention in Germany.[31] This obliges us to interrogate the way our own cultural assumptions shape the questions we ask and the answers we find convincing. Do we want to understand why Italy has apparently high rates of political corruption or why the UK has apparently low ones?[32] Do we seek to explain why the Italian system of criminal justice has relatively more built-in leniency than the Anglo-American system or the opposite?[33] Why did Blankenburg find the unusually low rate of litigation in Holland more puzzling than the exceptionally high rate of litigation in Germany?

This question of starting points is often left begging because of the implicit collusion between the writer and her audience which privileges what the audience wants to know as if it is what it *should want to know*. What therefore tends to

---

[29] J. K. Winn, 'Relational Practices and the Marginalization of Law: Informal Practices of Small Businesses in Taiwan' (1994) 28 *Law and Society Review* at 193–232.

[30] E. Feldman, 'Patients Rights, Citizen Movements and Japanese Legal Culture' in *supra* n. 1 at 215–236.

[31] N. Lacey, and L. Zedner, 'Discourses of Community in Criminal Justice' (1995) 22 *Journal of Law and Society* at 301–320.

[32] D. Nelken, 'Judicial Politics and Corruption in Italy' in M. Levi and D. Nelken (eds.) *The Corruption of Politics and the Politics of Corruption* (Oxford Blackwell 1996) at 95–113.

[33] D. Melossi, 'The Economy of Illegalities: Normal Crimes, Elites and Social Control in Comparative Analysis' in D. Nelken (ed.) *The Futures of Criminology* (London Sage 1994) at 202–219.

be highlighted are those aspects of the society under investigation which seem especially relevant in confirming or disconfirming previous audience expectations. One result of this is that it can often be instructive to read comparative work, whatever its purported aims, not for what it says about the country or culture being observed, but for what it reveals about the cultural viewpoint of the observer and her home audience (as if we were looking through the other end of the telescope). It is easy for us to see that what an Italian scholar finds strange and problematic about law in the USA is likely to tell us at least as much about Italian assumptions about the role and rule of law as it is does about how things are organised in the USA.[34] We are less quick to appreciate that the same is true in reverse. Much of the voluminous American research on the specificity of Japanese Criminal and Civil justice, for example, can be criticised for attempting to explain as distinctive features of Japanese legal culture matters which should rather be attributed to the Continental European models which shaped and still shape legal institutions in Japan.

Sometimes the natives whose views we are trying to understand make judgements which are themselves explicitly comparative. Take for example the claim by an Italian from Palermo that Northern Europeans 'have the state in their hearts'.[35] It is important to see how this judgement tells us something *both* about the observer's own preconceptions and about those he is observing. This accusation (which is more likely, I think, to leave Northern Europeans puzzled rather than offended) expresses all the contradictory feelings of someone brought up in the South of Italy and in Sicily, parts of Italy which have, on the one hand, regularly experienced external and internal colonisation, and on the other hand, can with reason lament continued neglect and abandonment by an absentee state. Hence such strong feelings about the state as an object of love and hate: to have *such* a state in our hearts would indeed be worthy of reproach. But most Northern Europeans, and especially those used to Anglo-American political discourse in which the term 'the state' hardly appears, do not think of their relationship with government in these terms. Still less would they accept that it is this background sentiment—which they are unaware of having—which both explains their relative law abidingness and permits their individualistic expressions of nonconformity. Perhaps though 'we', have indeed internalised the state at such a deep level of our hearts and minds that we simply can no longer recognise this (as Foucault would well have agreed).

As this suggests, cultures are themselves reflexive. Indeed they often define themselves in part through and against encounters with other cultures (or more specifically their 'idea' of other cultures.) The formation of identity is usually in part also a product of denial. Faced with legal developments to protect copyright on the continent, Britain in the nineteenth century reinvented its law of

---

[34] M. R. Ferrarese, 'An Entrepreneurial Conception of the Law? The American Model Through Italian Eyes' in Nelken *supra* n. 1 at 157–181.

[35] D. Nelken, 'Telling Difference: Of Crime and Criminal Justice in Italy' in Nelken *supra* n. 6 at 233–264.

copyright so that it became possible to claim that a specific British approach had always existed.[36] In the 1980s the appearance of league tables of relative levels of incarceration may have induced Finland to move towards the norm by reducing its prison population (and Italy to do the opposite). Whether East European cultures can come to resemble Western legal cultures, assuming this to be desirable, depends on whether their citizens believe they can escape the patterns inherited from the past.[37] Conversely, for some scholars rooted in Chinese traditions, what others describe as the welcome spread of 'the rule of law' is criticised as the marginalisation of the importance of 'quing', or the appeal to others' feelings, towards an over empasis on 'li' or reasonableness.[38]

5. NATIONAL LEGAL CULTURES, AND BEYOND

The search to explain or interpret legal culture at the level of the nation state (as in the 'Japanese approach to law', 'Dutch legal culture', 'French criminal justice' etc.) continues to be an important ambition of comparative law and comparative sociology of law. There are ingenious efforts to unsettle stereotypes of which nations are supposedly most or least litigious.[39] But is national legal culture a valid unit for comparison? It is undeniable that legal culture is tied in many ways to its own past, and that national authorities deliberately use law to impose institutional and procedural distinctions, for all sorts of political and legal reasons. Differences between legal cultures may also mobilise or reflect wider social and cultural similarities which roughly coincide with political boundaries. But any direct experience of the myriad differences *within* another society soon demonstrates how unwise it is to talk in stereotypes. Crossing the road in Trento in North Italy is a much safer enterprise than doing so in Naples! And, if the worst actually happens, there are also important differences in the time it takes to get accident damages from the Tribunals in these cities. Nor is legal culture necessarily uniform (either organisationally or meaningfully) across different branches of law. The purported uniformity, coherence or stability of given national cultures will often be no more than an ideological projection or rhetorical device.[40]

National legal cultures do not remain the same over time. The Italian legal system currently suffers from extensive legal delays for which it is routinely

---

[36] B. Sherman, 'Remembering and Forgetting: The Birth of Modern Copyright Law' in Nelken *supra* n. 1 at 237–266.

[37] M. Krygier, 'Is there Constitutionalism after Communism? Institutional Optimism, Cultural Pessimism, and the Rule of Law' in (1997) 26, 4 *International Journal of Sociology* at 17–47.

[38] S. W. Man, and C. Y. Wai, 'Whose rule of law? Rethinking (post) colonial Legal Culture in Hong Kong' (1999) 8 *Social and Legal Studies* at 147–170.

[39] E. Feldman, 'Blood Justice, Courts, Conflict and Compensation in Japan, France and the United States' in (2000) 34, 3 *Law and Society Review* at 651–702.

[40] Coombe, *supra* n. 3.

condemned by the Strasbourg Court of Human Rights.[41] But two generations before this judges were getting through more work than was coming in. What has mainly changed is the number of cases they were asked to handle. Likewise, relying on ideas of national character would make it difficult to reconcile the defiance of law in Weimar Germany as compared to the over deference to law of the Fascist period. Political changes are the obvious missing factor. The Dutch penal system was rightly celebrated for its 'tolerance' from the 1960s onwards in keeping its proportionate prison population well below that of its European neighbours.[42] But, shortly after gaining such praise, Holland engaged in a massive programme of prison building which took it back towards the levels of the 1950s, when its relative level of incarceration was comparable to the rest of Europe. The criminal justice elite who pioneered the 'Utrecht' approach were sidelined by the pressures of gaining popular political consensus in the face of Holland's growing drug problem.

Rather than limiting ourselves to national legal cultures both a narrower and larger focus will often be more appropriate. At the level below that of the nation state it may be fruitful to study the culture of the local courthouse, of different social and interest groups and professional associations, as well as the roles and relationships of individuals in engaging or avoiding disputes. Law will have a different, and changing, role and significance in different social arenas, settings, and for different groups and classes. On the other hand, we may also want to explore wider cultural entities; not only the Civil law and common law (or 'Anglo-American') worlds long identified by comparative lawyers, but also more idiosyncratic categories such as so called 'Latin legal culture',[43] or even 'modern legal culture' with its alleged converging tendencies.[44] It is also increasingly important to explore so-called 'third cultures' of international trade, communication networks and other trans-national processes.[45] Recent developments in opening up the world to trade and communication mean that many people increasingly have the sense of living in an interdependent global system marked by borrowing and lending across porous cultural boundaries which are saturated with inequality, power and domination. On the other hand 'increasing homogenisation of social and cultural

---

[41] D. Nelken, 'Comparing Legal Cultures' in A. Sarat (ed.) *The Blackwell Companion to Law and Society* (Oxford Blackwell forthcoming 2003).

[42] D. Downes, *Contrasts in Tolerance: Post War Penal Policy in the Netherlands and England and Wales* (Oxford Oxford University Press 1988).

[43] A. Garapon, 'French Legal Culture and the Shock of "Globalization"' in Nelken *supra* n. 20 at 493–506.

[44] L. Friedman, 'Is there a Modern Legal Culture?' (1994) *Ratio Juris* at 117.

[45] Y. Dezalay, and B. Garth, *Dealing in Virtue* (Chicago University of Chicago Press 1996); F. Snyder, 'Governing Economic Globalisation: Global Legal Pluralism and European Law' in (1999) 5 *European Law Journal* at 334–374; G. Teubner, 'Global Bukowina: Legal Pluralism in the World Society' in G. Teubner (ed.) *Global Law without a State* (Aldershot Dartmouth 1997) at 3–38; G. Teubner, 'Legal Irritants: Good Faith in British Law or How Unifying Law Ends up in New Divergences' (1998) 61.1 *Modern Law Review* at 11–32.

forms seems to be accompanied by a proliferation of claims to specific authenticities and identities'.[46]

Nation states are increasingly interdependent. Indeed, with the advance of globalisation the pre-eminence of the positive law of the nation state could be seen as no more than a temporal fusion of law's globalising and localising elements. Different legal systems participate in world or regional bodies and in common projects or trends such as the attempt to construct a 'Fortress Europe' or combat political corruption or money laundering. Each respond in their own way to Europeanisation, Americanisation and globalisation, and each are affected by the culture of modernity (or postmodernity). Thus the boundaries between units of legal culture(s) are fluid and they intersect at the macro and micro level in ways which are often far from harmonious. But, in spite of what critics allege, this untidiness, as well as the attempts to conceal or resolve it, are all part of the phenomenon of living legal cultures rather than evidence that the concept is otiose.

A problem that is ever more relevant is the question in what sense a national legal culture can be considered the product of the nation state in which it is found rather than the outcome of contingent processes of legal transfer. Transplants which derive from other places and other times can range from single laws and legal institutions to entire codes or borrowed systems of law.[47] Many non-European countries have mixed or pluralistic legal systems which testify to waves of colonial invasions as well as imitation.[48] Nearer to home, some of the disputing institutions, which people in Holland think of as most typically Dutch, are in fact a result of German imposition during the occupation and have been abandoned in Germany itself.[49] Law may (or may not) be remade by wider national culture but it can also itself help mould that culture. In advance of empirical investigation it would be wrong to assume any particular 'fit' between law and its environing society or culture.

The implications of these processes for theory and practice in the sociology of law emerge most clearly once we recognise that most legal transfers must be seen as attempts to bring about an imagined and different *future*, rather than to conserve the present (as the transplant metaphor might suggest). Hence ex-communist countries try to become more like selected examples of the more successful market societies, or South Africa models its new constitution on the best

---

[46] M. Strathern (ed.) 'Introduction' in *Shifting contexts: Transformations in Anthropological Knowledge* (London Routledge 1995) at 3.

[47] Nelken, *supra* n. 5; D. Nelken, 'Towards a Sociology of Legal Adaptation' in Nelken and Feest *supra* n. 12 at 4–55; D. Nelken, 'Beyond the Metaphor of Legal Transplants? Consequences of Autopoietic Theory for the study of Cross-Cultural Legal Adaptation' in J. Priban and D. Nelken (eds.) *Law's New Boundaries: The Consequences of Legal Autopoiesis* (Dartmouth Aldershot 2001); D. Nelken, 'Rethinking Legal Transfers' in Legrand and Munday (eds.) *Comparative Legal Studies: Traditions and Transitions* (Cambridge Cambridge University Press 2002).

[48] A. Harding, 'Comparative Law and Legal Transplantation in South East Asia' in D. Nelken and J. Feest *supra* n. 12.

[49] A. Jettinghoff, 'State Formation and Legal Change: On the Impact of International Politics' in Nelken and Feest, *supra* n. 12.

that Western regimes have to offer rather than on constitutional arrangements found in its nearer neighbours in Africa. The hope is that law may be a means of resolving current problems by transforming their society into one more like the source of such borrowed law; legal transfer becomes part of the effort to become more democratic, more economically successful, more secular or more religious. In what is almost a species of sympathetic magic, borrowed law is deemed capable of bringing about the same conditions of a flourishing economy or a healthy civil society which are found in the social context from which the borrowed law has been taken.

The adoption of dissimilar legal models is perhaps most likely where the legal transfer is imposed by third parties as part of a colonial project and/or insisted on as a condition of trade, aid, alliance or diplomatic recognition. But it has also often been sought by elites concerned to 'modernise' their society or otherwise bring it into the wider family of 'civilised' nations. Japan and Turkey are the most obvious examples. There is much discussion of whether or not such transfers can succeed. But even when they do succeed to all apparent purposes, this may be at a high price. There is for example continuing controversy in Japan about the significance of the 1890 reception of Western Law. Some indigenous scholars say Japan has an underlying culture which is incompatible with modern Western law, others reject this argument, alleging that it is an invention of the power elite by which the people are led to believe in their non-litigiousness (and lack of interest in rights) so as to leave power holders undisturbed.[50] But, more subtly, because Japan achieved its incredible modernisation not by Western law but through bureaucratic authoritarianism, there are some who feel that Japan has 'not yet achieved the modern'.

Thus, according to one leading Japanese scholar, 'Japan is experienced by the Japanese as a kind of double layered society. On the surface it is an industrialised society with necessary modern paraphernalia, while at bottom, or I would rather say, at the core, it is a hollow yet to be filled by the modern substance'.[51] Having achieved modernisation without 'the modern', which they were told was necessary, Japanese have a sense of guilt, and engage in a compulsive search for the modern which only leaves them frustrated. 'As examples of the consequent ambivalent approach to law Tanase points to the stigma attached to using legal remedies amongst neighbours as well as to a special concern with deciding what source of legitimacy other than law itself can make something count as legal. Interestingly, however, Tanase's conclusion is not that Japanese culture is irreducibly different but that postmodern man will increasingly come to resemble the Japanese, 'the decentred man with a hollow core inside who negotiates flexibly his relation with others and improvises workable arrangements ad hoc'.[52]

---

[50] T. Tanase, 'The Empty Space of the Modern in Japanese Law Discourse' in D. Nelken and J. Feest, *supra* n. 12.
[51] *Ibid.*
[52] *Ibid.*

Many of those participating in the new law and development movement focus on the techniques appropriate for transferring legal and political institutions as if these can be abstracted from culture and from wider social change; 'today's development policy assumes that a country must adapt the proper institutions to facilitate growth and that institutions can be transferred across borders'.[53] Currently many international organisations, such as the International Monetary Fund, are seeking to reshape societies according to a supposedly universal pattern of political and financial integrity. Some of these reforms have or are intended to lead to important changes. Others may be mainly symbolic; a way of marking willingness to accept 'rules of the game' of the wider global economy. This explains the adhesion to intellectual property or anti-trust provisions of the World Trade Organisation by countries who have few ways of enforcing such rules or little need to do so.

But some scholars return from missions abroad all the more convinced that law only makes sense in terms of its own (national) environment. One leading constitutional scholar reports that his experience in China confirmed him in the view that the type of administrative law used in the USA would not be currently workable there. This is because of its interdependence with wider features of American society, above all the presence of a litigious culture and the presumption that party involvement by numerous interest groups can be counted on to comment on and improve bureaucratic regulations. He argues that recommendations for change must rather draw on identifiable features of existing Chinese society.

> [B]y a sort of double reflection, the characterisation of American law that China's distance illuminates, becomes a way of perceiving what the underlying characterisation of a Chinese law would be. That law draws upon the hierarchy, centralisation and governmental prestige in the Chinese system. It would create governmental supervisory agencies, independent of other agencies, but possessing the full power and prestige of government, to enforce statutorily and required procedures.[54]

The current so-called globalisation of law is a complex process which is likely to produce increasing social and economic differentiation as much as harmony.[55] Assumptions of necessary convergence risks underestimating the continuing importance of culture and resistance (even if such resistance itself increasingly comes to be organised globally).[56] But one of the most important

---

[53] T. Ginsburg, 'Does Law Matter for Economic Development? Evidence from East Asia' (2000) *Law and Society Review*: 829–856 at 833.

[54] E. Rubin, 'Administrative Law and the Complexity of Culture' in A. Seidman, R. Seidman and J. Payne (eds.) *Legislative Drafting for Market Reform: Some Lessons from China*, (Basingstoke Macmillian 2000) at 108.

[55] B. de Sousa Santos, *Towards a New Common Sense* (London Routledge 1995); D. Nelken, 'The Globalization of Crime and Criminal Justice: Prospects and Problems' in M. Freeman (ed.) *Law and Opinion at the End of the 20th Century* (Oxford Oxford University Press 1997) at 251–279; W. Heyderbrand, 'Globalization and the Rule of Law at the end of the 20th Century' in A. Febbrajo, D. Nelken, V. Olgiati (eds.) *Social Processes and Patterns of Legal Control: European Yearbook of Sociology of Law 2000* (Milan Giuffrè 2001) at 25–127.

[56] Friedman *supra* n. 44.

tasks of the comparative sociologist of law at the present time is to try and capture how far in practice globalisation represents the attempted imposition of one particular legal culture on other societies. Importing countries are offered both the Anglo-American model whose prestige is spread by trade and the media, and national versions of the Continental legal system embodied in ready packaged Codes. The Anglo-American model is seen to be characterised by its emphasis on the care taken to link law and economics (rather than law and the state), procedures which rely on orality, party initiative, negotiation inside law or more broad cultural features such as individualism and the search for 'total justice'. Only some of these elements are actually on offer in legal transfers and much of this model does not accurately describe how the law operates at home (much of the American legal and regulatory system relies on inquisitorial methods). Much of what was represented by the 'rule of law' itself, as a way of providing certainty and keeping the state within bounds, seems increasingly outdated for the regulation of international commercial exchange by computer between multinationals more powerful than many of the governments of the countries in which they trade.[57]

More than any particular feature of legal culture, however, what does seem to be spreading is the common law ideology of 'pragmatic legal instrumentalism', *the very idea that law is something which does or should 'work'*, together with the claim that this is something which can or should be assessed in ways which are separable from wider political debates. Only time will tell what consequences this may have. How far, for example, will the NAFTA Treaty succeed in altering a legal culture such as Mexico where, we were told, not long ago (by an author who has since joined the Mexican executive!), that 'law institutes without regulating'?[58]

---

[57] W. E. Scheuerman, 'Globalization and the Fate of Law' in D. Dyzenhaus (ed.) *Recrafting the Rule of Law: The Limits of Legal Order* (Oxford Hart Publishing 1999) at 243–266.
[58] S. Lopez-Ayllon, 'Notes on Mexican Legal Culture' in Nelken *supra* n. 20 at 477–492.

18

Conclusion: Law and Sociology

REZA BANAKAR and MAX TRAVERS

T HE CONTRIBUTORS IN this book have demonstrated that sociology of law is
a rich and complex subject that contains a wide range of theoretical
approaches which can be used to study law. There are, however, fundamental
disagreements over how sociology of law should develop. In this chapter, we
will review these debates, and examine the institutional obstacles which prevent
it from developing in the same way as the sociologies of education, science or
medicine. We will end by presenting our own views on why law students should
study sociology of law, and why sociologists should pay more attention to law
and legal institutions.

1. FOUNDATIONAL DEBATES ABOUT SOCIOLOGY OF LAW

Numerous review articles have been published about sociology of law, which
reflects the fact that there continues to be considerable disagreement about the
nature of the subject, and how it should develop. Some of these disputes are
caused by the interdisciplinary make-up of sociology of law: by the confrontation between the academic concerns and aspirations of sociology and the instrumental approach and expectations of policy-makers and the legal system.[1]
These debates often have parallels in interdisciplinary sub-fields such as the
sociologies of medicine, science and religion. Other disputes are caused by the
fact that sociology of law has a smaller institutional base than the related fields
of policy-oriented socio-legal research and critical legal studies. It is, perhaps,
only natural that they should sometimes appropriate the term 'sociology of law'
for their own purposes. We would, however, argue that sociology of law is best
understood as a sub-field of mainstream sociology.

---

[1] R. Cotterrell, 'Law and Sociology: Notes on the Constitution and Confrontation of
Disciplines' (1986) 13 *Journal of Law and Society* 9–34.

Sociology of law as a policy science

Since the Enlightenment, the social sciences have always been employed to serve the interests of national governments. Although it prides itself on being independent from the executive, the legal profession is part of this state apparatus. Certainly, most funding for research about law and legal institutions comes from government departments.

This dependence on the state has had two consequences for the kind of research that gets pursued. Firstly, it is usually politically conservative, or at least unreflective about alternative ways of interpreting or contextualising the data.[2] It is necessarily geared to the practical questions that interest the civil servants who have commissioned the research. To give an example, British researchers were, for many years, concerned with how to increase access to public services, because this was the political objective of governments at the time. Today, however, the agenda has shifted to saving money by rationalising services or improving quality. In each case, academics have to design projects that narrowly address these questions, in order to obtain research funding.

Dependence on government funding has also resulted in most researchers conducting empiricist research, in which the objective is to produce clear-cut 'facts' that result in recommendations which solve social problems. This does not mean that researchers have to employ quantitative methods, since qualitative data can also be collected and analysed within this framework. It has, however, usually resulted in a bias towards survey methods since these are cheaper and appear to result in more 'objective' findings, and a reluctance on the part of funding bodies to support qualitative research.[3] It also means that researchers have generally been reluctant to think critically about method, even within the quantitative tradition.

From the perspective of policy researchers, most sociological theorising is irrelevant to the needs of government. There is, therefore, an increasing tendency for empiricist, policy-oriented research to present itself as sociology of law. There is, however, nothing sociological about this literature, since it does not address wider scientific questions about the role of law in society.

A theoretically 'undeveloped' field?

Some scholars dissatisfied by the theoretical state of the field often formulate the above debate in a more pointed fashion. John Manzo argues, for example, that

---

[2] For critiques of policy research, see C. M. Campbell and P. Wiles, 'The Study of Law and Society in Britain' (1976) 10 *Law and Society Review* 547–78; M. Travers, 'Sociology of Law in Britain' (2001) 32 *The American Sociologist* 26–40; A. Sarat and S. Silbey, 'The Pull of the Policy Audience' (1988) 10 *Law and Policy* 98–166.

[3] For discussion of the positivistic bias of policy research in Britain, see R. Watson, ' "Interpretive" Sociology in Great Britain: The State of the Art' in (2000) 26:3 *Swiss Journal of Sociology* 507–529.

contemporary sociological studies of law to a large extent conceptually adhere to the basic assumptions of the founders of sociology, but fail to live up to the visions or aspirations of classical sociology.[4]

Such complaints about the theoretically underdeveloped and non-innovative state of the field have provoked reactions among some law and society scholars. Brian Tamanaha, for example, discards them as the 'over-zealous doctrinal policing, of self-appointed theoretical sophisticates looking down upon their supposedly less aware half-brethren'.[5] He also finds the complaints strange because '[s]ocio-legal studies pieces are filled with references to fancy theories and theorists'.[6] Yet, Tamanaha paradoxically hastens to add that these references to theory often 'pay insufficient attention to the compatibility of the different theoretical sources identified, or are taken on at the beginning and the end of a study without being well integrated into the study itself'.[7]

The internal/external debate

Underlying this debate about the place of theory in sociology of law is an epistemological tension between two radically opposed ways of viewing law and legal institutions. The first approach is based on a juristic standpoint, which prioritises the *modus operandi* of positive law and/or takes the claims and concepts of legal positivism for granted. In a sense, this approach can be regarded as 'internal' to law. It uses sociology in so far as it serves its legal objectives and as an auxiliary instrument for collecting and processing data. The second approach, is driven by sociological concerns and views the law from without, questioning the taken for granted assumptions of positive law and legal practitioners. This approach which is based on an 'external' view of law and legal practice studies law in the same fashion as the founders of sociology, such as Durkheim, as a means of expanding sociology's insight into the social organisation of society.

This distinction between internal and external views is hardly new in sociology. One can, for example, see the same debate in the sociology of religion, where the insider or the subject's perspective is regarded as 'experience-near' and different from that of the outsider or the analyst which is 'experience-distant'.[8] This also indicates that the difference between these two perspectives is one of degree, i.e. they are not necessarily polar opposites.[9]

---

[4] J. Manzo, 'Ethnomethodology, Conversation Analysis, and the Sociology of Law' in M. Travers and J. F. Manzo (eds) *Law in Action* (Aldershot Ashgate 1997) at 3.
[5] B. Z. Tamanaha, *Realistic Socio-Legal Theory: Pragmatism and a Social Theory of Law* (Oxford Clarendon Press 1997) at 18.
[6] *Ibid.*, at 17.
[7] *Ibid.*, at 18.
[8] C. Geertz, 'From the Native's Point of View' in R. T. McCutcheon (ed.) *The Insider/Outsider Problem in the Study of Religion* (London Cassell 1999) at 38–50.
[9] R. Banakar, 'A Passage to "India": Toward a Transformative Interdisciplinary Discourse on Law and Society' (2001) 92 *Retfærd* (The Nordic Journal of Law and Justice) at 3–21.

Other scholars have, however, reformulated the tension between these two perspectives in terms of the possibility of accessing the law's 'truth'.[10] The question underlying this debate is whether sociology (representing the external/experience-distant view on law) is a prisoner of its own conceptual apparatus and can understand the world only in terms of its own concepts, definitions, and assumptions. If this is the case, then it becomes unable to provide insights into legal ideas and clarify questions about legal doctrine, as a result of which the essence of law and legal thinking (i.e. the internal/experience-near view of law) becomes inaccessible to it. Simply put, the question is whether sociology is able to climb out of its own skin and get inside the law to understand and explain the law's 'truth', ie the motives and meanings of legal phenomena from within.[11]

Sociology of law as critical theory

The main opponent to the empiricist, and usually unreflective and conservative, kind of policy research that gets funded by government departments is critical legal studies. This has been the largest area of growth in legal scholarship in recent years. New journals, such as *Social and Legal Studies*, exclusively publish critical research. Established journals like the *Law and Society Review*, and *Law and Social Inquiry*, increasingly publish articles informed by different traditions in critical theory. The main law and society textbooks, by Cotterrell, Anleu and Mansell, also have a critical bias.[12]

Critical legal scholars all draw upon sociological ideas and perspectives in making the political point that law benefits the economically powerful. Nevertheless, they are not much interested in sociology as a scientific discipline. Roger Cotterrell, in fact, explicitly recommends that sociology of law should not become a branch of academic sociology. Instead, he presents it as a 'continually self-reflective and self-critical enterprise of enquiry aspiring towards ever broader perspectives on law as a field or aspect of social experience'.[13]

The problem with this position, from a sociological point of view, is that it does not sufficiently acknowledge the argumentative nature of the subject, or the principled ways in which sociologists disagree over how to study the social world.

Less charitably, one might argue that Cotterrell, and other critical legal scholars, want to incorporate or assimilate insights and perspectives from the rest of sociology into the conflict tradition. They generally do this from a philosophical

[10] Cf. R. Cotterrell, 'Why Must Legal Ideas be Interpreted Sociologically?' (1998) 25 *Journal of Law and Society*, and D. Nelken, 'Blinding Insights? The Limits of a Reflexive Sociology of Law' (1998) 25 *Journal of Law and Society* 407 and D. Nelken (ed.) *Law as Communication* (Aldershot Dartmouth 1996).

[11] R. Banakar, 'Reflections on the Methodological Issues of the Sociology of Law' (2000) 27 *Journal of Law and Society* 273–95.

[12] For discussion of the critical bias of law and society studies, see chapter 1 in Tamanaha *supra* n. 5.

[13] R. Cotterrell, *The Sociology of Law: An Introduction* (London Butterworths 1992), at 310.

perspective, which reflects their own disciplinary allegiances and training, and have little interest in conducting empirical research, or in the methodological and theoretical debates that concern sociologists.

Sociology of law as a sub-field of sociology

Our own view is that sociology of law should be viewed as a sub-field of mainstream sociology. This is partly because the various traditions and perspectives covered in this volume cannot easily be made to fit into the categories of policy research or critical legal studies. It will be apparent, for example, that all the traditions we have examined are concerned with broader issues and questions than the fairness or cost-effectiveness of public services. Similarly, by no means all sociological approaches are 'critical', in the sense of being motivated by liberal or left-wing political values.

More fundamentally, we believe that sociology of law can only develop as an empirical discipline if it engages with theoretical and methodological debates in mainstream sociology, which include theoretically sophisticated attempts to address the relationship between 'internal' and 'external' perspectives. The best work in the field has resulted from this kind of engagement, through researchers taking up ideas or questions from different sociological traditions and applying these to law. It would be unfortunate if sociology of law became separated from developments in the rest of the social sciences in the name of transcending disciplinary boundaries.

From this perspective, it is important to note that most of the research published in law and society journals is not sufficiently sociological, in the sense that it does not engage with the mainstream discipline. Papers on all kinds of empirical topics are presented at the Law and Society meetings each year, but there is usually little explicit discussion of theory or method. The majority of academics who attend meetings of the Law and Society Association and the British Socio-Legal Studies Association belong to law departments; so there are, in practice, only limited opportunities to engage in intellectual dialogue with sociologists. The same also applies, though to a lesser extent, to the meetings of the Research Committee for the Sociology of Law.

2. INSTITUTIONAL OBSTACLES

One does not have to look far for the main reason why sociology of law has failed to develop as a sociological sub-field internationally. This is simply because there are very few sociologists working in law schools, and very little sustained intellectual contact between the two disciplines. At the same time, sociology of law is not usually taken seriously, or taught as a standard part of the curriculum, in departments of sociology.

One can contrast this with the position of the sociologies of education and medicine in the United Kingdom where not only are options in these fields offered on most sociology degrees, but departments of education, medicine and nursing also employ sociologists in large numbers to teach undergraduates and engage in research.[14] Moreover, research in these sub-fields is regularly published in mainstream journals, and is also the site for methodological discussion and debate that can influence other areas of sociology.

Sociology in the law school

If you consider the currriculum in your local law school, it will be apparent that very few courses outside the black-letter curriculum are offered, and that very few non-lawyers, or academics trained in other disciplines, are represented in the teaching staff. There are, of course, some well-known law schools that are committed to developing inter-disciplinary programmes, and there are also new developments like law and society degrees for non-lawyers.[15] Most legal education remains, however, narrowly focused on the core subjects, and learning legal rules. It also appears that this is what the legal profession wants from lawyers: although it may be that they simply value degrees from the older, established universities, which are more likely to offer a traditional curriculum.

Perhaps the greatest challenge facing those who want a more prominent place for sociology in the law school curriculum is the issue of research methods training. It is often forgotten in law schools that a central objective of the sociology degree is to teach students how to conduct empirical research. This will usually involve taking courses in quantitative methods (using the software package SPSSx) and perhaps collecting and analysing data in a small social survey. It will also involve learning about qualitative research methods such as ethnography and interviewing. Although it is often difficult to do in practice, students are also required to relate issues in data-collection and analysis to wider theoretical and methodological debates. To give two examples, they are encouraged to think critically about the relationship between quantitative and qualitative methods, and about the epistemological issues in analysing research data.

Given that the traditional law degree usually only offers non-law subjects as options at third year level (with the exception of a survey course in jurisprudence), it will be apparent that there is no easy way to incorporate research methods training. This can again be contrasted to how students taking degrees in education, health studies, and even management, are often required to complete empirical projects.

[14] For a comparison between sociology of law and medical sociology, see R. Banakar, 'Reflections on the Methodological Issues of Sociology of Law' (2000) 27 *Journal of Law and Society* 273–95.

[15] These include the inter-disciplinary programmes at Berkeley, Santa Barbara and Amherst college in America, the Sociology of Law Institute at Lund University in Sweden, and law departments which have a contextual bias such as Kent and Lancaster in the United Kingdom.

This gap in the law school curriculum becomes particularly evident at post-graduate level, in applications for PhD studentships by candidates who wish to undertake socio-legal research. These are few in number and often lack methodological rigour. The Economic and Social Research Council has identified this as a problem affecting research across the field.[16] We would argue that this cannot adequately be addressed by postgraduate summer schools, but that graduates doing empirical research in law departments need a year of intensive training, in order to make up for the fact they missed out on social science in their undergraduate degree.

Law and the sociology curriculum

If you look at the curriculum in your local sociology department, you are likely to find options offered on the sociology of the media, culture, science and technology, racial and ethnic relations, and stratification, but not usually an option on sociology of law. Here, it needs to be acknowledged that criminology is a booming subject at undergraduate level in many countries, and has benefited from the fact it deals with an interesting subject matter, and that governments have poured money into criminological research. There is usually some sociology taught on these degrees, but the focus is necessarily on criminal justice and criminal law. Moreover, the trend in this field, whether the subject is taught in sociology departments or law schools, is towards policy-oriented research. One suspects, for example, that methods teaching on these degrees is biased towards the statistical methods favoured by government departments.

It is also apparent from the major sociology journals that there has been a shift away from an interest in the state and law towards culture, new technologies and the media. The best sociological studies about law in Britain arguably resulted from the collaboration between academic lawyers and sociologists in the 1970s and 1980s. Today, there are far fewer sociologists who are interested in law, partly because major funding opportunities have moved to different fields.[17]

3. WHAT SOCIOLOGY OF LAW HAS TO OFFER

The attraction of sociology as a subject, in our view, is that it offers a good preparation for citizenship. Even when it is taught at a basic level, it should make you think critically about your everyday activities, and the nature of social institutions that we normally take for granted. It is a deeply political subject—

---

[16] See L. Mulcahy, 'Making the Most of Methodology' (1999) 28 *Socio-Legal Newsletter* at 1–2; and M. Adler, 'The Precarious Position of Socio-Legal Studies in the Competition for ESRC Studentships' (2001) 35 *Socio-Legal Newsletter* at 1–2.

[17] One reading of the history of British sociology is that academics have followed research funding, but also what is perceived to be the prospects for intellectual excitement or theoretical debate offered by a particular sub-field.

in the sense of making you think about how societies work, and have developed, and how they could be different—but there is no need to apologise for this, at a time when young people have little involvement in politics, and there is less discussion or debate about serious issues in the media.

Why law students should study sociology

It seems remarkable that law remains the only professional occupation where it is possible for students to avoid any social science courses whatsoever (aside from legal philosophy, for historic reasons, which only has a marginal place on the curriculum). This can perhaps be justified in the United States, where students do a general degree before studying law at postgraduate level. Even here, however, one does not need to be a Karl Llewellyn to feel a sense of disquiet that students are being sent out into practice with no understanding of the relationship between lawyers and wider society.

How one does this in the law degree remains a matter for debate in that one could just as easily teach courses on law in context, policy research or critical legal studies instead of sociology of law. Our own view is that sociology of law, particularly if combined with sociologically-based research methods training, offers the most academically rigorous route, and also one that offers more political balance. We would be worried about only offering students policy courses because they encourage conformism, and critical legal studies courses because they usually involve preaching left-wing politics (a dangerous enterprise educationally since students often have quite right-wing views).

What can sociology of law offer mainstream sociology?

Finally, looking back on the perspectives presented in this book, it seems unfortunate that so few contemporary sociologists are interested in studying law and legal institutions. The chapters in this book bear witness to the fact that law is a multifaceted social phenomenon, which manifests itself in different forms at different levels of society. Not only does it permeate the everyday lives of ordinary people, but it also operates as one of the primary factors shaping the structural organisation of society. It can be studied empirically at the micro or macro levels using the methodological tools that sociologists employ in investigating other areas of social reality. It is a body of rules, but also a source of norms and a specific form of social practice. It is a political instrument for bringing about social change, or securing justice, but also an institution concerned with the preservation of established rights and vested interests. It is an academic subject, but also the basis for one of the largest and most influential professional bodies in modern society. These are only a few of the sociologically intriguing features of law, and they can be studied from a variety of theoretical perspectives.

Index

Lightning Source UK Ltd.
Milton Keynes UK
10 October 2009

144769UK00001B/45/A